D1612387

THE ANGLICAN DIOCESE OF CYPRUS & THE GULF

THE UNFOLDING STORY

Angela Murray

THE ANGLICAN DIOCESE OF CYPRUS & THE GULF
The Unfolding Story

Published in 2020 by Gilgamesh Publishing
Email: info@gilgamesh-publishing.co.uk
www.gilgamesh-publishing.co.uk

ISBN 9781908531612
CIP Data: A catalogue record for this book is available from the British Library

Text Copyright: The Anglican Church (Cyprus) Ltd © 2020
Author: Angela Murray

Graphic Design:
Cover and layout concept - Marcia Dallas
Project layout - Brilston Francis Pavanathara

Maps: Eleni Lambrou, pages 10-14, Quentin Morton, page 84

Photographs and illustrations, pages: amazon.com, 150, 158; Andy Bowerman, 192; Anetta Stylianou, 269; Angela Murray, 102, 104, 105, 107, 114, 119, 183, 186, 194, 197, 206, 230, 236, 240, 250, 264, 314, 315, 325, 335, 341, 346, 355; Bapco, 99, 10; Bill and Edith Schwartz, 289; Bishop Michael Lewis, 336; BP, Abu Dhabi, 122; Caltex Corporation, 95, 247; Charles Gervais, 208; Charles Milner, 215; Chevron, 96; Christ Church Jebel Ali, 316; Christopher Butt, 132, 361; Cyprus Press and Information Office, 42; Diana Markides, 23; Diocese of Cyprus & the Gulf, 18, 36, 41, 169, 216, 218, 219, 226, 229, 242, 245, 255, 275, 277, 279, 285, 287, 295, 296, 300, 301, 303, 308, 317, 322, 339, 348, 360; Diocese of Jerusalem, 177, 178; Hampshire archives, 239; Hielke van der Wijk, 62; Holy Trinity, Dubai, 125; Imperial War Museum, London, 55; JEMT trustees, 33, 38, 71, 72, 81, 86, 89, 91, 93, 136, 139, 141, 143, 200, 209, 213; JPP Photography, 293; Kuwait Oil Company, 108, 110; Larnaca chaplaincy, 201; Leonard Brown, 154; Louis Andrew Katsantonis, 224; oikoumene.org, 147; Patricia Kingston, 184; Paul Armerding, 67; Penny Calder, 260; Peter Crooks, 330, 357; Peter Delaney, 270; RCA archive, 60, 68; Retreats Ministry, 327; Richard Brown, 288; Ronald Codrai, 117; Royal Collection Trust, 51; Sarah Maybury, 353; St Andrew's church, Abu Dhabi, 121; St Andrew's church, Kyrenia, 166; St Barnabas church, Dhekelia, 188; St Christopher's Cathedral, 252; St Mark's church, 351; St Martin's church, 358; St Paul's Cathedral, Nicosia, 20, 30, 35, 44; Stuart Plowman, 333; Wellcome Library, 28

Printed and bound in India by Imprint Press

CONTENTS

FOREWORD

Claims of uniqueness are to be treated with caution, but as the fifth Bishop of the Diocese of Cyprus and the Gulf I have no hesitation in affirming that it is quite fascinating and truly special, and its history absorbing.

In its present configuration, covering multiple nations, the diocese came into existence only in 1976. But the lands and places it now includes were served with Anglican presence, ministry, and churches long before that year. This book records those origins and traces the diocese's sometimes surprising evolution. Its worshippers have always been predominantly expatriate migrants, living as resident aliens in countries of which they are not citizens, even as its churches' doors have always been open for indigenous Christians and any who care to enter. Now, we are of a very large number of national and ethnic backgrounds and socio-economic groupings, and we are proud of our rich internal diversity.

Apart from a most interesting memoir in diary form by the Right Reverend John Brown, third bishop in Cyprus and the Gulf, the diocese has gone mostly unrecorded in any accessible form. But from a wealth of written documents in files, cupboards, magazines, and elsewhere, and from the oral testimony and correspondence of a variety of enthusiastic and knowledgeable contributors and collaborators, Mrs Angela Murray MBE, lay Canon of St Christopher's Cathedral, Manama, Bahrain, has assembled a comprehensive account from earliest beginnings, and we owe her a very great debt of gratitude for her industry and her meticulous attention to detail.

I make mention here of the Reverend (now Canon) Dr Matthew Rhodes, then Vicar of Maney in the Diocese of Birmingham and now of St John Ranmoor in the Diocese of Sheffield, who as a sabbatical project, assembled materials on the diocese some years ago, at the time when this diocese celebrated the fortieth anniversary of its 1976 designation.

Finally I have real pleasure in recording the crucial cooperation afforded to Mrs Murray by three people in particular: my predecessor, Bishop Clive Handford CMG; the Dean of Bahrain and Archdeacon in the Gulf, the Very Reverend and Venerable Dr Bill Schwartz OBE; and Mrs Georgia Katsantonis, my secretary and PA, as also to successive bishops before me. All of them have served long in the diocese and have a capacity for accurate memory to which I can only aspire.

Bishop Michael Lewis
Diocese of Cyprus and the Gulf

ACKNOWLEDGEMENTS

When Bishop Michael Lewis asked me in June 2016 if I might help him to develop a history of the Diocese of Cyprus and the Gulf and produce a book, little did I imagine that my task would transcend into a journey lasting almost three and a half years. More than one hundred people have generously contributed their time to assist my research and offer valuable suggestions, and to all I am most grateful.

Although I have not attempted to compile a definitive list of acknowledgements, a number of people do require special mention: Bishop Michael Lewis for his meticulous editorial oversight, advice and unwavering encouragement; Bishop Clive Handford for mentoring me up a fairly vertical learning curve, and adding depth to the narrative by drawing on his first-hand experiences which span more than fifty years; and Archdeacon Bill Schwartz, a fount of diocesan knowledge, always available to offer advice and assist with problem-solving.

Many days spent exploring diocesan records in Nicosia were only possible with the help of Georgia Katsantonis and Anetta Stylianou, members of staff for more than thirty years and so oral testimony contributors too. Dr Helen Perry has provided immeasurable help. Felicity Christofides, the Reverend Kent Middleton and the Reverend Justin Arnott devoted much time to search through registers at St Paul's Cathedral to answer my questions.

Throughout Cyprus, other people in particular have graciously answered a flow of requests, supplied photographs and/or offered oral history testimony: in Nicosia, Archdeacon John Holdsworth, the Very Reverend Jeremy Crocker, Maggie Le-Roy, Pat Baulch, Sarel and Cheryl du Plessis, Michelle Arnott and Julia Lewis; in Paphos, the Reverend Tony Jeynes, Jacquie Hammond and the late Patricia Kingston; in Limassol, the Reverend Canon Derek Smith, Charles Dodds and Christine Taylor; in Larnaca, Deborah Graham and Susan Mantovani; in south-east Cyprus, the Reverend Canon Paul Maybury, the Reverend Peter Day and Heather Crookes; and in Kyrenia, the Reverend Wendy

Hough, Dr John Worton-Griffiths and Linda Smith. I also thank the Reverend Peter King, British Forces Chaplain at Dhekelia garrison, for granting me access to the archives at St Barnabas church, and for arranging my visit to St Columba's church in the UN Buffer Zone.

In the Gulf archdeaconry I especially mention: Dawlat Abouna in Baghdad; the Reverend Michael Mbona in Kuwait; the Very Reverend Christopher Butt in Bahrain; the Reverend Canon Andrew Thompson and Helen Verghese in Abu Dhabi; the Reverend Tim Heaney and the Reverend Charlotte Lloyd-Evans in Jebel Ali Dubai; the Reverend Canon Dr Paul Burt and the Reverend Canon Andy Bowerman serving the Mission to Seafarers in Dubai; the Reverend Drew Schmotzer in Sharjah; and in Aden, Mansour Khan.

To those in the UK I am indebted to the Venerable Dr Ian Young, Shirley Eason (Administrator of JMECA), John Clark (Chairman of JEMT), Canon John Banfield and Mary Banfield, Charles Milner and Sally Milner, the Reverend Canon Alan Hayday, the Reverend Peter Crooks and Nancy Crooks, Thanos Petouris, Professor Jonathan Warner, David Blake (Curator of the Museum of Army Chaplaincy); and in Australia, the Reverend Zinkoo Han.

As for the book itself, graphic designer Marcia Dallas devised the cover and layout concept; Eleni Lambrou created the splendid maps; and project designer Brilston Francis Pavanathara patiently undertook the layout, more complicated than either of us envisaged. Scrupulous proofreading by Alexandra Newby ensured that mistakes were corrected. I especially thank Sibella Laing for suggesting Gilgamesh in London as a possible publisher, and therefore Max Scott for his willingness to add this work to his list and oversee its publication.

My husband Grant lost count of the weekends I deserted him to work at my computer. Not for the first time have I been humbled by his immense understanding and support. Thank you.

Canon Angela Murray MBE

PRIMATES (PRESIDENT BISHOPS)

The Episcopal Church in Jerusalem and the Middle East

Comprising four dioceses:
Cyprus and the Gulf,
Egypt and North Africa with the Horn of Africa, Iran, Jerusalem

1976 - 1986	**The Right Reverend Hassan B Dehqani-Tafti** *Initially known as Bishop President; chose to retain the title The Right Reverend throughout his primacy* Bishop in Iran
1986 - 1996	**The Most Reverend Samir Kafity** Bishop in Jerusalem
1996 - May 2000	**The Most Reverend Ghais Abd el Malik** Bishop in Egypt and North Africa with the Horn of Africa
May 2000 - 2002	**The Most Reverend Iraj Mottahedeh** Bishop in Iran
Feb 2002 - April 2007	**The Most Reverend Clive Handford CMG** Bishop in Cyprus and the Gulf
May 2007 - May 2017	**The Most Reverend Dr Mouneer Anis** Bishop in Egypt and North Africa with the Horn of Africa

28 September 2014: Central Synod of the Episcopal Church in Jerusalem and the Middle East resolved that the Primate (President Bishop), and the Bishop of the Diocese of Jerusalem, shall during their terms of office bear the title Archbishop.

17 May 2017: in respect of the coming five-year period, Central Synod unanimously elected Primates to serve successive terms of two-and-a-half years each.

May 2017 - Nov 2019	**The Most Reverend Suheil Dawani** Archbishop in Jerusalem
Nov 2019 - May 2022	**The Most Reverend Michael Lewis** Bishop in Cyprus and the Gulf

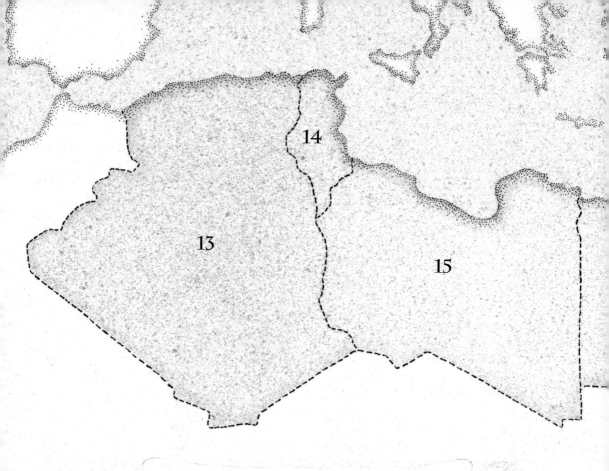

EPISCOPAL CHURCH IN JERUSALEM & THE MIDDLE EAST
The Four Dioceses

CYPRUS & THE GULF
1. Cyprus
2. Iraq
3. Kuwait
4. Bahrain
5. Qatar
6. United Arab Emirates
7. Oman
8. Yemen

JERUSALEM
9. Palestine & Israel
10. Lebanon
11. Syria
12. Jordan

EGYPT & NORTH AFRICA
13. Algeria
14. Tunisia
15. Libya
16. Egypt
17. Eritrea
18. Ethiopia
19. Djibouti
20. Somalia

IRAN
21. Iran

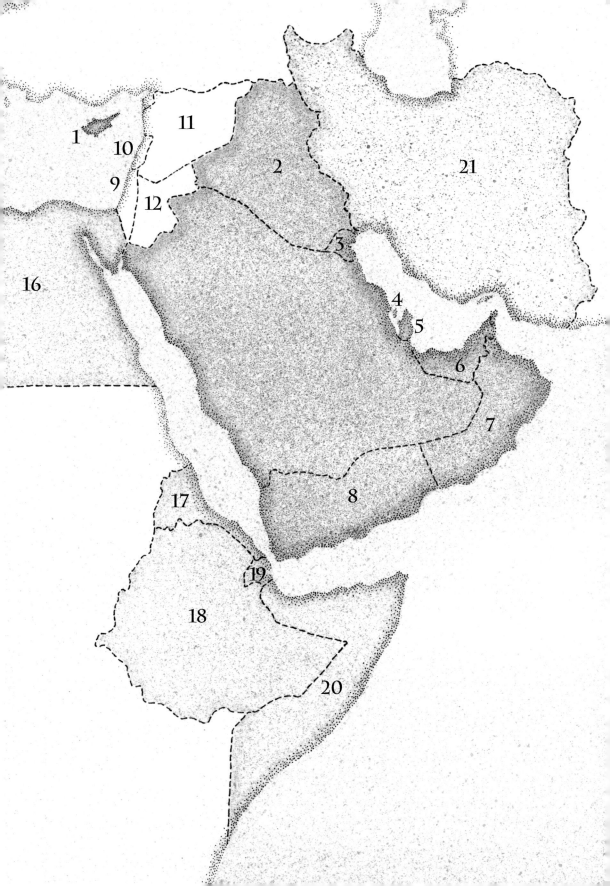

ANGLICAN DIOCESE OF CYPRUS & THE GULF
Church Locations

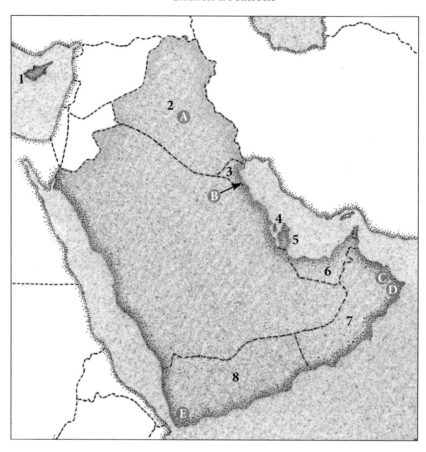

ANGLICAN CHURCHES IN CYPRUS

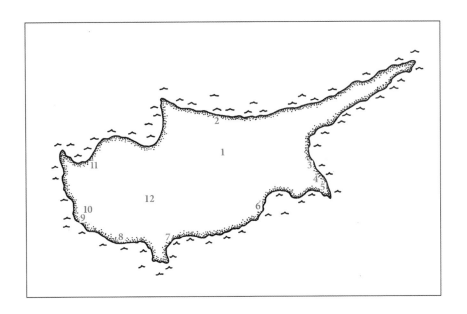

1   Nicosia: St Paul's Cathedral
2   Kyrenia: St Andrew
3   Famagusta: St Mark
4   Deryneia: St John the Evangelist
5   Ayia Napa: Christ Church
6   Larnaca: St Helena
7   Limassol: St Barnabas
8   Pissouri: St Lazarus
9   Kato Paphos: Ayia Kyriaki Chrysopolitissa *
10   Tala: St Stephen
11   Prodromi: St Luke
12   Troodos: St George in the Forest

* *With permission from the Greek Orthodox Church, Latin Catholic and Anglican congregations share use of this church sited within an archaeological site administered by the Department of Antiquities.*

ANGLICAN CHURCHES IN THE GULF REGION

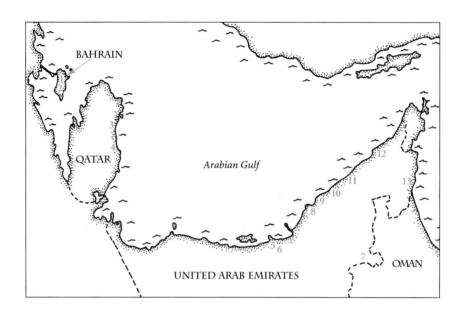

14

BAHRAIN
1   Manama: St Christopher's
     Cathedral

2   Awali town:
     *The church is owned by the
     Bahrain Petroleum Company
     and its use shared by different
     denominations*

QATAR
3   Al Khor: Anglican congregation
4   Doha: Church of the Epiphany

UNITED ARAB EMIRATES
Abu Dhabi emirate

5   Abu Dhabi city: St Andrew
6   Mussafah: All Saints
7   Al Ain: St Thomas

UNITED ARAB EMIRATES
Dubai emirate

8   Jebel Ali: Christ Church
9   Dubai: St Catherine
10   Bur Dubai: Holy Trinity

Sharjah emirate
11   St Martin

Ras al Khaimah emirate
12   St Luke

Fujairah emirate
13   St Nicholas

PART ONE

SETTING THE SCENE

While this book charts, and indeed celebrates, the evolution of the Diocese of Cyprus and Gulf since its institution on 5 January 1976, the scope of the story can only be fully appreciated with an insight into the remarkable warp and weft of its origins.

Some of the issues faced prior to and during this diocese's formative years continue to remain significant today. One is the need for sensitive respect in host countries where Islam is the national religion, and in Cyprus where the Greek Orthodox Church prevailed throughout the island until its partition in 1974, and since then south of the Green Line.

Other circumstances, including persistent financial challenges and transforming political events in countries within the diocese's geographical parameters, have always required prudence and vigilance to be exercised. The diocese has often had to cope with circumstances outside its control, whether or not it welcomed or accepted them. Yet, with exceptions in some locations, the Diocese of Cyprus and the Gulf remains free to offer Anglican ministry as it chooses so that chaplaincy (parish) life may thrive and, in modern conflict zones, simply survive. Part One provides an essential foundation for the tale to be told.

Central design of the marble altar front
installed at St Helen's church, Larnaca, in 1907
Agisilaou & Spyrou Photography Ltd, Nicosia. Diocese of Cyprus & the Gulf archive

Chapter 1

ANGLICAN PIONEERS IN CYPRUS

1878 - 1973

In 1878 the Ottoman Empire, with Constantinople as its capital, was politically and economically dominant throughout eastern Europe and many countries in the Near and Middle East, including Cyprus. Christians living on the island were almost entirely Greek Orthodox. Anglicans were few and far between, most being merchants and occasional visitors. As proselytising was illegal, opportunities for Christian missionaries to be active in Cyprus did not exist. On 4 June 1878, these seemingly unrelated circumstances began to converge with the signing, in Constantinople, of the Convention of Defensive Alliance Between Great Britain and Turkey, with Respect to the Asiatic Provinces of Turkey. In effect, Cyprus became a British Protectorate under Ottoman suzerainty, meaning that the British Government assumed responsibility for the island's security and the administration of its civil internal affairs; the Ottoman Empire retained control of the island's foreign policy and international relations.

This arrangement had been hastily agreed, in secret so it transpired. It was not until 7 July 1878 that the Convention was first made public, almost five weeks after it had been signed, not in Constantinople as might have been expected but in Berlin. This intrigue very much surprised many people in England, including Anglican Church authorities and especially those who a few days earlier had attended the first sessions of the 1878 Lambeth Conference between 2 and 4 July. Crucially, the announcement in Berlin had presented the Anglican Church with an unexpected opportunity and a logistical challenge, to both of which it responded without delay. During Part Two of the conference, 22 to 24 July, the subject of Anglican chaplains and chaplaincies abroad was discussed again.[1] Suffice it to say that the Right Reverend Charles Sandford, Bishop of Gibraltar, was eager to assume the challenge.

In his *Pastoral Letter to Clergy and Laity 1878*, he eloquently defined his task:

"If a considerable number of Englishmen should settle in the Island, it will be necessary to provide for their wants by …. the erection of a church which I trust may be worthy in all respects of our Church and country ….

"It will be felt by all Christian Englishmen that on arriving in this new land, which our Queen [Victoria] and country have just taken under their charge, we should bring with us the ordinances of our religion; and that an English church should soon be seen rising on the shores which were the first to be hallowed by the steps of the great Apostle to the Gentiles, when he had embarked on his earliest missionary journey."[2]

The Right Reverend Charles W Sandford
Bishop of Gibraltar, 1874-1903
St Paul's Cathedral archive, Nicosia; reproduced with the dean's consent

Meanwhile in June 1878, the first contingent of a British expeditionary force sailed from Malta, a vanguard of seven ships under the command of Vice Admiral Lord John Hay. This deployment arrived at the bay of

Larnaca on 4 July, followed by the arrival on 22 July of the main bulk of the troops under the command of Lieutenant-General Sir Garnet Wolseley. Highly regarded as a career soldier he had been appointed as the first High Commissioner of Cyprus and charged with the task of forming a Civil Administration. The perceived wisdom of the British public was that the whole campaign had been ill conceived. For example, except for some sailing charts, the British had neither proper maps of the island nor any helpful concept of the landscape.

> "Nobody on the flagship spoke Greek or Turkish and no staff officer was familiar with the island. … It was the hottest season of the year, but the British arrived with warming pans and coal boxes, which they abandoned on the beach at Larnaca Bay."[3]

Sir Garnet Wolseley was "appalled at the inadequacy of the preparations and wrote irritably in his diary that the disembarkation had been 'very unsatisfactory'".[4] His mood worsened when he discovered the ninety mule carts (shipped from Malta) scattered in pieces on Larnaca beach alongside the discarded coal boxes.[5] The carts could not be assembled because the quartermaster had overlooked to arrange for the vital "link pins" to be packed in the same consignment. Thus, on 28 July 1878 - in searing summer heat, with no available overland transport and inappropriate clothing - this substantial body of troops dressed in standard issue red woollen tunics and thick trousers had to march for several miles from the beach to the shore of the Salt Lake south-west of Larnaca, the site where they pitched their tents and established Camp Ciftlik Pasha.[6&7] On their way, sadly but not surprisingly, news was received that four members of the previous day's advance party had died from heat apoplexy. During that summer, at any one time, a quarter of Wolseley's troops were incapacitated by sunstroke and malaria.[8]

Before long, the Reverend David Nickerson, an Army Chaplain to Her Majesty's Forces, also arrived in Cyprus. At the request of Bishop Charles Sandford, Nickerson kindly agreed to extend his services to the few English civilians who had arrived on the island until a Civil

Chaplain could be appointed.[9] This arrangement was not without controversy, the main issue being that Army chaplains were members of the Army Chaplains Department, under the charge of the Chaplain-General as their spiritual head. One commentator robustly expressed his view:

> "The assistance of Navy and Army chaplains is often generously given to the civil chaplains and gratefully received. But the fact that the Bishop of Gibraltar neither has jurisdiction over the Forces (or their chapels), nor is responsible for ministrations to them wherever they may be within the geographical limits of his Jurisdiction needs plain recognition."[10]

As it turned out, the assistance was short-lived. By the end of December 1878 the Reverend David Nickerson had left Cyprus to pursue his Army career elsewhere. Meanwhile, on 13 December the Bishop of Gibraltar arrived in Cyprus for a three-day visit, part of his itinerary during a prolonged tour of his diocese (begun in the previous September and not expected to end until June 1879). He carried with him a letter of introduction from the Archbishop of Canterbury, the Most Reverend Archibald Campbell Tait, addressed to Archbishop Sophronios, Head of the (Greek Orthodox) Church of Cyprus, the text of which also extended the Archbishop's brotherly respect and courtesy greetings.[11]

On the last day of his visit, 15 December, Bishop Charles Sandford celebrated divine service in Larnaca, in the Church Room, "an iron building which had been lent for the purpose by the owner, Mr Watkins of the Ottoman Bank, and suitably furnished by some English ladies residing in the town".[12] This was the first formal civilian Anglican service to take place in Cyprus.

However, as the Church of England's colonial bishoprics had been disestablished in 1873, Bishop Charles Sandford's authority had its limits, possessing "a purely moral, voluntary, or consensual character" which could not be enforced by law.[13] The Bishop recognised that congregations under his remit would not be solely Anglicans, and therefore he welcomed those of non conformist denominations as long as Anglican discipline was not undermined.

His Beatitude Sophronios,
Archbishop of Cyprus

*Source: Sendell in Cyprus
1892-1898, p 54;
Copyright: Diana Markides*

A founding principle of the Diocese of Gibraltar (formed in 1842), and an important priority for Bishop Sandford, was that of "advancing those friendly relations and that mutual understanding between our Church and the Orthodox Churches of the East".[14] (This principle still remains an important part of the life of the Anglican Diocese of Cyprus and the Gulf.) In his *Pastoral Letter to Clergy and Laity 1878* Bishop Sandford also stated:

> "It should be remembered that the Chaplaincies which the Church of England maintains abroad are not for the purpose of making converts among members of other Christian communities. Our work is strictly confined to our own people."[15]

The fact that the Anglican Church overseas was disestablished meant that with a few exceptions, there was no funding from the British Government for chaplaincy work in its foreign territories. In Cyprus, limited financial support came from Anglican church members living on the island but, as most were employed in Government service for fixed tours of duty, the transient nature of the British community caused fluctuations in this source of funding. Instead, the Bishop was obliged to seek grants from two missionary societies based in Great Britain: the Colonial and Continental Church Society (C&CCS), and the Society for the Propagation of the Gospel in Foreign Parts (SPG). His quest was a success, thus by early 1879 it was possible to initiate civilian Anglican ministry in Cyprus: in Limassol, and jointly in Larnaca and Nicosia. These two developments which commenced more or less within a week of each other, and their immediate outcomes, evolved very differently.

Funding for the first Anglican chaplain in Limassol was provided through the Colonial and Continental Church Society. By September 1878 it had already collected £200 towards a stipend to support a mission "in this very special land [Cyprus] given its associations with St Paul and St Barnabas".[16] The Society had also engaged the Reverend Dr Hunter Finlay "who held a very high opinion of his ability and was possessed of a fervent mission as a clergyman".[17] Unfortunately, Finlay's eagerness and the C&CCS's enthusiasm to expedite the appointment proved to be a flawed and naïve combination.

Before Dr Finlay departed from England, the Chaplain-General of the Army Chaplains' Department had given him a letter of introduction to present to the British High Commissioner in Cyprus. On 22 January 1879 the Right Reverend Piers Calverly-Claughton, Chaplain-General, informed the C&CCS's committee that he presumed there would be chaplaincies in Larnaca and Famagusta, one supported by the C&CCS and the other by the SPG. But, he emphasised, the final decision was to be made by the Bishop of Gibraltar, and only after he returned to England at the end of his tour. The snag was that Dr Finlay landed in Larnaca a week later on 29 January 1879, proceeded to Limassol and lost no time in establishing himself as a stirring presence in the town's municipality hall. There he preached and held services every Sunday in the morning or afternoon, depending on when the Presbyterian minister held his service. Finlay later recorded that Sunday, 30 March, had been "a great day for the Church of England in Limassol".[18]

> "At 10.30 am the doors of the temporary Church of St Barnabas were thrown open. Members of the Royal Engineers based in the town entered first under the command of Lieutenant Wisley; the church filled up and many had to stand. The Archimandrite of the Orthodox Church attended along with two other priests and the 'service was exceedingly hearty' although there was no music as the Harmonium organ had not arrived."[19]

Such was the momentum generated by Dr Finlay that the C&CCS instructed him to purchase a plot of land on behalf of the Society on which to build a church, a school and a parsonage. A site was chosen and a deposit paid. But, even before the service on 30 March, doubt concerning the chaplain's appointment had been expressed. The Bishop of Gibraltar was informed. In March 1879 he wrote to the C&CCS saying that he wished to take the opinions of the residents of Limassol before licensing Finlay as chaplain there. Arrogantly, the C&CCS Committee resolved to tell the Bishop that this was inappropriate since it was paying the Chaplain's salary![20]

25

Finlay's behaviour began to discredit the church. Two letters of concern were sent to the Chaplain-General (in the United Kingdom): one was from Colonel F Warren, District Commissioner of Limassol, dated 16 April 1879; another, dated 3 May, was written by the High Commissioner's Private Secretary. Even though it seems that the texts were not specific, the Bishop of Gibraltar made it clear to the C&CCS that it had acted unwisely, and that "if he had been consulted the Reverend H Finlay would never have gone to Cyprus".[21]

Perhaps part of the Bishop's rationale was his knowledge that Finlay had an attitude problem. He been reluctant to study and sit the necessary exams prior to his ordination believing that as a medical doctor "he was already rather better qualified than most priests".[22] Although Finlay did overcome his reluctance and was ordained deacon in 1874, it was not until just before his appointment to minister in Limassol that he was priested by the Bishop of London.

The outcome of the various misgivings was that Finlay was recalled to England, returning on 17 June 1879 less than five months after arriving in Cyprus. Coincidentally, Colonel Warren wrote to the Bishops of London and Gibraltar on the following day:

> "I should for the sake of the good name of our religion and specially for the good name of its ordained priests be sorry to see Dr Finlay back here. … I must say that Dr Finlay was guilty of no immorality and that the earnest and interesting style of his sermons always attracted considerable congregations."[23]

Although Warren's opinions were not entirely critical, Bishop Sandford had made up his mind. Having completed his diocesan tour, he interviewed and appointed the Reverend Avidis Garboushian to assume Anglican ministry in Limassol, supported by the C&CCS. Mr Garboushian - an Armenian by birth, a native of Antioch, naturalised as a British citizen and held in very high regard - arrived in Cyprus on 22 December 1879 with every hope that he would be accepted by the congregation and feel comfortable in his new role. His ministry also extended to the British troops based at the new Polemidia Camp and Army Headquarters, established during 1879 a few miles inland from Limassol.[24] When the Army Chaplain departed in March 1880, Garboushian was also appointed Acting Chaplain to the Forces.

However, his ministry to the St Barnabas congregation was less sure. On 26 April 1880 he wrote to the C&CCS "expressing doubt that he would be able to continue with the Evening Service given that so many of the Congregation attended the Presbyterian Church".[25] The C&CCS insisted that the service must continue, even though attendance declined further. It also refused Garboushian permission to take more than fourteen days leave that summer.

Most likely he was relieved in more than one way to spend three months, July to September, ministering at the civilian and military summer camp in the Troodos mountains, now in its second season. Sir Garnet Wolseley had initiated this scheme in 1879 so that Government employees and their families living in Nicosia, and troops based at sea level, could enjoy a cooler summer climate.

After the Reverend Avidis Garboushian returned to Limassol, numbers at his services did not increase with the outcome that from October 1880 he ceased to celebrate Morning Service on Sundays. By the year-end the C&CCS in London was facing financial difficulties. Members of the Grant Meeting of the General Committee met on 20 January 1881 agreed to discontinue support for the chaplaincy in Limassol from 30 June that year. Surprised, and with regret, Mr Garboushian accepted the decision. Before leaving Cyprus he arranged to sell the church furniture, books and communion plate. All were returned to Liverpool in England. The harmonium was left in the care of Sergeant Major Steele. The land which had been bought by the C&CCS for the intended church, school and parsonage was sold. In effect, the embryonic Anglican chaplaincy in Limassol fell into abeyance until new financial arrangements could be made to support it. Until then, between 1881 and almost the end of the century, military chaplains based at Polemidia Camp provided ministry for Anglican civilians living in Limassol and Paphos, and during their stays in Troodos.

Mr Garboushian's future was more sorrowful. After briefly serving in Reigate, Surrey, he accepted the post of Consular Chaplain at Malaga in 1885. Unexpectedly, he died in Marseille that year, aged thirty-four.

The story now reverts to the latter months of 1878 by which time the Society for the Propagation of the Gospel in Foreign Parts (SPG) had managed to raise sufficient funds to appoint a chaplain in Cyprus. On 6 February 1879 the Reverend Josiah Spencer, aged thirty-seven, disembarked at Larnaca port. Unlike Dr Finlay (who it will be recalled had landed at the same port a week earlier with no episcopal reference) Spencer arrived having been "commended to Archbishop Sophronios by the Bishop of Lincoln, the Right Reverend Christopher Wordsworth"[26] (a literary figure as well as a clergyman and nephew of the poet William Wordsworth). Three days later on Sunday 9 February 1879, already licensed by the Bishop of Gibraltar as Anglican Chaplain in Cyprus, the Reverend Josiah Spencer celebrated his first service on the island.

From the outset, he sought to encourage the Anglican congregation in Larnaca. By the beginning of February, the Church Room was in regular use. On 13 February Spencer convened a meeting of church members, a church council was formed, within two months plans for building an Anglican church in the town were underway, and an appeal fund was launched. Financial statements and a report were approved and forwarded to the SPG in London to comply with its rules. Although these plans stalled indefinitely, the lack of an Anglican church building in Larnaca (until 1907) did not deter the congregation.

Initially, Josiah Spencer lived in Larnaca, but was also responsible for Anglican ministry in Nicosia. This required him to travel between the two locations in a horse-drawn coach, an arduous journey on unpaved roads, through villages and forests, over river culverts and rocky terrain.

Street scene in Larnaca, Cyprus, 1878
Wellcome Library, London

(Today, the direct distance between Larnaca and Nicosia by motorway is 28 miles/45 kilometres.) After a few months, Spencer found it more convenient to live in Nicosia, but still ministered regularly in Larnaca, and occasionally in Famagusta and Kyrenia.

The chaplain's rented home in Nicosia was close to Paphos Gate, one of three entrances to the old city within the 16th century Venetian ramparts. A room in the house was used for services. It so happened that one of the churchwardens was Lieutenant Horatio Kitchener. (He later found fame as Field Marshal the 1st Earl Kitchener of Khartoum, the British military commander in Sudan and South Africa; Consul General in Egypt, 1911-1914; and British Secretary of State for War, 1914-1916). In 1879 Kitchener had arrived in Nicosia with the brief to prepare the first scientific land survey and modern map of Cyprus:

> "He toured the island with his team of Royal Engineers and was confronted by bad roads, an arduous climate, and suspicious villagers - he was shot at twice. His scientific survey was published on sixteen sheets in 1885 in London under the title: 'Trigonometrical Survey of the Island of Cyprus'. It was and it is still regarded as a masterpiece of cartography."[27]

Small though the Anglican congregation in Nicosia was in 1880, the Bishop of Gibraltar and the SPG - and no doubt the Reverend Josiah Spencer - decided that rather than embark on a fund-raising appeal to build an Anglican church in the city they would seek to restore an old church thought to have been dedicated to St Nicholas of the English, then used by its Turkish owner as a stable and granary. The plan failed for two reasons: leasing difficulties, and the withdrawal of British Government support because the building was too close to a mosque. When the Special Fund offered by the SPG in support of the chaplaincy also failed, Mr Spencer was without a stipend. Reluctantly but with no choice he left Cyprus on 14 August 1880 to rejoin his family in England until a solution could be found.

It was during this interim period that the Reverend Avidis Garboushian, based in Limassol, found himself ministering as the sole civilian Anglican chaplain in Cyprus.

Less than four months later, on 3 December 1880, the Reverend Josiah Spencer returned to the island, this time accompanied by his wife Bessie and their young family. Having secured a part-time salaried appointment as Director of Education he was able to resume his ministry as Chaplain in Cyprus as well. During his first period as chaplain he had received little financial support from the congregation in Nicosia, and initially upon his return there was negligible change. He was obliged to cover the cost of church expenses himself and hope that the offertory would be sufficient for him to be reimbursed.

The Venerable Josiah Spencer
1842-1901
*St Paul's Cathedral archive, Nicosia;
reproduced with the dean's consent*

One parishioner, Major A Gordon (Commander of Police and the Pioneer Force), took remedial action by calling a parish meeting. This was held on 8 March 1881 at the home of the High Commissioner, Sir Robert Biddulph, whose wife Constance Lambert was the daughter of a clergyman. Whether or not she influenced the outcome, Major Gordon's initiative achieved some success with Sir Robert's support. Even so, payment of the chaplain's stipend of £50 per annum often fell into arrears. Spencer bore this graciously and waived payment when church finances were needed elsewhere.[28]

A year later in March 1882, during the Bishop of Gibraltar's second visit to the High Commissioner in Cyprus, a firm decision was taken to build an Anglican church in Nicosia. A committee was formed and fund-raising began, but for almost three years no suitable site could be found. Eventually in 1885 the so-named Nicosia Church Committee chose a site offered by the Government: a two-acre plot on St George's Hill (near the Secretariat) which was no longer required for a hospital. The plot contained the site of a former Christian church, and the hill ensured that a new church building would be clearly visible. William Williams, a young draughtsman employed by the Public Works Department who styled himself as Assistant Architect, was asked to design the church in the Victorian English Gothic Revival style typical of that period. It was emphasised, the church would be for the English and would not interfere with the local Greek Orthodox Church.

On 6 May 1885 the High Commissioner laid the foundation stone. By then, £900 of the expected £1200 cost of building the church had been collected. Building progress was such that, with the Bishop of Gibraltar's permission, the first service in the new church was celebrated on Christmas Day 1885. On Easter Tuesday, 27 April 1886 and with due ceremony, the church of St Paul in Nicosia was consecrated by the Right Reverend Charles Sandford. Among those present were His Beatitude Sophronios, Archbishop of Cyprus, together with other representatives of the Greek Orthodox Church.

Bishop Sandford's visit to Cyprus for the consecration was to be his last, although he had not anticipated this. In 1887, after considerable deliberation and with sorrow, he "surrendered" Anglican canonical authority in Cyprus, under his charge in the Diocese of Gibraltar, to that of the recently reformed Diocese of Jerusalem. The origins for this change began in 1841 when the Diocese of Jerusalem was first formed as an Anglican/Lutheran joint venture under the auspices of Queen Victoria (United Kingdom) and King Frederick William IV (Prussia). This status continued until 1881 when the Diocese of Jerusalem fell into abeyance; in 1887, it was dissolved and then reconstituted as an entirely Anglican entity. In the same year, the Right Reverend George Francis Popham Blyth was appointed as Bishop in Jerusalem.

As a result, on 27 January 1887, the Archbishop of Canterbury, the Most Reverend Edward Benson, asked the Bishop of Gibraltar if he might consider this proposal: that Cyprus should be transferred to the reformed Diocese of Jerusalem. In reply on 9 February 1887 Bishop Charles Sandford wrote:

> "On personal grounds I should be extremely sorry to surrender Cyprus. On the three occasions I have visited the Island I have received a hearty welcome and very great kindness from the authorities of the Greek Church as well as from my own countrymen residing there. But owing to the great distance of the island from all other places committed to my charge I think it right to be transferred to the care of the Anglican Bishop (for Jerusalem)."[29]

The Reverend Josiah Spencer was very sorry to learn of the bishop's decision and wrote to him accordingly. Sir Henry Bulwer, High Commissioner in Cyprus (since 9 March 1886), was equally dismayed. On 10 April 1887 he wrote to the Bishop of Gibraltar: "it is with very great regret I have received your letter telling me of the termination of your episcopal connection with Cyprus".[30] Mindful of these concerns, the Archbishop of Canterbury "exercised great care" in restoring the Diocese of Jerusalem and any alarm felt beforehand by either the British or the Greek Orthodox Church proved unfounded under the episcopate of the Right Reverend George Francis Popham Blyth, 1887-1914.

Almost immediately upon his appointment in 1887, the Bishop in Jerusalem would have understood that he could not hope for a contribution from the British administration in Cyprus to help fund chaplaincy ministry on the island, let alone the building of churches. During 1887 the harvest in Cyprus failed miserably due to severe drought. The implications were far-reaching. One reason why Great Britain had assumed responsibility for the administration of Cyprus in

1878 was to relieve the British and French treasuries, obliged for the previous two years to pay influential British and French bondholders the annual interest on the 1855 Crimean War loan, because the Sublime Porte (the central government of the Ottoman Empire) had defaulted on its repayments in 1877.[31] The much-needed revenue was raised in Cyprus through heavy taxation, primarily a percentage of the annual wheat harvest collected as a tithe called the Tribute. (This remained in force for fifty years until its repeal in 1927, causing many Cypriots to blame the British for their impoverishment and exploitation.) Thus, when the harvests failed in 1887, tax arrears strained the civil administration's budget further. There was no surplus of wealth.

Two years later the Bishop would have received more unwelcome news. During 1889 cracks appeared in the walls of St Paul's Church,

The Right Reverend George Francis Popham Blyth Bishop in Jerusalem 1887-1914

JEMT, reproduced with kind consent of the Trustees

soon worsening and appearing in some of the arches. By the year-
end the building was declared unsafe so causing services to be held
elsewhere. It was hoped that repairs would solve the problem. Instead,
during 1890 the cracks extended and opened further. On 25 November
that year, at a meeting of church members chaired by the British High
Commissioner Sir Henry Bulwer, in the presence of Bishop George
Popham Blyth during his first episcopal visit to Cyprus, it was agreed
to dismantle the church and rebuild it to the same design on a new site
beside Byron Avenue, using all the original materials. On St George's
Day in 1896, 23 April, St Paul's Church was reconsecrated by the Bishop.

Meanwhile in Kyrenia, on the north coast of Cyprus, a small British
civilian community had begun to establish itself, despite an inauspicious
beginning in 1878. Within a month of the British expeditionary force
establishing Camp Ciftlik Pasha in Larnaca, the site was deemed so
badly chosen and unhealthy that decisions were made to relocate the
troops. The contingent of the 42nd Royal Highlanders (Black Watch)
regiment was among the first to move, sailing on 17 August for Kyrenia
with orders to establish a new camp above the town. But, typically of
the chaotic planning so far, on 9 November 1878 the regiment was
ordered to abandon its new camp and relocate to Gibraltar. (During
the same month, troops based at Camp Ciftlik Pasha moved to Camp
Mathiati, a temporary cantonment in the foothills of the Macheras
mountains south-west of Nicosia, where other troops stationed on
the island stayed until Camp Polemidia near Limassol was established
in 1879.)

Several British personnel remained in Kyrenia and others arrived.
Among them were the newly appointed District Commissioner of
Kyrenia, Captain Walter Holbech of the 60th Rifles regiment, together
with the new Assistant District Commissioner and Chief of Police,
Lieutenant Andrew Scott-Stevenson, accompanied by his wife Esme.
Kyrenia, with a population of around six hundred, remained "a sleepy
provincial town under the charge of the resourceful Holbech and his

energetic assistant".[32] From time to time until the end of the nineteenth century, the Reverend Josiah Spencer made the journey from Nicosia over the northern mountain range to minister to the few Anglicans living in Kyrenia.

In 1899, Spencer's clerical status was raised when Bishop Popham Blyth appointed him as Archdeacon in Cyprus. Only then was he given the help of an Assistant Chaplain in Nicosia and a Chaplain in Limassol. But already the Venerable Josiah Spencer's health was fragile. He had "shouldered the responsibility of his spiritual office alone for most of his ministry in Cyprus. The solitary nature of his position was only alleviated by the presence and continual support of his family who were with him in Cyprus from December 1880".[33] On 21 April 1901, at the age of fifty-nine and while en route to England by steamer, Josiah Spencer passed away at sea near Marseille.

He was survived by his wife Bessie, their eldest son Cyril and six of their seven daughters: Edith, Mary, Florence, Alice, Beatrice and Ida. Two children had pre-deceased their parents: Reginald, aged almost two, in April 1887; and Lilian (Lily), aged nineteen, in March 1901.

35

Mrs Josiah Spencer, née
Bessie Ellen Perry
1844-1917

*St Paul's Cathedral archive,
Nicosia; reproduced with the
dean's consent*

Bessie continued to live in Cyprus. Between 1905 and 1915 five of her daughters celebrated their marriages in St Paul's church.[34] Whether or not Cyril and Edith married is not known, nor if they remained in Cyprus. Mrs Spencer died in 1917 at the age of seventy-three, commemorated on a headstone in the historic cemetery in Nicosia.

Stained glass window, St Paul's Cathedral, Nicosia, Cyprus

"To the glory of God and in loving memory of Josiah Spencer, Chaplain of Nicosia and Archdeacon in Cyprus who died 21st April; 1901. This window is placed here by his widow and children."

Agisilaou & Spyrou Photography Ltd, Nicosia. Diocese of Cyprus & the Gulf archive

During the last decade of Mrs Spencer's life, three more Anglican churches were built in Cyprus: St Andrew in Kyrenia; St Helen in Larnaca and St Barnabas in Limassol, the latter two designed by the same architect. These achievements most certainly would have delighted the Venerable Josiah Spencer had he lived to see them.

The church building of St Andrew in Kyrenia owes its existence to George Ludovic Houston (1846-1931), the sixth and last Laird of Johnstone in Scotland. He had made his fortune from the coal and limestone mines on his estate before he and his wife settled in Cyprus. "Although an eccentric and not popular with the British Administration",[35] Houston was a generous philanthropist. He financed and established several community projects, including the local hospital, and in 1913 purchased a plot of land on the hill above the harbour, then donated it to the Colonial and Continental Church Society in London to be held in trust for the Anglican Church. At that time Mr Ernest Eldred McDonald, District Commissioner of Kyrenia, was a licensed Reader ministering to the small congregation of St Andrew, as yet with no church building. It is not known whether Houston and McDonald discussed this matter; nevertheless Houston's donation of land enabled Mr and Mrs McDonald to erect a two-roomed building on the site.

In a letter dated 15 December 1913, McDonald recorded "that we had our opening of the Church Room last Sunday and it was a very good start".[36] The congregation consisted of thirty-three persons: the usual nine Anglican communicants, supported by several Greeks living in Kyrenia and members of the Orthodox Church who added joy to the occasion. Mr McDonald continued to serve as a Reader until 1927.

Elsewhere in 1906 on the south coast of Cyprus in Larnaca, the church of St Helen was built, largely due to the generosity of Thomas James Greenwood, District Commissioner of Larnaca, and his wife Chloë Adelaide Greenwood. The architect George H Everett Jeffery had designed the church, a small stone building in the Byzantine style, cruciform in shape and with a domed cupola. George Jeffery was Curator of Ancient Monuments in Cyprus, a post which he held from 1903 until his death in 1935. However, his principal work so far had been to design the Collegiate Church of St George the Martyr in Jerusalem, built in

1891 (and since 1976 known as St George's Cathedral). The first service to take place in the church of St Helen was held on Christmas Day 1907.

St Helen's church, Larnaca, line drawing by the architect George Jeffery, 1905
Source: Bible Lands, reproduced with the consent of JEMT's Trustees

To the west in Limassol, the congregation of St Barnabas had worshipped for more than thirty years in a cottage shared with the Scottish Presbyterian Church. In 1912 the Society for the Propagation of the Gospel in Foreign Parts (SPG) purchased a new plot of land on which to build a church. It had sold the original site in 1881 to relieve its financial difficulties. The Reverend Canon Frank Newham, founder of the English School in Nicosia, and Director of Education in Cyprus (1900-1930), was granted authority to act on the SPG's behalf. As might be expected, George Jeffery designed the church, a stone building with a pitched roof and an apse at the east end. Polycarpos Michaelides was the building contractor. The first service in the new church was held on 12 September 1915, and on 31 October 1915 it was dedicated jointly by Canon Newham and the Reverend Edward Herbert Taylor, chaplain in Limassol and serving the British garrison in Polemidia.

The First World War, then known as the Great War, was now in its second year. Already it had affected the political status of Cyprus. On 5 November 1914 Great Britain and France had declared war against Turkey, simultaneously causing the annexation of Cyprus into the British Empire under military administration status, and the abrogation of the 1878 Convention of Defensive Alliance Between Great Britain and Turkey. Cyprus was no longer under the suzerainty of the Ottoman Empire which itself was beginning to fracture. Following the end of the Great War in 1918, although Cyprus remained under British administration, the island's immediate future status remained unsure.

> "Around this time letters from Philhellenic academics appeared in *The Times*, urging that 'Cyprus, which was offered to Greece in 1915, should now be transferred to her keeping'.[37] Their views were taken seriously and renewed doubts over government plans for the colony meant that for the next two years the Anglican church was unable to recruit clergy to serve in Cyprus because of 'uncertainty as to what was going to happen there'[38]."[39]

Amid continuing indecision "the cogs of the imperial machine cranked on".[40] Then on 1 May 1925 the Commissioner for Nicosia, Charles Hart-Davis, stood in front of the law courts in Konak Square and announced that Cyprus was now a British Crown Colony. For six years there was an undercurrent of dissatisfaction and tension. Finally, during the night of 21 October 1931, several thousand protesters converged on Government House and set it ablaze. Fortunately the Governor, Sir Ronald Storrs, his family and staff were not harmed. The speed and intensity of the uprising shocked and alarmed the colonial administration, as well as Cypriot community and religious leaders. Calm was restored but the seeds had been sown for the political landscape of Cyprus to be transformed once again, culminating in a complex narrative during the 1950s, described presently.

As far as the life of the Anglican Church was concerned, there had been a new positive development prior to the uprising. It was in

September 1927 that the military authorities suggested to Sir Ronald Storrs and to the Right Reverend Rennie MacInnes, Bishop in Jerusalem, that it would be very desirable to have an Anglican church on Mount Troodos. For several years services in Troodos had been held in the recreation room or some other building in the barracks.

> "There was a growing feeling that this arrangement was unfitting as well as inconvenient. At first a simple building of wood or corrugated iron was proposed, but, after considerable deliberation, it was decided that such a building would not be worthy of its purpose, and that a stone church should be erected. … A local committee was appointed under the chairmanship of Archdeacon Buxton, who by his labours and his generosity, is responsible more than anyone else for the existence of Trödos [sic] Church."[41]

George Jeffery was invited to draw up plans. However, as he was not allowed on medical advice to stay at the mountain altitude, he declined the invitation. Instead, the acclaimed British architect William Douglas Caröe (1857-1938) was approached. It so happened he had been visiting Cyprus on behalf of the Ecclesiastical and Church Estates Commissioners for England. He generously agreed to design the church in Troodos, refusing to accept any remuneration.

A site was selected on forest land opposite the nearby barracks parade ground, for which a nominal sum of money was paid. In January 1928 Caröe's plans were received, and as soon as the snow cleared the Public Works Department began to prepare the site. On 27 October 1928 the foundation stone was dedicated by HE Sir Ronald Storrs, Governor of Cyprus. During 1930, with help from the Corps of Royal Engineers based at the barracks, the church walls were built and the roof installed. In 1931 the interior was finished, but not fully furnished, in time for Bishop MacInnes to consecrate the church of St George in the Forest on 3 June 1931, ready for use during that summer season.

In an article published in the January 1937 edition of *Bible Lands,* the Reverend Thomas S B F de Chaumont, chaplain at St Paul's in Nicosia from 1932 to 1937, reflected:

"The writer of these lines who has had the privilege of being in charge of the new church for four out of the six years it has been in use, can pay full tribute to the wisdom and faith of those who faced considerable opposition and criticism in their determination to erect a really worthy House of God, even though it is only open for a few months in each year."[42]

Line drawing by the architect William Douglas Caröe

Main illustration: the church interior as envisioned in 1930,
the nave, balcony and main entrance viewed from the sanctuary

Diocese of Cyprus & the Gulf archive

The complex political narrative in Cyprus gained pace during the 1950s. There was an intensified clamour by Greek Cypriots for enosis (union of Cyprus with Greece) combined with a brutal campaign conducted by EOKA[43] freedom fighters. Turkish concerns were expressed both peacefully and less so by supporters of the militant separatist organisation *Turk Mudya Teskilat* (TMT). Inter-communal clashes were numerous. Negotiations continued over the extent of British Sovereign Bases in Cyprus, with NATO keenly monitoring regional balances of power. On 17 September 1955, during one episode of anti-British rioting, the British Institute in Nicosia was burned to the ground.

Less than three weeks later, on 3 October, Field-Marshal Sir John Harding arrived in Cyprus to assume his appointment as Governor. Instructions he had received stated two priorities. One was "to crack down hard on the insurrection using military measures to restore order"[44]. The other was to start direct negotiations with Makarios III, Archbishop and Primate of the Church of Cyprus.

Governor Sir John Harding and Archbishop Makarios prior to their third round of negotiations at St Paul's vicarage during 1956; John Reddaway (with moustache), Administrative Secretary in Cyprus, on the right behind Harding

Copyright: Cyprus Press and Information Office

Harding wasted no time. During the day after his arrival he initiated the negotiations, in the card room of the Ledra Palace Hotel a short drive away from St Paul's church and its vicarage, the residence of the incumbent priest who was also the archdeacon. This became the venue for further sessions which John Reddaway, the colony's Administrative Secretary, recalled with painful feeling:

> "Subsequent meetings took place in considerable discomfort at the home of the Anglican Archdeacon in Nicosia[45], seated on straight-backed rush-bottomed chairs which tilted forward 'forcing you to sit more and more on the hard front edge of the seat and changing discomfort into torture'."[46&47]

The negotiations transpired to be "one of the most protracted and complex exchanges in the history British decolonisation after the Second World War".[48] Rising Arab nationalism especially in Egypt, the Suez crisis in 1956 (which forced the Reverend John Brown, later the third Bishop in Cyprus and the Gulf, to leave his incumbency in Jordan), and the revolution in Iraq on 14 July 1958 "were all to play a part in directing British policy in Cyprus during this period".[49]

Eventually, on 11 February 1959 in Zurich, agreement was reached on the future of Cyprus, spelled out by three documents: the Basic Structure of the Republic of Cyprus; a Treaty of Alliance; and a Treaty of Guarantee (whereby the British Sovereign Base Areas of Akrotiri and Dhekelia were to be retained as a British Overseas Territory). None of these had been drafted "by the colonisers or the colonised"[50] but by the Greek and Turkish Foreign Ministers. Arrangements were hurriedly made for the Greek and Turkish delegations to attend a conference at Lancaster House in London where details were to be finalised. On 17 February tragedy intervened. The aircraft carrying the Turkish delegation to London crashed in thick fog at Gatwick airport and burst into flames causing several fatalities. The Turkish Prime Minister survived and was admitted to The London Clinic. Two days later he received the Prime Ministers of Greece and the United Kingdom "bearing an appropriately grand silver inkpot".[51] With this as the centre-piece of a simple ceremony in a hospital room, the three men signed the official documents which inaugurated the Republic of Cyprus.

On 1 March 1959 Archbishop Makarios, who was to be the first president of the new republic, flew to Cyprus from London in an aircraft provided by the Greek shipping magnate Aristotle Onassis. As protocol demanded he was greeted by the Governor of Cyprus, the District Commissioner of Nicosia and the Anglican Archdeacon in Cyprus "before being enveloped in the ecstatic communal embrace of 200,000 of his compatriots, little short of the island's entire adult Greek Cypriot population."[52] During the next eighteen months the transitional arrangements prior to the declaration of independence proceeded peacefully, although with nervousness among the expatriate communities. At midnight on 16 August 1960, at Government House in Nicosia, a simple ceremony formally ended eighty-two years of British administration on the island.

St Paul's Church, Nicosia, Cyprus, circa 1952
St Paul's Cathedral archive, Nicosia; reproduced with the dean's consent

During the following fifteen years Anglican parish life in Cyprus continued under the canonical oversight of the Diocese of Jerusalem, by now one of five constituent dioceses within the Archbishopric of Jerusalem, itself created in July 1957.

While Cyprus enjoyed a period of relative calm until July 1974, other countries within the remit of the archbishopric were dramatically affected by the Arab-Israeli war during June 1967. Although the consequences were not the prompt to reconfigure Anglican diocesan structures within the Archbishopric of Jerusalem, their long-term impact could not be ignored.

By the late 1960s deliberations began and during the early 1970s consultations evolved which culminated in the formation of a new province within the Anglican Communion: the Episcopal Church in Jerusalem and the Middle East. It was in this context that the Right Reverend Leonard Ashton CB, Assistant Bishop in Jerusalem, arrived in Cyprus in January 1974 to prepare the way for the formation of the Diocese of Cyprus and the Gulf as a constituent member of the new province. With no comparable precedent to guide him, Bishop Ashton embraced what he later described as "this chance to create something from the beginning"[53] - a new era of Anglican Church life in Cyprus, and also in Iraq and the Arabian peninsula.

The Lord's Prayer in Arabic

Chapter 2

VENTURING INTO ADEN & MUSCAT

1839 - 1970

Today, the Gulf archdeaconry in the Diocese of Cyprus and the Gulf embraces Iraq, the geography of the entire Arabian peninsula and the archipelago of Bahrain. Eight political jurisdictions occupy this vast area of land which predominantly features desert landscapes and numerous mountain ranges particularly in southern Arabia. Although some characteristics are common to all of those jurisdictions - such as densely populated urban developments, Arabic as the most widely-spoken language and Islam as the official religion - distinct regional variations in political development and expressions, including attitudes towards the presence of Christian ministry, are to be found.

This chapter, and the three which follow, attempt to convey the complex diversity of those circumstances: a chronicle of when, where and how a mixed denominational presence evolved within what became the Gulf archdeaconry in the new Anglican Diocese of Cyprus and the Gulf, instituted on 5 January 1976. There is only scope in these chapters to present a flavour of that diversity. Nevertheless, they aim to offer an insight into it: a constantly changing pattern and sequence of elements which shaped the identity of Anglican presence in Arabia and Iraq, beginning in the nineteenth century, first in Aden (southern Yemen), second in Muscat (now the capital of Oman), and in Iraq; then during the first half of the twentieth century in Bahrain, Kuwait and the southern Trucial States[1] in Arabia (as they were politically until 1971).

Where it is appropriate, references to other ministries are included, for example, those of British military chaplains who served in Iraq and at stations in Arabia from the mid-nineteenth century; the fieldwork of the British-based Church Missionary Society (CMS); and the outreach of the Arabian Mission[2], officially organised in the USA on 1 August 1889 under the auspices of the Dutch Reformed Church in America

(RCA), as approved by its Board of Foreign Missions and Central Synod, now General Synod. In due course, the Arabian Mission's outreach led to presence in Bahrain, Iraq, Kuwait and Oman. These ministries are not mainstream to this narrative, yet they do require and deserve recognition in context.

The oldest Anglican church building in the entire Diocese of Cyprus and the Gulf is in Aden, a port city located at the south-western tip of Yemen and some 106 miles/170 kilometres east of the Bab al Mandeb Strait at the southern entrance to the Red Sea. Christ Church was consecrated in 1864. But the establishment during 1839 of a British settlement in Aden had required tenacious persistence to overcome devious and violent opposition.

By 1829 the British Government and the East India Company considered Aden to be strategically important enough for it to "entertain the notion of making Aden a coaling station, but the idea was abandoned owing to the difficulty of obtaining labour"[3]. Six years later, the government changed its mind. By 1835 America had developed such an appetite for coffee that it dominated all trade in Mocha, a coastal town north-west of Aden on the Tihama plain bordering the Red Sea. The coffee trade did not concern Prime Minister, Lord Palmerston, but rather the news that "Egypt's Muhammad Ali, who after invading Tihama seized Mocha and now had his sights trained on Aden."[4] Captain Stafford Bettesworth Haines of the British Indian Navy, then conducting a survey of the southern coast of Arabia, was despatched immediately to Aden with instructions to negotiate its purchase. Sultan Muhsin of Lahej transpired to be a tricky character to deal with. In short, if the British were ever to establish a coaling station in Aden to service its commercial steamers, Haines and his superiors in London and Bombay decided that an international incident of sufficient gravity to warrant their retribution would be the only way to achieve their goal.

In January 1837 that opportunity occurred when the *Duria Dowlat*, an Indian sailing ship flying British colours, ran aground on the

Yemeni coast and almost immediately was boarded by tribesmen who plundered her valuable cargo, then grossly mistreated her passengers by drowning some who included Haj-bound pilgrims and parading several Indian matrons on the deck like slaves. The British considered its response. Eleven months later on 28 December 1837 Captain Haines revisited Aden to "avenge the insult". The Sultan denied that he had any knowledge of the plundering of the ship yet the property was being sold from his warehouse in the Crater bazaar "and there was some evidence that there had indeed been a conspiracy between the agent in charge of the ship and the Sultan's family to wreck the ship and seize the goods".[5] After much discussion and various attempts to intimidate Haines, cargo valued at nearly 8,000 Maria Theresa dollars[6] was returned, and a bill was signed by the Sultan to pay the remainder.

> "Negotiations stalled. Sultan Muhsin's hot-headed son, Hamid, gathered a tribal following that was adamantly opposed to any land sale, and hatched a plot to kidnap Haines. It was foiled. Downcast but still not defeated, Haines sailed away to consider his next move."[7]

He returned in October 1838 authorised to complete the cession of Aden. The negotiations were not friendly, and finally the port was blockaded. Hence in January 1839 forces of the British Royal Navy mounted the Aden Expedition and took the peninsula and its harbour[8] by assault. At last, the much-needed coaling station was established, thus enabling vessels owned by the Peninsular and Oriental Steam Navigation Company to refuel during their passages between Europe and India (and to the Far East).

Aden Settlement began to grow. In 1839 its population was 6,000. By 1842 it had risen to 15,000 (exclusive of military)[9], most of whom were immigrant Arabs and Africans. During the next twenty years or so, a succession of more atrocities, tribal resistance and outrages committed by aspiring leaders required a strong British military presence to protect British interests. During that time "the British garrison was drawn from the Indian Army, and its pastoral care devolved upon chaplains of the Indian Ecclesiastical Establishment"[10] primarily those serving in the Anglican Diocese of Bombay (itself formed in 1837).

49

Steamer Point. The Inner Harbour and Landing Pier. Aden.

Source: vintage postcard

The first Anglican church to be built in Aden was situated in the old suburb of Crater, on the east side of the peninsula. (Also known as Kraytar, and officially named Seera, this district was so named as it is located in the crater of a dormant volcano which forms the Shamsan Mountain.) The church "seems to have been a primitive affair … and was known as the Divine Shed".[11] Some miles away, west of the old town in the aptly named new suburb of Steamer Point, or Tawahi, it was decided to build a "handsome"[12] church.

Funds to pay for its construction were "partly raised by public subscription (chiefly on board the Peninsular and Oriental Company's steamers, where many passengers to India must recollect seeing a box labelled 'Aden Church'), and partly by Government contribution".[13]

Christ Church opened for worship in November 1863. Less than two months later on 10 January 1864 the Bishop of Bombay, the Right Reverend John Harding, consecrated the building, large enough to "accommodate 350 persons"[14].

> "In the early days money was short: for the first twenty years of its life the Church possessed no organ. However, the years brought increased affection for the building from individuals and regiments: on its walls there are memorials to members of the Royal Garrison Artillery, The Queen's Regiment, The South Wales Borderers, and Bombay Regiments of the Indian Army."[15]

In 1868 the British Government extended its sovereignty in Aden by purchasing the peninsula of Little Aden to the west of Steamer Point and Tawahi,[16] and before long the government also decided to build a second church, this time in Crater. Thus, on 7 November 1871, St Mary the Virgin was consecrated by Bishop Harding's successor, the Right Reverend Henry Douglas. Although configured differently from Christ Church - a shorter nave with transepts extending from it - St Mary the Virgin could also seat about 350 people.

51

Christ Church, Steamer Point, Aden, circa 1875
Copyright: Royal Collection Trust, UK, reproduced with consent

An account of the "ecclesiastical arrangements" in the "British Settlement of Aden" in 1887 records:

> "Both of the churches are served by a chaplain, who is appointed and paid by Government. A service is held once every Sunday in each month, and occasionally on weekdays. In the absence of the chaplain, prayers are read by one of the officers in the garrison."[17]

A few interesting statistics provide a surprising perspective. In 1856 the total population was 20,738 including military. In 1872, the year after the second church had been consecrated, a new census of Aden revealed that its total population was 22,722 (including 3,433 military), of which only 208 civilians were European (including British), plus just one American. Therefore, during the previous sixteen years the population of Aden had grown by only 2,000. Of that increase the majority was attributable to immigration from Aden's surrounding district by local people who were dissatisfied with Turkish rule[18], and not because of commercial growth after the opening of the Suez Canal in 1869. None of the 5,024 Indians and Burmese were Christian, nor most likely were any of the Africans, Arabs and Asians who totalled 14,000.[19] A logical conclusion is that most worshippers at Christ Church and St Mary the Virgin were living in the garrison, or associated with it.

Almost half a century later, in 1933, the "legal union"[20] between the Church of England and the Church of England in India was dissolved. At that time the Government of India still provided chaplains for the two civil chaplaincies at Aden from the Bombay Cadre of the Indian Ecclesiastical Establishment, paying the stipend of one chaplain, and one quarter of the other. The Air Ministry paid the balance.

In December 1934 British politicians, in consultation with Indian counterparts, presented a bill before the British parliament to provide the basis for negotiations so that India might gain formal independence. The Government of India Act was passed in August 1935 and became law. This determined, among other consequences, that the political and ecclesiastical status in Aden would change. As for the provision of chaplains, on 5 May 1936 the British Resident in Aden stated (in an enclosure to a memorandum) that as at least three-quarters of the members of the Church of England in Aden belonged to the Army and Royal Air Force, the Air Ministry "ought to pay three-quarters of the total costs of the ecclesiastical establishment" and continue to pay its annual contribution of nine hundred Indian rupees for the maintenance of churches and cemeteries in Aden[21]. Whether or not that happened has not been determined.

Esplanade Road, Crater, Aden, late 1930s
Source: vintage postcard

On 1 April 1937 Aden was established as a British Crown Colony, and its tribal hinterland divided into two protectorates: the Eastern Protectorate extending through the Hadramaut to Mahra and including the Socotra archipelago of four islands, and the Western Protectorate extending to the Red Sea and some twenty miles north towards the city of Taiz. Aden's direct linkage with India was discontinued and ecclesiastically the colony passed from the Diocese of Bombay to that of the Sudan. Almost thirty years later, on 18 January 1963, the colony was reconstituted as the State of Aden within the new Federation of South Arabia. Coincidentally, later that year Christ Church celebrated its centenary. To mark the occasion the Reverend G S Marshall recorded:

"Until very recent years, the acquaintance of Army chaplains with Aden was limited to what could be seen from the deck of a troopship. Most were happy that this was so. …. The Royal Air Force had increasingly supplanted the Army in the defence of Aden and the Protectorates, and its chaplains now became responsible for ministrations at Christ Church. The Church is now the Station Church of RAF Steamer Point, in addition to being the Parish Church of Aden. Since the establishment in recent years in Aden of the joint headquarters of the Middle East Command, the Army has returned to the picture, and the Senior Chaplain Land Forces has been allotted a stall in the Church. Since Christ Church also offers hospitality to the Navy, not only do members of all three services worship in the Church, Sunday by Sunday, but also on occasion chaplains of all the service departments officiate.

"Externally the Church is not impressive. As with other buildings in Aden, function and consideration of comfort prevail over aesthetics. Windows are small and the building appears to be all roof. Expense in the early days disallowed a tower or spire (the climate discourages the art of bell-ringing), and there is nothing to catch the eye. So that it is a surprise, as well as a pleasure, in an area notably deficient in visual beauty, to find the interior of the Church so spacious and dignified. The Church is immaculately kept (itself a triumph in the heat, humidity and dust of Aden) and its Centenary is to be marked by the addition of new altar ornaments and sanctuary furnishings, so that the Services in Aden have indeed a Church of which to be proud."[22]

By the mid-1960s other Anglican churches serving the British military and their families were well established, among them St Martin in the Sands, and Twynham Prefabricated Hut, a temporary building on another site pending the completion of a cantonment church. On 12 December 1965 the Venerable Ivan D Neill, CB, OBE, Chaplain-General to the Forces, dedicated All Saints at Falaise army camp in Bir Fuqum, Little Aden, and St Christopher in Radfan Camp. It can be reasonably assumed that he had no inkling of an impending bombshell announcement by the British Government which would render those developments abruptly and irreversibly redundant.

Dedication of All Saints, Little Aden, 12 December 1965
The Venerable Ivan D Neill, CB, OBE, Chaplain-General to the Forces, gives the blessing
Copyright: Imperial War Museum, London

The first indication became evident in 1966 with the publication of a Defence White Paper: a major review of the United Kingdom's defence policy centred on the need to support NATO in Europe. In 1967 the pound was devalued by fourteen percent, thus sparking an economic crisis which led to budget cuts. Later that year and in 1968 the government published two supplements to the defence review in which the withdrawal of British forces deployed east of Suez was announced. (A UK defence presence was to be retained in Singapore and Malaysia.)

The Reverend Peter Crooks, who served at Christ Church during recent years,[23] reflected with raw honesty in his memoir:

> "By 1954 there would be a total of ninety treaties in place for a population of less than half a million people extending across an area almost as big as Britain. Keeping Aden was a costly exercise and one which would, in the end, be given up with unseemly haste and little concern or provision for those locals who had served it most faithfully. The last thousand British troops left in the early afternoon of 29 November 1967. In the brief, bleak words of one British official in Aden at the time, 'it was not a moment to bring tears to any eyes, or lumps to any throats unless you happened to be one of Aden's thousands of middle-class Indians, for example, or a sultan of one of the former protectorates, humiliated and furious at Britain's betrayal of their treaties'[24]."[25]

The last troops to leave were the Royal Engineers. The final withdrawal of the British from Aden, after having been stationed there for 128 years, took place on 30 November 1967. High Commissioner Sir Humphrey Trevelyan boarded an aircraft at RAF Khormaksar after a short handover ceremony. On that date the Federation of South Arabia (which included the State of Aden) became the nascent People's Republic of South Yemen. RAF Khormaksar was transformed and became Aden International Airport.

All this was a blunt and bruising end to official Anglican ministry in Aden - for a quarter of a century, as it transpired. Nevertheless, after 30 November 1967 "a substantial number of British people stayed behind in Aden, including bankers, businesspeople and even a number of military advisers who helped create the South Yemeni Air Force, and so on"[26]. It is likely that a number of Anglicans were among those who remained in Aden.

Ecclesiastically, although Aden remained within the Diocese of Sudan until its transfer to the Diocese of Egypt in 1975, that was of little relevance. An internal coup during 1969 in South Yemen (called the Glorious Corrective Move) allowed a more radical faction of the regime to come to power. Thus, on 1 December 1970 supporters of the National Liberation Front (NLF) formed the People's Democratic Republic of Yemen (PDRY). The Marxist-led government soon made its presence felt, resulting in the severance of ties with the old colonial power and the West in general, and the requisition of church buildings in Aden for other uses.

All Saints, already turned into as a mess for the soldiers of the Yemeni army who occupied Falaise army camp after the British departure in 1967, became squat accommodation. Distressingly, the former church of St Mary the Virgin in Crater - having been properly decommissioned by the British in 1950 to become the Legislative Council building - was deployed as a CID headquarters and interrogation centre. This acquired a most "unsavoury reputation"[27]. (Now renovated, it is a museum and community hall.) Christ Church was pressed into service as a storage facility and later a gymnasium.

When the Diocese of Cyprus and the Gulf was formed in 1976, any prospect of public Christian worship being reinstated in Aden remained bleak. Nevertheless, in 1978, Central Synod of the Episcopal Church in Jerusalem and the Middle East[28] decided to transfer south-west Arabia and North and South Yemen from the Diocese of Egypt to the Diocese of Cyprus and the Gulf. Fifteen more years were to pass before Christ Church could be restored for Anglican worship.

This chronicle now ventures to Muscat, some 1,162 miles/1,870 kilometres north-east of Aden, and reverts to the late nineteenth century. While Muscat is at the centre of the following significant episode, its focus of interest is the Right Reverend Thomas Valpy French, born on 1 January 1825. After serving as the first Bishop of Lahore for ten years, he resigned his See in 1887, returned to England in early 1888 and within a year began to set his sights on being a pioneer Anglican missionary in Arabia, which he did in 1891. Sadly he died in Muscat just a few months after his arrival, his already fragile health weakened by fever and exhaustion over a long time. Valpy French's legacy was profound and is still celebrated.

The immediate background to this story began with a British Act of Parliament in 1877 which established the Anglican Diocese of Lahore to include Delhi, East Punjab, Kashmir, and what is now Pakistan, with some responsibility for the south-eastern areas of Arabia. The Archbishop of Canterbury, the Most Reverend Archibald Tait, having been asked by the British Prime Minister to suggest a candidate to become the new diocese's first bishop, unreservedly recommended the Reverend Thomas Valpy French. He appears to have been "everyone's choice. French was ecumenical before his time and was acceptable outside as well as inside his own church."[29] On 21 December 1877 in Westminster Abbey, London, he was consecrated as the first Bishop of Lahore by the Archbishop of Canterbury.

The Right Reverend
Thomas Valpy French
Bishop of Lahore, 1877-1887

Thomas Valpy French had arrived in India in 1851, aged twenty-six, in the service of the Church Missionary Society; later the CMS appointed him to co-found St John's College in Agra which opened in 1853, but soon he was forced by ill health to return to England to recuperate. In February 1862 he accepted another CMS commission, this time to initiate mission work in the Derajat region but in December that year he was found collapsed in the jungle and became so seriously ill that the doctors treating him "thought that he would never be able to work in a hot climate again.[30] Again Valpy French returned to England and re-joined his wife and family.

By 1867 he had persuaded his doctor to let him return to India, and on 14 March 1869 he reached Lahore to initiate a project to establish a Divinity School. This opened for classes on 22 November 1870. Valpy French was regarded as a pioneer in theological education. Four years later and again in ill health, he returned to England once more. It is therefore remarkable that he had adequate stamina to sustain himself during his ten-year episcopate.

> "For more than two years before he actually resigned he had been thinking about it and discussing it with his colleagues and superiors. He was obviously killing himself in his endeavors to meet the requirements of his office but he was unwilling to relinquish the burden until he knew a worthy successor would be appointed. His choice was his Archdeacon, Henry Matthew."[31]

Fragile health was not the only reason why Valpy French resigned his See at the age of sixty-two. He had been in India for almost forty years, the last ten of which as Bishop of Lahore where he built a cathedral[32]. Not comfortable with confining his efforts to the expatriate British and those within their immediate ambit, he wanted to have dialogue and discourse with Muslims, rather than just giving them tracts. Therefore he very deliberately sought a place where he could so. After returning to England just before Easter 1888 and being reunited with his wife and family, his thoughts soon became restless. Already he had become deeply concerned about the almost total lack of Christian witness in Arabia. But there was another compelling reason why Valpy French chose Muscat.

Alexander Mackay, a Scottish Presbyterian missionary who had been sent to Africa by the CMS, had observed slaves being forcibly taken from Uganda by Arab traders. He later identified Muscat as the economic headquarters for their slave trade. In August 1888, while in

Usambiro on the south side of Lake Victoria, Mackay wrote an article in which he pleaded that:

> "Muscat which is, in more senses than one, the key to Central Africa, be occupied by a *strong* mission. .... I do not deny that the task is difficult; and the men selected for work in Muscat must be endowed with no small measure of the Spirit of Jesus, besides possessing such linguistic ability as to be able to reach not only the ears, but the very hearts of men."[33]

Mackay termed Arabia as "the cradle of Islam".[34] Bishop Valpy French began to think about the project. On 3 November 1890 he said goodbye to his wife and sailed from England, not imagining that he would never see her or his native land again. He first stayed in Tunisia, and then on 9 January 1891 he left Suez on board a Turkish vessel bound for Aden. It so happened that the Reverend Samuel Zwemer was a fellow traveller.

The Reverend Samuel Zwemer, 1867-1952
RCA archive

They began to talk of their settling down in Muscat. Zwemer later reminisced: "we travelled down the Red Sea both in quest of God's plan for us in Arabia".[35] When the vessel stopped at the pilgrim port Jeddah, Valpy French mailed a letter to his wife: ".... but, as I tell him [Zwemer], I have pledged myself to the CMS to report on its suitableness for founding a mission, according to Mackay's urgent entreaties, and that I preached in the bazaars there [Muscat] in 1884 as being part of my diocese."[36]

After leaving Aden, where the bishop replenished his stock of Arabic Bibles, the steamship proceeded to Bombay, then berthed in Karachi where Valpy French's successor, Bishop Matthew, unexpectedly came aboard to see him. At last, on 8 February 1891, Valpy French reached Muscat. Having allowed himself a few days to settle into his new surroundings, on 13 February he reported to the CMS:

> "I arrived here on Sunday last with Mr Maitland, of the Cambridge Delhi Mission, whom I met in Egypt. We did not like throwing ourselves on the British Consul here, as we thought it might embarrass him to entertain Christian missionaries on their first arrival here; and we had very great difficulty in finding even the meanest quarters for the first day or two, but are now in quarters in an adjoining village, more tolerable as regards necessary comforts, belonging to the American Consul. I have written to India for a Swiss-cottage tent[37], as a resource in case of no possible residence being available here, or Persian caravanserai[38]. In the adjoining hills such a tent might give shelter during the hot weather, if the Arabs will tolerate the presence of a Christian missionary. … Of possibilities of entrance of a mission, I feel it would be premature to speak yet. ….".[39]

61

The bishop and Mr Maitland had met the American Consul, Mr Mackirdy, during their steamer passage. Their decision to accept the consul's offer to let the upper floors of his house in the town of Muttra was only made after two days of "fruitless endeavour" to find suitable accommodation in Muscat, three miles away by boat. While writing to Mrs French on 22 February, her husband enthused:

> "The house is in the midst of a dense population, yet as it out-tops them all and has a roof which makes a little promenade, …. it is really just the kind of mission house we want; and I have got a fairly respectable servant, a decent cook - he would almost have suited you - for ten rupees a month."[40]

Not surprisingly, the bishop's long letters despatched to his wife during the next two months revealed more about his situation in Muscat than the shorter, stiffer reports he compiled for the CMS. That written on 22 February 1891 is a fine example. In this the bishop described having discovered a few schools for boys and girls, a fair number of people who could read, and bazaars chiefly in the hands of Baluchis, Persians and Hindus, "but the bulk of the population is Arab, and Arabic is the colloquial. I decline to talk any other language myself."[41] As yet, the bishop had not met many "thoughtful and encouraging hearers" or people wishing to receive Bibles and Testaments. He had encountered people being aloof, and even occasionally showing bitter and angry opposition, "but not as much as I have often met with in Lahore. I must at least thank God that even the first fortnight I have been able to secure so much patient attention and real opening up of the great truth of the Gospel. I could hardly have expected to get as far as this."[42] Valpy French ended this letter to his wife with characteristic candour:

> "I have now Bishop Matthew's authority [received in Karachi] besides the archbishop's blessing, and am preparing a report of the capacities of Muscat for the CMS. … Though if the CMS refuse to recognize my connexion with them formally, I shall beg the archbishop to put my work here into some official connexion with his Board of Missions; this is what I propose to myself at least. Colonel Mockler [the British Consul] still does all he can to dissuade my selecting Muscat for a centre.

> "Now I must close, grieving only that I cannot send you a brighter letter; still I have much to be thankful for. I cannot expect an effort like this to be easy and everything ready to hand. It is all *pioneering* work."[43]

Early in March 1891, by now a month after his arrival, the bishop decided that he and Mr Maitland should visit the Sultan of Muscat, a nephew of the Sultan of Zanzibar. Colonel Mockler arranged and attended the introduction. Valpy French later confided to his wife: "The Sultan must be about thirty years of age, dignified, courteous, and affable … so friendly as to offer me one of his forts to reside in! I am afraid it would not have attracted you, else I might have given it a second thought."[44]

Muscat harbour: (left to right) al Jalali Fort, the British Consulate and other buildings
Postcard photo by A R Fernandez, circa 1900
Reproduced with kind consent of Hielke van der Wijk, omanisilver.com

The bishop was subsequently to realise that there was an unstated sub-text to the gracious offer, though he was already aware of the Sultan's wish to monitor his activities.

In mid-March Mr Maitland left Muscat. Soon afterwards, writing on 18 March, he conveyed reassurances to Mrs Moulson, the bishop's daughter, that her father was very well, that he felt much stronger than at any time since he had left India and worked hard each morning on his Arabic, and then explained her father's routine. After dinner, at about four o'clock, the bishop would go out sometimes alone to preach or read to the people. He never allowed Maitland to go into the bazaar with him when he preached, yet from other sources Maitland gathered "that the people sometimes listened well, sometimes opposed, and occasionally were rude". Sometimes the bishop would walk with him into the country behind the town, or to a village in the neighbourhood, often engaging in conversation with the people. They would return at nightfall, and after tea conduct the service of evensong together.

Just five days after Maitland had written to the bishop's daughter, Valpy French wrote less optimistically to his wife about his task:

"It is premature to speak of the prospects of a mission being founded here. I am often amazed and startled to find the message borne with as it is, and sometimes listened to with profound attention by the Arabs, though I go out trembling every day, and wondering what will come next. As it is more and more understood and noised about what I am come for, and the growing clearness of my diction and ease of speech arrest more attention, the opposition is likely to be more organized and embittered."[45]

The opposition which Valpy French referred to in his 23 March letter to his wife was not confined to local attitudes. On 20 April he complained in a letter to the Reverend Robert Clark that "I can't get the Society [CMS] to identify themselves with the work here".[46] Four days later, the bishop explicitly conveyed his situation to the CMS:

"Patience here, as elsewhere (and more than in most scenes I have visited), is a great prerequisite. ... I cannot get many - very few, indeed - to come to my house and read, which is naturally one of my great objects. They ask me into their shops and houses sometimes, to sit and discuss on the great question at issue between us and them, some Beluchees [Baluchis], mostly Arabs ... There are some Hindus in the crowded bazaars ... rather a large proportion of educated men and women too; the latter take special interest in religious questions, and sometimes lead the opposition to the gospel. ... Chiefly, however, I reach the educated men by the roadside or in a house-portico, sometimes even in a mosque. ... Still there is considerable shyness ... yet bright faces of welcome sometimes cheer me and help me on.

"If I can get no faithful servant and guide for the journey into the interior, well versed in dealing with Arabs and getting needful common supplies (I want but little), I may try Bahrein, or

Hodeidah and Sennaa [Sana'a], or if that fails, the North of Africa again … But I shall not give up, please God, even temporarily, my plans for the interior, unless, all avenues being closed, it would be sheer madness to attempt to carry them out."[47]

That missive was dated 24 April 1891. Yet, on 3 May he scribed these optimistic reassurances to his wife:

"I love to think of possibly being with you about this time next year. I hope to feel my way cautiously and warily and [not] push on rashly. For the present I shall be by the coast. … Colonel Mockler has really tried to help me, and says he has really done his best to support my interests, but he is bound to keep the Sultan here acquainted with all my movements. This may render me safer, but the work suffers, I fear, in consequence. … I hope while at the sea-coast little town of Sib for the next two or three weeks I shall be able to get letters regularly despatched by private messengers to Muscat, but you must not be anxious at not hearing sometimes, for there is no official post despatch."[48]

That was to be the last letter which Mrs French would receive from her husband. He never reached the interior, although three days later he did set off for Sib (Seeb) with that resolve, accompanied by two shaikhs from two of the most influential tribes. They had been appointed by the Sultan to offer the bishop close protection "whichever way he turned"[49]. What Valpy French did not tell his wife in his final letter to her was that he was weakened by fever. Already, "once or twice he had gone into the Residency in Muscat almost prostrate, but had quickly revived to some extent when he had been induced to take food and a little stimulant".[50]

Valpy French left Muttra during the morning of 6 May in an open fishing boat with no protection except an umbrella. In the afternoon he arrived in Sib village, twenty-eight miles away where he hoped he would find cooler weather. After resting under trees near the shore until sunset, he walked three-quarters of a mile to the house placed at his disposal: a light two-roomed thatched structure, made of wattled screens of date palm leaves. It offered protection from the sun but not from the hot air which blew through the sides.

During the next day, with the two shaikhs and the son of the local wali (protector of local affairs) who had arrived, Valpy French walked for three miles to visit the wali and then returned to his house. This took its toll. On 8 May he went outside with some books, later to be seen by some men who told Kadu, the bishop's servant, that his master was asleep in the date palm grove. Presently, Kadu heard the bishop clap his hands for help and ran outside to find him, then unconscious. On 9 May, persuaded by the shaikhs, Valpy French agreed to return to Muscat but was not well enough to travel until the following evening.

Back in Muscat he hired a room near the British Residency and told Kadu to tell no-one. But indirectly he did. Two days later on 13 May, a Dr Jayaker visited the bishop and found him unconscious. After Valpy French revived, he consented to being taken to the British Residency and was carried there in a cot. Dr Jayaker arrived at about 8 am on 14 May to find the bishop quite unconscious again, and at 12.30 he passed away. That evening the funeral took place. The coffin was covered with the British flag and the service was read by Colonel Mockler. The first telegram sent to England with news of the bishop's death gave sunstroke as the cause. But later during a conversation which Mr Maitland had with Dr Jayaker, he concluded:

> "So far as I can judge it was not any special piece of exertion or exposure that killed him, but the whole task he attempted was beyond his physical powers."[51] On 22 May 1891 the *Civil and Military Gazette* of the Punjab recorded the depth of the impression Bishop Valpy French had made upon "the larger world of men. ..... His was indeed a saintly character, utterly self-denying and unwordly."[52]

Bishop Thomas Valpy French's grave is located in a cemetery at the bottom of a narrow ravine set back from a cove in a bay south of Muscat. This is normally reached only by boat although intrepid walkers may venture there over land. The cemetery has some three dozen graves, mostly of sailors and officers of the Indian Marine and the Royal Navy. Initially, the bishop's grave was marked by a wooden cross and protected by a cement covering. Later these were replaced with an elegant tomb of white marble, crafted in Jaipur and shipped from Karachi.

Bishop Thomas Valpy French's grave in a cove south of Muscat
Copyright: Dr Paul Armerding, reproduced with consent

Appropriately and poignantly, near to Valpy French's grave rests the body of an American missionary, the Reverend George E Stone who, on 26 June 1899 at the age of twenty-eight and after only a short period of service in the field, succumbed to heat apoplexy at the coastal town of Birka a few miles east of Muscat.

In 1893, the Reverend Peter Zwemer, younger brother of the Reverend Samuel Zwemer, had established himself in Muscat, and on 27 May 1896 he assumed guardianship of eighteen boys aged between seven and thirteen who had been rescued from an Arab slave ship by the British frigate *HMS Lapwing*. "The younger Zwemer pledged to the British political agent and consul in Muscat, Captain F W Beville, that he would feed, clothe, house, educate and prepare the boys for adult life."[53] In September 1896, a second capture of two dhows brought a draft of 183 slaves into Muscat, among them fifty boys of a suitable age to be educated at the Arabian Mission School.

These actions, largely a response to Alexander Mackay's plea, were to be tinged with sadness. The exertions involved combined with Muscat's fierce climate so weakened Peter Zwemer that he had to return home to Michigan where he died on 18 October 1898, six weeks after his thirtieth birthday. The Mission Church built in Muscat in the 1930s was dedicated to his memory.

The Reverend Peter Zwemer
1868-1898
RCA archive

Since the days of Bishop Valpy French and the Reverend Peter Zwemer, Christian ministries in and around Muscat have evolved, including a shared arrangement between the RCA and Anglicans, formalised in 1978. A later chapter takes up that story. On 5 November 2016, the 125th anniversary of Bishop Thomas Valpy French's "Final Journey to Oman" was celebrated in the new church building called Bait An Noor[54] in the compound at Ruwi. The Right Reverend Michael Lewis, fifth Bishop in Cyprus and the Gulf, presided and preached at a commemorative Anglican Eucharist. The occasion was distinguished by the presence of Their Royal Highnesses the Prince of Wales and the Duchess of Cornwall. Indeed, the memory of Bishop Thomas Valpy French as a respected Christian Anglican pioneer lives on.

Bishop Thomas Valpy French
1825-1891
RCA archive

Chapter 3

FOOTPRINTS IN IRAQ

1842 - 1973

Mesopotamia is an ancient region to the east of the Mediterranean Sea. Its name originates from the Greek meaning "between the two rivers", the Euphrates and the Tigris. The region corresponds to modern-day Iraq, and also parts of modern-day Iran, Syria and Turkey. It was known to Arabs as Al Jazirah (the island), later referred to as the Fertile Crescent by the Egyptologist J H Breasted. Iraq is the eastern part of the Fertile Crescent which stretches in an arc from the head of the Gulf to the south eastern extremity of the Mediterranean.

Anglican interest in the area of what is now Iraq and neighbouring regions may be traced particularly to the ministry of the Reverend George Percy Badger (1815-1888), who from 1842 to 1845 travelled as the representative of the Archbishop of Canterbury, the Most Reverend William Howley, to the Assyrian Christians of the Church of the East in Mesopotamia and Kurdistan.

Also of significant interest is the Assyrian Mission sponsored by a later Archbishop of Canterbury, the Most Reverend Edward White Benson. He requested Mr Athelstan Riley FRGS, a layman, to undertake a journey in the autumn of 1884 to North-Western Persia and Kurdistan "to ascertain the condition of the Assyrian or Nestorian Christians, and the state of the Mission sent thither in 1881 by the late Archbishop Tait[1] and the Archbishop of York".[2] Riley later submitted his *Narrative of a Visit to the Assyrian Christians in Kurdistan*.

The consequence was that clergy were sent to help the Church of the East through teaching and medical care. It was active until the Great War, 1914-1918. A significant leader of the Archbishop's Assyrian Mission was Canon William Ainger Wigram.

Even though the Church of the East was held to be Nestorian in its theology and therefore in one sense strictly not orthodox, Archbishop Benson was careful to forbid proselytism: the Anglican contribution was to be one of education and service to an ancient branch of Christianity that deserved respect for its persistence through the hardest of times.

Before the Great War, the Assyrians who acknowledged the authority of Mar Shimun, the Patriarch of the East, dwelt partly in the mountains of Kurdistan, partly in the highlands of Asiatic Turkey, especially near Lake Van, and partly around Urmia in Persia (modern-day Iran). Another large percentage, usually known as Chaldaeans, and sometimes by others termed as one of the Uniate churches with their Patriarch in communion with Rome, lived in the plains of Mosul some 250 miles/400 kilometres north of Baghdad.

Other smaller groupings and ethnicities included, then as now, Armenians, Shabakis (Sabaeans), Circassians, Turkmen, Mandaeans and Yazidis. The two main ethnic groups in Iraq are Arabs and Kurds. Today, around ninety-seven percent of the country's citizens are Muslims. Its Christian population is now estimated to be around half a million, or fewer. In the late nineteenth century that population was substantially larger though still firmly in the minority.

In that context the Church Missionary Society (founded in 1799), working with the Anglican Communion and Protestant Christians around the world, founded a mission in Baghdad during 1883, and in 1896 established a hospital there. A second hospital was established in Mosul during 1901. After the Great War began in August 1914 the mission workers were interned by the Turkish authorities, then expelled to Egypt where they continued to work. After the war ended the CMS chose not to resume its mission in Iraq.[3]

From Baghdad, Iraq's capital and largest city, the river Tigris runs south to Basrah. This former great inland port is located near the confluence of the Euphrates and Tigris rivers, 90 miles/145 kilometres up the

Shatt Al Arab waterway and inland from the head of the Arabian Gulf. By 1914 it had three distinct areas: Ashar, host to banks, consulates, major commercial houses and the main bazaar; Old Basrah City, 5 miles/8 kilometres inland on the other side of the waterway from which, in due course, lay the road to the RAF Camp at Shaibah and the oilfields in the desert; and Ma'qil, the port area about 5 miles/8 kilometres up river from Ashar where the airport was later built.

It was in Ashar that the Anglican church of St Peter was constructed in 1917 by sappers serving in the Great War, soldiers responsible for tasks such as building and repairing roads and bridges, laying and clearing mines. Unusually, and with splendid effect by all accounts, the building materials used were mud bricks and teak. About this time, the Missions to Seamen established a Rest House in Ma'qil, some 6 miles/10 kilometres away from St Peter's. Its military chaplain was also Honorary Chaplain to the Missions.

St Peter's Church, Basrah
Source: Bible Lands, reproduced with consent of JEMT's trustees

Following the defeat of the Ottoman Empire during the Mesopotamian campaign (6 November 1914 to 14 November 1918), a proposed British Mandate for Mesopotamia was awarded on 25 April 1920 at the San Remo conference in Italy, but was not yet documented or defined. A draft mandate document was prepared by the British

Colonial Office in June 1920. However, the mandate faced difficulties, principally a nationwide Iraqi revolt during that year. This prompted the foundation on 23 August 1921 of the Hashemite Kingdom of Iraq under British administration, after which on 10 October 1922 the Mandate was enacted via the Anglo-Iraqi Treaty of Alliance. Hence the kingdom was also known as Mandatory Iraq. The Treaty of Alliance was designed to allow for Iraqi local self-government while giving the British control of foreign and military affairs.

In 1922 British forces departed from Iraq, as did military chaplains who had served at St Peter's. They left the church under the care of the civil chaplaincy of Basrah and the Persian[4] Gulf. This included Kuwait, the islands of Bahrain, and the Trucial[5] State of Sharjah.

Also in 1922 a civil chaplaincy was established in Baghdad. For fifteen years the congregation was granted one of the new Iraqi Government's properties to use as a church, free of charge.

St George's Church, Baghdad (1922-1936)
Source: Bible Lands, reproduced with consent of JEMT's trustees

In all other respects the chaplaincy was entirely self-funded by collections and donations thereby enabling it to support a resident chaplain, without a break, for many years. During 1932 the Reverend David Colin Dunlop began his two-year incumbency, also serving from 1933 as the British Embassy chaplain. In that year he wrote:

"Since 1923, the civil congregation of Baghdad has worshipped in a building of exceptional suitability and charm. St George's Church was, until the British occupation of the city, the old [Turkish] gate-house of the South Gate. Yet a visitor entering the church for the first time would find it difficult to believe that the building was not deliberately designed for Christian worship. Indeed, many prefer it vastly to the general run of churches built for the use of small congregations in foreign parts. It has the dignity of age, and an unconventionality and quaintness which do not in the least limit its practical convenience."[6]

Meanwhile, Iraq's oil industry had been born, far away from the diplomatic and political epicentre of the country. One of the preliminary drilling sites was at Baba Gurgur, about six miles north-west of the ancient town of Kirkuk and some 200 miles/322 kilometres north of Baghdad, in what was primarily a Kurdish region.

"There, for thousands of years, two dozen holes in the ground had been venting natural gas, which was always alight. They were thought to be the 'burning fiery furnace' into which Nebuchadnezzar, King of Babylon, had cast the Jews. ...

"And it was there, at 3:00 a.m. on October 15, 1927, from a well known as Baba Gurgur Number 1 - in which the drill bit had barely passed fifteen hundred feet - that a great roar was heard, reverberating across the desert. It was followed by a powerful gusher that reached fifty feet above the derrick, carrying in it rocks from the bottom of the hole. The countryside was drenched with oil, the hollows filled with poisonous gas. Whole villages in the area were threatened, and the town of Kirkuk itself was in danger. ...

"Finally, after eight and a half days, the well was brought under control. It had flowed, until capped, at ninety-five thousand barrels per day. The leading question had been answered. There were petroleum resources in Iraq."[7]

On 31 July 1928, nine months after the initial discovery on 15 October 1927 and after six years of negotiations and wrangling, the full contract of an agreement was signed, allocating ownership of the oil. Royal Dutch/Shell, the Anglo-Persian Oil Company (APOC), the Near East Development Company (created to hold the interests of the American companies), and the French each received 23.75 percent. The Armenian self-styled "business architect" Calouste Gulbenkian received five percent. On 8 June 1929 the Iraq Petroleum Company (IPC), previously the Turkish Petroleum Corporation, was formed. At first, the IPC's concession was for the territory of Iraq east of the Tigris River, comprising the Kirkuk oilfield. When the extent of IPC's infrastructure grew, including an export pipeline and pumping stations along its length, the Anglican chaplaincy of the Iraq Petroleum Company was established and its evolution is described in due course.

Until 1931 the pastoral ministry of the chaplain in Baghdad encompassed British residents in the capital along with those living in other areas of Iraq, such as the oilfields of Kirkuk and Khaniqin, and also the administrative centres of Mosul and Diwaniyah. Pastoral care in the south of Iraq was the responsibility of the Anglican chaplain in Basrah. At that time, both chaplains were appointed by the Archbishop of Canterbury, who was also the diocesan bishop of their "parishes".[8]

In 1932 the Archbishop decided to adjust this arrangement. On 24 June that year the Right Reverend George Francis Graham Brown OBE was consecrated as the sixth Bishop in Jerusalem. Previously Principal of Wycliffe Hall, Oxford, and a great evangelical teacher, he had already made notable contributions to peace and mutual understanding between Arab, Jewish and Christian communities. From 1927 until his consecration, the future bishop had taken students to Palestine. During these visits he was able to study at first hand the Churches of the Near East, and later became a recognised authority on them. These credentials were among the reasons why, in the year of his consecration, the Archbishop of Canterbury asked him to undertake, on his behalf but in consultation with him, episcopal supervision of the chaplaincies in Iraq[9]. The bishop discharged this duty with characteristic thoroughness, paying constant visits, in addition to visiting the rest of his large bishopric which embraced Palestine, Syria, Transjordan, Cyprus and part of Turkey. In due course, the same thoroughness was also true of the Venerable Weston Henry Stewart who as Archdeacon in Palestine, Syria and Transjordan (1928-1943) also travelled extensively and spent much time ministering in Iraq between 1940 and 1942.

Meanwhile, during November and December 1931, the Venerable Harold Buxton, Archdeacon in Cyprus, visited Basrah. He noted that the land on which St Peter's stood was owned by the Iraqi government which, it was hoped, might be generous enough to donate it to the church. That required King Faisal I to grant permission. The government's proviso was that a company should be formed in whose name a firman (a sovereign's edict) could be issued. In 1932 the King fulfilled his promise. The land on which the church stood was handed to St Peter's English Church Company.

The year 1932 was encouraging for Iraqis too. Since the end of the Great War Great Britain had been entrusted by the League of Nations, founded on 10 January 1920 as a result of the Paris Peace Conference, with the work of "setting the freed people of Iraq upon their feet, and helping them to govern themselves".[10] Now that task was completed. On 3 October 1932 the Kingdom of Iraq was granted full independence and British executive authority in the country came to an end. The Reverend David Colin Dunlop remarked a year later:

> "Nevertheless there is still a fair-sized British community in Baghdad, and probably always will be, for even when the British Advisers to the Government finally leave the country, there will be the British staff of the Iraq railways (a large body), a considerable number engaged in trade, and very likely an increasing number connected with the three big oil companies. …

> "Great therefore was the dismay and sadness when it became known that the church was to be demolished. The development of Baghdad towards the south appears to the city authorities to demand the absence of St George's Church. …. The congregation of Baghdad is anxious that the new church shall be a memorial of the countless lives laid down on Mesopotamian soil."[11]

The Baghdad Civil Chaplaincy Association decided to construct a substantial church on land leased from the British Embassy. It was to be named the Mesopotamian Memorial Church of St George the Martyr in commemoration of the 41,115 British officers and other ranks who had given their lives in Iraq during the Great War, and in the troubled times following the Armistice of 11 November 1918. Dunlop's report published in the October 1933 edition of *Bible Lands* was also a fund-raising appeal:

> "It is hoped that the character of the memorial will be emphasised in the decoration of the building, which we want to be such that it will … be a real 'historic monument'. We do not on this account propose to be extravagant or to erect an elaborate building. All showiness is to be very much shunned, while we only aim at spending about £4,000. It will not be easy to raise this sum in Baghdad, where the people are already heavily taxed in maintaining (with no grants from outside) a permanent resident Chaplain. We are hoping that the church-people at home will help us. …. Lastly, we want to build a church in this city of domes and minarets which will be a witness that the British people care about their religion."[12]

Concurrent with those developments, the Arabic-speaking Anglican community in Baghdad became the subject of a bold and brave episcopal experiment. This community, and that in Mosul, had been formed before the Great War by CMS missionaries serving in Iraq. After their expulsion from Iraq and the CMS's later decision not to resume its presence in the country, both communities continued but with no clergyman in charge. The community in Baghdad declined offers from other church groups to provide, at no cost, a clergyman of another denomination; and it turned down inducements to join other bodies. For some eight years and with great effort during the 1920s it raised £1,000, and with this sum built a church of its own. Worship took place every Sunday led by an Arabic-speaking layman.

During June 1933 Bishop Graham Brown and Archdeacon Stewart visited the Arabic-speaking Anglican congregations in Baghdad and Mosul. Each had a church council, and each wished to have an Anglican clergyman to minister to them. The American missionaries under whose nominal care the two churches had been left after the CMS's departure were prepared for them to have an Anglican priest. In Baghdad some thirty families made up the Arabic-speaking Iraqi Protestant Church congregation which were prepared to contribute towards such a priest's stipend.

The Most Reverend Cosmo Lang
1864-1945
Archbishop of Canterbury, 1928-1942

Portrait painted by Philip Alexius de László, MVO

Source: en.wikipedia.org

On 6 July 1933 the bishop wrote to the Archbishop of Canterbury, the Most Reverend Cosmo Lang, to seek his advice. It had been suggested that a lay-worker of the Church Missions to Jews (CMJ) who had attended a shortened course at St John's College in Highbury[13] might be ordained for work in Baghdad. The American Mission thought that a "Baghdad Jew convert" would be acceptable to the Arabic-speaking Church, whereas a Muslim convert would not. The bishop remarked in his letter to the Archbishop: "it is a striking opinion but I can see the reason for it. I do not know whether Your Grace would wish this congregation to be encouraged in this desire to obtain a priest."[14]

The person being considered was Mr Alfred Cohen Karmouche, a Baghdad-born Jew living in Jaffa who for some years had been studying with a view to entering Christian ministry. The other protagonist in forthcoming events was Mr Abdulkerim Issa (as spelled on his letterhead), proprietor of the English Pharmacy on Badawi Street in Baghdad. Significantly he was Chairman of the local Iraqi Protestant Church Committee (IPCC).

On 2 February 1934 Bishop Graham Brown wrote to Mr Abdul Karim (the spelling used in letters) informing him that if satisfactory agreement could be made between Mr A C Karmouche, the CMJ and the IPCC, then the CMJ would request the Archbishop of Canterbury to instruct him, the Bishop in Jerusalem, to proceed with the ordination of Mr Karmouche. The Archbishop did grant his approval, providing that the Examination for Deacon's Orders were passed. All proceeded to plan. Then, too soon, the relationship between the IPCC and the deacon broke down.

Karmouche had been educated in America and in London and his wife was a Russian Jewess. He was determined to live as a Westerner with the result that, in the bishop's view, he was thought to regard himself as superior both to the Jew and to the Arab. Both groups considered his attitude to be one of patronising contempt. Within three months of the Reverend Alfred Karmouche's arrival in Baghdad he refused to minister any more to the Arabic-speaking congregation. An anonymous article published on 15 January 1935 in the *Alwehda* newspaper had sparked controversy by claiming that "Abdul Kerim Issa sits among his friends and talks about his authority and powers over the Protestant Church and how he exercised this authority, even upon the Pastor and worshippers, in front of the altar".[15]

In early 1935 the Reverend Charles John Fortescue-Thomas arrived in Baghdad as the new British chaplain to the English-speaking congregation, and honorary chaplain to the British Embassy. Almost immediately he set about trying to introduce a semblance of discipline among the Iraqi Protestant Church congregation, particularly as it was "quite unaccustomed to Anglican liturgy"[16]. As a start, Fortescue-Thomas's suggestions for Easter celebrations and the form of service he would conduct were readily accepted. So were his suggestions that the congregation might organise a reredos, a frontal for the altar and candles to place upon it, although not all were implemented immediately. This prompted him to write to the General Secretary of the CMS, the Reverend Prebendary William Wilson Cash[17], to ask if it might be possible for the CMS to re-engage its interests in Iraq by sending an Arabic-speaking missionary to serve the Arabic-speaking Anglican community. For emphasis he added that the Bishop in Jerusalem showed a deep personal interest in its future. The upshot was that on 17 May 1935 Wilson Cash responded, first to the bishop rather than to Fortescue-Thomas, to say that although restarting a CMS Mission in Baghdad was, so he thought, "quite out of the question for some years to come"[18], he could try his best to secure a grant of £50 a year to help with the appointment of a Baghdadi or Palestinian native pastor.

Meanwhile, Bishop Graham Brown had been trying to "compose the differences" between Mr Karmouche and the IPCC, recognising that serious mistakes had been made on both sides. In the end both were adamant that no further attempt should be made to bridge the gulf between them. On four occasions the bishop gave pastoral support to Alfred Karmouche, but by June 1935 Karmouche was on the verge of a nervous breakdown. Medical advice was that he should "be transferred to a less trying climate for duty"[19], a euphemism meaning that he and his family should leave Iraq almost immediately to take six weeks' holiday, during which time plans would need to be made for them.

The bishop explained all of this in a seven-page analysis written on 25 June 1935, addressed to the Archbishop of Canterbury. He characterised the situation as "the outward failure of the experiment of combining Jewish and Arabic work in Baghdad by a Baghdadi Hebrew-Christian".[20] Its failure was due, in his view, to the personalities involved, not the concept. "The opposition on all sides is great but there are unmistakable signs of a spirit of enquiry."[21]

In that same letter the bishop conveyed his immediate plans to resolve the crisis in the Iraqi Protestant Church congregation. His first two proposals were that the British chaplain, Fortescue-Thomas, would hold a service of holy communion for the Arabic-speaking congregation once a month, and the IPCC would invite him and the two churchwardens to advise them on matters dealing with church governance, administration and procedure. It may be assumed that Fortescue-Thomas had some influence in those plans.

A month earlier in May 1935 he had written to the bishop to offer his personal view: that the aim should be for a new policy and basis of work in Baghdad, hopefully in place when he departed at the end of 1936. If he could leave "with a beautiful new church built, possibly a small school for Christian children and also a chaplain's house all on the same site, with the Arabic church troubles settled"[22] his time spent in Baghdad would not have been in vain.

The bishop's third proposal conveyed to the Archbishop of Canterbury was a commitment to provide the Iraqi Protestant Church congregation with an "Arab layman who will be in the position of Lay Reader and Catechist and will minister to them".[23] Thus Mr Aziz Domet, a Palestinian Arab who had lived in Germany for some years, arrived in Baghdad at the end of July 1935. He was employed by the IPCC for an initial two-year term, on condition that the congregation contributed towards his salary, to be supplemented, it was hoped, by a CMS grant.

The British chaplain's desire for a "beautiful new church" to be built before he left Baghdad was indeed not in vain. On 10 February 1936, Lieutenant-Colonel J Ramsay Tainsh CBE VD, Director of Railways in Iraq, laid the foundation stone for the Mesopotamian Memorial Church of St George the Martyr. The stone had been sourced from a quarry near the so-called Solomon's Quarries in Jerusalem. Bishop Graham Brown conducted the service, having flown to Baghdad by courtesy of the RAF.

The design of the church was a simple cruciform, with two aisles and very small transepts, and a low tower rising in the centre. Yellow brickwork was used for the exterior walls. The plain pointed bricks of the interior walls were left uncovered to the level of the roof of the aisles. The main barrel roof was finished in white plaster. Electric lamps concealed behind the cornices allowed light to be reflected from the roof throughout the building.

Laying the foundation stone for the Mesopotamia Memorial Church of St George the Martyr
by Lieutenant-Colonel J Ramsay Tainsh, CBE, VD, on 10 February 1936
with the Right Reverend George F Graham Brown (left) and the Reverend A G Kayll, RAF
Source: Bible Lands, reproduced with consent of JEMT's trustees

The church, 90 feet/27 metres long, and 40 feet/12 metres wide, was expected to seat one hundred and fifty people, with room for extra chairs if needed.

By July 1936, ten stained glass windows and five teakwood panels had been promised as memorials by units of His Majesty's Forces at home and in India, and by relations and friends of those who had died in Iraq. So far £3,600 had been contributed towards the building cost, including £1,400 from residents in Iraq, and £280 from the "Scots Kirk" in Baghdad. To acknowledge this latter gift the St Andrew's Cross would be flown on the church every St Andrew's Day, 30 November. The money in hand was expected to pay for the building's completion, but more funds were needed for the furnishing, landscaping the grounds and, if possible, to build a chaplain's house. These details were set out in an article published in *Bible Lands*[24]. It ended (no author credited): "the Baghdad Civil Chaplaincy is supported entirely by contributions from residents and there is no endowment."[25]

In January 1937, Archdeacon Weston Henry Stewart and his wife arrived in Baghdad to work with the churchwardens and the church council to arrange the Service of Dedication and the following reception. On Saturday 6 March 1937 Bishop Graham Brown dedicated the Mesopotamian Memorial Church of St George the Martyr. As expected, the church was full with many people standing.

The service was conducted with the usual ceremonies. "An augmented choir rendered the musical part exceptionally well"[26], with Air-Commodore Leigh-Mallory among its eighteen members. Visiting clergy present were the Armenian Prelate for Iraq, Bishop Reuben Manassian, with an attendant priest; the Assyrian Bishop Mar Sargis, Bishop of Jilu, Baz and Rekan, also with an attendant priest; the Reverend Rahad Yacoub, a Syrian Jacobite priest; Herr Frizz, German pastor from Beirut; and two RAF Chaplains, the Reverend G W N Groves (Anglican) and the Reverend J K W Haswell (other denominations).

Bishop Graham Brown was attended by Archdeacon Stewart together with the two newly-arrived chaplains, the Reverend F W Bowyer and the Reverend R A Lowry, and Mr Aziz Domet. The document of dedication was signed by the bishop in the presence of the congregation, with a quill pen provided by the British Ambassador. To complete the formalities, on the following day, Sunday 7 March, he "licensed and instituted to their charges Mr Lowry to Baghdad and Mr Bowyer to Basrah".[27]

Parallel to building developments in Baghdad, the mud floor of the church of St Peter in Basrah had been covered with honey-coloured tiles, a new system of lighting had been installed, and the entire east end had been beautifully panelled, the cost being borne by Sir John Ward, one of the church's oldest and staunchest friends, who was the chaplain's warden and Basrah's Port Director. The church was used by the British community, by airmen from the Flying Boat Squadron at Ma'qil, and by a certain number of local Iraqi and Indian Christians. "Situated on a site of increasing importance, St Peter's, Basrah, thus continues to witness to the Christian Faith amid the polyglot inhabitants of Iraq's only port."[28] The Reverend Francis William Bowyer reflected shortly after his departure from Basrah in 1939:

"The Mesopotamia campaign cost many thousands of British lives, and many hundreds of men must have made their last communions in this church - for them a veritable out-post of Christianity. …. The church has continued to function, and a chaplain has been supported, almost without a break. St Peter's, Basrah, probably represents the smallest community in the Anglican Community [sic] maintaining its own church and chaplain."[29]

On 3 September 1939 the United Kingdom and France declared war on Germany following its invasion of Poland two days earlier. Very soon the theatre of war had spread to other parts of Europe, particularly the east. In November the Reverend Arthur Adeney was inducted as chaplain of the civil chaplaincy of Basrah and the Persian Gulf, with duty at the RAF Squadrons at Ma'qil and Shaibah. Soon he found himself busy looking after British refugees who had fled from the Balkans and were waiting in Basrah for shipping to repatriate them to the UK. During his two-year ministry there, despite wartime constraints, he was able to visit places in the Gulf region within the remit of his chaplaincy.

83

In 1940 the bishop charged Archdeacon Stewart with the added task of serving the chaplaincy of the Iraq Petroleum Company. This area included the export pipeline, vividly described by the archdeacon in the October 1940 edition of *Bible Lands*.

"The pipeline from Iraq's oilfields to the Mediterranean was in form like a slightly distorted letter Y laid on its side with the stem eastward and the two arms westwards. The stem represents the single line from the fields round Kirkuk to the point where the line crosses the Euphrates at Haditha, after which comes the bifurcation of the northern or T line, running mainly through Syrian (French mandated) territory to Tripoli, and the southern or H line, which passes from Iraq into the British mandated territories of Trans-Jordan and Palestine, and ends at the port of Haifa."[30]

The system lay across bare desert, with pumping station townlets at intervals of about 70 miles/112 kilometres.

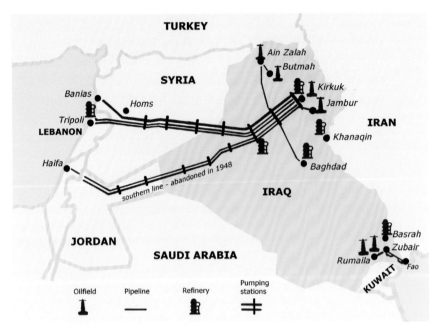

Each pumping station townlet had perhaps six European families with considerable numbers of locally recruited labour, of which a large proportion were Christians of various denominations. The "parish" of Kirkuk consisted of three camps where there were larger numbers of European residents. The chaplain's duties extended to outlying groups near Mosul, Basrah and even as far as the Arabian Gulf. By using the oil company's aeroplanes, the archdeacon had, in about four months, visited every station at least twice (except on the French part of the line, which was visited by a Roman Catholic priest), and had conducted services in sixteen different centres.

He was invariably warmly welcomed on these fleeting visits, and it was clear that his ministrations were deeply appreciated. In most of the stations services were held in messrooms or similar places with no regular church furniture, but, to quote the Archdeacon, 'the very absence of conventional church fittings, if (perhaps because) it puts a great tax on the officiant's powers of concentration, may, and sometimes does, increase the sense of relevance and reality in the services.'[31]

During 1941 the Reverend Arthur Adeney was transferred from Basrah to Port Said. He was replaced in December that year by Archdeacon Stewart who arrived to serve as acting chaplain. His ministry in Basrah ended abruptly when news was received that Bishop Graham Brown had been killed in a car accident in Palestine on Monday 23 November 1942. He had been hurrying back from Syria to Jerusalem to take part in a refresher course for Army padres, a night journey in the blackout which meant continuous travelling for fourteen hours, covering a distance over difficult roads of some 550 miles/885 kilometres.

> "At 5.30 p.m. he reached the Lebanon-Palestine frontier at *Ras el Nakoura*. Here a Moslem Arab policeman of Palestine and a Jewish ex-Legionnaire asked for a lift southwards and the Bishop moved over into the right corner of the back seat and took them in with him. About 6 p.m. the car was struck by a train in the darkness near Az Zib. Thus when the Bishop met his death he was with members of the two races for whose reconciliation he had striven."[32]

The bishop's car had been overturned by a goods train on a new level-crossing. His chauffeur was unhurt, and the two passengers to whom he had given a lift were only slightly injured. He himself sustained fatal head injuries and died almost immediately. *The Times* obituary notice began: "The Bishop in Jerusalem (Dr G F Graham Brown) was an outstanding leader of the Anglican Church overseas and one of the most widely and deeply beloved".[33]

Archdeacon Stewart was appointed Bishop Designate and returned to Jerusalem. Because of wartime travel restrictions his consecration at Westminster Abbey in London was delayed until 21 September 1943. Meanwhile, from late 1942 until 1944, British Army padres ministered to the congregation of St Peter's and the many members of the Forces who worshipped there. In the new year of 1943 the Reverend D Denton White arrived in Basrah to serve as the Missions to Seamen chaplain. He later took over the work of the civil chaplaincy of Basrah and the Persian Gulf in May 1944.

The year 1943 was at a critical time when a flood of supplies to Russia was beginning to pour through Iraq and Persia. A recreation hall in the grounds of St Peter's church had been enlarged to create a popular canteen and leisure club for all serving in the British Forces and the merchant navy, many of whom regularly worshipped at the church on Sundays. Denton White recorded:

> "The heat and humidity of Basrah are notorious, and there have been a number of deaths among the crews of the ships which become steel ovens in the summer, so that a great need was fulfilled in providing shore sleeping accommodation for the seamen, and recreational facilities which were then almost non-existent in the port area."[34]

Also in 1943, St Peter's suffered a great loss in the death of Sir John Ward, the Port Director, who had been a churchwarden and a pillar of the church for over twenty years. The Missions to Seamen secured a lease on his house and grounds which enabled it to open its Institute on the premises during that summer. The chaplain in Basrah also made periodic visits to Fao, a sandbar at the mouth of the Shatt al Arab which had to be kept clear for shipping by a fleet of five dredgers. Some sixty British officers were constantly deployed on this monotonous chore.

The Missions to Seamen building among the date palms at Fao
Source: Bible Lands, reproduced with consent of JEMT's trustees

Their only spiritual ministry was that offered by the chaplain during his visits. By the end of the Second World War in 1945 Denton White summed up the situation:

> "What the future will bring is unpredictable, but with the promise of commercial expansion, particularly in the oil fields, the British community in the area is not likely to lessen, and the Bishop hopes that there will eventually be another Gulf Chaplaincy with its centre at Bahrein[35] but it is certain .... that whatever peace-time conditions may bring, there will be an adequate ministration for members of the Anglican community in the area, and the opportunities for spiritual work and expansion will ever be numerous."[36]

In February 1947 the Reverend Edward Matchett became Civil Chaplain of the Basrah and the Persian Gulf chaplaincy, and Port Chaplain for The Missions to Seamen, Basrah. By 1948, a new Flying Angel[37] Institute was set up at Maʻqil providing seamen with air-conditioned rest areas as respite from hot ships. After the British Army left Iraq in October 1948, RAF units remained in Basrah at the Shaibah and Maʻqil camps, and in Bahrain and Sharjah. As RAF chaplains no longer served in any of those stations, Matchett assumed honorary RAF chaplain duties, taking services at Shaibah twice a month, and offering monthly communion at Maʻqil. Well into the early 1950s, the Anglican chaplain in Basrah also made pastoral visits to the oil company's hospital outside the city at Makina, and continued long journeys to Fao and the oil terminal to conduct services there.

Meanwhile, new developments had taken place in the chaplaincy of the Iraq Petroleum Company. On 6 November 1947 Bishop Weston Stewart recorded: "Only a few days ago, in the Kirkuk oilfield, perhaps where the Magi of the Epiphany story came from, I dedicated a temporary Church of the Wise Men".[38] Registers of Services archived at All Hallows by the Tower in London[39] document continuous activity at the church from 1939 to 1960.

All proceeded well in Basrah until 26 January 1957. During that night the church of St Peter was gutted by fire. The Honorary Secretary of St Peter's Church Association, Norman Jenkins, wired the news to the bishop, who was then in Jerusalem, adding simply: "grateful if you can visit Basrah sometime". In a measured letter to the bishop dated 29 January 1957 Jenkins wrote: "I realise that you have your difficulties and problems in current world affairs but if you can spare the time to visit us we shall be heartened and comforted. .... With kind regards from us all in Basrah."[40]

Just over a week after the fire, Bishop Stewart arrived to inspect the damage. On 11 February 1957 he recorded his three-day visit:

> "For all practical purposes, it is true that the church is totally destroyed, though in fact it seems there was no wind on the night of the fire and though the roof and the east end collapsed altogether, the west end, north and south walls and, strange to say, the teak uprights of the whole building, are still standing, I had no idea that wooden beams could possibility have withstood the furnace which the church must have been [sic] …

> "Thanks to some really remarkable enterprise and energy on the part of Norman Jenkins, assisted by representatives of the Port Directorate and the Basrah Petroleum Company, a very effective temporary chapel has been fitted up by knocking together the library room in the chaplain's garden and the canteen room adjoining it. When I reached there on Tuesday, 5 February, it seemed impossible that this could be ready for use by Friday. But in fact it was, and I celebrated there that morning, with thirty-six communicants present. I have nothing but admiration for the way in which the situation has been handled, and the speed with which the work was done."[41]

All parties, including the insurance company involved, were agreed that there was no evidence as to the cause of the fire, "still less as to any malicious activity"[42]. The general consensus was that the cause was a fault in the electrical wiring. The bishop advised that any idea of arson should be dropped. The next question was how and where to rebuild.

The Right Reverend Weston
Henry Stewart,1887-1969
Bishop in Jerusalem, 1943-1957

*Source: Bible Lands,
reproduced with consent of
JEMT's trustees*

A few weeks later he suggested that "the best plan will be to dispose of the site altogether: the very facts of noisy dock and commercial surroundings, which make it rather unsuitable today for a church, give it a very considerable market value, and it may be possible to sell it for a sum sufficient not only to buy a quieter site in a more residential area, but also to build a better church and parsonage."[43] That suggestion formed part of The Bishop's Letter published in the April 1957 edition of *Bible Lands*, written on 26 March while he was at the IPC Guest House in Kirkuk. Although the bishop did not say so, that date was eleven days after his seventieth birthday. Already he had planned to retire:

> "This is probably the last letter that I shall write for *Bible Lands* as Bishop in Jerusalem: the July number, when it comes, will I hope begin with a first letter from my successor. The Archbishop of Canterbury has already announced his identity - Angus Campbell MacInnes, elder son of the Bishop under whom I first served in the East. …."[44]

This was a reference to 1926 when, as the Reverend Weston Henry Stewart, he had arrived in Jerusalem to be a staff member at the Collegiate Church of St George the Martyr.

After serving in the Diocese of Jerusalem for more than thirty years, Bishop Stewart resigned his See on Saturday 29 June 1957 and retired. By this date, the Archbishop of Canterbury, after due consultation with Metropolitans of the Anglican Communion and other bishops, had approved a revised system of jurisdiction for the bishoprics and congregations in the Middle East. This was enacted at Lambeth Palace on 8 July 1957 when the Right Reverend Campbell MacInnes was invested by the Archbishop of Canterbury as the eighth Bishop in Jerusalem, with the title Archbishop in Jerusalem and Metropolitan.

Just over a year later, on 14 July 1958, a political watershed occurred when King Faisal II was overthrown in a military coup led by Abd Al Karim Qasim. This signalled the end of the monarchy in Iraq, and made the position of many people in the country extremely difficult.

In Basrah, the English-speaking Anglican congregation faced a challenging time with many leaving the country at short notice after being relieved of their jobs. Hope of rebuilding St Peter's church had been abandoned. The new plan was to improve and adapt the temporary building then being used as a church, and to remain on the same site.

By the end of 1960 there were serious clerical gaps in all Anglican chaplaincies in Iraq. Canon Bernard Hall Coombs Wilson (Church of the Wise Men, Kirkuk), Canon Haydn Parry (St Peter's, Basrah) and the Reverend William Benjamin Farrer (St George's, Baghdad) had all left during the year, Farrer to take up his appointment as Archdeacon in Cyprus. It was not easy to find replacements, but in February 1961 Archbishop MacInnes visited Iraq to institute two new chaplains: the Reverend John de Chazal at St George's and the Reverend Harold Marcus Wilson at St Peter's. He also licensed Mr Albert Brown as Reader in charge of the ministry at Fao.

The next blow was when the Government closed the Seamen's Institute in Basrah and took over the property. By early 1962 alternative facilities had not been provided, so the chaplaincy made plans to build premises for the seamen's use on the site of the gutted St Peter's church. These were thwarted by new turmoil in Iraq when, between 13 and 18 November 1963, pro-Nasserist Iraqi officers led a military coup within the Ba'ath Party. Uncertainties and frustrations abounded throughout the country. The application to open a new centre for seamen was turned down once again by the authorities. Since the closure of the Missions to Seamen's Institute at Ma'qil, all attempts to persuade the Government to allow the church to open premises to serve the seamen's recreational needs had failed.

Archbishop Campbell MacInnes (centre) and Canon Haydn Parry prepare to visit tanker crews at Fao, seen off by Mr W Manning, Chairman of the Missions to Seamen, Basrah
Source: Bible Lands, reproduced with consent of JEMT's trustees

The dynamics had changed in Albert Brown's ministry too. As the Missions to Seamen's representative in Fao, he had until now travelled to Basrah each month to conduct a service at the church. By 1966 use of the main oil terminal had dramatically declined because tanker owners were avoiding having to pay port levies for the berthing of their vessels there. Instead, most of the big tankers were directed to anchor at Khor Amaya, an artificial island some distance out to sea, south of the Shatt al Arab. As few ships now used the terminal and Mr Brown could only occasionally visit Khor Amaya, his job had become very frustrating. Archbishop MacInnes therefore decided, with the agreement of the Missions to Seamen, that Albert Brown should move to Basrah and live in the Chaplain's House with the hope that his ministry would be more fulfilling by working among seamen who came to the main port in Basrah itself. With the help of the oil company, he would also be able to make weekly visits to Fao and Khor Amaya.

In mid 1965 there was better news in Baghdad. Archbishop MacInnes reported: "We are fortunate in having an excellent chaplain in Baghdad, Alfred Cooke, who was an army chaplain in the war. He and his wife are having the whole of Iraq to look after, including Kirkuk and Basrah."[45]

On 6 January 1967, the Feast of the Epiphany, a week before the Reverend Alfred Cooke was due to leave Baghdad, his successor the Reverend Clive Handford arrived to be the next chaplain at St George's. Thirty years later he was to become the fourth Bishop in Cyprus and the Gulf. He recalls: "Alfie had visited Kirkuk each month and Basrah every three months. I maintained the pattern with Kirkuk but at the request of the local congregation and with the encouragement of the two pastors of the American Mission, began going to Basrah each month."[46]

As things turned out, it was not to be an auspicious Epiphany. Between 5 and 10 June 1967, the Six-Day War, also known as the June War, the 1967 Arab-Israeli War, and the Third Arab-Israeli War, was fought by Israel and her neighbours Egypt, Jordan and Syria. Bishop Handford reflects:

"As a result of this war, Iraq severed diplomatic relations with the UK, USA and West Germany. Like my predecessors, as the honorary Chaplain to the British Embassy, I was put on the diplomatic list and reckoned as a diplomat. This worked well until the breaking off of relations. While all Americans left within twenty-four hours, there were people of a number of different nationalities, including UK citizens, who were not leaving. There was, therefore, still a viable congregation at St George's.

"During the week before the final convoy out of Baghdad, I tried to get my status changed. Sadly, this proved impossible and so I had to leave. We went to Iran, the nearest safe place. Jane, my wife, was already at the church there having left on the first convoy. We were in Iran for almost three months while the Swedish Embassy in Baghdad, which was looking after British interests, negotiated with the Iraqi government to try to get us back. In the end the answer was 'No' and we moved to Beirut.

"Before I left Baghdad, I asked the English Churchwarden, Larry Gaines, an accountant with IPC, to conduct evening prayer every Sunday evening until I was able to return. In the event, Larry continued to do this and when he was going on leave instructed others to take the service. They even started to sing the service and maintained the pattern until Colin Davies arrived in the autumn of 1968."[47]

The Mesopotamian Memorial Church of St George the Martyr, Baghdad
Source: Bible Lands, reproduced with consent of JEMT's trustees

It is remarkable that this even became a possibility. On 17 July 1968 yet another coup took place in Iraq. Ahmed Hassan Al Bakr replaced Abd Al Rahman Arif as President of Iraq, and thereafter for a number of years he governed Iraq in concert with the Ba'ath Party leader Saddam Hussain. Nevertheless, the government granted permission for an Anglican priest to serve in Iraq again. The Reverend Colin Davies was licensed and installed in St George's on 28 October 1968, to minister in Baghdad, Basrah and Fao. His ministry during the next five years was fraught with unsurmountable challenges, particularly Iraqi government censorship. The future was unpredictable.

Also during 1968 Archbishop MacInnes declared his intention to retire, having accepted that his ministry was now too onerous for his poor health. He was succeeded on 10 March 1969 by Archbishop George Appleton. Soon, he too had to face difficult decisions about Iraq. On 13 December 1969 the Reverend Colin Davies informed Mr Jim Wilson, Secretary of the Jerusalem and the East Mission Trust[48], that the Archbishop in Jerusalem had approved his suggestion that St Peter's House and Church in Basrah should be placed in the care of the French Carmelite Fathers who worked in Baghdad and Basrah and were well established in Iraq.[49] Only on 31 August 1972 was the Reverend Colin Davies granted General Power of Attorney. This provided for a document to be drafted whereby the Chaplain at St George's Church, Baghdad, would agree to transfer by way of a gift to the Latin Church, the plot in Basrah then in the name of St Peter's Church. On 12 February 1973 Mr Wilson informed Archbishop Appleton that he had received a copy of the draft.

Bishop Handford asserts that the "property in Basrah never was transferred to the Carmelites, which would have been a good thing"[50] to ensure its continued use for ecclesiastical purposes. At the end of 1973 the Reverend Colin Davies was expelled from Iraq. The chaplaincy in Baghdad was suspended, leaving St George's with only expatriate members and no resident chaplain. For many years, services were led by lay people. The chaplaincies in Basrah and Kirkuk fell into abeyance.

It was not until early in the twenty-first century that the Anglican chaplaincy in Baghdad at St George's was meaningfully, and differently, restored. For the time being the chaplaincy of Basrah remains defunct. A cautious hope is still held that one day it may be possible to re-establish Anglican presence not only in Basrah, but elsewhere in Iraq too, besides Baghdad.

Chapter 4

NEW ERAS IN BAHRAIN & KUWAIT

1932 - 1975

Thehe peninsula of Arabia is the largest in the world. The Red Sea lies to the west, the Gulf of Aden and the Arabian Sea to the south, the Gulf of Oman to the north-east, and the Arabian Gulf[1] along its eastern coast. From early times inhabitants of the peninsula have often called it *Jazirat al Arab* (Island of the Arabs).

Along the peninsula's eastern coast, the archipelago of Bahrain had for centuries served as a trading entrepôt. Its indigenous natural pearl-fishing industry had thrived, as had that in Kuwait, and similarly at the small communities of Abu Dhabi and Dubai. Natural pearls found in oyster shells and molluscs fished from the Arabian Gulf were prized as some of the best and most precious in the world.

Pearl merchants in Bahrain, circa 1950s
Caltex Corporation archive, reproduced with permission

In 1893, Mikimoto Kokichi, a Japanese entrepreneur, was successful in creating the first cultured pearl. By the early 1920s commercially-viable harvests created fierce competition for the Gulf-based natural pearl-fishing economies and caused their decline. The collapse of the New York stock market on 29 October 1929 precipitated the global Great Depression. This compounded the economic woes of Bahrain, Kuwait, Abu Dhabi and Dubai. It also spawned a clamour by Anglo-American oil corporates to acquire additional oil exploration rights in the Arabian peninsula, and seek extensions to existing concessions, all with the hope that commercial success would follow.

Major Frank Holmes
Chevron archive

At the end of the Great War one person had declared his conviction that significant deposits of oil lay undisturbed far below the desert sands of Arabia. His name was Major Frank Holmes[2], a rugged New Zealander who wrote home to his wife in 1918:

"I personally believe that there will be developed an immense oilfield running from Kuwait right down the mainland coast."[3]

Holmes had sound reasons for this assessment. Trained as a mining and metallurgical engineer and having gained considerable international expertise in his discipline, at the age of forty in 1914 he found himself serving as a quartermaster in Abyssinia (now Ethiopia) arranging supplies to be sent through Aden to the British Army serving in Mesopotamia. In so doing he visited Arabia for the first time and became interested in the oil seepages which he observed.

After his demobilisation, Holmes registered the Eastern and General Syndicate Limited in London on 6 August 1920 as a consortium of British businessmen to acquire and operate oil concessions in the Middle East. In May 1923 he signed an agreement with Ibn Saud, then Sultan of Nejd, whereby the syndicate was granted a concession in al Hasa area of eastern Arabia, and in May 1924 was granted a concession in the Kuwait-Nejd neutral zone. When a Swiss geologist engaged to evaluate the land claimed that searching for oil in Arabia would be a gamble, banks and oil companies were discouraged from investing in Arabian oil ventures.

Holmes remained confident and undeterred. On 2 December 1925 he signed a concession with Shaikh Hamad bin Isa Al Khalifa, Ruler of Bahrain that allowed him to search for oil there. On 11 January 1929 the Bahrain Petroleum Company (BAPCO) was registered in the Canadian city of Ottawa as both a British company and a wholly-owned subsidiary of the Standard Oil Company of California (SOCAL), itself registered in San Francisco. This convoluted arrangement was necessary to comply with the Red Line Agreement, signed on 31 July 1928, negotiated to formalise the corporate structure of the Iraq Petroleum Company (IPC). Its American, British and French shareholders were prohibited from independently seeking oil interests in territories which had been within the former Ottoman Empire. The agreement was so named because at one meeting during the negotiations, Mr Calouste Gulbenkian, an Armenian businessman who owned five percent of IPC's shares, had allegedly called for a large map of the Middle East, taken a red pencil and drawn a line along the boundaries of the now defunct empire.

During May 1930 detailed survey work began in Bahrain. Fred A Davies, a SOCAL geologist (who later became Chairman of the Arabian American Oil Company), detected "a large definitely closed domal structure (anticline)"[4] at the foot of Jebel Ad Dukhan (Mountain of Smoke)[5], so named due to heat hazes which often shroud it. There he built a cairn of stones to mark the site for oil well Number 1. On 16 October 1931 the Deputy Ruler of Bahrain worked the first blows of the drill as the well was "spudded in".

Oil flowed on 1 June 1932, followed on Christmas Day that year when well Number 2 "came in" with a rush. As a result, Major Frank Holmes gained the sobriquet in Arabia of *Abu Al Neft*, Father of Oil.

Encouraged by this success, SOCAL was granted an exclusive concession on 29 May 1933 by Ibn Saud who, less than a year earlier on 23 September 1932 had been proclaimed King of Saudi Arabia. On 8 November 1933, SOCAL formed a new subsidiary, registered in Delaware in the name of the California Arabian Standard Oil Company (CASOC)[6], later the Arabian American Oil Company (ARAMCO).

On 22 February 1934 the tanker *El Segundo*, owned by SOCAL, dropped anchor off Bahrain's east coast adjacent to Sitra island on which it was planned to construct three fuel oil storage tanks and a jetty. For three-and-a-half months the tanker was used as a freighter, storehouse and floating dormitory. On 7 June it was loaded with the first shipment of Bahrain crude and set sail for Yokohama in Japan where, on 9 July, it docked and discharged its cargo, then voyaged home to San Francisco. At the end of the year, on 23 December 1934, Shaikh Ahmad Al Jaber Al Sabah, the Ruler of Kuwait, granted an oil concession to the Kuwait Oil Company (KOC). This was formed as a partnership between the Eastern Gulf Oil Company registered in Kentucky and the Anglo-Persian Oil Company (APOC), later known as British Petroleum (BP).

Almost three years later, on 11 December 1937, His Highness Shaikh Hamad bin Isa Al Khalifa officially opened the Bahrain refinery. On 22 February 1938 oil was discovered in the Burgan field of Kuwait, followed by news from Saudi Arabia on 3 March 1938 that Dammam well number 7 had begun to produce oil in commercial quantities.

It is well known that these discoveries were the catalysts for rapid economic development in the upper Gulf region, replicated later in Qatar, the Trucial States and Oman. Less well known, this process created unique opportunities for Christian presence to grow in those host jurisdictions which allowed freedom of worship in their burgeoning expatriate communities. Oil companies, in particular BAPCO and KOC, were leaders in the provision of church buildings for their Christian employees and their families.

The mounted camel guard at Bahrain refinery in 1938
BAPCO archive

By the mid-1930s a number of Anglicans were living in Bahrain, some in the capital of Manama, but most in BAPCO's evolving township of Awali. There was no organised body of Anglican church members in Bahrain, and no specific church building available to Anglicans living in Awali or Manama. As explained in the previous chapter, spiritual and pastoral oversight of Anglicans living in Kuwait and Bahrain was the responsibility of the incumbent priest of the Basrah and Persian Gulf[7] chaplaincy. Since the Reverend Francis William Bowyer's arrival in Basrah during October 1936 to take charge of that chaplaincy, it had "weighed heavily"[8] on his conscience that Bahrain lacked a church council or committee and regular church services. In January 1937 he visited to remedy the situation.

At that time the Political Agent in Bahrain was Lieutenant-Colonel Gordon Loch. He was not an Anglican but, for political reasons, he wished Bahrain to be linked ecclesiastically to Basrah and thence to Jerusalem/Canterbury. During Bowyer's visit, Loch encouraged him to form a church council. A preliminary meeting attended by some twenty Anglicans was held on 8 January 1937 at the home of Mr Charles Belgrave, Adviser to the Ruler of Bahrain, and his wife Marjorie.

Those present included Mr Edward Skinner, General Manager of BAPCO. It was decided that the chaplain in Basrah should try to visit Bahrain three times a year and hold services in the Arabian Mission Church, the use of which had been offered by the RCA missionaries running the mission's school and hospital in the capital. The meeting discussed how the chaplain's journeys would be funded and elected a church committee. This met for the first time on 16 March 1937.

When the Reverend Francis Bowyer returned to Bahrain in December that year he found that another committee had been formed, in Awali and under the chairmanship of Dr Louis Dame, a former RCA missionary. In January 1937 he had been appointed as BAPCO's doctor. This committee was holding non-denominational services every Sunday in a converted school-room, conducted by another RCA missionary, the Reverend Gerrit D Van Peursem, and assisted by Norman Dodds, formerly a Reader in the Anglican Diocese of Durham. Bowyer persuaded the Awali committee to combine with that in Manama, and to hold an Anglican service of evensong in Awali once a month. In turn, he was asked to increase his visits to six times a year.

By 1938 the new auditorium of the Awali cinema/theatre was being used for church services by all denominations. Alas, a BAPCO rule stated that "no Indians or black people were allowed to enter the building"[9]. Charles Belgrave and the Manama Anglicans objected to this discrimination by refusing to attend services there. Although Awali and Manama continued to be represented on the same church committee for some years, as the Awali congregation was mainly nonconformist this created tensions and a difference in outlook.

A visit between 13 and 20 June 1938 by the Right Reverend George Francis Graham Brown, Bishop in Jerusalem, gave impetus to the view that a new basis for Anglican organisation in Bahrain was required. During that time, services were held in the BAPCO auditorium and at the American Mission Church in Manama. On 16 July 1938 the bishop reported to the Archbishop of Canterbury, the Most Reverend Cosmo Gordon Lang, that he had spoken to the British Political Agent in Bahrain, by now Mr Hugh Weightman, about the need for a British Anglican chaplain to serve BAPCO's community. Although the company was prepared to finance this appointment, no suitable candidate was available and so the momentum was lost. Even during the Second World War Anglican clergy from Basrah travelled to Bahrain every quarter, and the Bishop in Jerusalem endeavoured to come once a year. (On 23 November 1942 Bishop Graham Brown died in a car accident in Palestine. His archdeacon, the Venerable Weston Henry Stewart, was immediately named Bishop-designate although not consecrated until 21 September 1943.)

By 1950, BAPCO had constructed a church to serve its community. Over the years it has been extended and enhanced but, essentially, it remains much the same today. At the east end behind the altar, a striking stained-glass window depicts Jesus Christ holding a lantern. It is derived from the allegorical painting "The Light of the World" by the Pre-Raphaelite artist William Holman Hunt.

During the 1940s a determined effort was made to enable an Anglican church to be built in Manama. Sir Geoffrey Prior was a key instigator.

Awali Church, photograph dated 28 May 1950
BAPCO archive, reproduced with permission

Although he was now British Political Resident in the Gulf based in Bushire, he had served as the Political Agent in Bahrain from 1929 to 1932. On 20 October 1943 he wrote to Bishop Stewart suggesting that an appeal fund should be launched to raise funds to pay for the church.

As it turned out, most of the money needed was raised in Bahrain through events held by the expatriate community.

Already Prior had the Reverend Norman Sharp in mind as a possible architect. He had arrived in Iran during 1925 as a CMS missionary, then served as pastor in Yazd for eleven years. He observed that he had "never seen places of worship so uninspiring and devoid of architectural merit, and of art and beauty, as the churches we had in Isfahan, Yazd and Kirman".[10] His resolve to remedy this situation became a passion. During 1928 he designed, fundraised and founded a new church in Yazd; in Shiraz after moving there in 1938; and in 1944 he designed churches in Qalat and Bushire. In all of these he incorporated decorative tilework and designed the windows to include coloured glass reused from abandoned or demolished Persian houses, former homes of the Qajar dynasty (late eighteenth to early twentieth century).

As Sir Geoffrey Prior was living in Bushire at that time, almost certainly he had seen Norman Sharp's creative expertise. In 1944 they

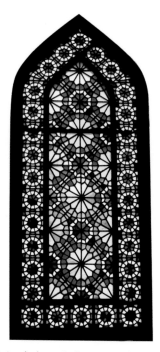

One of nine Persian stained-glass windows at St Christopher's church, Bahrain
Copyright: Angela Murray

met to discuss the Bahrain project. Within a year, Sharp had completed his designs and submitted them to the church council. Unfortunately, his concept was thought to be too elaborate and expensive and so the council decided to postpone progress until a resident chaplain was appointed. To that end, several people were approached, most at the recommendation of Bishop Stewart. None accepted, most of them unwilling to live in Bahrain. Awali members of the church council suggested that a Free Church minister should be chosen. Those in Manama insisted on an Anglican.

The church council despaired of ever finding a suitable candidate from Europe and so decided to recruit a priest from Australia or New Zealand. The rationale was that as the brother of the secretary to the council was a priest serving in Australia, he might help. Five applications were received. Eventually, the Reverend Robert Gorbutt Rickells, a British national who since 1945 had been a vicar at Greytown in New Zealand, accepted the bishop's offer to appoint him as the first Anglican chaplain to serve in Bahrain. He and his wife Norah, an accomplished musician and organist, left New Zealand on 11 October 1951 aboard a tanker owned by Caltex[11] and arrived in Bahrain on 8 November "at the end of the best sea-trip we have ever had."[12] Their home was a rented apartment above a grain store in Manama. Robert Rickells also served as chaplain to the RAF based on Muharraq island and to the Royal Navy at HMS Juffair on the north coast of Manama, the capital.

By now there were plans to build a church and a chaplain's house in Bahrain. Two years earlier the Ruler, His Highness Shaikh Isa bin Salman Al Khalifa, had donated a large plot of land in Manama, sited between the police fort and a Muslim cemetery. The title deed dated 30 August 1949 is in the name of the Jerusalem and the East Mission Trust. Preparation of the site began in August 1952 and the foundation stone laid on 24 November 1952. On 13 March 1953 Bishop Weston Henry Stewart consecrated the building and dedicated it in the name of St Christopher, the patron saint of travellers. Sir Charles Belgrave, largely responsible for the building's design, became a churchwarden.

The revised external appearance of the church was simple, with no tower, transepts or a porch to relieve its basic box-like shape.

The decorative enhancements were nine windows containing handmade stained-glass in delicate colours, thought to be some two hundred years old. The Reverend Norman Sharp had found the windows, removed from an old Persian house before its demolition, for sale in a carpenter's shop in Yazd. He donated the windows to Sir Geoffrey Prior who had them sent to Bahrain by dhow during the Second World War. They were stored in Manama until they could be installed.

Processing alongside St Christopher's church to the west door, circa1955
Bishop Weston Henry Stuart (at the back), churchwardens Sir Charles Belgrave (left)
and Neville Pocock, the Reverend Canon Alun Morris, and crucifer (unidentified)
Source: author's collection

Construction of a single-storey villa on the compound began in 1954 to serve as the vicarage, but not finished before Robert and Norah Rickells left Bahrain in April that year. Their successors were the Reverend Alun Morris and his wife Edith. When they moved the furniture and the air-conditioner from the rented apartment, they soon discovered that an infestation of weevils from the grain store had been transferred too. "It took us quite a long time to repulse the invasion."[13]

Alun Morris discerned that to improve awareness of the Anglican church in Bahrain he needed to be easily associated with it. His neatly trimmed black goatee beard and moustache, and black polished shoes with silver buckles worn on formal occasions and when visiting Rulers, were distinctive idiosyncrasies. But they were not obviously the dress of a priest. He wrote:

> "It had become clear to me that St Christopher's was not as well-known as it should be and that I should have to be my own PRO [Public Relations Officer]. So I went to Ghulam Mohammed in the souk and got his very expert cutter, to copy my white cassock, in light-weight material, and that was my dress for ten years, except on the golf course. … I never regretted my decision."[14]

Chaplain's House with the church bell on the roof
Canon Alun Morris with St Christopher's School students and teachers assembling outside the church hall, early 1960s
Source: author's collection

In 1953, Captain Kendall, a friend of Charles Belgrave, offered the parish the gift of a church bell. Eventually, this was cast in a foundry in Loughborough in England and shipped to Bahrain in July 1956. It was supposed to have been hung in the church tower but this was never built. According to Alun Morris, experts calculated that if the bell were to be attached to a wall of the church, "it would probably bring the whole edifice down when it was rung, as a church bell should be, so it was decided that carefully set on the vicarage roof, with only vertical thrust, which the structure could absorb, it would probably do no harm except to the occupants below, and so it was.

Depending on the direction of the wind, the ringing could be heard a mile or more away. To the consternation of some, the amusement of others, and the pious approval of many, I was accustomed to ring the Angelus [call to prayer] on appropriate occasions and times, and before church services."[15]

In Manama, as yet there was no place where St Christopher's could hold large meetings and social functions. During 1959 a church hall was built between the church and the chaplain's house, large enough to house a badminton court as requested by Mrs Morris who was a keen player. A decent floor, stage, storage space and lighting were installed to meet the need for a multi-purpose function room. Alun Morris had something else in mind for the new hall. Until 1961 the custom was that British expatriate parents living in Manama sent their children back to the UK to attend boarding school. But, as he observed:

> "They soon began to miss them terribly, perhaps even more than the children missed their parents, and generally speaking the families involved were new to the stresses and strains they were discovering. Becoming conscious of this as a pastoral problem, I reasoned that, somehow, we should do as a community what BAPCO were doing as company policy. We had not their resources, but I felt that the evident need could be met by some organised good-will. ….

> "After some debate and not a little opposition, the school idea got off the ground. Our initial advantage was that we already had the hall to use. We started with about two dozen children and the affair snow-balled. We discovered plenty of teachers among expatriate wives, all technically qualified, all enthusiastic and loyal. The various firms and companies soon realised the benefit of what was going on and rallied round financially. We all had lots of headaches and lots of fun, and the rest, for me, is history."[16]

St Christopher's School was opened in February 1961. Initally, each class was held in a private house. At Easter that year the school moved to the church hall. By the end of 1963 a single-storey school had been built next to the church, and a second storey added in 1965. In 1972 the school moved to larger premises in Manama, and has since evolved at other sites, independently from the church. Nevertheless, the chaplain of St Christopher's has continued to serve as an *ex officio* governor of the school, now in his role as Dean of St Christopher's Cathedral.

St Christopher's church and church hall, early 1960s
Source: author's collection

In 1962 the Reverend Alun Morris was appointed Archdeacon in Eastern Arabia and the Gulf, the first archdeacon in the Diocese of Jerusalem to be granted that title, and to be resident in the Gulf region. Episodes from that ministry are narrated in the next chapter. The Venerable Alun Morris CBE and his wife Edith left Bahrain in 1964.

When oil was discovered in Kuwait in 1938, the country was "a quaint, quiet, sandy little desert town whose main livelihood was the sea".[17] This was the observation of Dr Lewis Scudder in 1939, after he and with his wife Dorothy, a nurse, arrived to serve as RCA medical missionaries at the Arabian Mission's hospital in Kuwait.

At that time the few Anglicans living in the country were served by the incumbent chaplain in Basrah who visited periodically. At first, the Kuwait Oil Company's facilities were basic: a few tents in the desert, gradually replaced by Nissen huts. "Where in 1945 there was nothing but a struggling acacia bush on a ridge in the sandy desert"[18], by 1950 KOC's township of Ahmadi had become a large development, two-and-a-half miles across, some 20 miles/32 km south of Kuwait town, and about 6 miles/10 km inland from the Arabian Gulf. As KOC continued to expand its workforce, the Christian congregations grew in size too. In 1949 the Reverend Raymond Pearson was appointed as the first Anglican chaplain in Kuwait, his stipend paid by KOC.

By now there were a number of permanent buildings in Ahmadi, including the Guest House where Pearson was able to hold Sunday services in one of the rooms. Before long KOC allocated a large Nissen hut for exclusive use as a church. A brass eagle lectern, cross and candle holders, a sturdy wooden altar table, harmonium, a small marble font and other fittings were shipped from the UK. The big signboard in front of the hut advertised: Church of England Chapel. The misleading wording was not changed until 1955. Within five years the Nissen hut church was too small, and considered to be "a slight reproach on the town itself"[20]. A purpose-built church was proposed.

The Nissen hut Church of England Chapel in Ahmadi, Kuwait
Ahmadi Guides, Brownies, Scouts and Cubs on parade
Kuwait Oil Company archive, reproduced with permission

By now the estimated number of Anglican and Protestant church-goers was about fourteen hundred, with the average attendance ninety. The peak in any one congregation was one hundred and fifty, particularly on Remembrance Sundays.

> "[Editions of] *The Kuwaiti* newsletter of the late forties and fifties describe an almost nostalgic era in which the expatriate British workers in the Kuwait Oil Company tried to recreate a typical English village community in the middle of the desert. Amidst the weekly reports of cricket scores, fashion reviews from London, [and so on], the chaplain's weekly sermon was printed under his column *Ask the Padre*."[19]

In April 1955 a model of the proposed church was displayed. KOC invited constructive feedback. By June a new site was chosen. Already it had been decided that the new church should be dedicated in the name of St Paul, the only apostle known to have visited Arabia. Construction began in August 1955. A congregational decision was made that a new signboard should stand in front of the new church stating: St Paul's Protestant Church, Ahmadi. In November the name was changed again to be St Paul's Church, Ahmadi. That remains so today, although not stated on a signboard outside. During 1955, the Reverend Raymond Pearson was succeeded by the Reverend Richard Ashton. Although the dedication of the church was postponed until November 1956, Bishop Stewart granted his permission for it to be used and so the first service was held on 7 July 1956. Richard Ashton described the church:

> "By general consent, it is the most beautiful building in the place, and although it retains the traditional basilica form with side-aisles and an apse, the treatment is entirely modern. There is seating for about 170 in the nave and 30 in the choir. The nave seats are specially designed chairs, and the pulpit, lectern, reading-desk and choir stalls have all been locally made in teak. The floor is also of polished teak. The walls are eggshell blue, and the roof a deeper blue, with white pillars and a white apse. In summer the air-coolers are most efficient, and it is the one place where people have to bring something to keep warm!"[21]

The church committee, by constitution, consisted of a proportional number from each denomination represented in the English-language service. The electoral roll listed 622 names, 66.5 percent of which described themselves as Church of England, 19 percent Church of Scotland, 9 percent Methodist, 2 percent Baptist, 1.5 percent Congregationalist and 2 percent other denominations. An inter-congregational committee was also set up to represent the five different groups which used the church: English-speaking, Assyrian, Malayalee, Syrian Orthodox and Telegu. Attendance grew so fast that in early November KOC agreed to extend the building by adding a choir vestry and a basement for storage.

On 16 November 1956, the Right Reverend Weston Henry Stewart, Bishop in Jerusalem, dedicated St Paul's church in Ahmadi. He and Mrs Stewart had flown to Kuwait direct from England. The Bishop in Iran and his wife arrived from Isfahan, and Bishop Jacob travelled to represent the Church of South India. For reasons which Richard Ashton did not explain, other clergy in the Gulf region could not be present.

St Paul's church in Ahmadi, Kuwait, as it was on 16 November 1956
Source: Kuwait Oil Company, reproduced with permission

However, "it was good to have the support and presence of the Reverend G E de Jong, the RCA missionary pastor resident in Kuwait town."[22]

The service began with prayers at the font, reading desk, pulpit, chancel steps and altar. At the lectern, Bibles in the languages of those congregations which used the church were presented to the bishop. He then signed the Deed of Dedication together with the General Manager of KOC and the British Political Agent in Kuwait. The choir, for the first time robed in blue gowns, sang an anthem. A new Compton Electrone two-manual organ had been installed. Bishop Stewart dedicated the church and preached the sermon. The Bishop in Iran read the lesson. Bishop Jacob, with Mr de Jong, said prayers. Referring to himself, the Reverend Richard Ashton added: "the chaplain, as the only common-or-garden parson present, filled the gaps!"[23]

A few months later Bishop Stewart announced his decision to retire. At Lambeth Palace on 8 July 1957, the Right Reverend Campbell MacInnes took office as the 8th Bishop in Jerusalem. He was also invested with the title Archbishop in Jerusalem and Metropolitan by the Archbishop of Canterbury, the Most Reverend Geoffrey Fisher.

Almost four years later, on 19 June 1961, Kuwait was proclaimed as a sovereign state, independent from British protection and a relationship which had been formed in 1899. Kuwait was the first Arab state in the Arabian Gulf region to establish a constitution and a parliament.

The next key event at St Paul's church occurred in 1966 when Archbishop MacInnes dedicated three stained-glass panels set in the east end. The figures in the windows portray the Ascension of Jesus. These originated from St Peter's church in Winchester, described by the Reverend Canon Andrew Thompson[24] as a fine old Victorian church which had been closed and fallen into disrepair:

> "The chaplain in Kuwait at the time [1962-1966], the Reverend Harvey Roydon Phillips, acquired the stained-glass window from St Peter's and commissioned the glaziers Albert Goldie and Joseph Porter to reset the figures in the modern setting of Ahmadi."[25]

The Reverend Keith Johnson, the last KOC-appointed chaplain, left Kuwait in 1973.[26] He was succeeded by the Reverend John Pragnell, his stipend paid by the Anglican chaplaincy of Kuwait. At the end of 1975, the Kuwait Oil Company was nationalised.

This was a major watershed for Ahmadi and St Paul's, as the Reverend Clive Windebank[27] reflects. His ordained ministry began at St Paul's in 1979 as a Non-Stipendiary Assistant Priest, though he had been a KOC employee for almost ten years, having arrived in 1968 with his wife Marian and their young family.

> "The older British couples had been there many years, several coming from India, so there was a distinct atmosphere of the Raj. At that time we were the youngest there, in our mid-20s, and quite bemused by visiting cards and offers to play bridge! Our children along with those of everyone else in Ahmadi went to the Anglo-American School situated next to St Paul's and there was a strong relationship between school and church. ... The chaplain was treated as an oil company employee, lived in a company house for senior staff. ... Prior to 1975, he would fly in the company plane with other staff to play cricket or other sport, with other oil companies in Bahrain, Ahwaz [in Iran], and, most coveted of all, Beirut. Of course, this gradually changed after 1975."[28]

The KOC's expatriate community became more diverse with growing numbers of workers arriving from Asia. Today, a thriving Mandarin-language Anglican congregation is one example of that diversity.

Chapter 5

OPPORTUNITIES IN EASTERN ARABIA

1954 - 1972

After the breakup of the Ottoman Empire at the end of the Great War, Qatar came within the British sphere of influence. The first onshore oil concession in Qatar was awarded in 1935 to the Anglo-Iranian Oil Company (AIOC). But, because the terms of the Red Line Agreement determined that AIOC could not operate the concession, it was transferred to a new associate company of the Iraq Petroleum Company, Petroleum Development (Qatar) Limited (PDQ). In October 1938, oil well Dukhan Number 1 was spudded in, and by January 1940 it was yielding flows in commercial quantities. However, due to the Second World War, oil development in Qatar was paused until 1947.

Throughout the 1950s PDQ employed a chaplain to minister to its workforce and their families. Most were stationed at its headquarters in Umm Said on the south-east coast of the Qatar peninsula. The Ruler's capital, Doha, lay some 40 miles/64 km further north, then the only considerable settlement on the peninsula.

In a letter dated 11 June 1954, published in the July edition of *Bible Lands*, Bishop Weston Henry Stewart wrote that the Archdeaconry of Iraq and Eastern Arabia "is one of the most interesting archdeaconries in the whole of the Anglican Communion"[1]. He had recently visited several places within it, firstly Kirkuk and the IPC oilfield chaplaincy, secondly Basrah, and then Qatar where the Reverend Kenneth Jenkins was based. The bishop remarked: "Not many years ago there were but twenty Europeans in Qatar: now the padre is in touch with at least one thousand! Economic expansion in the Gulf is phenomenal. I believe that we are only at the beginning of things commercially in Iraq and Eastern Arabia. Great opportunities await us all."[2]

During his ten-day stay, Bishop Stewart visited many people in Qatar. He took services of Holy Communion and Evensong at Dukhan on the west side of the Qatar peninsula, and at Umm Said on the east coast. Some people travelled from as far as Doha for Evensong at Umm Said. On the Sunday evening the bishop and the padre did the reverse. Setting out from Umm Said, they "motored for one hour across the barren desert" to take a Holy Communion service at the residence of the political agent in Doha, "this astonishing and rapidly expanding coastal capital".[3]

Bishop Weston Henry Stewart
Source: author's collection

Two years later, the Reverend Kenneth Jenkins explained exactly what his workload entailed, physically and spiritually. His parish was vast, embracing Qatar, all the Trucial Coast states, and the Sultanate of Muscat and Oman. The total population was estimated to be one million, of which five thousand formed the international Christian community. This was distributed within seventeen centres, the biggest concentrations being in Qatar at Doha and Umm Said, and along the Trucial Coast. Jenkins elaborated:

> "The chaplain resides at Umm Said, Qatar, but it would be more correct to say that he lives in a suitcase. His main problem is concerned with travelling the enormous distances in the parish, and the time involved. Perhaps some idea of its extent can be gauged by the fact that about 2,000 miles are covered by road transport and about 5,000 miles by air transport every month. This means that the more populated areas are visited about once every two weeks, and the least populated areas about once every six or seven weeks. The work suffers from a lack of continuity."[4]

With the exception of the Royal Air Force chapel at Sharjah, there was no church building in the parish and still no prospect of one being constructed. Instead, services were conducted in "all sorts of places", such as clubs, houses, bars, tents and in the open. The sense of isolation Jenkins experienced throughout his work was very real. Therefore, the Christian fellowship he enjoyed and shared with Bishop Jacob of the Church of South India, the archdeacon, and Canon Alun Morris during their visits was among "the chaplain's happiest memories of 1955. … The spiritual help gained is very deep and indeed indispensable."[5]

In the 1930s the main settlement of Abu Dhabi was a fishing village, only accessible by land via a hazardous road from Dubai. Other small communities and date plantations were sited inland within the oases of Liwa and al Ain. During 1936, IPC created a subsidiary company called Petroleum Development Trucial Coast (PDTC). On 11 January 1939 this obtained a seventy-five-year concession to explore the whole area of Abu Dhabi. When the Second World War intervened, development was put on hold until the early 1950s.

Almost as soon as the Reverend Alun Morris arrived in Bahrain in October 1954, he planned a visit Abu Dhabi so that during Christmas time that year (date unknown) he might offer Communion "to whoever I could find there."[6] He recalled:

> "We were five in the end, the British Political Agent, the Honourable Martin Buckmaster; Mr Tim Hillyard, BP's man in charge of offshore exploration; and two Indians. I stayed with Tim, and we had our service in the Agency. It had been arranged for me to call on the Ruler and so Martin and Tim took me along. There were no roads in Abu Dhabi then. Only four-wheel drive trucks could move across the sand. Shaikh Shakbut [bin Sultan Al Nahyan] arrived at his desert white four-turretted fort at the same time as we did, by the great front door. ... The Shaikh indicated I should step across the threshold. I protested that he must go first. He said no, I must. After a few more polite gestures to each other, he took me by the hand and we stepped across the threshold hand in hand. I saw him frequently on other occasions and always he was unchanged in his welcome and kindness. ... I shall always remember him with the greatest affection and admiration, a Muslim gentleman, an Arab prince."[7]

By this time Shaikh Shakbut had granted a concession to Abu Dhabi Marine Areas Limited (ADMA), jointly owned by BP and Compagnie Française des Pétroles (later Total). Das island was its operational offshore base which Alun Morris visited frequently too. Years later he recalled that BP, and all the Gulf-based oil companies, were most generous with invitations to visit their camps, the provision of transport and hospitality, and every facility.

> "Das, when I first went there, was very much a frontier area, all personnel reminiscent of that among wartime infantry up at the sharp end, with one marked difference. The Das commissariat tended to produce high cuisine rather than biscuits and bully [corned beef].[8]

"At first I was [air]lifted down on de Havilland Doves, which later became Herons, and after them Viscounts. … Doves were hair-raising enough. The airstrip was so short that a few yards beyond the last oil drum was the sea."[9]

During 1957 the small Christian congregation in Abu Dhabi talked about an Anglican priest possibly being able to conduct a service around Christmas time that year. A proposal was made to Peter Tripp, then the British Political Agent in Abu Dhabi. He agreed to fund the cost of flying in Alun Morris from Bahrain. Tim Hillyard and his wife Susan lived in a BP company house overlooking the sea. Within eight days of Christmas Day in 1957 (date not known) some twelve people gathered in the villa's living room where Morris celebrated a Christmas service. For a few years thereafter, a similar service was held in the British Agency in Abu Dhabi.

Abu Dhabi Fort and the British Agency compound, 1962
Photographed by Ronald Codrai
Copyright: Department of Culture and Tourism, Abu Dhabi

117

In 1958 ADMA began drilling in the Umm Shaif field. Oil was struck. This discovery was followed in 1959 when PDTC's onshore well Murban Number 3 also struck oil. Thereafter, Abu Dhabi's petroleum industry developed rapidly. When the Reverend Alun Morris visited Shaikh Shakbut on another occasion he recalled that, "among other things, he hoped that all the people flooding into his country would say their prayers, and that I must provide a church. He followed this up in due course by saying he would give a site for a church, and consulted maps with his advisers."[10]

The early history of Anglican presence in Abu Dhabi is interwoven with further developments in Qatar. The chaplaincy of Qatar, the Trucial States, Muscat and Oman was formed in 1960. In practice, access to Muscat and Oman was not easy because Sultan Said bin Taimur bin Faisal Al Busaidi, a feudal traditionalist, resisted foreign interaction.

After the Reverend Kenneth Jenkins left Qatar, Petroleum Development Qatar (PDQ) appointed the Reverend John Howells to serve at its headquarters at Umm Said. From there, he visited PDQ personnel who were developing the new fields at Dukhan in the west. He also visited Abu Dhabi and Dubai, proving the need for a reconfigured chaplaincy, or chaplaincies, to serve those growing communities.

Meantime, as mentioned in the previous chapter, at the end of June 1957 Bishop Stewart retired. On 8 July the Right Reverend Angus Campbell MacInnes succeeded him as 8th Bishop in Jerusalem, and was invested with the title Archbishop in Jerusalem and Metropolitan. Keen to develop Anglican ministry in Arabia, he soon recognised the extensive ministry of the Reverend Alun Morris. In 1960, Archbishop MacInnes appointed him as an Honorary Canon of St George's Collegiate Church in Jerusalem. Then in 1962 he collated Canon Morris as Archdeacon in Eastern Arabia and the Gulf. Aside from serving as chaplain in Bahrain, his archidiaconal duties required him to visit Qatar, Sharjah, Kuwait and Iraq, including Basrah, Baghdad and "adjacent hinterlands", referring to IPC's oilfields. Years later Morris admitted:

"I never much liked flying, but it had to be done, and I got to know Gulf Aviation very well. ... Many of the pilots were ex-RAF, slightly hair-raising, completely resourceful, unable to appreciate the qualms of groundlings like me."[11]

Archbishop Angus Campbell MacInnes and
The Venerable Alun Morris at St Christopher's church, Bahrain
Source: author's collection

On 13 May 1963 he and Archbishop MacInnes were flown to Abu Dhabi, met by Colonel Hugh Boustead, the Political Agent, who drove them to a meeting with Shaikh Shakbut. Their purpose was to ask formally if he might provide a plot of land on which to build an Anglican church in Abu Dhabi. Already he had gifted land to the Roman Catholic Church for the establishment of a church and school. The archbishop recorded:

"After a pleasant interview with the Shaikh in his desert fortress, he offered to give us a plot of 40,000 square feet and left us free to choose the site. In the afternoon we selected a central position on the sea front on the town draft plan, and an agreement was drawn up by which the land could be made over for us. Next morning the Ruler graciously signed the document just half an hour before our plane was due to take off. In reply to his query as to when we should begin to build, I told him that I hoped to begin as soon as there was a passable road to the site."[12]

Just over two weeks earlier, on 26 April 1963, the Reverend Richard Matthews began his ministry as chaplain of Qatar, the Trucial States, Muscat and Oman, based in Abu Dhabi, having moved from Bahrain where he had been serving as Assistant Curate. Archbishop MacInnes had assigned him the task of working towards creating a new chaplaincy to be based in either Qatar or Abu Dhabi. The grant of land by Shaikh Shakbut sealed the decision. The oil company PDTC constructed a prefabricated bungalow on the assigned plot to serve as a "vicarage". Until the church was built, services were held at the Abu Dhabi Marine Areas Training Centre.

When the oil company in Qatar ceased to employ a resident chaplain (the date is not known), Matthews began to make monthly visits from Abu Dhabi. The Christian congregations were small but "deeply appreciative and were mainly oil company staff, diplomats, bankers and a growing number of Indian Christians".[13] In 1967, after Matthews returned to England he was replaced by the Reverend David Elliot. He maintained the pattern of monthly visits to Qatar where the focus of church life was shifting from Umm Said to Doha. He also continued to serve the small congregation at the oilfield camp in Dukhan which still involved arduous and time-consuming drives across the peninsula.

In Abu Dhabi, work began during March 1967 to construct the proposed Anglican church on the corniche. David Elliot later reported:

"We all watched it growing and were terribly disappointed whenever we met any setback, which unfortunately turned out to be quite often. The Arab-Israeli War in June did us most harm

120

but fortunately sufficient work was done to enable us to have an absolutely thrilling carol service in the incomplete church last Christmas [1967]. … This being our first church in the Trucial States, it brought home to us more fully that we had a great responsibility for ensuring that Dedication Day would be a great focal point in the life of the church. … No effort was spared."[14]

Its modern and unusual design was the creation of Mr Gordon Jones, a Beirut-based architect. Glass could not be seen anywhere as all the lighting was indirect. There was a noticeable absence of colour. A grained effect was produced by different densities of light contrasted with very strong shadows in certain places. The altar was set in one of the points of the almost square shape, with not a curve in sight. Outside, a tall white concrete cross stood as a landmark, designed to shine out over the sea at night when a spotlight illuminated it.

121

The first church of St Andrew in Abu Dhabi, then on the Corniche
St Andrew's church archive, reproduced with permission

Construction of the church of St Andrew had been made possible by the generosity of many. The Jerusalem and the East Mission had provided a grant. Substantial gifts had been received from the Anglican Church of Canada, the church community in Aden, the Diocese of Leicester, many individuals in Abu Dhabi, and throughout the world.

15 February 1968 - HH Shaikh Zayed bin Sultan Al Nahyan, Ruler of Abu Dhabi, leaving the church of St Andrew with Archbishop Angus Campbell MacInnes

Copyright: BP archive, Abu Dhabi

These included a splendid pair of silver candlesticks made and presented by Mr Algernon Asprey, the renowned British silversmith. A huge carpet for the sanctuary was air-freighted from London at the expense of a friend. The church was intended to seat about one hundred and twenty. With extra chairs, four hundred people filled the church on Dedication Day, Thursday 15 February 1968. Among them were members of British, American and Canadian Western tradition churches, and a number from the Greek and Syrian Orthodox Churches of the east. People living hundreds of miles away who were served by the chaplain, and thereby felt part of the one church, made sure they were there. A contingent from Qatar chartered their own aircraft.

The band of the City of London Regiment, 1st Royal Fusiliers, then stationed at the British garrison in Sharjah, had been flown in by the RAF. At 4 o'clock a fanfare of trumpets, and a guard of honour formed by Brownies, greeted the Ruler of Abu Dhabi, His Highness Shaikh Zayed bin Sultan Al Nahyan. (He had succeeded his brother Shaikh Shakbut in August 1966).

Shaikh Zayed, with Sir Stewart Crawford, the British Political Representative in Abu Dhabi, and other dignitaries, accompanied the Most Reverend Angus Campbell MacInnes, Archbishop in Jerusalem, to the main door of the church on which he knocked three times, saying: "Lift up your heads, O ye gates". The archbishop reflected: "The Dedication Service was an experience never to be forgotten. The Shaikh stayed beside me, then took his seat in the front of the church. … I spoke in Arabic, explaining briefly what we were doing, and assuring him of our gratitude to God that it had been possible to put up the building on land given by the [previous] Ruler."[15]

Shaikh Zayed was presented with a large mother-of-pearl jewel case made in Bethlehem, and then escorted out of the church. Archbishop MacInnes gave the final Hallowing of the altar, and delivered his address in English.

The Anglican chaplaincy of Dubai and Sharjah was formally constituted on 5 April 1970. Like that of Qatar and Abu Dhabi, its early history is another pioneering story. In 1966, oil was first discovered in Dubai at the offshore Fateh field. Historically, the Emirate of Dubai had been inhabited only on the coast and a little inland down the creek known as Bur Dubai, the small downtown area and seat of government. By the late 1960s this had become a prosperous and thriving community, with a single-track toll bridge linking it to Deira, the commercial centre.

The two townships faced each other across the entrance to the creek. Deira was connected to the outskirts of Sharjah by a tarmac strip, always at the mercy of high tides and so frequently under water. A sand track linked Sharjah to Ras al Khaimah, but only at low tide. British, other European and American residents "made occasional forays"[16] to St Martin (established in 1926) within the British garrison in Sharjah.

A small group of Indian Christians felt unable to do likewise, not least because transport was unavailable. In Dubai, church services were held in a house when it was known that the chaplain in Abu Dhabi could visit. Tony Foulger arrived in 1968. Previously he had served in Winchester as a licensed Reader. Soon he decided, with two Tanzanians, to seek permission from Archbishop MacInnes to attempt to establish a church in Dubai. The trio formed a committee, joined by four others, chaired by Foulger.

By late 1968 they had raised enough funds to contemplate employing a chaplain. By now, services were held every Sunday evening in the court room at the British Political Agency. Evensong was led by Tony Foulger or Vic Aubrey, and 1662 Communion was celebrated when an army or RAF chaplain was available to travel from Sharjah. On special occasions and festivals when more space was required, services took place outside on the Agency's tennis court. In his book, *Christianity in the UAE*, Andrew Thompson explains how events evolved:

> "In 1969, it was resolved to revise and adopt the informal constitution, and to seek permission form HH Shaikh Rashid bin Saeed Al Maktoum, then Ruler of Dubai, to build a church for all Christians to use. A request was also made for the appointment of a chaplain to care for the spiritual welfare of the expatriate Christians living in Dubai, Sharjah and the northern Trucial States. Shaikh Rashid not only acquiesced to the request for land, but himself laid the foundation stone of Dubai's Holy Trinity Church".[17]

The Reverend Kenneth Ridgewell, appointed as the first Anglican chaplain to serve in Dubai, arrived in November 1969. His "parsonage" was an apartment above a printing shop in Cinema (now Nasser) Square in Deira. He assumed responsibility for the English-language worship while his congregation set out to raise the funds necessary to complete the church building. Construction began in January 1970. The timber for the roof was donated by Shaikh Rashid, "and even the Muslim foreman in charge of the work pledged a week's salary".[18] On 13 December 1970, the church was dedicated by Archbishop George Appleton. He had succeeded Archbishop MacInnes in March 1969.

It had been agreed that the building would not be consecrated, and that its title of dedication should be particularly chosen to signal a truly catholic embrace of all Christians. Holy Trinity was the chosen name. At that time, the church was situated well away from the populated areas, a drive of some 3 miles/5 km into an area of the desert. In due course the location became the Oud Metha district. The church is a unique edifice, some say built to resemble a bishop's mitre, or as Ridgewell suggested, a Bedu tent.

He described the roof rising forty feet into the air in a cruciform pyramidal shape. Relating the building to its environment, the altar was a large block of local stone standing on a short circular plinth. The four peak faces of the high white painted interior were "embellished with 20-feet high raised crosses, delicately shaded by light reflected from the narrow-slit embrasure windows, or from the cylindrical lights which are fixed around the walls on a timber facia which conceals the air-conditioning duct … The vaulted faceted roof, timber cladding a steel frame, forms a sound box which gives surprising resonance and depth to even the smallest organ."[19]

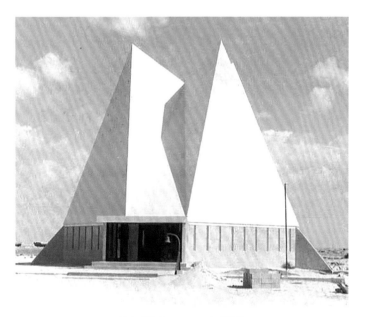

Holy Trinity, as seen in 1970

Holy Trinity archive, reproduced with permission

When the Reverend Kenneth Ridgewell departed in 1971, Dubai had grown in importance as a maritime centre. It had been agreed that the chaplaincy of Dubai and Sharjah should form a shared ministry with the London-based Missions to Seamen which would assign a chaplain, paid and accommodated by the chaplaincy. The charity would fund the building of a house for the chaplain at the Holy Trinity compound. In late 1971, the Reverend Canon Haydn Parry MC arrived to launch the scheme. His assessment was this:

> "The next chaplain will have the spiritual oversight of the church and congregation of Holy Trinity and also the care of the souls of seamen of all the nations that visit Port Rashid. ... I have been the Missions to Seamen Chaplain in several ports but the ease of access to docks and ships at Port Rashid has been the best in my experience. I have just completed an honorary chaplaincy-stay of five months and look back upon it as a valuable and enjoyable experience, but a permanent chaplain needs a strong and fit body, particularly because he also has the spiritual oversight of Sharjah (12 miles distant) and Ras al Khaimah (70 miles away). His prayer life too must be strong and his patience and sense of humour as fathomless as the sea."[20]

Away from the port activity, Canon Parry found profound spiritual solace inside Holy Trinity. His reflections are moving and eloquent.

> "The interior has its own intrinsic atmosphere unaided by ikon [sic], statue, shrine or picture. ... At times the altar position and surround recall a Quaker session or a conclave for free church elders or a place made ready for an Old Testament sacrifice, but always suggesting that it is the meeting place of heaven and earth. The communicants are Christians of various expressions of Christianity, almost all known denominations this side of heaven. The church itself is a lovely house of God and its utter simplicity is penetrating."[21]

Canon Haydn Parry's brief, but valuable, ministry was followed immediately by that of the Reverend Phillip Sturdy who arrived in 1972. Initially he and his wife lived in the Deira apartment, then moved to the new chaplain's house on the Holy Trinity compound. In his dual role as parish priest and the Missions to Seamen's chaplain in Dubai's rapidly expanding port, Philip Sturdy soon identified an urgent need to provide a base for visiting seafarers. He drove the initiative to make this happen. Eventually, on 11 September 1976, the Dubai International Seafarers' Centre was officially opened.

Meanwhile, as narrated in Chapter 2, far-reaching British defence cuts in the mid-1960s had caused its military forces to vacate Aden, which were completed by 30 November 1967. Then, on 16 January 1968, Prime Minister Harold Wilson announced that, due to a balance of payments crisis in the UK, the British government would withdraw all its military forces from Arabia by the end of 1971. The Rulers of Bahrain, Qatar and the Trucial States were dumbfounded by this announcement. Only three months earlier they had been reassured by the British Foreign and Commonwealth Office that it had no intention of ending its defence commitments in the Gulf region.[22] Faced with no choice, the ruling shaikhs and their advisers therefore decided to form a federation, albeit with British advice. Saudi Arabia and Kuwait were invited to support the concept, but declined since both were already sovereign entities. On 25 February 1968 the Rulers of the Trucial States - Abu Dhabi, Ajman, Dubai, Fujairah, Ras al Khaimah, Sharjah and Umm al Quwain - and of Bahrain and Qatar, convened in Dubai for their first constitutional conference and formed a Supreme Council. By mid-1970 there was speculation that Bahrain and Qatar might opt out.

Oman was on the precipice of transition itself. The British government had become frustrated with Sultan Said bin Taimur bin Faisal Al Busaidi's imperfect leadership and "overreliance on British military support".[23] It also viewed the Sultan's deposition as the only viable way to defeat Oman's growing communist insurgency. On 23 July 1970, at the Al Husn Palace in Salalah, Sultan Said bin Taimur was overthrown, forced to sign a declaration of abdication and then flown to London by the RAF. (There he lived in exile until 19 October 1972 when he died peacefully in his suite at the Dorchester Hotel on Park Lane.[24]) Qaboos, his son, was determined to modernise Oman, but his vision was that this process would evolve at a measured and appropriate pace. Therefore, on 20 October 1970, His Excellency Tariq bin Taimur bin Faisal Al Busaidi, the Prime Minister and uncle of Sultan Qaboos, declared that Oman would not join the federation, although it might form an association with some of the emirates at a later date.

During a broadcast on 14 August 1971 His Highness Shaikh Isa bin Salman Al Khalifa proclaimed Bahrain's independence as a sovereign state. On 1 September 1971, Qatar also declared its independence as a sovereign state. Three months later, on 2 December 1971, Abu Dhabi, Ajman, Dubai, Fujairah, Sharjah and Umm al Quwain announced the creation of the United Arab Emirates (UAE), with Shaikh Zayed bin Sultan Al Nahyan as president. Ras al Khaimah joined the federation on 10 February 1972 after resolving its main concerns.

By now British forces had vacated their bases in Arabia. In Sharjah responsibility for the garrison church of St Martin devolved upon the Anglican chaplaincy of Dubai and Sharjah. The Reverend Ralph Lindley had completed his final military-service posting as Senior Chaplain at RAF Muharraq in Bahrain. On 4 December 1970 he was installed as Anglican chaplain at St Andrew in Abu Dhabi, and also as Archdeacon in the Gulf. A few months later he remarked about the Gulf region:

> "Here Christians far from home can maintain the continuity of their faith amidst a world that still worships faithfully in response to the call from the minaret. Each in their way can discover they have something to offer to each other as they come to know each other better. Here, where Western Christianity lives alongside Eastern Christianity and both live as guests in a Muslim world, all stand to gain from the faith of each other."[25]

Those sentiments remain true today.

PART TWO

THE DIOCESE OF CYPRUS & THE GULF

The Diocese of Cyprus and the Gulf, instituted on 5 January 1976, is one of four dioceses in the Episcopal Church in Jerusalem and the Middle East, a constituent province of the Anglican Communion.

The other three dioceses in the Province are the Diocese of Egypt with North Africa and the Horn of Africa, the Diocese of Iran, and the Diocese of Jerusalem.

From the outset the Diocese of Cyprus and the Gulf has evolved in an environment of constant change and frequent challenge, not least because within it are approximately ten political jurisdictions, several of which are among the most politically troubled in the world. Yet, throughout its history so far, the diocese has been determined to embrace opportunities, remain united in its diversity, and be driven and enriched by a common mission. The second part of this book documents that narrative.

The throne of the Bishop in Jerusalem,
the Cathedral church of St George the Martyr

Copyright: the Very Reverend Christopher Butt

Chapter 6

PRELUDE

1943 - 1973

The story of the Diocese of Cyprus and the Gulf cannot be told without awareness of its complicated and often controversial genesis. To all intents and purposes this began in 1881 when the Anglo-Lutheran bishopric of Jerusalem fell into abeyance, was dissolved in 1887, and then in the same year was refounded and reconstituted as a purely Anglican entity. The Right Reverend George Francis Popham Blyth, then aged fifty-five, was appointed as the fourth Bishop in Jerusalem. His jurisdiction stretched from Syria to Egypt and later included the Sudan and Iran. Also in 1887, Bishop Charles Sandford of the Diocese of Gibraltar reluctantly agreed with Bishop Blyth that ecclesiastical oversight of Anglican ministry in Cyprus would make more geographical sense if it were to be assigned to the Diocese of Jerusalem. Hence, in that year canonical oversight of Cyprus was transferred from the Bishop of Gibraltar to the Bishop in Jerusalem.

The wording in the previous sentence prompts comment. In his tribute to Bishop Blyth who died on 5 November 1914, the Venerable Beresford Potter explained:

"Bishop Blyth has always been called Bishop 'in' Jerusalem, not 'of' Jerusalem; and his Archdeacons have taken their titles in the same form, which serves the purpose of emphasizing the fact that the Church of England does not, by serving her own people in the East, or undertaking missionary work there, desire to interfere with or act in any antagonistic spirit towards the National Churches already existing in those countries."[1]

That protocol remains the same today and is certainly applied throughout the Diocese of Cyprus and the Gulf.

Bishop Blyth was eager to provide firm financial support for the Diocese of Jerusalem and so in 1888 established the Jerusalem and the East Mission as a fund to support his diocese's maintenance and its development. As it turned out, this mission fund continuously served the Anglican Church in the Middle East for eighty-eight years, until a change in name and a new constitution became effective on 6 January 1976, the same day that the new province of the Episcopal Church in Jerusalem and the Middle East was inaugurated.

The subject of this and the following chapter is the process by which the Diocese of Jerusalem together with the dioceses of Egypt, Iran and the Sudan became the Archbishopric of Jerusalem in 1957, and was reconfigured with a new constitution during the early 1970s. In 1976 a new province of the Anglican Communion was inaugurated, consisting of four dioceses, one of which was the Diocese of Cyprus and the Gulf.

The prelude began in 1943. Following the death of Bishop Graham Brown in a car accident on 23 November 1942 in Palestine, Archdeacon Stewart was appointed to serve as the seventh Bishop in Jerusalem. Due to wartime travel restrictions his consecration in London was delayed until 21 September 1943. Nevertheless, the Bishop Designate already knew the diocese well having served as Archdeacon in Palestine, Syria and Transjordan[2] since 1928, and had visited Iraq on numerous occasions. During the formative years of his ministry he had rapidly acquired a knowledge of Arabic so that with good pronunciation he could take services acceptably in that language, and in due course honed his spoken-Arabic fluency.

The constant pressure under which Bishop Graham Brown had worked at all times was intensified after the outbreak of the Second World War by heavy additional duties arising due to the presence of armed forces in the bishopric, and general staff shortages. Throughout this period Archdeacon Stewart continued to be the bishop's second-in-command, relieving him of much detail in his workload and thereby gaining considerable insight into what were to be his own episcopal responsibilities. An article written by the Reverend Canon Charles Thorley Bridgeman[3] published in the January 1943 edition of *Bible Lands* clearly defines the demanding role:

"The office of Anglican Bishop in Jerusalem is one of particular difficulty and demands so many first-rate qualities that it is almost impossible to find a man capable of measuring up to them all: he has to be a Father in God to three major racial groups within the jurisdiction, each with its distinctive and often clashing backgrounds; he has to represent the Anglican Communion as a whole vis-à-vis the great Churches of Christendom, all of which are found in the Holy Land; … the presence of Moslems and Jews in such overwhelming numbers in Palestine imposes upon him the need for entering into friendly and helpful relations with them both, even when they are most bitterly opposed in political aims to each other. The work of the jurisdiction lies in five foreign countries other than Palestine, and so he needs to keep in touch with the Governments and movements in those countries in so far as they affect the life and work of the Church and her people. The immediate work of the Bishopric lies in the fields of evangelism, pastoral care, education, medical work, literature and social conditions. …

"No-one except a spiritual superman can meet all these requirements with equal adequacy. But it is amazing to what a degree the late Bishop succeeded in bringing spiritual freshness to all who had to deal with him in these manifold relations. The secret lay in his profound humility before God and his modesty before men."[4]

Bishop Weston Henry Stewart perceived Jerusalem as the centre to which the whole Christian world should look, and St George's Cathedral - formally named the Collegiate Church of St George the Martyr until 1976 - as having a special part to play in the Anglican Communion.

"No small part of his time in those early days was spent in trying to work out a constitution for the Diocese [of Jerusalem] which would take proper account of the needs and aspirations of Arab members of the Church who were organized in what was then known as the Palestine Native Church Council (PNCC), later known as the Arab Evangelical Episcopal Community. He was an excellent draughtsman and showed the greatest patience as he worked on successive drafts in an attempt to meet the many objections which were made."[5]

It is noteworthy that Bishop Stewart was responsible for working out the Prayer Cycle for the Communion, later adopted at the Lambeth Conference of 1948. Throughout his episcopate, he travelled extensively throughout an area already known to him and always had most cordial relationships with other Christian leaders both Eastern and Western. This experience also enabled him to realise how helpful it might be to have a closer association with neighbouring dioceses in the region, "though his vision of an Archbishopric did not materialize until after his resignation".[6]

The Right Reverend Weston Henry Stewart
Bishop in Jerusalem
1943-1957
Source: Bible Lands, reproduced with consent of JEMT's trustees

During the years immediately following the Second World War when various commissions were trying to solve the Palestine problem, Bishop Stewart gave evidence before both the Anglo-American Commission and the United Nations Special Commission on Palestine (UNSCOP). "He had the gift of putting a case with simple clarity which was one of the reasons why his sermons were not easily forgotten. ...

He was acutely aware of the injustices suffered by the Arabs and did what he could to make their case known."[7] These remarks, and those which follow, were the observations of Bishop Stewart's successor, Bishop Campbell MacInnes.

In 1948 after a truce had been agreed, Bishop Stewart went to London to attend the Lambeth Conference. At that Conference and at the Anglican Congress at Minneapolis in 1954, and at the second assembly of the World Council of Churches at Evanston, people were impressed by what he had to say:

> "One of the results of Minneapolis was that the Jerusalem Bishopric became a responsibility of the whole Anglican Communion, to meet which every Province paid a quota, thus relieving the British missionary societies who had been contributing to the Bishop's stipend. In 1948, with the creation of the State of Israel and the ensuing war between the Arabs and the Jews, many were displaced, and refugees abounded."[8]

In 1954 the Anglican Communion acknowledged the Bishop in Jerusalem as its formal representative there. Two years later during 1956, the Majma'[9] in Jordan[10], the assembly of diocesan representatives, unanimously passed a resolution advising the Archbishop of Canterbury to appoint an Arab priest as the next Anglican Bishop in Jerusalem. The reaction of Archbishop Geoffrey Fisher of Canterbury took the form of two positive decisions: firstly to bring into existence the Jerusalem Archbishopric, and secondly to create a new diocese which included Jordan, the diocesan of which would be an Arab bishop.

In 1957 Bishop Stewart's vision of an Archbishopric of Jerusalem became a reality, formed out of four existing Anglican Dioceses: Egypt, Iran, Jerusalem, and the Sudan. The archbishopric was extra-Provincial and under the metropolitical jurisdiction of the Archbishop of Canterbury. However, a few months before that was implemented and well in advance of his seventieth birthday on 15 March 1957, Bishop Stewart had made the decision to retire.

At the start of his last letter as Bishop in Jerusalem published in the April 1957 edition of *Bible Lands,* he wrote:

> "The July number when it comes, will I hope begin with a first letter from my successor. The Archbishop of Canterbury has already announced his identity - Angus Campbell MacInnes, elder son of the bishop under whom I first served in the East. ...

> "Eight years ago he was seriously wounded by an irresponsible sniper when on an errand of mercy with his wife during the fighting in Jerusalem that followed on after the end of the British Mandate. A year or more later he underwent a series of operations in the endeavours to save the sight of one eye and it was after those that the doctors forbade him for the time to return to the Holy Land. I cannot sufficiently express my admiration of his courage in returning now to fill a post which seems to grow more exacting and more difficult every year, but which by common consent he is better qualified to fill than perhaps any man living."[11]

Thus the Right Reverend Angus Campbell MacInnes, Suffragan Bishop of Bedford in the Diocese of St Albans, was appointed to become eighth Bishop in Jerusalem, and the first Anglican Archbishop in Jerusalem. He was a natural choice, his father the Right Reverend Rennie MacInnes served as fifth Bishop in Jerusalem between 1914 and 1931. Campbell MacInnes had spent much of his youth in the Middle East, and after study and ordination in England he returned to serve in Jerusalem as a CMS missionary, then two years later as Principal of the Bishop Gobat School[12] where he worked for fourteen years. Then followed ten years of service as Secretary of the CMS in Palestine (1940-1950). During most of that time (1943-1949), he also served as Bishop Stewart's right-hand man, following in his footsteps as Archdeacon of Palestine, Syria and Transjordan.

On Saturday 29 June 1957 Bishop Stewart resigned the Bishopric in Jerusalem in the fourteenth year of his episcopate, and after thirty-one years in the Holy Land. Thus ended a chapter in the history of the Anglican Church in the Middle East which had begun with the consecration of Bishop Popham Blyth seventy years earlier.

The Archbishop of Canterbury, after consultation with his fellow Metropolitans of the Anglican Communion and with the Anglican bishops and others in the geographical areas concerned, had approved a revised system of jurisdiction for the bishoprics and congregations in the Middle East.

The Most Reverend Campbell MacInnes
8th Bishop in Jerusalem, and
1st Archbishop in Jerusalem, 1957-1969
Source: Bible Lands, reproduced with consent of JEMT's trustees

When on 8 July 1957 the Right Reverend Campbell MacInnes took office as the eighth Bishop in Jerusalem, the Archbishop of Canterbury invested him with the title of Archbishop in Jerusalem and Metropolitan. His primary tasks were defined in a statement issued by Lambeth Palace. He was required to summon and establish an Episcopal Synod consisting of all the bishops under his metropolitan jurisdiction, that is to say, the Bishop in Egypt and Libya, the Bishop and the Assistant Bishop in the Sudan and the Bishop in Iran.

"He will also exercise the diocesan jurisdiction hitherto belonging to the Bishop in Jerusalem with one important exception. Before summoning the Episcopal Synod, the Archbishop in Jerusalem will, by direction of the Archbishop of Canterbury, create a new Bishopric of Jordan, Syria and Lebanon and will consecrate a Bishop thereto who will become a member of the Episcopal Synod. ...

"In view of the historical associations of Jerusalem itself and owing to the fact that its political boundaries have not been finally decided, it has been thought right that for the time being the Archbishop in Jerusalem shall exercise diocesan jurisdiction over Anglican congregations and establishments in Jerusalem. With that exception, jurisdiction in Jordan, Syria and Lebanon which has hitherto belonged to the Bishop in Jerusalem, will be transferred to the new bishopric as soon as it has been created."[13]

The provisions did not in any way change the traditional recognition given by the Churches of the Anglican Communion to the position and jurisdiction of the Patriarch, Archbishops, Metropolitans and Bishops of the Ancient Churches in the regions concerned. Rather, the Anglican representatives in the Middle East were expected to endeavor at all times to strengthen their fellowship with them and with all other Christian people.

The aim of the provisions was to strengthen the pastoral work and witness of the Anglican Communion in the areas concerned and to provide a largely self-directing system suitable for meeting developing needs and flexible enough to respond to fresh demands as they may arise in a rapidly developing part of the world.

Meanwhile in April 1957 a delegation from the Palestine Native Church Council (PNCC) visited the Archbishop of Canterbury at Lambeth Palace. The PNCC, founded in 1905 by the CMS, and "more recently described as the Arab Evangelical Episcopal Community"[14] was generally known as the Majma'. The purpose of the visit was to discuss their problems, the focus of which was considerable anxiety about the status of Jerusalem and various other points in the Archbishop's plan to implement an Archbishopric of Jerusalem. For that reason, after Archbishop MacInnes arrived in the city in August 1957 he led several days of discussion to try and resolve the situation, all this before his enthronement. Eventually an understanding was reached by members of the discussion group.

"The Majma' accepted the result of our deliberations and in token of the wider responsibilities which it would assume in the new diocesan plan, decided to delete the name 'Arab' from its title. Finally, it unanimously nominated Canon Cuba'in as its choice as the first Bishop in Jordan, Lebanon and Syria."[15]

On 6 January 1958 the Archbishopric of Jerusalem welcomed the Right Reverend Najib Cuba'in on the occasion of his consecration as its first Arab-born bishop of the new Diocese of Jordan, Lebanon and Syria. Bishop Cuba'in, a Jordanian whose home town was Salt west of Amman, had jurisdiction over Jordanian-controlled East Jerusalem, but not over the See of Jerusalem. His offices were in the city at the Collegiate Church of St George. (Bishop Cuba'in served for eighteen years until 1976, the entire duration of what transpired to be the new diocese's relatively short existence.)

The Right Reverend Najib Cuba'in
Bishop of Jordan, Lebanon and Syria
1958-1976
*Source: Bible Lands, reproduced with
consent of JEMT's trustees*

The five dioceses now forming the Archbishopric, and their diocesans, were: Jerusalem, the Most Reverend Campbell MacInnes, CMG; Iran, the Right Reverend Hassan Dehqani-Tafti; Egypt with Libya and North Africa, then vacant; the Sudan, the Right Reverend Oliver Allison CBE; Jordan, Lebanon and Syria, the Right Reverend Najib Cuba'in.

By 1968 Archbishop MacInnes was finding life more difficult as ecclesiastical troubles accumulated and his health deteriorated. He had never fully recovered after being wounded during the 1948 Arab-Jewish war having found himself on the front-line in Jerusalem.

He was repatriated to England to undergo several operations, none of which were wholly successful. Later he lost the sight of one eye due to a detached retina which could not be fixed, the injury having occurred while driving to Beirut. Yet he remained active, embarking on many long and tiring journeys to visit chaplaincies in Iraq and the Gulf countries. His fluent Arabic and knowledge of Arab customs ensured that he was always welcomed by those Rulers whom he visited. But during 1968 Archbishop MacInnes was aware, as were others, that his ministry had become too onerous, and so he decided to resign and retire. Who might succeed him, and what was expected of the new incumbent?

As Archbishop and Metropolitan in Jerusalem he was President of the Synod of the Bishops of the dioceses forming the archbishopric, and as diocesan Bishop in Jerusalem he had oversight of its Anglican congregations. The Archbishop was also responsible for ensuring that Christianity was worthily presented to non-Christian peoples in the area, and was also *ex officio* President of the Jerusalem and the East Mission, the organisation which ensured that he had the necessary staff and funds to support his ministry.

The Most Reverend George Appleton, then Archbishop of Perth and Metropolitan of the Province of Western Australia, was chosen to succeed Archbishop MacInnes. Although he had not lived in the Middle East, he offered a depth of international experience including service for many years in Rangoon (now Yangon) then the capital of Burma (today Myanmar), and in Australia. Throughout this service he maintained his connectedness with the Church of England. He had earlier served as Archdeacon of London and as a Canon of St Paul's Cathedral. Other reasons why Archbishop Appleton was chosen to lead the Archbishopric of Jerusalem are offered by two bishops. Bishop Michael Lewis, currently fifth diocesan in Cyprus and the Gulf, suggests:

> "Archbishop Appleton was well known for his deeply spiritual stature, and as a widely loved and read writer on prayer. In the late sixties, with growing demands in Jerusalem for indigenous leadership, he was perhaps thought best fitted by his nature and his connections to hold the archiepiscopal role in the years when the new province was being contemplated."[16]

Bishop Clive Handford, fourth diocesan in Cyprus and the Gulf, was in 1969 a comparatively young chaplain serving in Beirut and closely associated with contemporary developments. Reflecting on that era he believes that several other factors may have led to Archbishop Appleton's appointment:

"He was an experienced Archbishop, coming near to retirement. The Jerusalem appointment came as a surprise to him. Given his age, it was clear (if not stated) that he would not be in post for many years, which fitted the situation well.

"Archbishop Appleton was significantly involved in inter-faith concerns. He had written on the subject, notably a book on Christian relations with Buddhism, fed by his time in Rangoon. When he worked in London, he developed good relations with the Jewish community. He was also involved in the ecumenical scene and was a close friend of a number of its leaders. He was known to be flexible in his thinking and open to fresh ideas."[17]

143

10 March 1969, the Most Reverend George Appleton (right)
with the Most Reverend Donald Coggan, Archbishop of York, at Lambeth Palace
Source: Bible Lands, reproduced with consent of JEMT's trustees

On 10 March 1969 in Lambeth Palace Chapel, London, the Archbishop of York - commissary to the Archbishop of Canterbury who at that time was in the West Indies - presented Archbishop Appleton with his mandate investing him with jurisdiction as Archbishop in Jerusalem. A week later he entered the Collegiate Church of St George the Martyr, Jerusalem, in the presence of the leaders of Jerusalem's historic Christian communities. "This formal occasion is unique to Jerusalem and normally takes place on the day of arrival of any new Heads of Churches"[18] in their principal place of worship.

On this occasion the ceremony took place on the day following Archbishop Appleton's arrival "to allow for any vagaries of the aircraft" in which Archbishop Appleton travelled. The service was simple: the *Te Deum*, prayers, an address, followed by prayer and the blessing given by the new Archbishop. During a much more elaborate and lengthy ceremony on Passion Sunday, 23 March 1969, the Archbishop was enthroned by the Reverend Canon Harold Adkins who had served as Vicar-General during the vacancy. His full account ends with these memories: "A great occasion, moving, dignified and full of meaning, a family occasion, an ecumenical occasion, a Jerusalem occasion."[19]

The Synod of the Anglican Bishops of the Middle East - in short form, the Episcopal Synod - met in Cyprus in October 1969. Among their various deliberations, Archbishop Appleton recorded that he and his fellow bishops looked together "at the need to strengthen the episcopal pastoral care of our people and recommended to the Archbishop of Canterbury that an assistant bishop should be consecrated to help me with the work of the Jerusalem Diocese."[20] That was implemented on 15 February 1970 with the consecration of Bishop Kenneth Cragg as Assistant Bishop in the Archbishopric with special care and responsibility for the relationship with Islam.

Also at that time in Lebanon, a Palestinian Arab cleric, the Reverend Samir Kafa'ity, was serving as Chaplain to the Arabic-speaking congregation at All Saints in Beirut, while the Reverend Clive Handford, an Arabic linguist too, was chaplain to the English-speaking congregations residing in the city. Their clerical careers followed a notably similar pattern, each being appointed at different times as

Archdeacon and then Bishop in different dioceses within what became the province of the Episcopal Church of Jerusalem and the Middle East, each finally serving as its President Bishop.[21]

With recall of that period and of later events, and by drawing on his archive Bishop Handford has documented how and why the Diocese of Cyprus and the Gulf, and the new Province, were created:

> "Soon after taking up his post Archbishop Appleton became aware of the strong desire of the Arab (Jordanian and Palestinian) congregations in the Dioceses of Jerusalem, and Jordan, Syria and Lebanon, as well as that of the Egyptians in the Diocese of Egypt, that the indigenous Christians of the Church should assume the leadership role without undue delay. The Archbishop had considerable sympathy with this sentiment. Archbishop George Appleton also considered it was timely to reconsider the arrangement of the Archbishopric and draw into one Province the key regional geography of the Near East and North-East Africa and thereby reconsider the configuration of the dioceses within it."[22]

145

Thus, another outcome of the Episcopal Synod in October 1969 was that Archbishop Appleton established a Commission to study and report on what might be the future structure of the Archbishopric. The membership of the Commission was quite small: the Right Reverend Leslie Brown, Bishop of St Edmundsbury and Ipswich in England, with long missionary experience, and formerly Archbishop of Uganda, Rwanda, and Burundi with experience of having handed over responsibility and leadership to an indigenous church; the Reverend Canon John Satterthwaite, General Secretary, Church of England Council on Foreign Relations; and the Reverend Canon Edward Every who since 1952 had been a Canon Residentiary at the Collegiate Church of St George in Jerusalem and so had considerable experience of association with the Eastern Churches in that city.

Two external representatives were chosen: Maitre Habib Sa'id, a veteran layman of the Anglican Church in Egypt and an acknowledged worker for Christian literature; and Mr Fu'ad Saba, an Arab layman from the Anglican church in Beirut. The Reverend John Wilkinson was appointed as secretary, having recently taken charge as Dean of Studies at St George's College, the residential centre adjacent to St George's Collegiate Church offering short-term pilgrimages and study courses on the Holy Land to lay and clergy alike. Bishop Cuba'in served as consultant for the indigenous churches and the Very Reverend Harold Adkins, appointed Dean of St George's Collegiate Church by Archbishop Appleton in 1970, was consultant and adviser concerning chaplaincy work.

Although the then Reverend Clive Handford was not a member of the Commission, he and his wife Jane entertained its members when they held their first meeting in Beirut during 1970, and thereby became aware of the ideas under discussion:

> "The Commission proposed a Diocese of Jerusalem which could include Cyprus, and a Diocese of Beirut which would include the Gulf region. The Council of the Church in Cyprus was to be asked to which Diocese it preferred to belong. Subsequently there was a suggestion that Cyprus should be transferred to become part of the Diocese of Egypt. This was not the first time this idea had been suggested, and nor was it to be the last. In 1968 the Archdeacon in Cyprus had reported fears in the island when it was suggested that Cyprus might become part of the Diocese of Gibraltar. In 1970, the firm response of the Church in Cyprus to the new proposals was that it did not wish to be part of Egypt or Gibraltar. Subsequently, the clear view in Cyprus was one of regret at the proposed abolition of the Archbishopric and a strong desire for a Western rather than local episcopal leadership.

> "Another initial suggestion was that a diocese of Cyprus and the Gulf should also include the chaplaincies in North Africa, Ethiopia and Eritrea but subsequently they were assigned to the Diocese of Egypt when Sudan left the Archbishopric in 1975 to form its own province."[23]

By the summer of 1970 an interim report was available for study. In January 1971 the Episcopal Synod next met in Khartoum and accepted the main principles drafted in the report but felt that further thought was needed about diocesan boundaries and draft constitutions. The Commission also had power to invite consultants.

The Right Reverend Kenneth Cragg
Source: oikoumene.org

When its second meeting was held in Nicosia during 1971, Bishop Kenneth Cragg was living in Cairo, always in principle holding a wider brief in support of the Archbishop. It is likely, therefore, that the bishop was invited to serve as a consultant to the Commission. He presented a controversial proposal for consideration. The gist of it was this:

> "A Diocese of Jerusalem St George should be established with the Bishop's seat in St George's Cathedral to comprise all the Arabic speaking congregations within two existing dioceses: Jerusalem, alongside Jordan, Lebanon and Syria. And that a Diocese of Jerusalem St John, possibly based on Bethlehem, should comprise all the expatriate congregations residing in the same two existing dioceses."[24]

Bishop Handford recalls that Bishop Cragg's idea gained little acceptance, perhaps not surprisingly given its divisive implications.

When the Episcopal Synod next met in January 1972 plans for the development of the Archbishopric into an autonomous Province had been formed. At the Synod's following annual meeting, this time between 16 and 24 January 1973 in Isfahan, its members had the benefit of the Report of a Working Party which the Archbishop of Canterbury had convened to advise on the nature of Anglican Presence in Jerusalem. The chairman of the working party, the Right Reverend and Right Honourable Robert Stopford, Bishop of London, *ex officio* Chairman of the Jerusalem and the East Mission, and an Episcopal Canon of Jerusalem, was present to explain the report and act as consultant about constitutional developments. The four archdeacons of the archbishopric were also present at this episcopal synod.

The result was a simple plan for the future pattern of work in the Middle East. Among the key principles were those which spelt out the envisaged configurations of the constituent dioceses within a new province. Constitutionally, a minimum of four dioceses was required.

- The diocese covering Jordan, Lebanon and Syria, and the diocese covering Jerusalem and Israel (but without Cyprus and the Arabian Gulf region), were to be united to form a reconfigured Diocese of Jerusalem.

- A new diocese would be created (referred to by some at the time as a "chaplaincy diocese") titled the Diocese of Cyprus and the Gulf.

- The Egypt bishopric was to be revived.

- The Diocese of Iran would remain in its current form.

- The Diocese of the Sudan would be permitted to withdraw from the constitution when the time was ripe to form an independent province.

- Finally, a council with a President elected by itself from among the diocesan bishops would have authority delegated by the Archbishop of Canterbury for Mandates and Consecrations and similar constitutional functions.[25]

Without delay the plan in the form of a draft constitution was submitted to the existing five dioceses for their acceptance or rejection. The Diocese of Jordan, Lebanon and Syria accepted the plan, as did the Dioceses of

Egypt and Iran. The Diocese of the Sudan was already consulting with the Archbishop of Canterbury about an early date for returning to his direct jurisdiction, in preparation for becoming a separate province.

The decision of the Diocese of Jerusalem was more complicated to achieve, particularly as it had no constitution to follow. Therefore, the proposed plan was submitted to a tripartite representative council of parish, clergy and representatives for Israel and Jerusalem, the Island Council in Cyprus, which did have its own constitution, promulgated by the Archbishop in Jerusalem on 8 March 1972[26]; and the Archdeaconry Council in the Gulf, formed in 1972. [27]

This meant that the Diocese of Jerusalem voted in three sectional meetings. The Majma' of the Evangelical Episcopal Church in Israel[28] accepted the plan by large majorities. Vigorous debates within the Cyprus Island Council and the Gulf Archdeaconry Council were protracted over several months, in many instances couched in language - recorded in minutes - which today would be viewed as racist and uncompromisingly resistant to change. These views were in the minority but nevertheless caused division. Drawing on his archive once again, Bishop Handford has summarised:

> "In Cyprus the proposal was agreed with votes being 10 in favour and 3 opposed. It was felt that the Bishop should be based in Cyprus because 'ecumenical affairs there were developing promisingly' and it would also be easier to keep in touch with Jerusalem. In the Gulf Archdeaconry Council it was concluded that Cyprus was the right base for the Bishop because the Gulf was too expensive. But, again after discussion in the congregations, much regret was expressed at the proposed demise of the English [sic] Archbishopric. In the end, the proposals were approved with 20 members in favour and 2 opposed."[29]

Meanwhile, Archbishop Appleton recognised that although the new constitution had been worked out, it required amplifying and codifying. Much work remained to be done concerning legal trusts and financial matters, and this was expected to take some time even after the Archbishop of Canterbury decided to implement the plan, and before he could fix a date for the final handover. In the Spring of 1973 Archbishop Appleton wrote: "One preparatory step for this will be my own retirement which should come early in 1974, particularly as both my wife and myself are now in our seventy second year."[30&31]

Soon afterwards the Bishop of London, the Right Reverend and Right Honourable Dr Robert Stopford, himself already seventy-two years old, announced his retirement effective on 11 June 1973. This automatically required his retirement as Chairman of the Jerusalem and the East Mission, and so he became its Vice-President. The significance of all this was not announced until later in the year, although undoubtedly Archbishop Appleton and the Most Reverend Michael Ramsey, the 100th Archbishop of Canterbury, had already planned their next move.

The Most Reverend Michael Ramsey, 100th Archbishop of Canterbury and the Right Reverend and Right Honourable Robert Stopford (right)
Source: amazon.com

Meanwhile, the Anglican Consultative Council (ACC) met at Dublin between 16 and 27 July and agreed to recommend the draft constitution of the new province to Archbishop Ramsey without any change.

During his final summer sermon to the gathering of the Jerusalem and the East Mission, Archbishop Appleton said:

> "To me the most vital concern is the spiritual preparation - a spirit of trust between our people there and those who have supported them for so many years. …. A short period of intensive spiritual preparation could ensure the right working of the new pattern. I hope people will be ready for it, even ask for it. It is vitally important to give our brethren in the Middle East full fellowship, trust and support. They will need this more than ever before, as they take over greater responsibility."[32]

Archbishop Appleton's advice was prescient, although he could not have anticipated how, or why, "fellowship, trust and support" would become even greater prerequisites in the coming months; nor could he have forecast that the reorganisation of the Anglican Church in the Middle East would, suddenly, be at risk of possible disruption beyond both his and the Archbishop of Canterbury's control.

At 2 pm on 6 October 1973 Egyptian and Syrian forces launched a coordinated surprise attack against Israel on Yom Kippur, the holiest day in the Jewish calendar. In Egypt and Syria it was also the tenth day of Ramadan that year, one of the reasons why the Israeli army was shocked as it had not thought it possible that the Arabs would attack during the Muslim holy month when strict fasting is observed from dawn to sunset. Egyptian troops swept deep into the Sinai Peninsula, while Syria struggled to dislodge occupying Israeli troops from the Golan Heights. Israel counterattacked and recaptured the Golan Heights. This Arab-Israeli War - also known the Yom Kippur War, the Ramadan War or October War - was fought by a coalition of Arab states to repossess territory occupied by Israel during the 1967 Six-Day War.

On 16 October 1973 OPEC[33] responded to USA support for Israel during the current war by increasing the posted price of Arabian light crude oil by seventy percent on a "take it or leave it basis".[34] During the following day the oil ministers of the Organisation of Arab Petroleum Exporting Countries (OAPEC)[35], except Iraq, agreed to cut their crude oil production by a minimum of five percent with immediate effect, precipitating a sense of crisis as the Arab oil embargo began to "bite" internationally. Notably, all nine member countries of OAPEC were within the ecclesiastical jurisdiction of the Anglican Archbishopric of Jerusalem, as were four of the five member countries of OPEC, the exception being Venezuela.

Although a cease-fire was effected on 25 October 1973, the impact of the Arab oil embargo continued to be far-reaching, and worsened. By the end of the year the posted price of Arabian light crude oil had again more than doubled thereby tightening the grip of the embargo. To what extent all these events would change the political and economic landscapes of the Middle East was as yet very uncertain.

Yet, despite all these distractions, and no doubt mindful of them, the Archbishop of Canterbury stuck to his plan. Already he had decided that the constitution for the new council of the new province - the Episcopal Church of Jerusalem and the Middle East - could not be introduced until the full details had been fine-tuned. Clearly, this process would go beyond the date of Archbishop Appleton's retirement in March 1974. In anticipation of this, on 7 December 1973, the Archbishop of Canterbury issued an announcement to say that the Right Reverend Dr Robert Stopford had accepted appointment as Vicar-General, to hold office for not more than two years. His principal task was to supervise the planning of the new constitution and the transition to it and, in general, to be responsible for all the work now devolving on the Archbishop in Jerusalem.

As far as the new Diocese of Cyprus and the Gulf was concerned, those who were eager to know how this might take shape would have been pleased to read a press release[36] issued on 30 November: the Archbishop of Canterbury announced that he had appointed the Venerable Leonard James Ashton, recently retired Archdeacon for the Royal Air Force in the Church of England and Chaplain-in-Chief to the RAF, to be Assistant Bishop in the Jerusalem Archbishopric, with the charge of Anglican congregations in Cyprus and the Gulf. His consecration was to take place on 22 January 1974.

Chapter 7

TRAUMA & TRANSITION

1974 - 1975

Consecrations usually take place in cathedrals. However, on 22 January 1974, St Clement Danes on the Strand in London, the Central Church of the RAF, "provided adequate space for a widely representative congregation together with the intimacy of a family occasion"[1], in this case, the consecration of Bishop Leonard Ashton by the Most Reverend Michael Ramsey, Archbishop of Canterbury.

The damp and dull weather of the capital "emphasised rather than detracted from the beauty of the setting"[2] provided by the restored and beautified church. Bishop Ashton was presented for consecration by the current and previous archbishops in Jerusalem, the Most Reverend George Appleton and his predecessor the Right Reverend Campbell MacInnes. The representative nature of the occasion was further emphasised by the presence of Archbishop Toumayan (Armenian), Bishop Gregory (Greek Orthodox), Father Wissa (Coptic Orthodox) and Father Andrew Cloonan (Franciscan, Roman Catholic).

Also among the congregation were "a full detachment from No 12 Warwick Square"[3] - the registered offices of the Jerusalem and the East Mission - together with Mr and Mrs Williamson, representatives from Cyprus; from the Gulf, Mrs Ralph Lindley, wife of the Archdeacon in the Gulf; and Mr Stanley McGinley, an American citizen who in 1973 had been appointed by Archbishop Appleton as a Reader. He served the Canterbury Group[4] until his retirement in 2010.

Thus with due ceremony Leonard James Ashton CB was consecrated Assistant Bishop in the Jerusalem Archbishopric and Bishop-designate of the Diocese of Cyprus and the Gulf. It would take almost two more years to complete its formation.

The Most Reverend Michael Ramsey, Archbishop of Canterbury,
and the Right Reverend Leonard Ashton, at the Church of St Clement Danes
Source: collection of Leonard Brown, reproduced with permission

Within days Bishop Ashton had left the damp and dull weather of London behind and flown to Cyprus.

"The Island in the Sun - so shout the travel brochures. Here in mid-winter the snow-crowned mountains sweep down to the verdant plains, through dark green groves of oranges and lemons, trembling with the promised glories of the Spring. … Cyprus - the dream of tourists, the Mediterranean gem whose shores are

washed by the blue seas from which Aphrodite was born, whose ruined columns mark the highways where Barnabas and Paul urgently trod to preach the Gospel. Here I arrived in the early hours of a January morning, and it was two degrees colder than in England at the time of my departure at midnight!

"The Royal Air Force has very kindly provided me with temporary accommodation at Nicosia, but in a winter that has swept the Island with the welcome rains, the bungalow seemed cold and damp. In my first ten days I attended meetings and receptions and services, scarcely having time to chop a few logs and to crouch about the blazing fire for warmth."[5]

Already, Bishop Ashton had bought his first episcopal car, a second-hand purple Mini sold to him by a sergeant who was about to leave Cyprus. In the bishop's words: "Now mobile, with my modest little dwelling well furnished, and an old borrowed typewriter, I was able to begin building the structure of the new diocese."[6]

On Sunday 3 February 1974 the bishop was formally welcomed at a "Service of Presentation" at St Paul's church in Nicosia, during which he preached. In his honour, Mr and Mrs David Humphreys hosted an informal evening reception at their home. Mr Humphreys was Head Master of the English School and one of the four Managing Trustees of the Jerusalem and the East Mission Trust (Cyprus)[7].

Later that evening Archbishop Appleton arrived in Cyprus as part of his valedictory tour of the archbishopric. His week-long itinerary included a visit to the congregation in Kyrenia. On the last day of his stay, 10 February, he was the celebrant at the morning service and preached the sermon at St Paul's in Nicosia. In Limassol he attended Evensong at St Barnabas and, before bidding farewell, the archbishop dedicated the new organ. Bishop Leonard Ashton reflected:

"The departure of this great and good man created a sense of bereavement among all who had been enriched by his ministry. The Church in the Middle East will miss him and Mrs Appleton more than I can say, but his work will endure and his influence will continue for many years to come."[8]

After Archbishop Appleton had left Cyprus, Bishop Ashton with Archdeacon Lindley (also a retired RAF Senior Chaplain) embarked on a month's visit to several destinations in the Gulf archdeaconry: Abu Dhabi, Bahrain, Qatar, Dubai and Muscat. The bishop held his first confirmation service at the church of St Christopher in Manama, the capital of Bahrain. He was heartened by the kindly support and friendliness of His Highness the Ruler of Bahrain, the Prime Minister of Oman, the Governor of Muscat and the Minister of Islamic Affairs in the United Arab Emirates. At grass roots level the bishop was equally reassured by the exciting and dynamic support he received from the lay people of the Gulf. When he returned to Cyprus there was much work to be done, administrative matters inevitably had begun to multiply, and "the litter of files" had made his dining room look more and more like a diocesan office.

As part of the transitional process key events had taken place elsewhere in the Archbishopric of Jerusalem. In January 1974 the Diocese of the Sudan reverted to the metropolitical jurisdiction of the Archbishop of Canterbury as the first step towards the formation of an independent Province of the Sudan. Now, quite definitely, the envisaged province of the Episcopal Church of Jerusalem and the Middle East would have just four constituent dioceses.

At the end of December 1973 the Very Reverend Harold Adkins, having served in the Middle East for twenty-five years, retired as Dean of the Collegiate Church of St George in Jerusalem. His successor, jointly nominated by Archbishop Appleton and Bishop Cuba'in, was the Reverend Clive Handford. He had served in Baghdad and Beirut "with great effectiveness and devotion, earning the affection of all who have been in touch with him. He and his wife Jane, who has been such an able companion and hostess, will have the confidence of all who know them, especially as Clive has a good knowledge of Arabic, and Jane is a good organist and a successful inspirer of Sunday Schools".[9]

During January 1974 the Dean-designate and his wife moved to Jerusalem from Canterbury in England where he had spent 1973 as a

Research Fellow and staff member of St Augustine's College[10], then used by King's College, London. Archbishop Appleton, himself an alumnus of St Augustine's College, wrote in early 1974:

> "This will be my last letter as Archbishop, as the date of my retirement will be March 10th. May I thank you all for your interest and continuing support, as well as for the prayers of which so many of us have been conscious during these troubled years. The things that I have cared for most are deepening the spiritual life of our clergy and people, working for peace, trying to encourage responsibility of the indigenous Church, and uniting all together in the service of the Church to its own people, in its relationships with people of other faiths, and in its service to people in the community at large who need special affection and care. I know that all of you will have the same aims and hopes and I send a final blessing to you all, with affectionate greetings from my wife and myself."[11]

On 1 April 1974, at Lambeth Palace, London, the Archbishop of Canterbury, the Most Reverend Michael Ramsey, presented his official Mandate to the Right Reverend and Right Honourable Robert Stopford, KCVO DD, empowering him to act as his Vicar-General in Jerusalem and the Middle East.

Less than a week later, on Palm Sunday which that year fell on 7 April, Bishop Stopford was received officially in Jerusalem, and presented by Bishop Cuba'in at 9.30 am to the members of the Diocese of Jordan, Lebanon and Syria, and at 11 am to the members of the Diocese of Jerusalem. Bishop Ashton was also present, having travelled to Jerusalem for the first time so that he could greet the Vicar-General upon his arrival.

Commenting on the workload they both faced, the bishop recorded: "the daunting prospect of acquainting myself with the office files was more than balanced by the pleasure of meeting the staff of St George's and some of the Arab clergy. Before I returned to Cyprus a few days later, the Vicar-General was deeply involved in his massive programme of meetings and discussions and consultations."[12]

The Right Reverend Robert Stopford,
Vicar-General in Jerusalem, 1974-1975
Source: amazon.com

Abstracts from an article published in *Bible Lands* elucidate the Vicar-General's view of the task he had undertaken, his hope that the Jerusalem and the East Mission would continue to offer support, and his acknowledgement of Archbishop Appleton's valued contribution to life of the Church in the Middle East:

"For the past twelve years I have been privileged to be the Chairman of the Jerusalem and the East Mission and I know something of the devoted help in prayer and giving which you who support the J&EM have never failed to give. Now I write to you in my new capacity to ask you to intensify your support especially in this period of planning and transition. I am myself convinced that the new arrangements, to which the Anglican Consultative Council has given general approval, are right and necessary. I believe that they will give to the Anglican Church in Jerusalem and the Middle East a flexibility to meet the changing situations and a renewed sense of mission to the world. But the changes proposed are great, and they will need faith to work them out in detail, and the power of the Spirit to bring them to good effect. That is where we need the continued help of all those who have given so much through J&EM in past years.

"As I take on this new and strange, though temporary, responsibility, I am very conscious of the great work done by Archbishop Appleton not only for the Archbishopric in the narrower sense but also for the reconciling work of the church in this time of tension. He has worked ceaselessly for peace, for understanding between men of different Christian allegiances, and men of different faiths. The Church in the Middle East owes him a great debt of gratitude.[13]

The Dean of St George's Collegiate Church, the Very Reverend Clive Handford, worked closely alongside Bishop Stopford during the next twenty-one months, the duration as it transpired of the "strange, though temporary" phase of the Vicar-General's ministry.

Bishop Ashton regularly visited Jerusalem for consultations, either staying with the Vicar-General, or with the dean and his wife Jane, spending "quite a bit of time together, and, of course, talking about the future plans."[14] In May 1974 the bishop wrote his first epistle to the Jerusalem and the East Mission, choosing the setting of his bungalow in RAF Nicosia to compose his thoughts. His letter focused on the fact that although he had not yet been able to visit the entire area of the proposed new Diocese of Cyprus and the Gulf, and still had to embark on an extensive tour visiting other areas under the Vicar-General's jurisdiction, already he appreciated that his immense and varied work was "a tremendous privilege"[15], and involved great responsibilities.

He was astute enough too to realise that the new diocese would, from its outset, depend on generous financial giving by many who would not be among its parishioners. In a style which became a hallmark of his episcopate, in written and spoken forms, he carefully crafted his words so that when the punchline was delivered, he had fluently and persuasively stated his case.

"The vast geographical area presents difficulties of travel and communication, with long hours of waiting at airports and the frustrating delay in postal services. The differing culture and creeds over this area form a fascinating subject for study, and there is much that we can learn from one another; but there are differences of outlook and attitude which sometimes tend to create problems among Christians, and sometimes between Christians and those of other faiths.

159

"Indeed, with the present political tensions, I am astonished that the problems are not greater.

"Then there are serious financial problems in the new Diocese of Cyprus and the Gulf. We urgently need money to provide a chaplain for Muscat and help for Baghdad, and there is work for at least one other chaplain in Cyprus. The local churches are already hard pressed financially and cannot bear the burden alone.

"Can you help with your gifts as well as with your prayers? I make no apology for making a blunt financial appeal, because the work of Christ's Kingdom depends on us all. If you would like precise details of our needs, please do not hesitate to write to me."[16]

Already, too, the bishop had a foretaste of the challenges and frustrations he might encounter during his episcopate. The phrase in his letter "help for Baghdad" referenced the fact that the Anglican congregation at St George's no longer had the resources to support a resident chaplain. Until the expulsion of the Reverend Colin Davies from Iraq at the end of 1973 his stay had only been made possible because of a hidden IPC subsidy. Archdeacon Ralph Lindley had been warned by IPC's managing director that the subsidy would have to stop if he knew the end of Colin Davies's ministry "was in sight". As events turned out, his abrupt departure was not envisaged. Since then no visa had been granted to an Anglican chaplain to reside in Baghdad or to visit.

Undaunted, Bishop Ashton liaised with the British Embassy in Baghdad, his aim being to celebrate the forthcoming Easter at the Mesopotamian Memorial Church of St George. On 12 April 1974, Good Friday that year, Mr Ian McCluney, the British Chargé d'Affaires, sent a cable to the bishop: "Visa available on arrival Baghdad. Please advise flight details and we will meet." On Easter Sunday he did arrive at Baghdad airport, but was refused entry. "Within minutes"[17] of the RAF flying him away, the Director of Consular Affairs in the Ministry of Foreign Affairs (MFA) telephoned the British Chargé d'Affaires at his home to apologise for the bishop's "unfortunate experience".[18]

Those events, recorded three days later by Mr McCluney in a confidential letter to Bishop Ashton, prefaced the rest of the story:

> "On Tuesday 17 April Vice-Consul Saltwell was summoned to the Ministry for further apologies and told that had you been able to stay at the airport an hour longer you would have been allowed to stay. After the fairly determined treatment you received this seems laughable, but since I hope you will try to come here again in the not too distant future, it may be just as well if I set down the advice of the Ministry about a future visit. (There seems no alternative now but to treat the matter officially through the Embassy). …

> "We have said you are based in Cyprus and cover a range of countries from Morocco to the Gulf. Your title of Assistant Bishop in the Bishopric of Jerusalem is traditional and has no geographical significance. (The MFA has not suggested that this title is offensive, but it might be as well to avoid its use and any reference to Israel in dealing with Iraqi officials.) The MFA advise that you re-apply for a visa (through your travel agents in Beirut, I presume) and it will be granted."[19]

On 23 April, St George's Day, the bishop replied to McCluney's letter: "I was very sorry indeed about all the nonsense at Baghdad airport on Easter Sunday. I left for Kuwait feeling very frustrated and unhappy. … The rest of my tour was very profitable, and in Kuwait I was met by the British Ambassador just in time to preach at their evening service!"[20]

In May 1974 Mr Cecil Griggs, Chairman of the JEMT (Cyprus), was presented with an OBE by Mr Stephen Olver CMG[21], the British High Commissioner in Cyprus acting on behalf of Queen Elizabeth II who had bestowed the honour. Mr Griggs was a member of St Paul's Church Council and, as documented in later chapters, volunteered his part-time services in other ways until his sudden death in 1987. He and Bishop Ashton worked together, navigating their way through many tense situations, one of which had been simmering for four years.

Ever since the Cyprus Island Council had been asked to submit its thoughts regarding the possible reconfiguration of the Archbishopric of Jerusalem, some members had consistently held they did not wish to see Cyprus aligned with Jerusalem and would rather see it within a diocese in Europe, such as Gibraltar. The "old guard" - which included retired military personnel - wished to revert to the diocesan boundary arrangement of almost a century earlier. At a meeting of St Paul's Parish Council on 18 June 1974 the minutes record that at the last meeting of the Cyprus Island Council - attended by the Vicar-General and Bishop Ashton - "the new Constitution had come into effect in spite of the views repeatedly expressed by members of the church council"[22]. The nay-sayers had clung to their hope that the Vicar-General and the bishop, along with their colleagues, might eventually change their minds, and therefore reminded them that "there was provision in the Constitution for alteration of the boundaries of the Diocese if the intended arrangement proved unworkable".[23] Just over a month later myopic concerns about diocesan boundaries had paled at the appearance of an alarming and very visible boundary: a military-controlled zone across the landscape of Cyprus.

On Monday 15 July 1974 a *coup d'état* orchestrated by the Cypriot National Guard and the Greek military junta had ousted the incumbent president, Archbishop Makarios III. Five days later, on Saturday 20 July, Turkish troops landed on the north coast of Cyprus "to intervene". A letter sent to the JEMT (Cyprus) in 1975 defined this as the "Turkish Peace-keeping Operation of July-August 1974"[24]. Greek-Cypriot opinion defined this as an invasion, as did that of other nations. It is not for this narrative to comment on those interpretations which remain deeply sensitive. The incontrovertible fact is that the outcome of the military action resulted in the partition of the island.

Suddenly, Bishop Ashton found himself, and the bungalow in which he lived at RAF Nicosia, stuck on the front line. He was advised to take refuge with the RAF chaplain in his bungalow, both spending the first night sheltering in the central corridor while the Turks bombarded Nicosia over the weekend. By Sunday 21 July RAF Nicosia had become "decidedly unhealthy"[25]. Orders came to vacate the living quarters.

"We left Nicosia in a huge convoy of sundry military and civilian vehicles, watched over by RAF aircraft as we slowly made our way to the British army base at Dhekelia, some thirty miles south. ... I had with me very little in the way of clothing, except the trousers and shirt I was wearing, plus some of my robes and the pastoral staff which had been in my car. ... During the evacuation, even my little purple Mini which I was driving was hit and dented in the back by a service vehicle, when we were all supposed to be stationary!"[26]

For the next twelve days the bishop lived in the vicarage at Dhekelia garrison with several other refugees. He shared services at the church of St George with other military chaplains, broadcast talks on the Forces radio and tried to continue with his own chaplaincy work. On 2 August 1974 he was allowed to return to Nicosia where he lived in a hotel with few other guests, most being journalists from overseas. . In his words, "these were not easy days". The two full-time Anglican chaplains in Cyprus were on holiday in the UK and could not obtain immediate permission from the British FCO to return. In any case, commercial flights to the island had been suspended. Nicosia International Airport had been bombed and was out of action. Then, the only way to fly from the UK to Cyprus was by arrangement with the RAF on a military flight to Akrotiri. The Reverend Canon Hubert Matthews, although retired and living in Limassol, had agreed to continue ministry at St Barnabas until another chaplain was available. This left the bishop almost fully occupied taking services and dealing with pastoral matters among the other Anglican congregations. Fortunately, he was allowed to drive throughout Cyprus, including in the north, with permission of the Turkish authorities.

Meanwhile, on 25 July the foreign ministers of Turkey, Greece and the United Kingdom had met in Geneva, Switzerland, to start discussions pertaining to UN Security Council resolution 353 (1974). Five days later on 30 July the text of the Geneva Declaration concerning Cyprus was agreed. Thus, on 18 August the ceasefire line across the entire island became the United Nations Buffer Zone, commonly known as the Green Line. It remains in place today.

During August, the Reverend Basil Pitt and Archdeacon Jack Nicholls were allowed to return to Cyprus. This enabled Bishop Ashton to leave the island to attend the consecration of the new Bishop in Egypt at St George's Cathedral in Jerusalem. But to reach there, first he had to "hitch-hike" a lift from Larnaca to Tel Aviv in a small aircraft hired by journalists who were reporting on the Cyprus conflict, and then journey by road. On 2 September, four days after the consecration and still in the old city, Bishop Ashton explicitly and emotionally wrote:

> "We cannot begin to calculate the cost in human and material terms imposed on Cyprus by the tragic events of this hot dry summer. The young lives wastefully squandered, the pains of the wounded and the sorrows of the bereaved, the buildings destroyed, the villages burnt, the harvests lost, the economy perilously threatened - how can these things be added up and cast into statistics?

> "Even when we have worked out the numbers of the dead, listed the names of the wounded, and published the hard cold facts of economics in pounds and pence, the figures recorded are only figures written in pen and ink. They have no feeling, no tears, no sorrows, but those who have suffered and wept in the fields and mountains of Cyprus are people for whom God cares. ... It is for the Church to share in some small measure the grief and sorrow of these people, and to give itself in prayer and service to their suffering. What can the Church do in a practical way?

> "First of all, it must be the Church. Simply by being there it is a symbol to those who pass by and to those who stop and pray that God is and that He cares. .... Secondly, the Church is involved in reconciliation. ... Regrettably the Church has often failed in this respect. Sometimes it has built walls of division instead of breaking down the barriers that divide. But, when it follows its true mission in Christ, the Church may be a great healer. ... Thirdly, the Church exists to serve. In practice this means that the Church will do all it can to alleviate suffering and to bring specific aid to those in need. ... There are more than 200,000 refugees in Cyprus."[27]

Throughout the island, the Anglican Church itself needed help to recover. Congregations were likely to remain diminished for some time. In September 1974 there were still only two full-time chaplains in Cyprus: Archdeacon Jack Nicholls based in Nicosia, and the Reverend Basil Pitt on the north side of the Green Line ministering at St Andrew, Kyrenia. In the south at St Barnabas Limassol, the Reverend Canon Hubert Matthews had a particularly challenging problem: how to deal with the refugee families squatting in the vicarage, the church hall and elsewhere on the premises. Understandably they were reluctant to leave. The humanitarian need was great, so were the management issues.

Special postage stamps issued for the Cyprus Refugee Fund

On the whole, Anglican church buildings on the island appeared to be structurally sound, but broken windows and the scars of bullets and mortars on stonework needed repair.

The bishop was personally affected too: "My house at RAF Nicosia is inaccessible. During the invasion I had to leave most of my books and papers and personal effects, although it is hoped that these things will not be lost."[28] Bishop Handford believes that the possessions were recovered eventually. But, as other contemporary reports tell, homes and churches were looted, including St Paul's vicarage in Nicosia, and St Andrew's church in Kyrenia which the bishop inspected for himself later in 1974:

"We approached Kyrenia through the mountain pass from Nicosia. The indomitable chaplain of St Andrew's Church, the Reverend Basil Pitt, drove cautiously along the winding road and our Turkish escort sat silent in the back seat. …

"Morning sunshine laid bare the fiery destruction of man's pitiless and pathetic rage. ... Then we entered the town where the bleak sad streets were largely deserted, most of the shops shuttered or looted, all adding to the sense of desolation. ... During the next two or three days I met many members of the British community, and a more courageous bunch of people would be hard to find.

"In spite of the difficulties, the looting and the deprivations, they will stay, and it was only in their houses that I caught again a little of the laughter which Kyrenia has lost. ... The little church of St Andrew, damaged in the battle and subsequently looted six times, is one of the focal points of the community.

The church of St Andrew Kyrenia
Source: P C Collins, A Short History of St Andrew's English Church: 1913-1988,
digitally recreated in 2013, www.standrewskyrenia.org

"So I returned to Nicosia and the Greek sector. ... The work among refugees cannot be told in a single paragraph. ... The children in a tented camp near Nicosia clustered around me to have their photographs taken, while the Reverend Peter Cowen, full-time chaplain in refugee work, collected an enthusiastic teenage team of footballers to play on the dusty wasteland. ...

"The great need now is educational, cultural and social, and in this work the Church is very much involved and needs continued help and prayer."[29]

After Archdeacon Jack Nicholls retired and departed in May 1975, for the next few months the bishop lived in St Paul's vicarage where, in a store room at the back of the house, he re-established his office. To emphasise how vulnerable the vicarage and church had been during the conflict, the cease-fire line on part of the Venetian ramparts in the heart of Nicosia is only few hundred metres away. At first the Green Line bisected the Roman Catholic convent and church of the Holy Cross, a brisk five-minute walk from St Paul's grounds. Sense and negotiation prevailed to allow the entire Holy Cross premises to be as one, on the south side of the Green Line. (The nuns at Holy Cross convent now make and supply the communion wafers required by St Paul's Cathedral.)

While Cyprus had been the focus of international attention since July 1974, the Archbishop of Canterbury and the Vicar-General had been discussing the process of nominating and voting on the appointment of a Coadjutor Bishop and another Assistant Bishop to serve during the transition. On 29 August 1974 the Vicar-General consecrated the Reverend Canon Faiq Ibrahim Haddad as Coadjutor Bishop to minister within the existing Diocese of Jerusalem and the existing Diocese of Jordan, Lebanon and Syria, the intention being that he would be appointed bishop of a united Diocese of Jerusalem. His dual role was to assist both the Vicar-General and the Right Reverend Najib Cuba'in, Bishop in Jordan, Lebanon and Syria, in working towards a smooth formation of the new province.

On the same day, the Vicar-General consecrated the Reverend 'Aql 'Aql as Assistant Bishop in the Diocese of Jordan, Lebanon and Syria to reside in Amman. Sadly, in 1975 Bishop 'Aql died due to a heart attack "before he could see the culmination of his hopes. By his death the diocese suffered the grievous loss of his wisdom and experience and pastoral care."[30] He was succeeded by Bishop Eliya Khoury in 1979.

Meantime, in November 1974 Bishop Stopford consecrated the Reverend Ishaq Musaad as Anglican Bishop in Egypt to serve in the restored diocese, the first Egyptian appointed to that See. In the same month, the Most Reverend Michael Ramsey was due to retire on 15 November, the day after his seventieth birthday. Three weeks earlier on 22 October, during the annual service of the Jerusalem and the East Mission at Christ Church, Lancaster Gate in London, he preached what was to be one of his last sermons as Archbishop of Canterbury. He said:

"We have much in our hearts and minds the recent sad conflict in Cyprus, sad for all the people of that country and our alms, our offerings, today are going to go to Bishop Ashton to help him in the rehabilitation of Church life in Cyprus, and our prayers and love and admirations have been very much with him and his people in Cyprus in these last months.

"In the last period, the Anglican work in the Middle East has had the Archbishopric in Jerusalem as its centre and focus. … Bishop Stopford, as Vicar-General, now has the authority, hitherto belonging to the Archbishop, for the purpose of working out the new pattern … to be a Council of Bishops and Dioceses - four in number, Jerusalem, Egypt, Iran, Cyprus and the Gulf - and these dioceses, with their bishops joining together in council, will be a pattern similar to that which has developed happily and strongly in other parts of the Anglican Communion.[31]

Archbishop Ramsey conveyed the hope, too, that while each diocese would have its own constitution, and likewise the Council in general, so would St George's Cathedral in Jerusalem whereby it could serve the diocese of which it was to be a part, and the wider Anglican Communion. Bishop Clive Handford, then the Dean of St George's, explains one source of confusion and how it was resolved:

"From the time of Bishop Blyth, the cathedral was always known officially as the Collegiate Church of St George the Martyr, the thought being that the Cathedral of Jerusalem is the Church of the Holy Sepulchre, the Bishop of Jerusalem being the Orthodox Patriarch. The Collegiate Church had never had a constitution, yet in conversation it was always referred to as the Cathedral. With the planning of the new Province it was decided that it should have a constitution. When we mentioned to the Orthodox our problem over what the church should be called, they laughed and said 'Well, we always call it the Cathedral so why don't you?'

"So technically before 1976 the name was the Collegiate Church and afterwards the Cathedral. If one wishes to be ultra formal then it is the Cathedral Church of St George the Martyr but normally it is just called St George's Cathedral."[32]

The Cathedral Church of St George the Martyr in Jerusalem, circa 1976
Diocese of Cyprus & the Gulf archive

Meanwhile, during the latter months of 1974, Bishop Ashton continued to use Jerusalem as his main base from where he planned visits to Cairo, the north African chaplaincies, Baghdad and Bahrain. All this was expected to keep him busy until the end of the year. By the summer of 1975 the Vicar-General and those assisting him, including the Dean of St George's Collegiate Church and Bishop Ashton, had completed work on codifying the new Constitutions. Arrangements were in place to reunite the Diocese of Jordan, Lebanon and Syria with part of the Diocese of Jerusalem, and to institute the new Diocese of Cyprus and the Gulf. In June 1975 Bishop Stopford informed readers of *Bible Lands*:

> "My dear Friends, the new organisation, which is to be inaugurated on January 6th 1976, requires that I myself shall cease to be Vicar-General on January 5th. ... So the task which I went out to the Middle East to do is nearly completed."[33]

The planned structure of the new Episcopal Church in Jerusalem and the Middle East also involved profound changes in its supporting bodies in England, including transforming the character of the Jerusalem and the East Mission (J&EM). The Vicar-General believed these changes were wise, and after careful planning they were to be implemented according to the resolution of the Anglican Consultative Council which had met in Dublin during July 1973, and the advice of those who knew how the Anglican Communion worked in the Middle East.

Anglican Church property in various parts of the Archbishopric of Jerusalem was and remains owned by the Jerusalem and the East Mission Trust Limited incorporated on 27 December 1929, and by other entities[34]. A comprehensive J&EM paper titled *A New Partnership in the Middle East*[35] highlighted the fact that changing the registered ownership of lands and property is an expensive process and can only be justified in exceptional circumstances in cases not involving sale. Therefore, the entity of the Trust must remain unaltered.

The status of the Trust's supporting agency, the Jerusalem and the East Mission, was quite different: a registered charity at the service of the Archbishopric. For many years the word "Mission" had been a source of confusion and misunderstanding because the J&EM had never been a "Missionary Society" in the way that title is usually understood, and it had never been responsible for *sending* either money or people. Instead it had made all its funds available to the Archbishop in Jerusalem for *him* to send and employ where and how *he* liked within the Archbishopric.

Another source of confusion had been the relationship of the Mission with the Church of England, "by whom, to the Mission's undoubted gain, the Jerusalem and the East Mission was recognised as one of the 'Big Nine'."[36] The Mission, however, had always claimed that it was not exclusively a member of the Church of England but an Anglican agency. This inevitably resulted in a difficult balancing act in England and another cause of misunderstanding.[37] Therefore, the creation of a new province to succeed the archbishopric made it opportune to remove both "sources of trouble".

The upshot was that the Council of the J&EM agreed to change the title of the Mission, the charity, to become The Jerusalem and the Middle East Church Association (JMECA). This was to be instituted on 6 January 1976 simultaneously with the inauguration of the new province, and for that to be legally possible the charity's new identity required a new constitution, a draft of which had been approved.

There was a chain effect to all this. The Jerusalem and the East Mission owned 11 Warwick Square in London and had a long lease of number 12. Various flats and maisonettes in the houses had in the past secured a good return as investments in the form of rental income. Although number 12 offered the J&EM comparatively cheap office accommodation in central London, the building did "state an unfortunate and misleading appearance of opulence"[38] and represented a large capital sum tied up in an increasingly less economic investment. Regretfully, therefore, it had been decided that the entire property, which for sixty years had been the Mission's home, should be sold and that the new Church Association would start life in new premises outside London in a country town served by rail. Farnham in the county of Surrey was chosen, and is where the offices of JMECA remain today.

The author (not credited) of "A New Partnership in the Middle East" (published in *Bible Lands*) emphasised that these changes would, in fact, make the work of the Jerusalem and the East Mission more important. The Episcopal Church in Jerusalem and the Middle East needed more rather than less support as it set out on its new life. The new province came into existence at a time of excessive inflation in the Holy Land as well as in the United Kingdom.

171

A counterpoint to those remarks is relevant specific to the Diocese of Cyprus and the Gulf. In March 1974 the OPEC oil embargo had ended. Already during 1975 increased oil prices were spawning economic prosperity and development in the Gulf countries. Although the full impact would not manifest itself until later, this opportunity "created the employment context for the millions of expatriate/migrant workers who now make up the Church in the Gulf".[39]

During 1974 and early in 1975 further visa applications for Anglican clergy to visit Baghdad had failed. However, on 9 June 1975, the Reverend David Penman, temporary Anglican chaplain at All Saints in Beirut, offered Bishop Ashton a ray of hope. The Reverend Georg Richter, a German pastor living in the city, had telephoned him to say that after two years of trying to obtain a visa to travel to Iraq he had recently visited Baghdad and met some of the Anglican congregation there. He hoped to return in October or November and was "happy to be of service to us in any way we desire if we continue to be without a visa for entry".[40]

This breakthrough spurred Bishop Ashton to write almost identical letters to the Right Reverend Hassan Dehqani-Tafti, Bishop in Iran, and the Right Reverend John Satterthwaite, Bishop of Fulham and Gibraltar:

> "You may know that since Colin Davies was expelled from Iraq in December 1973, no Anglican chaplain has been able to enter Baghdad. …. I have since been refused entry, but I am trying again this year. … Meanwhile we are looking around to try to find any Anglican chaplains in neighbouring countries who might be available to visit Baghdad to take a service for the small English-speaking congregation."[41 & 42]

Bishop Ashton had in mind Philip Saywell at Ahwaz in Iran, and David Palmer in Ankara. Both were keen to help, yet months passed with no progress. Then, quite unexpectedly, the bishop received a cable from Beirut: "Penman has visa for Iraq and will conduct services at Baghdad on Sunday 9 November en route for [his homeland] New Zealand."

The Reverend David Penman was due to take home leave before moving to Australia to become Principal of St Andrew's Hall, a CMS training college in Melbourne.[43] Yet, in a letter dated 24 November 1975, Bishop Ashton informed the Reverend David Palmer in Ankara, via the FCO in London: "I am still waiting to hear if Penman made it from Beirut to Baghdad."[44] It is not known whether he did.

A complication was that, since the start of the civil war in Lebanon in April that year, airline traffic at Beirut airport was often disrupted. Also, because the bishop still had no fixed anode, post had to be sent to him c/o the Jerusalem and the East Mission at 12 Warwick Square in London. Nevertheless, the bishop would submit a further visa application to visit Baghdad in early 1976. By then he would be Bishop of the Diocese of Cyprus and the Gulf. Would that make a difference? Only time would tell.

Bishop Robert Stopford's ministry in Jerusalem was drawing to a close. Reflecting on this phase in his life, he wrote his penultimate letter for *Bible Lands*:

"For me the past eighteen months in which I have been privileged to work in the Middle East as Vicar-General have been full of stimulus and encouragement. Working out details of constitutions, sometimes on points for which there are few precedents, has not been easy - and there have been times when members of committees have disagreed with each other. But there has been a readiness to accept changes and to work for unity which gives me great confidence for the future of the new Central Synod and the new dioceses. Many problems remain to be solved and the challenge of contemporary events to our tiny Anglican Church in the Middle East is very great.

"I am writing this letter just before I leave for a round of farewell visits - to Iran, the Gulf (where I hope to dedicate a new church at Muscat), Beirut and Cyprus. It is difficult not to have a sense of sadness at the end of the Archbishopric in Jerusalem in its present form. Since it was created in 1957 it has given a new cohesion and purpose to Anglican work in this part of the world. ...

"I have no doubt myself that the changes which are being made are necessary and right. Under the leadership of the four Bishops, Hassan in Iran, Leonard in Cyprus and the Gulf, Ishaq in Egypt, and Faik in Jerusalem, I am confident that the Church will go forward with fresh life and vision, but the changes of structure of themselves will not alter the practical problems of politics, finance and personnel which face the Bishops. ... I would, therefore commend to you the reconstituted Jerusalem and the Middle East Church Association as it embarks on its new life as the Church's supporting agency in the place of the old Jerusalem and the East Mission which has served the Church so well for the last eight-eighty years."[45]

Bishop Robert Stopford did visit Muscat, the capital of Oman, during his farewell tour of the Archbishopric and, as he had hoped, on 12 October 1975 he dedicated the new Protestant Church building located in the modern commercial district of Ruwi. He was assisted by Archdeacon Ralph Lindley, the Reverend James Dunham, and the clergy of the Protestant and Orthodox communities in Oman.[46]

This event was resonant in two respects. Firstly, the existence of the Anglican Church in the Middle East depends on cordial relationships with host Rulers, and their generosity. An excellent example lay in the fact that the plot of land on which the new Ruwi church stood had been donated by His Majesty Sultan Qaboos bin Said Al Said in 1973 for the building of places of worship for Christians.

Secondly, Muscat was where almost eighty-five years earlier Bishop Valpy French had pioneered Anglican ministry in south-eastern Arabia. Bishop Stopford may well have mused on this during his visit. As Vicar-General he too had overseen a significant episode in Anglican pioneering, the results of which were to be inaugurated in Jerusalem on 6 January 1976.

Chapter 8

THE INAUGURAL YEAR

1976

O n Monday 5 January 1976, Evensong in the Collegiate Church of St George the Martyr, Jerusalem, was distinctly different from usual. The highlight of the service was the solemn institution by the Vicar-General of the Right Reverend Leonard Ashton CB as the first Bishop of the new Diocese of Cyprus and the Gulf. This act formalised the diocese's creation, a legal requirement prior to the inauguration of the new province during the following day. The Vicar-General had acted on behalf of the Archbishop of Canterbury who, at that point but not for many more hours, still exercised metropolitan jurisdiction over the Archbishopric in Jerusalem.

Also significant, at midnight on 5 January 1976 the Collegiate Church of St George the Martyr formally changed its name and became the Cathedral Church of St George the Martyr. In conversation it is generally called St George's Cathedral.

> "Though in no way detracting from the acknowledgement of the position of the Orthodox Patriarch of Jerusalem as the successor to St James as Bishop of Jerusalem, and the Church of the Holy Sepulchre as the Cathedral of Jerusalem, St George's under its new Constitution has the status of a Cathedral Church, serving not only the diocese, but also in a unique way the whole Anglican Communion, with which it is linked by the Episcopal Canons who have a share in the government of the Cathedral."[1]

All this was a preface to the grand processions and events which were to take place on the following day. On 6 January 1976, the Feast of the Epiphany, the Anglican Communion's newest province, the Episcopal Church in Jerusalem and the Middle East, was inaugurated amid glorious pageantry, and media attention.

The Reverend Samir J Habiby, a Palestinian Christian Arab refugee resident in California and Communications Chairman for the Episcopal Diocese of Los Angeles, was in the congregation. With passion and keenly observed detail he reported the proceedings for the Episcopal News Service in the USA:

> "The resplendent rites took place … with the triumphal fanfares of organ and ceremonial trumpets to herald a joyous new era in the life of the Biblical Middle East. Eastern Orthodox, Armenian, and Western Rite senior bishops, Archimandrites, and their chaplains in glittering copes and miters, with the golden miter-like crowns of the East; clergymen in colorful vestments; visiting dignitaries of the Reformed and Protestant communions; attendants such as vergers, crucifers, marshals and others robed in flowing copes; members of the Jerusalem Consular Corps and others added to the rich traditional stateliness and dignity that Anglicans throughout the world revere and look for in the orderliness of their liturgy."[2]

The focal point within the Eucharist at which the Vicar-General, Bishop Robert Stopford, celebrated and preached the sermon, was the reading by him in English, and Bishop Cuba'in in Arabic, of the legal document by which the Archbishop of Canterbury relinquished "all metropolitical, spiritual and episcopal jurisdiction over the Archbishopric of Jerusalem to the intent that the Central Synod shall exercise the jurisdiction hitherto possessed by him".[3] After the Vicar-General had made the formal declaration of inauguration, a new chapter began in the life of the Anglican Church in Jerusalem and the Middle East.

The ceremony and rites continued with the installation of the Right Reverend Faiq Ibrahim Haddad as the eleventh Bishop in Jerusalem. In the customary manner he knocked at the cathedral's "Great Doors" and asked to be admitted. The dean, the Very Reverend Clive Handford, met the bishop as the doors opened and responded in Arabic for the cathedral chapter and the seven-thousand five-hundred communicants of the diocese: "Right Reverend Father in God, we welcome you most gladly in the name of the Lord …"[4]

The Very Reverend Clive Handford, Dean of St George's Cathedral, welcoming
the Right Reverend Faiq Haddad at the cathedral's main entrance
Diocese of Jerusalem archive

177

Bishop Haddad, escorted by the dean and the cathedral chapter, made his way up the nave to be met at the crossing by his two immediate predecessors in office, Bishop George Appleton and the Vicar-General, Bishop Robert Stopford, together with Bishop Cuba'in. After taking the oath of office, Bishop Haddad was invested with the pastoral staff of the See of Jerusalem and escorted to the throne for installation by the dean.

It had been a poignant occasion for Bishop Cuba'in. The inauguration of the new province signalled the end of what had been for eighteen years his See of Jordan, Lebanon and Syria, those countries now being integrated within the reconfigured Diocese of Jerusalem. The end of the service officially marked the start of Bishop Cuba'in's retirement to Amman, Jordan.

During Evensong, and to conclude the day's ceremonies, the dean installed three episcopal canons of St George's Cathedral: Bishop Leonard Ashton, Cyprus and the Gulf; Bishop Hassan Dehqani-Tafti, Iran; and Bishop John Howe, General Secretary of the Anglican Consultative Council.

After the inauguration of the Episcopal Church in Jerusalem and the Middle East,
Front row, 3rd, 4th and 5th from the left: the Right Reverend Leonard Ashton CB,
the Right Reverend Faiq Haddad, the Right Reverend & Right Honourable Robert Stopford
Middle row, 5th from the left: the Very Reverend Clive Handford
Diocese of Jerusalem archive

Early next morning the Anglican bishops and delegates to the Central Synod travelled to Amman, making the difficult crossing that separates the West and East Banks of the Jordan. Their purpose was to meet in the Central Synod's first constitutional and legislative session later that day, 7 January 1976.

The Central Synod itself comprised sixteen members, of which six formed its Standing Committee: the four diocesan bishops; the secretary, then the Venerable Samir Kafity; and the treasurer, Mr Ibrahim Wakid, an Egyptian living in Cairo. The four dioceses were:

Cyprus and the Gulf embracing Cyprus, Iraq, Kuwait, the archipelago of Bahrain, the Arabian peninsula, and Das island within the emirate of Abu Dhabi

Egypt along with Algeria, Libya, Tunisia and Ethiopia, plus the French Territory of the Afars and Issas (now Djibouti), and in due course Eritrea and Somalia

Iran, the smallest in size and numbers

Jerusalem spanning Palestine, Israel, Jordan, Lebanon and Syria, including the city of Jerusalem, the Gaza Strip and the West Bank of the River Jordan

Metropolitical authority was to rest with the Central Synod - often referred to as the Provincial Synod - consisting of the four diocesans and representative elected clergy and laity. As part of its formational process in 1976, it was decided that there should be no fixed primatial See but that any of the four diocesans might be elected as Primate for a five-year term, with the title President Bishop. In secret ballot at that first meeting in Amman on 7 January, "the Central Synod elected as Bishop President the Right Reverend Hassan Dehqani-Tafti, the Bishop in Iran"[5].

That phrasing, used by Bishop Robert Stopford in a sermon he preached a week later, highlights a technicality: Bishop Dehqani-Tafti preferred and often used the title Bishop President, although not consistently. His successors in the primacy have always been styled as President Bishop. Another idiosyncrasy was that although he should have been correctly addressed The Most Reverend, he consistently retained the title "The Right Reverend" throughout his primacy.

The formal business of the Central Synod was now complete. Starting on the following day 8 January and continuing for four days, also in Amman, a Partners in Mission Consultation convened during which members of the synod and representatives from Anglican and Episcopal provinces in Australia, Africa, Canada, the UK and USA discussed plans for the future.

With his task as Vicar-General accomplished, Bishop Robert Stopford returned to Jerusalem for the last time and flew to London, no doubt thinking about the sermon he was due to preach a few days later. On 13 January 1976 at Holy Trinity Church, Brompton, a Service of Intercession and Rededication was held to mark the inauguration of the new Jerusalem and Middle East Church Association. Officially, this had happened on 6 January, the same day that the new province had been inaugurated. As most of those listening would not have been in

179

Jerusalem at that time, and since there were no international satellite television news networks, Bishop Stopford wished to convey a flavour of the occasion during his sermon, with a short history lesson too:

> "In the Deed of Relinquishment, the Archbishop of Canterbury handed over his authority not to a person but to a body, and for this I know of no precedent. There will not be an Archbishop. Instead there is a President elected by the Synod from among the four diocesan bishops, to hold office for five years with a possible extension for a further five years.[6] ... When I pronounced the inauguration, the great congregation rose to sing a solemn *Te Deum* with a sense of real thanksgiving. What was happening was the climax of 135 years of Anglican history in the Middle East."[7]

Bishop Stopford went on to explain that when Michael Solomon Alexander was consecrated in 1841 as the first Bishop of the Church of England in Jerusalem, his bishopric was unique in three ways. First, it was then the only bishopric of the Church of England outside the British Empire; secondly, it was the only bishopric of a Western Church other than the Latin Church in the diocese of an Eastern Orthodox Patriarchate; thirdly, Bishop Alexander had pastoral care not only of Anglican but also Prussian Lutheran clergy and laity. The purpose of the new bishopric was to be an Anglican presence in Jerusalem, not to create a new branch of the Church of England but to care for those Anglicans living and working in Jerusalem.

Over the years the numbers of those Anglicans had grown from a few chaplaincy congregations in trading cities like Alexandria and Aleppo to a rapidly increasing family within the Anglican Communion and, although the Anglican Church in the Middle East was small in numbers, it was great in potential influence, above all in the work of reconciliation. But, as Bishop Stopford emphasized:

> "This will need our help as never before, though in different ways. ... May I conclude by quoting some words of Cardinal Suenens[8] with which I ended my sermon at the Inauguration Service.
>
> 'To hope is a duty not a luxury.

'To hope is not to dream, but to turns dreams into reality.

'Happy are those who dream dreams and are ready to pay the price to make them come true.'" [9]

As a postscript, not long after preaching this sermon Bishop Stopford flew to Bermuda, a British Overseas Territory in the North Atlantic Ocean. There on 20 February he celebrated his seventy-fifth birthday. His purpose for being in Bermuda was to undertake a new assignment, but very soon after his arrival he was taken ill. Almost exactly six months later, having largely managed to complete the work he went to do, Bishop Stopford died on 13 August 1976.

What were Bishop Ashton's hopes and dreams for the Diocese of Cyprus and the Gulf? They were inspirational and radical, and he rarely allowed himself to be side-tracked from them.

As a start, already on 6 December 1975, the Feast of St Nicholas, the bishop had dedicated a new small stone chapel in the grounds of St Paul's church, Nicosia[10]. The chapel, a renovated and converted stone pump-house, provided "a place and an atmosphere"[11] for Sunday school prayer services, and served as a memorial to all children, both the living and the dead, hence its dedication to the patron saint of children St Nicholas. On 6 January 1976, the same day that the new province was inaugurated in Jerusalem, St Paul's church council held its first meeting that year, during which it was agreed, at a cost of £6, to buy a copy of an icon of St Nicholas to display in the chapel, which already was being well used, both by children and people of all ages seeking a quiet place for private meditation.

In September 1975 two members of St Paul's church council, Mr Cecil Griggs and Mr David Humphreys, had suggested to the bishop that the Reverend Peter Cowen, serving as chaplain to the refugees in Cyprus, might become the bishop's chaplain and later the chaplain at St Paul's church to fill the vacancy created by the departure of Archdeacon Jack Nicholls in early May 1975. Even by October the decision still rested with the Vicar-General. Eventually, Bishop Stopford did confirm the chaplain's appointment, and thus on Sunday 18 January 1976 Bishop Ashton installed the Reverend Peter Cowen as incumbent at St Paul's in Nicosia, not as Archdeacon in Cyprus. That post remained vacant, the bishop choosing to take his time to discern what the role under his authority should entail. The process took two more years.

As it was no longer practical for Bishop Ashton to lodge at St Paul's vicarage, once again he moved into a hotel. As few tourists were visiting Cyprus at that time, he was able to rent two rooms at a cheap rate. These remained reserved for him when he travelled away from Nicosia. Soon this arrangement became inconvenient, so the bishop rented a succession of apartments until he found one where he could receive and entertain visitors, and invite them to stay. The then Archbishop of York was one such guest. Jokingly, Bishop Ashton referred to Flat 3, Number 4 Andrea Zakou in the district of Engomi as "The Bishop's Palace". As explained later, this tongue-in-cheek description was later considered by some to be a semi-serious notion. In fact, Bishop Ashton's lifestyle was necessarily modest. Initially, he could not afford to employ a secretary and typed letters himself. His filing cabinet was a suitcase.

The bishop's credentials included a wealth of contacts accumulated during his long service with the RAF between 1945 and 1973. While ministering as Assistant Bishop in Jerusalem he had developed close cooperation with British military chaplains in the Sovereign Base Areas in Cyprus, and also with those who arrived to serve with the United Nations Forces after the partition of Cyprus in July 1974.

Not long after the diocese came into being in 1976 he began to draw on those contacts to recruit retired RAF chaplains to minister as civilian chaplains in Cyprus and the Gulf. One advantage was that, to save parish expenditure by not paying a stipend, the bishop was sometimes able to recruit such chaplains on a house-for-duty[12] basis. He was not afraid either to seek RAF support at the highest level when other needs arose, as the following story demonstrates.

The church of St Antony in Kato Paphos, in 2017
Copyright: Angela Murray

During the autumn of 1975 Metropolitan Chrysostomos, Orthodox Bishop of Paphos, granted permission for Anglicans and Latin Catholics to hold liturgies in the old Orthodox church of Ayios Antonios, then not in use. This ecumenical gesture allowed the two congregations to repair the little church in the old town of Kato Paphos, install electricity, fence off the grounds and plant trees around the perimeter. There was a snag: the interior was empty, and there were no funds to pay for furnishings. Thus, on 20 October 1975, Bishop Ashton wrote to the Reverend F Hawkes, Deputy Assistant Chaplain-General of British Near East Land Forces headquartered at Episkopi (the Sovereign Base Area near Limassol), to ask if the military might be able to supply some of the required furnishings from redundant stocks on the island. By January 1976 the bishop had received no response. Using the opportunity of a conversation with Air Marshal Sir John Aiken KCB RAF, Commander

British Forces Near East, he briefly mentioned his predicament. The bishop followed up with a letter on 26 January, apologising for bringing so trivial a matter to the Air Marshal's attention, yet wondering "if a gentle prod from above might get things moving again"[13]. The enclosure was a shortlist of desired equipment. RAF Akrotiri obliged, generously providing and presenting St Antony's church with an exhaustive inventory,[14] including chairs (there was space for thirty), kneelers, credence table, silver chalice and paten, brass altar cross and candlesticks, missal stand, lectern Bible, hymn and prayer books, even a wafer box and altar linen, and an American organ - albeit needing repair, and in Nicosia. St Paul's in Nicosia provided fifty Holy Communion books.

18 April 1976, Easter Day, Bishop Leonard Ashton outside the church of St Antony, with the Reverend Canon Hubert Matthews

Source: the late Patricia Kingston, reproduced with Philip Kingston's consent

On the evening of 18 April 1976, Easter Sunday that year, Bishop Leonard Ashton celebrated Holy Communion, the first Anglican service to be conducted in the church, assisted by the Reverend Peter Cowen visiting from Nicosia, and the Reverend Canon Hubert Matthews who, although retired, continued to minister at St Barnabas in Limassol during what had become an extended interregnum.[15] The large congregation overflowed into the grounds of the church, among them tourists from Britain, Germany and America, lay visitors from Nicosia and Limassol, and representatives from other churches.[16]

Thereafter on Sunday afternoons Canon Matthews drove west from his home in Polemidia near Limassol to Kato Paphos, a journey taking two-and-a-half hours along what was the main route through villages and along the hilly coast road. His destination was St Antony, and his purpose was to lead evening Anglican worship, a routine which his successors maintained for more than a decade.

185

Once a month, usually in summer, the chaplain at St Barnabas also drove north up to the Troodos mountains to take services in a secluded forest, at the church of St George. Its inspired design was that of the eminent ecclesiastical architect William Douglas Caröe (1857-1938).[17] He had waived his fee on one condition: in keeping with the international Arts and Crafts movement which flourished in the late nineteenth and early twentieth centuries, he insisted that the church interior should form part of a single coherent architectural design. "Virtually all the congregants' donations, including the altar, a copper cross and candlesticks, and the church weather vane, conformed to Caröe's aesthetic criteria."[18]

A fine eighteenth-century icon of St George, a gift from Sir Ronald Storrs CMG CBE, the Governor of Cyprus, is mounted on the balcony facade, He had laid the foundation stone of the church on 27 October 1928, and on 3 June 1931 the Right Reverend Rennie MacInnes, fifth Anglican Bishop in Jerusalem, conducted its consecration. (It will be recalled that his son Campbell Angus MacInnes became the eighth Anglican Bishop in Jerusalem, and first Archbishop in Jerusalem.)

Eighteenth century icon of St George,
mounted on the balcony of St George in the Forest, Troodos
Copyright: Angela Murray

For many years during the summer months, St George in the Forest served the British garrison based in Polemidia and the British administration headquartered in Nicosia during their camping seasons. Following the formation of the British Sovereign Base Areas in 1960, the church was used by military personnel while staying at the nearby Services Leave Camp in Troodos, and well into the 1980s the church was still "used almost exclusively by members of the British Forces who very kindly hold the key and keep the property clean"[19]. Bishop Ashton was invited to lead their special services at the church, particularly on Remembrance Day. St Barnabas-based chaplains also conducted occasional services at St George's.

One outcome of the civil war in Lebanon, beginning in April 1975, was that the church of St Barnabas became a magnet for migrant worshippers from Beirut, including members of Christian organisations previously based there, many from other denominations. Their arrival considerably swelled the congregation and spawned a fine Sunday school.

Less satisfactorily, the vicarage and the church hall remained occupied by refugees who had installed themselves after the partition of Cyprus in 1974. On 19 May 1976 Bishop Ashton wrote to His Eminence Bishop Chrysanthos of Limassol to seek his advice and help. "We should be very grateful if you regard our problem sympathetically, and I shall be very happy to visit you to discuss the matter if you so desire."[20] Although the Anglican Church did not wish to evict the homeless families from the St Barnabas compound, the vicarage was needed by the Reverend Walter Gunn, appointed as chaplain for Limassol and Paphos to fill the incumbency left vacant when Canon Matthews retired in 1974. In the autumn of 1976, the bishop reported that the problem had been resolved.[21] Although he did not explain how, it may be assumed that the Bishop of Limassol's response had been helpful.

Another consequence of the civil war in Lebanon was that Cyprus became the office location and conference venue of choice for the Christian Churches of the Middle East. The Middle East Council of Churches (MECC) and the Fellowship of Middle East Evangelical Churches relocated their offices to Cyprus. When Larnaca became the base for the Bible Society, its employees favoured St Helena's as their spiritual home.

In Nicosia, the congregation at St Paul now included UN personnel billeted in the former Ledra Palace Hotel just over half a mile away, joining other non-British church members, including diplomats, businesspeople, teachers, and journalists from organisations such as Reuters. As a result, the Sunday school at St Paul's was international, energised and expanding. The new youth club, one of the Reverend Peter Cowen's first initiatives at the church, was also hugely popular. On 5 October 1976, almost overnight, his workload expanded. On that day St Paul's church council agreed to Bishop Ashton's request that the Nicosia chaplaincy should assume responsibility for St Helena's church in Larnaca,[22] not as yet a separate chaplaincy. The bishop's thinking was a response to changed circumstances.

For several decades St Helena's had been served by chaplains from St Barnabas, Limassol. When the Reverend Canon Hubert Matthews retired in 1974 and no successor was appointed in the aftermath of the July crisis in Cyprus, that arrangement ceased. Instead, on the first Sunday evening of each month the Anglican padre at Dhekelia, the British garrison east of Larnaca, had led a Holy Communion service at St Helena's. He was available to be contacted at other times - his telephone number at the rectory in Dhekelia was displayed on a board outside the church. By 1976 his ministry also included serving those at 4 Mile Point, at Ayios Nikolaos south of Famagusta, also within the British Sovereign Base Area.

By now the Reverend Walter Gunn, recently arrived from Amman and installed at St Barnabas Limassol, was multi-tasking: trying to re-establish normality on the church compound now that the refugee squatters had left; serving as honorary chaplain to the new Missions to Seamen's club on church premises; caring for the growing congregation at St Antony in Paphos; and ministering at St George in the Forest, Troodos. Already at full stretch, he could not serve Larnaca too.

The garrison church of St George at Dhekelia, rededicated in 2005 to St Barnabas
St Barnabas Dhekelia vestry archive, reproduced with the consent of Padre Peter King

Combining the ministries at St Paul and St Helena seemed to be the best way forward. In fact, parishioners at St Helena's were spoilt for choice. The plan was to continue with the monthly evening service at St Helena's as this did not conflict with the morning service at St George's church in Dhekelia, only 7 miles/11 kilometres away.

Many parishioners at St Helena's worshipped there and were welcome to do so. In due course this relaxed arrangement ended when the Ministry of Defence in London implemented tight security controls.

In 1976 the focal point of Bishop Ashton's ecclesiastical jurisdiction, his See, was the church of St Paul in Nicosia. There were at this stage no plans to rehallow the church as a cathedral, so although he had been instituted on 5 January 1976 in Jerusalem as the Bishop in Cyprus and the Gulf, more than five years were to pass before he could be enthroned in his See. The main reason was the cost involved to reconfigure and refurnish the sanctuary to accommodate a bishop's throne and other stalls, and to partition the vestry properly to form a separate room.

More urgently the new diocese of Cyprus and the Gulf required synodical and financial infrastructures. However, its geographical size presented major logistical challenges. Its founding fathers therefore decided that it would have two archdeaconries: Cyprus, and one which embraced Iraq and the Arabian Gulf region to be named The Gulf. As for financial infrastructure, in 1976 the diocese of Cyprus and the Gulf had no legal foundation beyond its ecclesiastical and constitutional status as one of the four dioceses within the new province of the ECJME. The diocese did not own any property, and technically it still does not.[23]

Relevant to this narrative focusing on the diocese's inaugural year, it is helpful to provide background. On 27 December 1929, the Jerusalem and the East Mission Trust Limited had been incorporated in the UK as a non-profit limited company to administer the assets of the Mission, and a number of other related charities. This included land and church buildings, such as in Bahrain.

In 1973 subsidiary trustees were appointed in anticipation of a deed in the name of the Jerusalem and the East Mission Trust (Cyprus) - a charitable trust and not a limited company. This Declaration of Trust, signed and sealed on 2 March 1973 in London by notary public, Sydney Charles Crowther-Smith, was received on 12 March 1973 at the first meeting of the JEMT (Cyprus) Managing Trustees.[24]

At that time Anglican Church property in Cyprus included land and church houses in Nicosia, Kyrenia (also Houston Cemetery), Larnaca, Limassol and Troodos, land in Famagusta, and a lease on Blue Skies House in Troodos. (Later, the portfolio came to include apartments and some commercial property.) Anglican Church property on the island continues to be managed locally by the JEMT (Cyprus). Additional declarations and deeds have been signed over a number of years.[25]

Between 1973 and the formation of the Diocese of Cyprus and the Gulf in 1976, the four managing trustees of the JEMT (Cyprus) met four times each year. They were Cecil Griggs, then general manager of Atlas Copco in Cyprus; David Humphreys, headmaster of the English School in Nicosia; Charles Bennett, a banker; and Major Jack E Walliker, resident in Limassol and a member of St Barnabas church.

When the new diocese was formed these same four trustees were the constituent members of a new body known as the Diocesan Board of Finance (Cyprus). The Board's terms of reference included receiving and paying the bishop's stipend and diocesan expenses. The Board also administered income from several JEMT (Cyprus) properties and used it to top up the stipends for the clergy in Cyprus. A Diocesan Board of Finance (Gulf) was established, its *ex officio* members being the chaplain in Bahrain, the Archdeacon in the Gulf, and three nominated members.

The creation of a cohesive diocese depended upon other factors. Given its geographical spread, for ease of administration it was also decided to form two synods: the Diocesan Synod (Cyprus) and the Diocesan Synod (Gulf), each with its own House of Clergy and House of Laity, although in those early days they were not convened as formally as they are now.

As events turned out, the historic first synod was a meeting of the Diocesan Synod (Gulf), held between 26 and 27 February 1976 in an unusual setting: the VIP Lounge of the Abu Dhabi Petroleum Company (ADPC). Each day began with a service of Holy Communion in the church of St Andrew, then eight years old, located on the Corniche. All told, twenty-five people attended this first Diocesan Synod (Gulf):

the bishop, the Archdeacon in the Gulf and chaplain in Abu Dhabi; chaplains from Bahrain, Dubai, the Canterbury Group, Kuwait and Oman; eleven lay representatives and seven observers, including the Reverend Michael Pavey from RAF Masirah in Oman.

Bishop Ashton later remarked in his "Advent 1976 letter" to *Bible Lands* that "Archdeacon Lindley continues to blaze his enthusiastic way up and down the Gulf archdeaconry",[26] a statement which does not tell the whole truth. The challenges which he and the bishop faced were numerous, not least in the chaplaincy of Dubai and Sharjah. Congregations there were primarily British with a large percentage of Indian nationals, and other countries represented in smaller numbers. Exercising Anglican oversight was not easy. The new Chaplaincy House in Dubai, completed and occupied in January 1975, had rapidly proved its value to church life as a meeting place. Living in it, however, the chaplain now found himself having to deal with more callers arriving with their pastoral problems than had been envisaged. His front door on the church compound was more easily found than his former rented apartment in Deira.

Chaplaincy life in Sharjah was no less challenging, St Martin's church having suffered a serious setback in May 1975. The last British military presence in the area had already departed, the garrison having been the mainstay of church life in the emirate which was now developing very quickly. It was considered essential to maintain a Christian presence there, but the urgent question in 1975 was: where? New road developments meant that the church would be demolished within two years. The Ruler of Sharjah had promised to provide the congregation with a new church building, but as yet this had not happened.

Not only did the Reverend Philip Sturdy have his work cut out to cope with the parish workload, but also he served as port chaplain for the Missions to Seamen, a joint ministry with the chaplaincy of Dubai and Sharjah. Financially significant, the Mission contributed one third of his stipend, but for how long that arrangement could remain viable was doubtful. The new Dubai International Seafarers' Centre (DISC), built on land donated by the Ruler of Dubai, was opened officially on 11 September 1976.

When in due course the centre became fully operational, with many hundreds of seafarers using its facilities, the bishop realised that more staff would be needed.

Dubai International Seafarers Centre
Copyright: the Reverend Canon Andy Bowerman, reproduced with consent

Meanwhile, the first Diocesan Synod (Cyprus) met on 26 May 1976 in St Paul's Church Hall, Nicosia, preceded by Holy Communion in the church. In contrast to the Diocesan Synod (Gulf), just ten people were present: the Bishop, the chaplains from Kyrenia and Limassol, and seven others including the chairman of the Diocesan Board of Finance (Cyprus), Cecil Griggs. (The chaplain serving Nicosia and Larnaca was absent. The minutes do not explain why.) Bishop Ashton's finale to his presidential address was astute and prescient:

"Synod is not likely to prove to be an earth-shattering event, and will probably not even cast a great ripple across the placid waters of the Universal Church, but we are now firmly established. We have a chance to create something from the beginning.

"We need not allow ourselves to become tied with traditions and beset with the burdens which so often cripple other and ancient dioceses. We can experiment - administratively, ecumenically, liturgically. We shall make mistakes. We shall learn from our mistakes. We may, in our ignorance, omit things which are important. We may, in our innocence, include things which are trivial. But we shall learn, sometimes the hard way, and we shall be the better for it."[27]

A few months later the Primate of the ECJME, Bishop Hassan Dehqani-Tafti, made a limited tour of the Diocese of Cyprus and Gulf during which, in November 1976, he spent three days in Muscat, Oman. One evening he was invited to celebrate Holy Communion with two pastors assisting: the Reverend Dr Harvey Staal (RCA) and the Reverend Ibrahim Laal (Church of Pakistan). Bishop Dehqani-Tafti later remarked:

"As my luggage only reached me just as I was leaving Muscat I had to put on a white cassock of a lady priest (Lutheran). This was, so far, the nearest I have got to the question of Womens' Ordination!"[28]

Although his aside was not meant to be taken seriously, thirty-four years were to pass before Central Synod of the ECJME passed a motion in November 2010 which specifically allowed the Bishop in Cyprus and the Gulf, at his discretion, to ordain women to the priesthood. This provision did not apply, and still does not, to the bishops of the other three dioceses in the province.

The inaugural year of the Diocese of Cyprus and the Gulf had been busy, and replete with new initiatives. How they could be nurtured and sustained was among the challenges and opportunities which lay ahead.

A traditional Cypriot house in Kakopetria village, Troodos
Copyright: Angela Murray

Chapter 9

NEW BEGINNINGS

1977 - 1979

When Bishop Leonard Ashton began to envisage how he might craft the archdeaconries of Cyprus and the Gulf into a cohesive diocese, he will first have studied a large-scale map of the Middle East. Some statistics are helpful.

The island of Cyprus is moderate in size. The estimated driving distance from Kyrenia on the north coast to Larnaca on the south coast, via Nicosia, is 46 miles/75 kilometres; and from Larnaca driving west to Paphos, via Limassol, the distance is approximately 104 miles/166 kilometres. In 1976 the island's major towns were already linked by a reasonable network of paved roads - motorways were to be built years later. Therefore, as long as the bishop had a pass to cross the checkpoints on the Green Line, a pastoral tour of the island's Anglican churches could be achieved within days.

Travel elsewhere in the diocese involved much longer distances and travelling times. Supposing that the bishop was in Baghdad visiting the Mesopotamian Memorial Church of St George the Martyr, and from there he visited Kuwait, Bahrain, Doha in Qatar, Abu Dhabi, Dubai and Muscat, the direct distance as a bird might fly is 1832 miles/2949 kilometres. In 1976 there were few regional airlines and limited routing choices. Add to this the time taken to travel within chaplaincies, and the logistics involved. In 1977, for example, the bishop accompanied Archdeacon Lindley on a helicopter tour, touching down on several oil rigs in the Gulf, and arriving at Das island home to four thousand oil industry employees - where they held a service and remained overnight.[1] It takes little imagination to conclude that a pastoral tour as described would have taken weeks to accomplish, not days.

Although burgeoning cities were being built on desert landscapes, roads between city centres in the UAE, and to oil company camps throughout the region where Anglican ministry was offered, were basic. Wind blown sand often obscured tarmac surfaces. It was not uncommon for unwary travellers to find their vehicles stuck in soft sand with no equipment (a shovel and matting) to effect self-help. Wandering camels were hazards. A collision with one could be fatal, so it was best to avoid driving on unlit roads outside the cities after nightfall.

Touring the Gulf archdeaconry was also expensive before the days of regional budget airlines and discounted advance-booking fares. It is not surprising that on 24 February 1977, the first day of the second Diocesan Synod (Gulf), this time meeting in Dubai with Holy Trinity as the church focus, the bishop began his presidential address with a passionate statement about finance. He stressed to Synod that he had set up the new diocese "on a shoestring", with an inadequate budget, and was living off his RAF pension of £3,000 per annum. Later when inflation and cost-of-living expenses began to seriously devalue the pension, this goodwill gesture had to be reviewed. At several successive Diocesan Synods chaplains from both archdeaconries expressed serious concern at the insufficient provision for the bishop's stipend and the need to correct this.

Deploying a technique which became his trademark style, the bishop skilfully crafted his address into a powerful rallying call, while paying tribute to all those who were striving to make a success of the new diocese despite many challenges. With God's help the future was full of promise. He said:

> "On the whole, the churches have fared well, especially in the Gulf, but we cannot pretend that the year has been an easy one either pastorally or financially, especially for the churches in Cyprus and for the creation of a diocesan structure. ... The Diocese may be descended from a noble lineage, through the Anglican archbishopric in Jerusalem, but it was born in poverty. No impressive pedigree can alter the fact that in the first year the Diocese has been existing in rags and tatters, begging its way from month to month.

"But Cyprus and the Gulf also covers a geographical area that is not only vast, but fascinating. … Somewhere here is the legendary location of the Garden of Eden, whether on the traditional site where the great rivers Tigris and Euphrates move through Basra into the Arabian Gulf, or, as some archaeologists have contended, in the recently identified land of Dilmun … centred on the Island of Bahrain. Here, in this Diocese, occurred the flood of Noah in the land of the rivers. … Here lies the glory that was Babylon, about sixty miles south of Baghdad. … In the land of Oman, down the spice coast of Arabia, they will tell you that the magi collected their frankincense and myrrh (and maybe gold) as they began the long journey to Bethlehem.

Omani hand-painted clay burners, with frankincense - resin from boswellia trees
Copyright: Angela Murray

"As we reach across a thousand miles to the Mediterranean Sea we come to the other part of the Diocese, the lovely Island of Cyprus, where St Barnabas was born, and later, with St Paul, returned on their first missionary journey. …. Some of the myths of ancient Greece were allegedly enacted in Cyprus, and you may bathe where the goddess Aphrodite emerged from the sea foam; you may wander through ruined cities, visiting ancient mosaics, the tombs of kings, the temples and shrines of the gods, the amphitheatres and gymnasia of long forgotten people.

"But the diocese, although embedded in this rich setting of ancient history, is itself a living thing, made up of ordinary folk who have devoted their lives to the cause of the Kingdom of God. … It is as partners in this work that we meet together in synod. … God has been good to us, and I am sure that with His continued help the future will be bright with promise."[2]

Although eternally optimistic, the bishop was pragmatic too. One reason why he had said that the first year in the life of the new diocese had not been easy was because of staff shortages. He said: "We could do with another young chaplain in Cyprus" but there was no money available to pay a stipend and expenses. Four or five new chaplains were needed "to open up the new work in the Gulf", a direct result of oil boom development in the region and increasing numbers of expatriate workers.

In Kuwait, an increase in the British population was expected almost immediately in the oil town of Ahmadi, and already another chaplain was needed in Kuwait City.

High hopes for a new chaplaincy in Qatar, with its own chaplain, living in a house built on land given by the Ruler for a new school, had been delayed for lack of approval for such a project from the Ruler. He had promised an answer within six months, "which we all pray will be 'Yes'. Meanwhile, this thriving parish is without adequate pastoral coverage".[3] Nevertheless, the archdeacon in the Gulf visited for about three days each month holding services in the English School hall in Doha, the capital on the east coast of the Qatar peninsula, and in the oil encampment in Dukhan on the west coast. Although the locations are 53 miles/86 kilometres apart, then involving long journeys on rudimentary roads across desert terrain, the visiting archdeacon was never in doubt that his ministry was both greatly needed and appreciated.

Since 1972, the Reverend Philip Sturdy and his wife Mary had done "fine work" at Holy Trinity, but they were to leave during 1977. The new Dubai International Seafarers Centre (DISC) was fully operational. A new city, Jebel Ali, was being developed about 22 miles/35 kilometres from Dubai, including a huge seaport. By the end of 1977 the joint ministry between the chaplaincy of Dubai and Sharjah, and the Missions to Seamen, was too much for one priest. The emirate of Sharjah was developing rapidly, and the northern emirates were attracting more and more expatriates, particularly Ras al Khaimah. In the bishop's opinion, "a separate chaplaincy appears to be the only satisfactory answer, although no funds are as yet available".[4]

The need for more chaplains was about to increase. For many years, the British Royal Air Force had maintained a base on Masirah island which lies off the east coast of Oman. On 31 March 1977, soon after the second Gulf Synod, the base was to be closed and relinquished to the Royal Air Force of Oman. On behalf of Synod, Bishop Ashton thanked the RAF and their chaplains who had made such a valuable contribution to the work of the church in Oman but, for obvious reasons, he deeply regretted their imminent departure from Masirah.

In the Abu Dhabi chaplaincy, a clerical vacancy was only part of its impending problem, although there was no hint of this earlier in the year. On 19 February 1977, two days before the second Gulf Synod began, the bishop had officially opened the new St Andrew's Community Centre on the Corniche. By September 1977 sufficient funds had been raised to clear the debt. "No sooner finished, gathering rumours hardening into fact made it clear that the Government of Abu Dhabi intended a move of all the church sites on the Corniche to a site about two miles away"[5]

The existing Anglican and Roman Catholic church sites were needed for road redevelopment. Negotiations began, with assurances that there would be a generous grant of a new plot of land for St Andrew's and generous compensation. Suddenly, the parish council faced two challenges. How might it fund the construction of a new church, and who would lead all this? It was not to be Archdeacon Ralph Lindley, also chaplain at St Andrew's, as had been assumed. In November 1977, he announced that he would leave Abu Dhabi on 1 May 1978, not to retire but so that his wife Margot might enjoy better health in England's cooler climate. On 28 June 1978 while holidaying in the Scottish highlands, he replied to an enquiring letter from Bishop Ashton: "I will be glad to act as your Commissary for the Gulf. … You must know that anything I can do to help the Diocese I will do with joy".[6]

The Venerable Ralph Lindley CBE
Source: Bible Lands, reproduced with consent of JEMT's trustees

On 15 August the Venerable Ralph Lindley CBE began his new job as General Secretary of the Jerusalem and Middle East Church Association now based in Farnham, Surrey.

In fact it was the Dean of St George's Cathedral in Jerusalem, who would come to the new diocese to succeed Archdeacon Lindley. In October 1978, the Venerable Clive Handford, was installed as Archdeacon in the Gulf and chaplain at St Andrew's, and so began his massive task of leading plans to build a new church on a site in the al Mushrif district of Abu Dhabi island, and of raising funds to pay for the venture. Three years later in October 1981 a fund-raising committee was formed and the St Andrew's Endowment Fund was created to realise the vision for a new church, community hall, thrift centre and clergy accommodation, and to support their running costs and the maintenance of the fabric.

By coincidence a similar development was occurring in Cyprus. On 1 May 1978, the same day that Archdeacon Ralph Lindley left Abu Dhabi, the Reverend Douglas Northridge was installed as Chaplain of Nicosia and Larnaca, succeeding the Reverend Peter Cowen. Significantly, he was also appointed Archdeacon in Cyprus, the post which had remained vacant since May 1975. There was another parallel. Both archdeacons were retired senior RAF chaplains. In this, his first civilian ministry since retiring from the RAF, the Venerable Douglas Northridge was submitted to a baptism of fire, in Larnaca.

In summary, the managing trustees of the JEMT (Cyprus) decided early in 1978 that the seventy-one-year-old stone church of St Helena should be demolished so that the site could be redeveloped into a commercial complex of apartments and shops, to incorporate a new Church Centre on the ground floor of one block. One of the apartments would serve as a chaplain's residence. A sentence in a confidential report authored by Bishop Ashton, copied to Mr Cecil Griggs and the Venerable Ralph Lindley and dated 15 September 1978, sums up the thinking behind the proposal:

> "It was not good Christian stewardship to hold on to a plot of valuable land - even with a beautiful little Church which was used for only one hour once a month for a Sunday evening service - when the Anglican churches in Cyprus were perishing for lack of funds."[7]

201

St Helen's church, built in 1907
Source: Larnaca chaplaincy office, reproduced with consent

The managing trustees assumed that the rental income generated from the development would substantially solve this problem, and help to cover the diocese's administration costs generally.

This was not the first time a similar experiment had been mooted. In 1968, under the remit of the Archbishop in Jerusalem, a project to redevelop Anglican church property in Nicosia had been initiated.[8] In 1970 the building committee of St Paul's Church in Nicosia proposed to demolish the almost forty-year-old Chaplain's House (the vicarage) and construct an eight-storey building on the site to house shops, apartments and offices, and rather bizarrely not necessarily to include a new home for the chaplain. After the JEMT (Cyprus) came into being in 1973, the Nicosia project became its responsibility. In June 1974 the Electricity Authority of Cyprus expressed interest in leasing offices in the new development. Already, a London-based development corporation had contacted one of the managing trustees of the JEMT (Cyprus) to enquire about the possibility of financing and managing the project's development.[9]

A month later all hopeful plans and negotiations stopped, halted by the tragic Cyprus crisis in July 1974. In effect, this put an end to the Nicosia project. Its daunting cost, lack of financing and the implications of managing the commercial complex were unacceptable.

Notwithstanding this precedent, the managing trustees of the JEMT (Cyprus) believed that in 1978 it was possible to launch the Larnaca project "for which the capital expenditure was so much less than the Nicosia project and was obtainable."[10] A new dual-purpose church Centre had been designed, larger than the existing church, to be used for worship on Sundays and available on weekdays for religious and cultural activities, even to accommodate ladies' keep-fit classes - albeit with a wall-to-wall curtain drawn to hide the sanctuary. The premises were to be heated, air-conditioned and have kitchen facilities.

None of this dispelled the fears and frustrations of St Helena's congregation and its robust objections to the scheme. In early August 1978, a public meeting of St Helena's church was held at the Sun Hall Hotel in Larnaca. Mrs Susan Mantovani was among those present:

"The project was sold to us on the basis that 'you have an asset which we are going to redevelop and make an income for the diocese to support the development of the churches in the Gulf'.

Out of the deal, St Helena's would receive enough money to support a full-time chaplain whose responsibilities would extend to SE Cyprus, south of the Green Line crossing."[11]

Archdeacon Northridge and three of the JEMT (Cyprus) trustees - Mr Cecil Griggs, Mr David Humphreys and Mr Charles Bennett - were present to defend the diocese's plans, and listen to the acrimonious resistance. On Tuesday, 8 August 1978, the *Cyprus Mail* reported the protests. "The objectors say that the Larnaca municipality and the Antiquities Department should oppose the demolition of the church at Gregoris Afxentiou Avenue." Furthermore, if the diocese was not interested in keeping the old church, it should at least be offered to the Kitium Bishopric for conversion to Greek Orthodox use to serve Larnaca's increased population, namely an influx of displaced families following the partition of Cyprus in July 1974, and, since April 1975, the start of the civil war in Lebanon.

By late summer the intense controversy had escalated, prompting Archdeacon Northridge to write:

203

"My dear Bishop, Since early July this year it has been my unsought lot to sail uneasily between the Scylla[12] of the Cyprus Trustees, representing the Jerusalem and Middle East Church Association, and the Charybdis[13] of that group of St Helena's people whose spokesman has been Gordon Catlin.

"Notwithstanding the duties of an Archdeacon in relation to church fabric the main purpose of this letter is to request exemption from all further mediation and involvement with either side in what has sadly developed into a dispute; a dispute, that is, in relation to the wisdom of the plan to develop, and secondly, to the method of the plan's implementation."[14]

The archdeacon used his letter to place on record his own observations relating to the development scheme and the ensuing arguments. He agreed that the managing trustees had a duty to develop JEMT's resources and improve the church in Larnaca, and that everyone concerned should be grateful to them for trying to achieve that goal. However, with hindsight, it was now clear that "a wiser course of action" on their part would have been "to inform the church people at St Helena's … when plans were being drawn up, as to what was 'cooking.'" [15] Although the trustees were under no legal obligation to inform anyone, secrecy had caused suspicion; suspicion had bred mistrust; and mistrust had destroyed fellowship in the church community. The archdeacon concluded: "In the aftermath of antagonism it will be my task - more than anyone else's - to dispel that mistrust and to rebuild that fellowship. Therefore it is wiser, I feel, for me to disengage completely from the controversy at this late stage and not attend any Larnaca meeting arranged to restate plans and policy". [16] Whether or not the bishop agreed with this is not recorded.

In an "Occasional Letter" simply dated September 1978, Bishop Ashton did articulate his position. True to form, he pulled no punches, reminding his readers of theological imperatives:

> "This is addressed more particularly to the good people of Larnaca who attend the little Church of St Helena's. I know of your distress about the [proposed] demolition of the existing Church and I agree that it will be like a little bereavement to lose it. … Certainly if the Larnaca development does not proceed it is difficult to see how we shall be able to avoid a serious cutback in the work of the Church.

> "My concern is for the witness and worship of the Anglican community. I am not involved in the details of development projects; but I pray that we may be faithful stewards of that which God has entrusted to us so that His work may be free to expand. It may mean temporary inconvenience and some sacrifice but with your support and cooperation I am sure that we should make the venture in faith so that the project may prosper under the hand of God." [17]

In November 1978 the old church of St Helena was demolished to make way, as planned, for the site's redevelopment to include a new church centre, a chaplain's residence, and income-generating commercial property. The outcome was somewhat different. Mrs Mantovani recalls that the project ran out of money:

"By the time it was finished, the JEMT (Cyprus) owned one flat, the church, and three shops and a coffee shop from which it received rent."[18]

Bishop Ashton's prediction in his first presidential address that "we shall learn from our mistakes" had become a reality. The project had failed as a JEMT (Cyprus) commercial enterprise simply because most of the apartments and shops had to be sold to pay off escalated and unforeseen construction costs. No similar commercial experiment has been attempted in the diocese again. Yet by the end of 1978, Bishop Ashton, the Archdeacon in Cyprus, other decision-makers, and the congregation of St Helena's, did have three events to look forward to: the dedication of the new church, the formation of a separate Larnaca chaplaincy and the installation of its first chaplain. At the end of 1978, it was still too early to say when.

Meanwhile at the start of that year, a new beginning of a very different kind had taken place in Cyprus. During the evening of 21 January 1978, reported in the *Cyprus Mail* on the following day, the Limassol District Officer, Mr Ph. Zachariades, opened a Missions to Seamen Flying Angel Club in the grounds of St Barnabas church. The chaplain, the Reverend Walter Gunn, also Honorary Chaplain of the Mission in Limassol, had inspired this initiative with the support of the diocese and in particular Bishop Ashton. Naturally enough he was present at this prestigious opening, along with senior officials from the Sovereign Base Area, including the Air Marshal; and the First Secretary of the British High Commission in Nicosia, Mr George Romeril, together with his wife.

The Flying Angel Club in Limassol was the first to be established in the Mediterranean region, at that time one of three-hundred international clubs supported by the Missions to Seamen based at St Michael Paternoster Royal, College Hill in the City of London. (To reflect changing attitudes, in 2000 the charity's name was changed to the Mission to Seafarers.) The purpose of the clubs, then and now, is to cater for the physical and spiritual well-being of seafarers of all nationalities, races, languages and faith by providing prayer rooms, entertainment facilities such as television areas, books, newspapers, table tennis and light refreshments. Crucially, before the age of the internet, seafarers used the clubs' telephone services to contact their families. The new Dubai International Seafarers Centre was a larger version of such a club. Over the years, more centres have been established in ports within the Diocese of Cyprus and the Gulf, such as in Bahrain.

Stained-glass window at St Barnabas, Limassol
Copyright: Angela Murray

Another new initiative in the life of the new diocese was the idea of creating an "Association of Friends", or some similar body. This had also been suggested at the first Diocesan Synods in 1976. Initially there were some objections - the minutes do not state the reasons - but after animated discussion in the two archdeaconries, there was a positive consensus. The rationale was that a diocesan association would foster the growing communications between Cyprus and countries in the Gulf region, and would help to kindle and maintain interest among people who had lived in the diocese. By late 1977 the groundwork was prepared. The Reverend Jack Nicholls, former Archdeacon in Cyprus, would chair the association, and his wife Joyce serve as its secretary.

The Reverend Peter Delaney's support had a parallel significance. During 1977 he had been installed as the new Vicar of All Hallows by the Tower in London and had soon established himself as an energetic and inspired motivator with many links beyond church walls. For four years previously he had been the Precentor of Southwark Cathedral, south-west of All Hallows on the south bank of the River Thames. Bishop Ashton had already met Peter Delaney during his exploratory investigations to find a suitable host venue for the new association. But Father Delaney had more than this in mind: he wished to invite the Diocese of Cyprus and the Gulf to enter into a "Partnership in Mission" with the parish of All Hallows, and to do so he asked retired Bishop John Daly[19] to be his emissary.

In February 1978 Bishop Daly accompanied Bishop Ashton on a month-long tour of several chaplaincies in the Gulf archdeaconry, ending in Bahrain where between 21 and 22 February he attended the third Diocesan Synod (Gulf). On behalf of the people of All Hallows, Bishop Daly presented their Letter of Greeting which formally invited the Diocese of Cyprus and the Gulf to enter a mission partnership with them. A lively discussion prompted constructive suggestions, one being that All Hallows might help with "the Anglican project in Oman": a proposal being developed to form a shared ministry between an Anglican chaplain, and a Protestant pastor supported by the Reformed Church in America (RCA). As part of the "special project" in Muscat, during 1978 the Reverend Canon Alan Gates - a qualified social welfare

207

worker - became the first Anglican chaplain to minister in Oman, joining the Reverend Rodney Koopmans (RCA pastor in Ruwi) in the new joint ministry, himself a new arrival that year.[20]

Two other forward-thinking suggestions proposed at the Diocesan Synod (Gulf) in 1978 were that the Diocese of Cyprus and the Gulf might assist the parish of All Hallows in dialogue between Muslims and Christians; and that a dialogue on the definition of "mission" might begin, with particular reference to the pioneer ecumenism then being witnessed in the new diocese. Although it was too early to say how all this might be achieved, Bishop Ashton gladly accepted Peter Delaney's invitation. Five months later at All Hallows by the Tower, in July 1978, the Association of Friends of the Diocese of Cyprus and the Gulf was inaugurated. Within a year there were one hundred members.

All Hallows by the Tower, Byward Street, London
Copyright: Charles Gervais, www.BothHemispheres

Strictly speaking, the Association was not linked to the Partnership in Mission. Nevertheless, Father Delaney and his people considered that All Hallows was a common bond. When in March 1979 the Diocesan Synod (Gulf) met in Muscat, he emphasised in a follow-up letter that the venue was particularly significant to all at All Hallows "because we identify ourselves with the work in Muscat as a special project … because of our financial commitment to your work … also because we here had the joy [last year] of welcoming to our own community on Tower Hill people from different areas in your diocese."

Since then the Association of Friends of the Diocese of Cyprus and the Gulf has evolved, now meeting annually in three locations.[21] Its core focus was and remains centred on prayer and fellowship, with the annual reunion, AGM and Celebration Eucharist at All Hallows still considered to be the main event to which Friends have a standing invitation. *The Olive Branch,* published by the Association, continues to enhance and promote its original aims: "to foster the growing communications between Cyprus and countries in the Gulf region" and "maintain interest" among those who have lived in the diocese.

Two other new developments occured in 1978, distinctly different yet with a common theme: potential opportunities for the diocese to expand its ministry. In Cyprus, on 10 September 1978, Bishop Ashton "had the joy of presiding over his first ordination at St Paul's, Nicosia",[22] also the first in the Diocese of Cyprus and the Gulf.

209

Bishop Leonard Ashton and the Reverend Clive Windebank

Source: Bible Lands, reproduced with consent of JEMT's trustees

Clive Windebank, employed by the Kuwait Oil Company (KOC), had been for some time a licensed Reader serving the church of St Paul in the town of Ahmadi. Both the church and the town are owned by KOC. Following his ordination, while still employed and until 1983, the Reverend Clive Windebank served as a non-stipendiary part-time assistant chaplain at St Paul's Ahmadi where he was priested on 25 March 1979. (In 2003 he moved to Abu Dhabi where he served as chaplain at St Andrew's until retiring in 2010.)

The other notable event occurred in November 1978 when the Central (Provincial) Synod of the ECJME confirmed, during its meeting in Cyprus, that Anglican oversight in south-west Arabia and the two Yemeni republics[23] should be transferred from the jurisdiction of the Diocese of Egypt to the Diocese of Cyprus and the Gulf.

This meant that the entire geography of the Arabian peninsula was now under the young diocese's ecclesiastical remit. Clearly, the change in diocesan boundaries had been under discussion for several months. Eager as ever to make the most of the new opportunity, on 18 October 1978 the bishop had written to the First Secretary (Consular) at the British High Commission in Nicosia to say that already he was "exploring the possibility of visiting Sana'a, and perhaps Aden, going on to the Gulf states"[24] in February 1979.

British diplomatic advice was not encouraging. On 2 November and at the request of the British High Commissioner, Mr George A Romeril passed on the following briefing from the Chargé d'Affaires of the British Embassy in Aden. While he was pleased to read that South Yemen was now part of the Diocese of Cyprus and the Gulf and that Bishop Ashton was considering a visit, he wished to explain the situation in Yemen regarding a church presence so that the bishop could decide objectively whether or not to make his proposed journey to Aden.

"All missionaries and clerics have long since departed or been expelled from this totalitarian Marxist State and Christian churches, chapels and missions closed. The only exception to this is the Catholic Church at Steamer Point, Aden, which is still allowed to continue with a regular service under the ministry of its single Italian priest. The reason that this continues to be permitted is thought to be because of the UNDP [United Nations Development Programme] presence in Aden some of whose members attend that church. ... The Seamen's Mission in Aden no longer functions in any religious context. ... Christ Church at Steamer Point which was once the centre of Church of England worship in Aden has long been closed and has been used as a Government store for the last four years or so. One of the BP [British Petroleum] staff at the Aden Refinery Company (locally owned) conducts a short Carols and Lessons service at St Peter's Church at Christmas, but he is expected to leave Aden during the next few months."[25]

Such then was the picture of Christian activity in South Yemen in 1978, neither encouraging nor likely to improve any time soon. The bishop did not visit Aden as he had planned, yet no doubt he remained ever hopeful that a change in regime might make that possible. Eventually that was to happen but not during his episcopate. Instead, in February 1979, he did embark on his proposed tour of the Gulf archdeaconry, six weeks spent visiting Dubai, Abu Dhabi, Doha, Muscat, Bahrain, Kuwait and Baghdad. The main reason for his visit to Muscat was to preside at the Gulf Synod held during that month.

For four years the structures of the two Diocesan Synods had followed an annual pattern: the Gulf Synod meeting in February or March; Cyprus Synod meeting in May, with rare exception always in a different venue. The logic of the separate entities was questioned during the 1979 Gulf Synod. The general mood, recalled by the then Venerable Clive Handford, was "that as a demonstration of our unity as one diocese it would be good for the two synods to meet together as one from time to time. The proposal from the Gulf Synod was that we do it in 1980, if Cyprus agreed."[26] On 9 May 1979 the Cyprus Synod did agree, unanimously.

In an article published in the autumn 1979 edition of *Bible Lands*, the Reverend Evelyn Chavasse remarked: "in the life of most churches, the passage of five years is unlikely to make any noticeable difference. Even in Kyrenia, on this lovely northern coast of Cyprus, the same almost holds good."[27] Retired from a distinguished British military career and sharing ministry at St Andrew with the Reverend Sir Patrick Ferguson-Davie, both serving as honorary chaplains, Father Chavasse was well positioned to offer those observations, the introduction to the main thrust of what he had to say:

> "We have had our share of trouble, but under the good hand of God, we have long been back in business, proclaiming the Gospel and administering the Sacraments; and to a casual passer-by our lovely little church appears much the same as before. But it isn't quite.

> "It is now five years since bombs and shells and mortars and heavy machine guns of various warring parties, blasting away at each other but not at us, made a bit of a mess of the place. For two Sundays only we had to stay away from our rubble-filled, glass-shattered church, holed and pock-marked by military hardware. But now, all that is past. Alas, we now have to keep our doors locked during the week, but inside, all is decent and in order, and our twice-weekly worship, Sunday and Thursdays, proceeds without interruption. …

> "The fact is that until very recently - I write in June 1979 – Cyprus has long dropped almost entirely out of the world news, and people at home write to us: 'Of course it's all over now, isn't it … and everything must be settling down nicely, I'm sure?' I wish it were true."[28]

Physically the church was much reduced in size, not the result of the war but due to structural failings. In 1947 the box-like church had been enlarged by a spacious sanctuary and transepts. Since then, the addition had been "sliding inexorably toward the sea" one hundred feet below. It transpired that the new part had been built on rock sliding on a layer of wet clay. The decision had been taken to demolish the extension and replace it with a "just-adequate" sanctuary built of light brick, and no transepts. "Nuts and bolts! But what about the reality?"[29] wrote Evelyn Chavasse, meaning the worshipping and spiritual life of the congregation.

On an ordinary Sunday, congregations of twenty or so people were strengthened by the presence and prayers of Roman Catholics, Methodists, Presbyterians and Quakers, occasionally by Orthodox from among the eleven Greek Cypriots who still lived in Kyrenia, as well as Maronites and Armenian Christians. In the summer, tourists were arriving again, several of whom found their way to St Andrew's. To conclude his article, he summed up the situation: "Our numbers are small, our need is great. We want a full-time chaplain. By the time you read this, please God we may be on the way to getting one."[30] Prayers were answered. In January 1980, the Reverend Arthur Rider MBE began his ministry at St Andrew's where he served until retiring in 1987.

Bishop Leonard Ashton at St Paul's, Nicosia
with the Reverend Charles Buckmaster, chaplain, St Barnabas Limassol *(left)*;
the Venerable Douglas Northridge, Archdeacon in Cyprus *(2nd from right)*,
the Reverend Evelyn Chavasse, honorary chaplain, St Andrew's Kyrenia *(right)*
Source: Bible Lands, reproduced with consent of JEMT's trustees

At the church of St Antony in Paphos there too had been cause for celebration. On 17 November 1979, Winifred S Mogabgab, Honorary Secretary of St Antony's church wrote to the bishop: "I am sure that the people of St Antony's will be delighted that we now have your permission to become officially a separate parish from Limassol. This has been our desire and wish for a very long time, as you know".[31] The church council met on 3 December 1979 to discuss a new constitution. On 24 March 1980, the Annual Church Meeting of St Antony's approved and adopted the Constitution, with one amendment suggested by Bishop Ashton.

The last few weeks of any year is a time when Christmas letters are written, narratives of joys and sorrows experienced during the past twelve months. In 1979 Archdeacon Douglas and Mrs Hazel Northridge's Christmas Letter was in that mould, with one sobering difference. The Iranian Revolution which had ended earlier that year had, in one respect, touched them personally. In November 1979 they offered emergency refuge at St Paul's vicarage to the Anglican Bishop in Iran, the Right Reverend Hassan Dehqani-Tafti, and his wife Margaret.

The background to this had begun on 16 January 1979 when the Shah of Persia, Mohammad Reza Pahlavi, flew to Cairo leaving his duties to a regency council. On 1 February, at the invitation of the Iranian government, Ayatollah Khomeini returned to Tehran from exile in France. The Persian monarchy collapsed on 11 February when troops loyal to the Shah were overwhelmed in armed street fighting, bringing Khomeini to official power. Christian presence in Iran became more precarious, documented in the Northridge's Christmas letter:

"During October reports were coming through that our Primate (President Bishop) Hassan Dehqani-Tafti in Iran was being harassed, interrogated and threatened. Last January the Anglican chaplain in Shiraz, [the Reverend] Aristoo Sayyah, who had been with us in Cyprus two months previously for our central Synod, was brutally murdered - apparently by Islamic extremists. ...

"On 2 November, Bishop Hassan Dehqani-Tafti and his wife Margaret came to Cyprus, she with her left arm in a sling, within a few days of an attempt, on the part of Moslem fanatics, to murder him. Woken in the early hours of the morning the assassin had fired five bullets at the bishop's head at a two-foot range.

"A circle of holes in his pillow - around his head - was evidence enough of a miraculous escape; one bullet went through Margaret's hand as she tried to protect her husband. Through all this Bishop Hassan has shown no fear, and the quiet courage with which he faces possible martyrdom is an inspiration to all of us who have had the privilege of being with him in recent weeks. As a boy Bishop Hassan was converted from Islam and therefore to Moslems he is an infidel".[32]

In August 1980, at All Hallows in London, Margaret Dehqani-Tafti was asked: what had stopped the assassination? Her unequivocal response: "a wall of prayer".[33]

All Hallows by the Tower, Byward Street, London
Copyright: Charles Milner, reproduced with consent

6 January 1980 at St Helena's church in Larnaca

The Bishop of Kitium with Bishop Leonard Ashton
Behind, left to right: Cecil Griggs and David Humphreys (churchwardens) and
the Venerable Douglas Northridge, Archdeacon in Cyprus

Diocese of Cyprus & the Gulf archive

Chapter 10

MILESTONES

1980 - 1983

A new decade had dawned, and the next era in the young life of the Diocese of Cyprus and the Gulf. In Larnaca, the afternoon of Sunday 6 January 1980, the Feast of the Epiphany, was significant for three reasons: the new church of St Helena was dedicated by Bishop Leonard Ashton, assisted by the Archdeacon in Cyprus; the bishop inaugurated the chaplaincy of Larnaca; and he installed the Reverend Idwal Brian Bessant as its first chaplain.

Around one hundred and seventy-five people were packed into the church, not just parishioners but many people from the local community, including the choir from St George's garrison church in Dhekelia which added to the "worshipful spirit of the occasion".[1] All were "greatly honoured" by the presence of the Bishop of Kitium, representing Archbishop Chrysostomos who regretted not being able to accept the invitation to attend as he had duties that day in Limassol.

When speaking towards the end of the ceremony, the Bishop of Kitium likened the occasion to the star of Bethlehem. "As it drew certain people to worship the newly born Christ so let this Church be also a place which attracts people to worship God. …Let us all look forward to a second Pentecost when all Christians will worship the same God together".[2] He prayed that the ministry of the Reverend Brian Bessant would be blessed and fruitful.

Bishop Ashton was also feeling truly blessed. At the 1979 Gulf Synod he had remarked: "in the vast area of the Gulf archdeaconry, with thousands of expatriates from east and west … you can see how desperately we need yet another young chaplain with a roving commission".[3] Brian Bessant became that much needed young chaplain, thanks to the generous financial support of the Church Missionary Society. His licence included extended responsibility as Diocesan Chaplain to visit Christian groups in the Gulf archdeaconry who for one reason or another had no chaplain, such as those in Baghdad, and in Sana'a where Anglicans met privately in small groups.

Front of the marble altar from the original church of St Helena
Agisilaou & Spyrou Photography Ltd, Nicosia; Diocese of Cyprus & the Gulf archive

Although the furnishings in the original church had been stored prior to its demolition, upon recent inspection the bishop and Archdeacon Northridge had found that most were no longer of practical use. The marble altar was too small for the new building and would have looked incongruous. However, a section was preserved and is now mounted on one side of the church porch. The stained-glass window featuring St Helena was reinstated, Mrs Susan Mantovani having taken the broken top panel to London in her hand luggage to have St Helena's crown repaired. The lectern was renovated. Father Bessant, also a professional artist, made the large cross fixed on the wall behind the altar.

As Brian Bessant arrived in Larnaca, the Reverend Arthur Rider arrived in Kyrenia in that same month, January 1980. The numerical strength of incumbent Anglican chaplains in Cyprus had doubled, the other two being the Reverend Charles Buckmaster in Limassol, and the chaplain at St Paul's, also Archdeacon in Cyprus, the Venerable Douglas Northridge. In March that year, the four chaplains held their first "chapter meeting" in Nicosia. In his report for the year the archdeacon added a touch of humour: "The initials of the Christian names of the chaplains happen to be A, B, C and D, so the less formal designation is 'The ABCD Group'! We plan to meet once in each quarter in each other's parishes to share experiences, discuss plans and in a preceding act of worship to wait upon God".[4]

Stained-glass window featuring St Helena, the new church of St Helena
Agisilaou & Spyrou Photography Ltd, Nicosia; Diocese of Cyprus & the Gulf archive

Far away in the Protestant Church in Oman, the situation was rather different. The chaplains ministering in the joint chaplaincy had found the experience of working together "a mixture of pain, toil, frustration, stimulation, excitement and fulfilment".[5] They still, however, believed that "others will greatly benefit from the challenge that such a situation provides". The Reverend Alan Gates had announced that he would not renew his contract when it expired in August 1980. Nevertheless, the church council unanimously agreed to appoint a successor so that

that the "dual ministry" could be maintained. In a show of unity, Alan Gates and Pastor Rod Koopmans concluded their annual report to the forthcoming Diocesan Synod:

> "The responsibility for working out the Church's mission to Oman, to the expatriate community and to the world at large, is something that needs constant prayer and discussion. We hope that, however dim our light may at times be, our presence in this country as Christians is important to God in the development of His kingdom."[6]

On 8 and 9 May 1980 the first joint Synod of the Diocese of Cyprus and the Gulf met at the Splendid Hotel in Pano Platres, a village set amid forests on the southern slopes of the Troodos mountains. Bishop Ashton remarked:

> "This is my fifth presidential address since the formation of the Diocese of Cyprus and the Gulf, and it is the first that does not have to be repeated because of a fractured diocese. It's a splendid thing for the two wings of the diocese to meet in this way, thus emphasising our unity."[7]

These were prophetic words. Unity - in the form of landmark decisions and motions passed in one combined session - was certainly present during this first joint Diocesan Synod.

Financial topics were keenly discussed. Mr Cecil Griggs, Chairman of the Diocesan Board of Finance (Cyprus), pointed out that the Diocesan Fund (the central "pot of money") depended greatly on two sources of income. One was from the United Thank Offering (UTO), a ministry of the Episcopal Church in the USA (ECUSA) founded in the nineteenth century to provide grants for projects in needy parts of the Anglican Communion. The second was a one-off donation from the Royal Air Force. These sources amounted to nearly half of the Diocesan Fund's income. Although Mr Griggs cautioned that the ECUSA offering could not be depended upon he strongly suggested that the JEMT (Cyprus) should consider an immediate and generous increase in the Bishop's stipend, this having remained static since the formation of the diocese. (The Bishop asked that it be noted he had not prompted this request.)

Given that for some years several chaplains had been lobbying for such an increase, synod members unanimously agreed to this.

The President Bishop of the ECJME, the Right Reverend Hassan Dehqani-Tafti, was also present. He strongly recommended the establishment of a type of endowment fund to finance the bishop's stipend, remarking that it was "inconceivable" that Bishop Ashton "should receive less than some of his clergy, as at present". Others suggested that funding for the bishop's accommodation should be considered as part of this item. Thus, the managing trustees of the JEMT (Cyprus) were tasked to implement a world-wide appeal, urgently.

Archdeacon Douglas Northridge's report which followed, although not entirely unrelated to finance, certainly had an exciting visual slant to it. He drew the Synod's attention to the artist's impression and architect's plan displayed on a board. He presented the proposal that, at last, the church of St Paul in Nicosia should become the See church in which Bishop Ashton would have his official seat of authority, a *cathedra*, and that the church should be known as the "Cathedral Church of the Diocese". Furthermore, that the bishop would have an episcopal chair in St Christopher's Bahrain, and that church would be known as the Pro-Cathedral in the diocese. The archdeacon emphasised that no cost would be involved in approving these proposals. Bishop Dehqani-Tafti stressed the importance of having a cathedral as a focal point, adding that the Diocese of Cyprus and the Gulf was the only diocese in the province not to have one.

An architect had been engaged to redesign the church sanctuary of St Paul's. His fixed fee for creating working drawings and completing the scheme was GB£1,500, a considerable sum at that time. There would be little or no charge on the Diocesan Board of Finance (Cyprus), or the Diocesan Fund, as the trustees of the JEMT (Cyprus) were responsible for St Paul's property. Inevitably, concerns were raised about the potential cost of the schemes. Eventually, the proposal for St Paul's was agreed but with two votes against and several abstentions. The proposal for St Christopher's was unanimously agreed. How the schemes might be financed and planned were the more challenging questions. It was agreed not to consider these at this synod.

221

Those details notwithstanding, if all went well the Bishop in Cyprus and the Gulf would have not just one See church and *cathedra*, but two.

The significance of these approvals in one combined session at that first joint Diocesan Synod in 1980 was not lost on those present. The unanimous verdict was that the united format had been a great success and should be repeated always, as one annual Diocesan Synod held in Cyprus. (This practice has continued, except in 1999 when it met in the emirate of Ras al Khaimah, and in 2020 will meet in Abu Dhabi.)

Unity of an even deeper sort was to bind this first joint Diocesan Synod together in shocked solidarity. Exactly one week earlier on 1 May 1980, Jean Waddell, secretary to the President Bishop and to the Diocese of Iran, had been shot by two intruders while she was staying in the diocesan flat in Tehran. Although severely wounded, remarkably she survived.[8] Worse news received was that Bahram Dehqani-Tafti, aged twenty-four, had been murdered in Iran. He was the only son of Bishop Hassan and Margaret Dehqani-Tafti who themselves had narrowly escaped being murdered only a few months earlier. The response was a robust resolution unanimously passed:

> "That the Synod of this Diocese [of Cyprus and the Gulf] is appalled by the apparent persecution of our sister Church in Iran, which has included the murder of one of its priests, the seizure of the Church hospitals and the Institute for the Blind, and other Church properties and funds, the looting of the Bishop's house, the attempted assassination of the Bishop, the wounding of his wife, the attempt on the life of his secretary, and the murder of the Bishop's son. …"[9]

The resolution also implored His Excellency President Bani-Sadr of the Islamic Republic of Iran, "to protect the rights of religious minorities, including the Episcopal Church, in accordance with the stated policy of the Government of Iran and the Revolutionary Council. …. We are sure Your Excellency will help in trying to heal this wound."[10] The resolution was printed on diocesan letterhead and signed by Bishop Ashton on 14 May 1980. At the Diocesan Synod in 1981 he reported that no reply had been received, and he denounced "absurd" press reports in Iran which claimed that the perpetrators of the crimes were Armenians.

A further sadness was to touch the diocese a few months later. On 15 August 1980, while on holiday in England, the Venerable Douglas Northridge died very suddenly after a fatal heart attack. This was a tragic blow to his wife Hazel and their family. Bishop Ashton wrote in tribute: "The Parish, the Diocese and the Province are grieved and impoverished by his death. ... The many letters and telephone calls received indicate something of the impact of his life on those who came to know him"[11].

During the summer of 1980 in London, after a lead-time of almost five years, the Garter Principal of the College of Arms presented Bishop Ashton with the Patent for the Coat of Arms for the Diocese of Cyprus and the Gulf. The desire for the diocese to have its own coat of arms had begun as one element of "creating something from the beginning", referring to an aspiration in the bishop's address to the first diocesan synods in 1976. To implement a patent from the College of Arms in the UK is expensive, at that time £780. Although Gulf Synod members had been inclined to proceed, it was felt in Cyprus that this cost could not be borne by normal diocesan funds and so the project was put on hold.

When in 1977 both synods met again the bishop was delighted to say that an anonymous donor had generously met the cost. The Reverend Sir Patrick Ferguson-Davie had agreed to liaise with the College of Arms. In due course a proof was received. This time it was Gulf Synod members who stalled the project. Some people did not like the reference to the Crusades so the design was referred back to the College of Arms for amendment. At last, in 1979, the Garter Principal King of Arms approved the design and granted a coat of arms to the Diocese of Cyprus and the Gulf for use in all chaplaincies. Already several chaplains had suggested that plaques featuring the design should be available for sale.

Coats of Arms - Diocese of Cyprus and the Gulf
Artwork: Louis Andrew Katsantonis

A year later the bishop was presented with the patent. The key heraldic symbols of the coat of arms are as follows: for Canterbury, the pairle - a device representing the front of an ecclesiastical pallium, a liturgical vestment consisting of a broad Y-shaped form covered with crosses - is presented in gold, in heraldic language known as Or; for Cyprus, the island is signified by two lions rampant and crowned, facing each other on a background of fesslets of the Lusignan arms - a fesslet being a heraldically derived term to mean a single, narrow horizontal stripe. The Jerusalem cross established the link between Canterbury and Jerusalem; for the Gulf, the gold (Or) tinctured pallium with wavy outlines against the silver (Argent) and blue (Azure) background suggests the coastlines and general topography of the Gulf with its yellow(ish) sands. The whole is surmounted with the bishop's mitre and lappets - two narrow lengths of hanging fabric, usually silk edged with a fringe, attached to the back of the mitre.

In March 1981, once again Bishop Ashton embarked on a selective tour of the Gulf archdeaconry, this time to dedicate two new churches. In Sharjah, after the previous church was demolished to make way for road redevelopment, the Ruler of the emirate honoured his promise to provide another building for church use, albeit a derelict former mess facility requiring much renovation, near Sharjah Radio Station. In 1979, led by the Anglican chaplain the Reverend John Paxton, successor to the Reverend Philip Sturdy, a committee was formed in conjunction with others who would use the new church: the Mar Thoma Church, the Syrian Orthodox Church and Urdu-speaking congregations. Together they worked hard to convert the premises into what Bishop Ashton hoped would be a "worthy Church". Although the building should have been dedicated in 1980, twice the event was cancelled due to severe rains and flooding. Eventually in March 1981 Bishop Ashton hallowed the new church of St Martin.

Later that month, in Salalah the capital of the Dhofar Province in Oman, the bishop had the "joy" of jointly hallowing the Church of the Magi, along with Bishop Gremoli, the Roman Catholic Vicar Apostolic of Arabia. During the same visit Bishop Ashton deaconed the Reverend Samuel Masih who had been a "leading inspiration"[12] in building what was also known as the Salalah Ecumenical Church. Samuel Masih hoped to retire from employment in the Sultan of Oman's Land Forces (SOLF) in Dhofar to continue his theological training in England and return to Salalah in full-time ministry as an ecumenical pastor. Instead, he returned to Pakistan where he was priested by Bishop Alexander Malik in 1983.

Kakopetria in Cyprus is the highest village in the Solea Valley, nestled in the north-facing foothills of the Troodos mountain 34 miles/55 kilometres southwest of Nicosia, surrounded by fruit-bearing trees on the banks of the Kargotis and Garillis rivers. The Makris Hotel in this picturesque setting was the venue for the second joint Diocesan Synod on 14 May 1981. After welcomes, introductions and general news, Bishop Ashton came straight to the point:

"Synods must meet to transact the business of the Church - it is all part of the chores of administration, and I hope you won't find it too great a bore. But it is a short Agenda, and I hope we shall finish everything in one day - and then into Nicosia for the Service in St Paul's Church."[13]

To those listening, "the Service" needed no explanation. During the following day another milestone event in the life of the diocese would be celebrated, when St Paul's church would be rehallowed as the Diocesan Cathedral. To achieve this stage of readiness had been difficult. For nearly two years the project had suffered frustrating delays due to lack of funds and the death of the architect Mr Laurence King. Yet, on the day of the rehallowing service, the essentials were in place: a *cathedra*, adjoining stalls and a provost's stall, an ambo (pulpit), a screen properly separating the vestry from the body of the church, and reconstructed altar steps with new communion rails.

The bishop's throne and adjacent stalls in the cathedral church of St Paul in Nicosia
Agisilaou & Spyrou Photography Ltd, Nicosia; Diocese of Cyprus & the Gulf archive

Almost fifty percent of the work had been paid for by two generous donors, one being the Revered Sir Patrick Ferguson-Davie whose gift was the *cathedra*. Twenty-five percent had been contributed by the Trustees of the JEMT (Cyprus). The balance was made up of promised funds from the Friends of St Paul's, and from an appeal. The ambo was to be a memorial to the late Venerable Douglas Northridge. Thus, with due ceremony on 15 May 1981 the church of St Paul in Nicosia was rehallowed as the Diocesan Cathedral. The Right Reverend Leonard Ashton CB officiated, after which he was duly enthroned.

The bishop had already appointed the Reverend Bryan Henry to be Provost of St Paul's Cathedral, and Archdeacon in Cyprus. However, on the day of the rehallowing he was still serving as senior RAF Chaplain at Rheindalen, the Joint HQ for British military forces in Germany and the NATO Northern Army Group. Within ten days he had retired from the RAF and flown to Cyprus. On 25 June 1981 he was licensed and installed at St Paul's Cathedral and so became the Very Reverend Bryan Henry, the first provost in the Diocese of Cyprus and the Gulf.

During 1981, two other significant developments took place. Dubai seaport was growing rapidly so that even by the end of 1979 the Dubai International Seafarers' Centre was being visited by as many as two thousand seafarers each month. The new seventy-berth container port at Jebel Ali was expected to be completed early in 1982. It was to be one of the largest ports in the world. When the General Secretary of the Missions to Seamen had visited the UAE during late 1979, he observed that the Reverend John Paxton was doing a "splendid job"[14] both as chaplain serving the seafarers and as chaplain to the Christian communities in Dubai and Sharjah. Even so, he needed "high-calibre assistance as soon as possible."[15] By late 1980 it was decided that the joint ministry was no longer viable and should be separated. Unfortunately, the Dubai branch of the Missions to Seamen was not able to support a priest with a wife and young twin boys, and so having been offered the choice between remaining with the Dubai and Sharjah chaplaincy, appointed by the chaplaincy council, or transferring back to the UK to serve the Missions there, John Paxton chose the latter. Nevertheless, Missions to Seamen chaplains with ministries in UAE ports have continued to be representatives at Diocesan Synods.

In Bahrain, an exciting complementary initiative was evolving. In November 1981, Bishop Ashton approved a plan to establish the Bahrain International Seafarers Society (BISS) in association with the Missions to Seamen. The new society was granted Bahrain government approval to be managed by a body of local businessmen with shipping interests. The Reverend Michael Roemmele, chaplain at St Christopher's Pro-Cathedral and the key initiator of this development, became the Missions' first honorary chaplain in Bahrain.

During 1982 two more milestone events took place. The preliminary to the first of those took place in Abu Dhabi on 10 February when Mr Alan Horan, Chairman of the Fund Raising Committee, and Archdeacon Clive Handford, jointly signed a letter addressed to Friends of the St Andrew's Endowment Fund.[16] They explained that although compensation for the existing buildings had been received, additional funds were necessary to build the church, the vicar's residence, a community centre able to cater for staged productions with a multi-purpose area for smaller meetings and groups, the library and a Thrift Centre. Remarkably, within a year, this vision was well advanced towards becoming a reality. Meanwhile, on 24 April 1982, the Most Reverend and Right Honourable Stuart Blanch, Archbishop of York, laid the foundation stone for the new church of St Andrew on a plot of land next to the new Al Khubairat Community School, alongside a plot granted to the Roman Catholic Church for the rebuilding of St Joseph's Cathedral and School. Before the laying of the foundation stone, there had been unusually heavy rains. With the desert site now a sea of mud, the contractor had to bring in lorry loads of dry sand to enable the Archbishop and congregation to reach the assigned place for the ceremony.

> "A scroll, signed by the archbishop and congregation members, was placed inside the stone. Accompanying the scroll was a medallion of York Minster to link St Andrew's with the Archbishop's own church."[17]

24 April 1982 - laying the foundation stone of the new church of St Andrew, Abu Dhabi
by the Most Reverend and Right Honourable Stuart Blanch, Archbishop of York
Diocese of Cyprus & the Gulf archive

Bahrain was where the second milestone event in 1982 took place. Under the supervision of the Reverend Michael Roemmele, preparations were complete in readiness for the church of St Christopher to be rehallowed. A porch had been built on to the west entrance. The historic stained-glass Persian windows had been renovated and cleaned. A new organ and new nave windows had been installed. The chancel floor was now extended - and raised to reduce flooding during the rainy seasons - and the altar brought forward to create space under the east window to place a *cathedra,* generously donated by Major Gerald Green.

> "The overall plan was to reflect the unity of the diocese by the similarities in the sanctuary areas of both cathedral churches, and the work has been made possible by a grant of $6,000 from the Episcopal Church in the USA".[18]

A second storey had been added to the vicarage to create an apartment for the bishop to use as a base during his Gulf tours. Additional funding for all this had been raised by the congregations in Bahrain, with donations from some churches in the Gulf archdeaconry.

On 1 May 1982, as a continuation of his visit to the Gulf archdeaconry, the Archbishop of York rehallowed the church of St Christopher in Bahrain as the Pro-Cathedral of the Gulf. One hundred and eighty-eight people were present, including parishioners from the Anglican Church in Awali. The Archbishop's visit was noted too "for having provided a valuable opportunity to build upon the good relationships which exist between the Anglican churches and the other denominations represented on the island".[19]

Later in the year, on 25 October, Bishop Leonard Ashton was enthroned at the Pro-Cathedral. During the service, he dedicated the new stained-glass windows in the nave, crafted by the Goddard Gibbs studio in London to commemorate Sir Charles and Lady (Marjorie) Belgrave, their son James,[20] and Mr David Crawford CMG, British Ambassador at Bahrain who, a month after taking up the post, had suffered a fatal heart attack in September 1981.

Two of the Goddard Gibbs stained-glass windows in St Christopher's Cathedral, Bahrain
Copyright: Angela Murray

Since the first joint Diocesan Synod in 1980 much progress had been made to improve the diocese's administrative structure and address its cashflow. Mr David Hardacre had been appointed as an Administrative Officer, offering his services for one day a week. The framework for an international appeal to place the diocesan finances on a proper footing was established. Within a year, the Appeals Committee had been renamed as the Diocesan Committee, chaired by the bishop with Mr John Thompson as Vice-Chairman. Only those resident in the diocese were eligible to be members. The Sponsors Committee was comprised of people from outside the diocese. When Synod met in 1981, already Mr Thompson had visited America. Some individual parishes of the Episcopal Church in the USA (ECUSA) were not interested in contributing towards a single large endowment fund but instead preferred to make direct grants to support chaplains in the Diocese of Cyprus and the Gulf. By 1981 the scope of the Appeal had grown beyond that decided by the 1980 Synod, and it had been reshaped too.

The concept of a single Capital Assets Fund, totalling US$275,000, now took shape as *The Capital Fund*.[21] This was designed to ensure that St Paul's Cathedral in Nicosia would be fully supported, to give additional support in Bahrain for the Pro-Cathedral project, and to provide for the purchase of a Bishop's residence in Nicosia. "Since his arrival in Cyprus in late January 1974 he had successively lived in a military bungalow at RAF Nicosia, St Paul's vicarage lodging with the chaplain and his wife, sundry hotels, a borrowed house, and three different flats."[22] The Endowment Fund, totalling US$1,500,000, had been renamed *The Project Fund* to serve the ongoing work of the diocese, initially to help finance the proposed Diocesan Office and Cathedral Centre; and to support four unspecified chaplaincies in the Gulf.[23]

Bona fides for the Appeal was provided by the Archbishops of Canterbury and York, the Presiding Bishop of ECUSA and the Overseas Missions Society of ECUSA, all granting their blessing and support to the Appeal as a recognised activity. The target for completion of the project was June that year. Could this be achieved?

On 5 February 1982 at Lambeth Palace, the London residence of the Archbishop of Canterbury, the Diocesan Appeal was launched. Some one hundred guests attended a formal luncheon, including the Bishop in Cyprus and the Gulf, the Right Reverend Graham Leonard (Bishop of London), the Right Reverend George Appleton (former Archbishop in Jerusalem), and other bishops. Company representatives with business interests in the Arabian Gulf region were also present, significantly from the Inchcape Group which had generously paid for the luncheon. During his speech, Lord Inchcape offered £10,000 to start the Appeal.

231

According to plan, Bishop Ashton visited the USA during March 1982. By mid-year the UTO Fund of ECUSA had donated US$30,000, a third of the sum required to build a proposed Diocesan and Cathedral Centre within St Paul's compound. This was to replace rented diocesan offices elsewhere in Nicosia, and to create a fit-for-purpose church hall with Sunday school classrooms. As the donation was conditional on construction work starting within a year, it was decided that any funds raised through the Appeal which were not pre-assigned should be allocated towards making up the project's funding shortfall.

During the Diocesan Synod in 1982 the bishop once more deployed his persuasive oratory in an echo of his presidential addresses in 1977:

> "At this stage some reflections on Church finance may not be out of place. Let me make it quite clear that we do not get any money from the Church of England (except by way of donations from individual churches) and the Church of England is NOT financed by the State. We do need greater understanding about the significance of financial matters for the life and mission of the Church. ... I know we get all tense and on the defensive when we talk about money – but there is no need to do so. It is a fact of life and must be faced honestly and squarely."[24]

Pronouncing that "buildings are not an end in themselves", the bishop took issue with the ambivalent title on the Appeal Brochure - TO BUILD A CHURCH [sic]. Many people "think that we want to put up buildings. Certainly they are important but what we need is the Creation of a Living Church within our Diocesan structure."[25] He had chosen his phrasing carefully for a good reason. On other occasions he had talked about building "a Bishop's Palace" by which he simply meant a permanent residence for the bishop. Some potential donors to the Appeal Fund, especially in the USA, did not appreciate the jest and took him literally.[26] He continued:

> "I have been trying to work without adequate buildings and plant for the last eight years, and I know something of the difficulties and frustrations. ... Of course, people are more important - but don't tell me that buildings are of no importance. That is why,

two years ago, the Synod set up the Appeal Fund, and we are now moving into first gear. We are a young and, I hope, a vigorous diocese faced with great possibilities and opportunities. We cover countries rich in history and mythology; but we are non-traditional, we are not stuffy; we are colourful, bursting with life, exploding in size and enthusiasm, straight from the Acts of the Apostles. ... Our survival, by the grace of God, is not in question; we survive in order to participate in God's redemptive activity."[27]

These assertions prefaced another purpose: the bishop needed all Houses of the 1982 Diocesan Synod (Bishops, Clergy and Laity) to pass a motion to confirm constitutional amendments and structural changes to the existing Boards of Finance, a process initiated at the first joint Diocesan Synod in 1980. A majority passed the motion.

The Cyprus Archdeaconry Board of Finance (CABF) remained responsible for the administration of Anglican church funds in Cyprus, receiving money from various sources; and the Gulf Archdeaconry Board of Finance (GABF) remained responsible for the collection and administration of funds received from churches in the archdeaconry.

The main difference was that the Diocesan Board of Finance (Cyprus) would become the Central Diocesan Board of Finance (CDBF), charged with two main tasks: to continue administering church quotas channelled into it from CABF and GABF; and to administer the Diocesan Appeal Fund. Thus, the CDBF held, as separate accounts, the Diocesan Charities Fund and the Bishop's Discretionary Fund. It also retained details of the Diocesan Appeal Fund, itself held in a separate account in London managed by the Diocesan Appeals Committee in Cyprus. The Trustees of the Jerusalem and the Middle East Trust (Cyprus) continued as before to manage Trust property in Cyprus.

David Hardacre, the diocese's administrative officer, dealt with its funds and the Appeal Fund, giving as much time as he could, often more than his commitment of one day a week. Cecil Griggs, managing director of the Swedish company Atlas Copco Middle East, also volunteered one day a week in an executive role as Diocesan Secretary, Chairman of the CDBF and a Managing Trustee of the JEMT (Cyprus).

233

The constitutional amendments and revised financial structures for Cyprus and the Gulf approved by Diocesan Synod in 1982, ratified in November that year by the Central Synod of the ECJME, took effect at the 1983 Diocesan Synod held on 12 May. However, if anyone present at that gathering expected diocesan "business as usual", they were to hear otherwise. In the now familiar setting of the Makris Hotel in Kakopetria, Bishop Leonard Ashton announced:

> "As far as I can work out, this is the sixteenth time that I have given opening addresses at synods in Cyprus and the Gulf. But take comfort - it's likely to be the last. ... And, whatever decisions you make at this synod, bear in mind that you will undoubtedly have to bring them into effect without any help (or hindrance) from me. But my successor will soon take over .... ."[28]

One person not present knew all this, and regretted it. On 11 January 1983 Major Gerald Green, a warden at St Christopher's Pro-Cathedral, had written:

> "My v. dear Len, ... I am greatly saddened to hear that your leaving us is even being considered. Why? Have we proved to be empty vessels? You have worked so hard to set up the Diocese and have inspired others by your devotion. Surely now is the time to take things a little more easily and enjoy the fruits of your labour."[29]

The bishop replied: "I feel the time has come for me to retire. I think I have completed the initial work of crafting the new diocese which is what I agreed to do, and now that I am coming up to 68 years of age I am sure it is better for a younger man to try to cope with the travelling involved."[30]

Major Green countered:

> "What on earth are you talking about? Coming up to 68, which I will be come the 8th June this year, good gracious me, th'art nobbut a lad, as we would say in Cheshire. However, I do know how very taxing much travelling can be as the years advance. ... Happily, we can take heart in knowing that you will be involved in the work of the Jerusalem and Middle East Church Association and continue to take an interest in the Province and Diocese."[31]

Having announced his retirement at the 1983 Diocesan Synod the bishop turned his attention to three other developments in the diocese's life. First, he welcomed his guest Prebendary John Parkinson from the Diocese of Exeter in England, invited to deliver the devotional address. The bishop then divulged: "We are delighted that Exeter is entering into a "partnership in mission" relationship with us; they will share in our work, and we shall share in theirs."[32] This companion relationship had been forming for some time. The Diocese of Exeter, in the county of Devon, is one of the largest in England, now host to 490 parishes and 597 churches. Prebendary Parkinson, who held an honorary stall in Exeter Cathedral, was an influential advocate in forming the companion link. In 1983 he moved to the Diocese of Cyprus and the Gulf to take up an appointment as chaplain of the Pro-Cathedral of St Christopher in Bahrain, accompanied by his wife Joan. Together they continued to foster that link relationship over many years. Canon Parkinson, as he liked to be called, also succeeded the Reverend Michael Roemmele as Honorary Chaplain to the Missions to Seamen in Bahrain.

Second, Bishop Ashton conveyed the news that the Venerable Clive Handford and his wife Jane were imminently to leave the diocese having felt called to return to the UK. The bishop paid tribute to "Clive and his fellow workers"[33] for their achievements. With a terrific effort the Abu Dhabi chaplaincy had raised something like GB£600,000 to complete the rebuilding of St Andrew's and all its facilities.

Third, as Chair of the Diocesan Appeals Committee, the bishop reported that it was marking time pending the formation of a new committee, simply because most members had departed from the diocese, with the bishop soon to follow. "We owe a tremendous debt of gratitude to the Vice-Chairman of the Appeal, Mr. John Thompson, … and without his efforts little or nothing would have been achieved. … Money is still coming in, and at the time of writing C£70,000 is held. However, this is less than a fifth of our target figure."[34]

Obviously, the original targets had been hugely over-optimistic. Nevertheless, a grant from ECUSA had made it possible for a suite of offices in Nicosia to be rented as a modest secretariat for the diocese, and to serve as the registered premises for the JEMT (Cyprus).

235

5A John Clerides Street, Nicosia, offices for the Diocese of Cyprus & the Gulf, early 1980s.
The house was demolished two weeks after this photo was taken in July 2018.
Copyright: Angela Murray

The address was 5A John Clerides Street, half of a house owned by Greek-Cypriot politician and barrister Glafcos Clerides who in 1993 became the fourth president of the Republic of Cyprus. The house was accessed by its own entrance to the staircase which led upstairs, first to the secretary's office, then to the bishop's office occupying the big corner room. On the other side of the passage a smaller office was used by David Hardacre, and later by Michalakis Patsalides when he was employed as the accountant. The ground floor of the house served as a law office for a cousin of Mr Glafcos Clerides. This was where the monthly rent for the diocesan premises was paid.

Although by 1983 the administrative foundations of the diocese were fairly sound, Bishop Ashton admitted that the structure "shook" a little from time to time because "the staff was scarcely adequate to cope with the workload". Joan Nield, the part-time secretary, generally managed to cope with the typing, filing and office work, with occasional help from the Bishop who, in his own words, attempted "to do it all if the secretary is away".[35]

Not surprisingly, the bishop's valedictory presidential address was challenging and uplifting. He reminded his listeners how, as Christians, they should define treasures and wealth:

> "It will be possible for me to hand over three benefactions to my successor: an antique pectoral cross which bears the Coat of Arms of Pope Pius VII who reigned from 1800-1823 ... a second antique pectoral cross with six amethyst stones set in a Middle East silver design ... a very handsome antique crosier in silver and ebony. ... We also have two copes, one inherited from Bishop Robert Stopford and the other locally made out of curtain material! Such are our treasures. But of course we have other treasures - the unspeakable riches of the Gospel entrusted to us, the unfathomable wealth of Christ, the treasure which, as St Paul says, is contained in earthen vessels. This is what the Church is all about."[36]

On 26 May 1983, Bishop Ashton received a handwritten letter from Allan Brown at the HQ of the British Contingent, United Nations Force in Cyprus, to thank him "most warmly on behalf of the congregation of St Columba's for preaching and celebrating the Eucharist for us last Sunday. .... My churchwardens were struck by your remarks about the new bishop's need for robes etc and are now wondering how best a small contribution from us - say £50 - could be made towards these expenses. Finally may I, on behalf of the congregation here, wish you every happiness in your retirement."[37]

The bishop attended a farewell party held in his honour on 17 June 1983, and on 3 July was the celebrant at his final service at St Paul's Cathedral in Nicosia.

Who was to become the second Bishop of the Diocese of Cyprus and the Gulf? This was the first time there had been a Vacancy-in-See in the diocese. Mr George Meikle OBE, Deputy Chairman of the Diocesan Standing Committee, explained the appointment process.

237

The constitution of the Diocese of Cyprus and the Gulf stated: when it was known that the office of bishop was likely to fall vacant, the Diocesan Standing Committee shall inform the Archbishop of Canterbury and request him to nominate to the President Bishop a successor. When Bishop Ashton had declared his intention to retire, his standing committee had indeed informed the Archbishop of Canterbury, and received a mandate from the Central Synod of the ECJME which allowed the selection process to commence. In December 1982 the chaplaincies were informed and their chaplains invited to submit any representations to either of the archdeacons. However, Mr Meikle also said that as there were almost no indigenous Anglican Christians in the Diocese of Cyprus and the Gulf, and its Anglican community was largely transient, "it would be very difficult in such a situation for the churches to know where to begin to look for a possible bishop."[38]

Already there had been dismay in Cyprus about this "most undemocratic"[39] nomination process. Mr Cecil Griggs had written a week earlier on 5 May 1983 to Bishop Hassan Dehqani-Tafti, living in exile in the UK, to suggest that the selection should wait until Bishop Ashton retired and a Vicar-General appointed to allow the matter to be resolved "in a democratic manner"[40] This did not happen. As allowed by the constitution, the President Bishop accepted the Archbishop of Canterbury's recommendation received in a letter: "I was much impressed with Harry Moore and I would like formally to nominate him to you for appointment. I think he has all the right attitudes and a deep sense of our critical position in the Gulf Area".[41] Central Synod of the province had approved Archbishop Robert Runcie's nomination by postal ballot and issued a mandate for the consecration, the place and date to be chosen by the Bishop-designate.

The Reverend Henry Wylie Moore, born on 2 November 1923, was almost sixty years old. Following his ordination in 1952 and holding curacies in England, he served as the CMS Chaplain to the Khuzistan Oil Fields in the Diocese of Iran between 1957 and 1959. After returning to ministry and further study in England, he became Home Secretary of the CMS, then in 1980 was appointed CMS Deputy General Secretary and Executive Secretary.

On 27 June 1983 Diocesan Standing Committee decided,[42] with Bishop Ashton's agreement, that upon his departure from the diocese in July he should be regarded as being on terminal leave until the day before his successor's consecration thereby avoiding an episcopal interregnum. The chosen place was Winchester Cathedral in the county town of Hampshire in the UK and the date 29 September 1983, the Feast of St Michael and All Angels.

The Right Reverend Harry Moore, Bishop in Cyprus and the Gulf (*4th from the left*), after his consecration at Winchester Cathedral with brother bishops
Hampshire archives, reproduced with consent of archivist David Rymill

The ceremony, reported over several column inches in the *Hampshire Chronicle*,[43] was one of great splendour and unique: it was the first time a bishop had been consecrated in England by the Primate of an overseas province, namely the President Bishop of the Episcopal Church in Jerusalem and the Middle East, the Right Reverend Hassan Dehqani-Tafti who was by then serving as an assistant bishop in the Diocese of Winchester during his exile.

The dean and chapter of Winchester Cathedral welcomed "a large congregation made up of friends and supporters of the Churches in the Middle East". From far and near, other guest clergy included the presenting bishops, the Right Reverend Faik Haddad, Bishop in Jerusalem, and the Right Reverend Ross Hook, Chief of Staff to the

Archbishop of Canterbury. The Epistoller was the Right Reverend Kenneth Newing, Bishop of Plymouth, representing the Diocese of Exeter. The Gospeller was the Right Reverend Samir Kafa'ity, Secretary of the Central Synod of the ECJME and coadjutor Bishop in Jerusalem.

Present too were the Deans of St George's Cathedral Jerusalem and All Saints Cathedral Cairo; the Vicar-General in Egypt; the Very Reverend Bryan Henry, Archdeacon in Cyprus; and the Venerable Ralph Lindley CBE, General Secretary of the Jerusalem and Middle East Church Association. Bishop Leonard Ashton CB attended in his new role as Episcopal Consultant to the Province of the EJCME.

On 1 November 1983 Bishop Harry Moore was duly enthroned in St Paul's Cathedral in Nicosia. Five days later, on 6 November, he was presented with a new crosier, a gift from the congregation of St Columba's Church located in the UN buffer zone, not far from former RAF Nicosia. The heavy and distinctive hooked staff had been designed and made in Cyprus by 48 Command Workshop of the Royal Electrical and Mechanical Engineers.

The church of St Columba (a converted Nissen hut)
in the Nicosia sector of the UN buffer zone
Copyright: Angela Murray

Soon afterwards, Bishop Moore and his wife Betty began their first tour of the Gulf archdeaconry, arriving first in Bahrain where on 20 November 1983 the bishop was enthroned once again, this time in the Pro-Cathedral of St Christopher. He also visited the Anglican congregation at Awali church, the community church in the Bahrain Petroleum Company's township.

From there, he and his wife travelled to Abu Dhabi. In two services on 28 and 29 November 1983 the bishop dedicated the new St Andrew's Centre. The first service was honoured by the presence of representatives of HH Shaikh Zayed, President of the United Arab Emirates; Shaikh Shakhbut and members of the Diplomatic Corps. The second service, on the eve of the Feast of St Andrew, included the seventeen congregations of St Andrew, and representatives of those at Ruwais and of All Saints church on Das island.

The bishop's onward itinerary involved visits to Holy Trinity in Dubai, St Martin's in Sharjah, and the Protestant Church in Oman including a visit to Salalah. From there he travelled north to Qatar to attend an open-air carol service in Doha and to visit the small congregation in Dukhan, and then further north to Kuwait to celebrate a house communion in the city and visit St Paul's in Ahmadi.

Since 1974 it had been difficult, although not impossible, for clergy to gain visas to visit Iraq where the English-speaking congregation at St George's in Baghdad was still without a resident chaplain. The situation became even harder after Iraq invaded Iran on 22 September 1980, triggering what became a bitter eight-year war between the two countries.[44] Church members were therefore delighted when Bishop Moore and his wife Betty arrived in Baghdad in late December 1983. He was to preside at the Christmas Family Communion Service. A congregation of about two hundred filled the church, rejoicing with thanksgiving and no doubt praying for a blessed new year.

242

AN AIR LETTER SHOULD
NOT CONTAIN ANY ENCLOSURE;
IF IT DOES IT WILL BE SURCHARGED
OR SENT BY SURFACE MAIL.

Dennis Gurney,

Chaplaincy of Dubai & Sharjah,

P.O.Box 7415;

Dubai. U.A.E.

Sender's name and address

Second fold here →

رسالة جوية مظروفة

AEROGRAMME

8 AM
5 FEB
1985

35 UNITED ARAB EMIRATES

50 UNITED ARAB EMIRATES

UNITED ARAB EMIRATES

The Rt. Revd. Harry Moore,

Diocese of Cyprus & the Gulf,

5A John Clerides Street,

P.O.Box 2075;

NICOSIA.   Cyprus.

An example of an aerogramme: a lightweight piece of paper for writing a letter for
transit via airmail, in general use before the development of email technology.
The letter is written on the reverse of the foldable and gummed envelope.

Diocese of Cyprus & the Gulf archive

Chapter 11

CONSOLIDATION

1984 - 1987

During his first visit to the Gulf archdeaconry, Bishop Moore witnessed first-hand the impact of the regional economic downturn which had begun some two years earlier. After the price of oil peaked at US$35 per barrel in 1980, the glut which followed led to government panic in the Gulf economies and private sector collapse throughout the region.[1] The Christians whom the bishop had met were mostly from India, Pakistan, South Korea, and the Philippines, as well as the UK and USA. Many were Anglican, or from churches in communion with the Anglican Church, working in the Gulf countries in order to remit money home to support both their families and their local churches. The oil price collapse immediately led to social, religious and political pressures, but above all to an economic crisis which caused redundancies and other unwelcome moves by employers to lessen their payroll burdens. The bishop summarised the situation:

> "The expatriate Christian community is in the short term unstable. It may be reduced at any time and individuals sometimes return home at very short notice. Rapid reduction of expatriates means there is extra pressure on the Diocese, and that means the Bishop, to be present as much as possible or at least to be in touch regularly and effectively. …. Therefore, we should maintain the Church's presence wherever we can. … This means constant and costly visits by the bishop and the Archdeacon in the Gulf, and it also means good communications from the Diocesan office, which in turn needs to be efficient and effective in its work."[2]

These remarks were not a rallying call to anyone within the Diocese of Cyprus and the Gulf but are found in a long letter dated 3 January 1984 addressed to the Right Reverend Patrick Rodger, Bishop of Oxford. Bishop Moore was seeking the Diocese of Oxford's financial support so that his own diocese might build up its funds, and thereby "such reserves that we can continue the Christian presence in our diocese even when local factors reduce the number of Christians and therefore reduce the financial resources available".[3]

The letter had the desired effect. On 20 December 1984 Bishop Moore was very pleased to write: "Dear Patrick, I have just heard today that the second £5,000 of your promised gift to this diocese has been credited to our account in London. Please express our continuing gratitude to your diocese."[4]

The background to this correspondence had begun in late 1983 when the Venerable Ralph Lindley, General Secretary of the JMECA in England, had sounded out Bishop Rodger. In response, on 1 December he requested publicity material about the Diocese of Cyprus and the Gulf so that he could use this to help launch the Diocese of Oxford's outreach fund early in 1984.[5] The Bishop of Oxford intended to do this by way of a motion at his Diocesan Synod on 25 February 1984. The motion was well received.

In the context of Bishop Moore's earlier remark that his own diocesan office needed to be "efficient and effective in its work", early in January 1984 Mr Cecil Griggs interviewed Mrs Georgia Katsantonis to succeed Joan Nield. She had retired shortly before Bishop Ashton's departure. Georgia recalls being told that the job requirements were simple: an ability to speak English and Greek. More than three decades later, still the bishop's PA as well as Secretary to the ECJME's Central Synod, she recounts her introduction to the diocese on 1 March 1984:

"The secretary's office and equipment were basic: a manual typewriter, a small desk - which I still use! - a chair and a grey filing cabinet. As Bishop Harry Moore was on an extended three-month Gulf trip I did not meet my boss until about April of that year. … Archdeacon Bryan Henry came into the office about once a week to give me work to do as I was still learning. He would dictate letters which I would type and then post. Everything was sent by post. We had no telex machine. A fax machine was installed later when we moved to the new offices. My weekday working hours were from 9 to 12.30. Cecil Griggs also came into the office once a week to make sure that everything was all right.

"We had a telephone but communication with some other countries was difficult. If there was an emergency anywhere in the diocese, the archdeacon would come in and make the telephone call. …. While Bishop Harry was away I had no communication with him at all."[6]

Georgia Katsantonis in the diocesan office, 1980s
Diocese of Cyprus & the Gulf archive

In 1984 the Diocesan Synod met for the first time on the south coast of Cyprus, at the Lordos Beach Hotel a few miles east of Larnaca. Inevitably, Bishop Moore's experiences during the first few months of his episcopate had shaped his impressions, among them these conveyed in his first presidential address:

"Within the communities where we live, there are points of need and strain and tension. Whenever we can show a brotherly love, a caring interest, an accepting friendship and a helping hand to anyone of whatever nationality, language or religion, it is the Church's concern to do so.

"It is encouraging, as we travel the diocese, to discover so many ways in which our churches corporately, and our church members individually, are involved in caring and in charitable social efforts. This is how it should be - may it always be so."[7]

In 1985, Diocesan Synod met again at the Lordos Beach Hotel. Chaplaincies in the Gulf archdeaconry reported heartening successes during the previous year, despite their common experience of economic challenges.

In early April 1984, St George's church in Baghdad had marked the eighth anniversary of the resumption of Sunday services, led by some fourteen people during the course of the year. Sunday school was held monthly in the church hall. Holy Communion was celebrated during visits to Baghdad by the bishop, the Archdeacon in the Gulf, and the German pastor from Cyprus. At last in 1984, after a break of many years, it had been possible for a lay representative to attend the Diocesan Synod. That person was Mr B J Stops, Honorary Treasurer of St George's Church Council. Its secretary, Mr W L Muriel, joined Mr Stops in writing in February 1985 that the Anglican church in Baghdad now felt increasingly part of the diocesan family "and is very grateful for the encouragement and support that it is given in so many ways".[8]

Further south in Kuwait, 1984 had been a busy year breaking new ground, consolidating gains, replacing losses, and seeking new people, new finance and new opportunities for mission. The Reverend Michael Jones was unrestrained about one topic: "St Paul's was, and still is to a large extent, quite unknown. ... Unable to advertise itself, St Paul's [sic] problems of communication defy belief".[9]

Canon John Parkinson, chaplain in Bahrain, was forthright about one matter. In his 1984 report he noted that although the creation of the Pro-Cathedral and the enthronement of Bishop Leonard had given some substance to the concept of a Cathedral in the Gulf, it still remained true "that 'Pro-Cathedral' is a term which is not understood, untranslatable in Arabic and a lot longer to write than 'Church'."[10]

In Awali there were signs that its congregational life, which during 1983 reached its nadir, might now be recovering. "It was no longer just an oil town".[11] Housing was being allocated to other Government employees, such as those working in the Ministry of Housing, and at the aluminium smelter. Hopeful signs that Awali might be on the verge of an upsurge offered hope that the Anglican congregation at Awali church might recover in numbers too.

Awali town, with Jebel Ad Dukhan (Mountain of Smoke) on the horizon
Source: Caltex Corporation, reproduced with consent

By 1985, Canon Parkinson was exuberant. In his report to Synod that year he said that "the arrival of a second priest to take up the post of assistant chaplain had made history in Bahrain and the diocese. Of much greater importance is the opportunity this gives to further the work of the church. The Revered Ian Young has already established his position … to the point where it is difficult to imagine how the ministry was maintained by a single priest."[12]

In contrast, 1984 was a year of turbulence within the Anglican church in Doha. Major differences, dating back for sometime, reached a head when the Prayer and Praise group finally separated from the rest of the church to form the International Christian Fellowship. Unfortunately, this was not achieved without some bitterness on both sides. Later in the year, changes in leadership in both groups made some rapprochement possible thereby enabling "a very real sense of unity in the Church as a whole, to the extent that it has been possible to organise occasional joint services. We praise God for this reconciliation".[13] Differences between the 'Anglican' and 'Allied' members of the church remained but these were, by and large, covered by having alternating services led by various members, and by Archdeacon Michael Mansbridge during his monthly visit. The church in Dukhan held bi-monthly meetings. Although their numbers were down in recent years, moves were under way to increase support from Doha to help build it up again. All told, after a bad start to the year, the Anglican church in Qatar moved into 1985 "with a sense of hope and of purpose, and with a feeling of peace from the knowledge that the Christians in Qatar are members of one body".[14]

In the UAE, the Reverend Dennis Gurney arrived in Dubai on 13 October 1984 with his wife Naomi and twelve-year old twin sons Timothy and David. He settled in quickly, continuing the ministries which he had inherited at Holy Trinity, and at St Martin's in Sharjah. Every three weeks he drove with his family to the northern emirates of Ras al Khaimah and Fujairah to lead unpublicised home group meetings which he began to nurture. In particular, these took the form of worship, junior church gatherings and Bible study in the al Nakheel area of Ras al Khaimah, discreetly hosted by a family in their home.

The situation in the Cyprus archdeaconry was rather different where, almost without exception, regular publicised worship took place in church buildings. Even north of the Green Line steady growth was reported: at St Andrew in Kyrenia, mainly from the gradual expansion of Western tourism, especially British; and in Famagusta where low-key house services were held. The Anglican church of St Mark in Varosha, the southern quarter of Famagusta, had had to be abandoned after the division of the island. The church was subsequently demolished and Varosha remains in no-man's land under UN control.

South of the Green Line in the parishes of Limassol and Paphos, the Reverend Desmond Sheppard was buoyant. By the end of 1984 the two parishes were "in the happy position" of being able to increase their contributions to the diocese. In Nicosia, although parish life was thriving at St Paul's, it was frustrated by a stalled building project. This had begun when Bishop Ashton initiated his Appeal Fund and said that he would like to establish a Diocesan and Cathedral Centre. Unfortunately, the building contemplated would have cost more than the whole balance in the Appeal Fund and so the scheme was abandoned.

At the start of Bishop Moore's episcopate the idea was resurrected in a simpler and cheaper form: a two-storey prefabricated building on the church site, suitably disguised to look attractive. The plans were approved at the Diocesan Synod in May 1984. It was not long before the trustees of the JEMT (Cyprus) faced a new setback. The Nicosia Municipality informed them that building permit rules in Nicosia had changed: prefabricated buildings were no longer permitted within the city limits, and all existing ones had to be demolished and replaced by permanent structures. Revised architectural plans were submitted and the budget adjusted. Even with a grant from ECUSA, funding from the JEMT (Cyprus), and from the Cyprus Archdeaconry Board of Finance, this created a serious cash flow challenge, worsened by ECUSA's requirement that the building had to be completed within six months. In addition, the JEMT (Cyprus) was "not allowed any local borrowing facilities whatsoever".[15] The final cost of the project was US$92,000.

At the Diocesan Synod, held from 9 to 10 May 1985, a motion was passed that the shortfall of US$33,230 to complete the church hall on the ground floor should be the responsibility of St Paul's Cathedral; and that the shortfall of US$13,250 to complete the diocesan offices above should be funded by the Central Diocesan Board of Finance.

At last, on Friday 28 June 1985, Bishop Harry Moore dedicated the distinctive two-storey brick building designed in a version of traditional Greek architectural style. A cause for relief was that the cathedral council had rejected a proposal by the Nicosia Municipality that a parking layout could be created by felling many of the old and beautiful cypress trees in the church compound. Today, the trees still grace and shade the gardens around St Paul's Cathedral, the Deanery, the diocesan offices and the church hall.

St Paul's church hall (ground floor) and the diocesan offices (second floor)
Copyright: Angela Murray

More landmark decisions had taken place at Diocesan Synod in 1985. First, a resolution to consolidate the Central Diocesan Board of Finance and the Gulf Archdeaconry Board of Finance into one Diocesan Board of Finance (DBF) was unanimously approved. This created a need to amend the Diocesan Constitution, consolidate accounts and restructure the membership of the DBF.

Second, developments in the House of Laity election results were significant. The norm in previous years had been for the two Houses of Laity to meet separately, each having their own culture: Cyprus members were mostly retirees while, on the whole, Gulf members were employed and younger, often accompanied by their families. In 1985 it was agreed that the Houses of Laity should thereafter hold joint meetings and become one House of Laity with two elected co-chairmen. The change was timely because George Meikle, Chairman of the House of Laity (Cyprus) was not seeking re-election as he was about to retire. Peggy McGinley was seeking re-election as Chairman of the House of Laity (Gulf) having earlier in the year succeeded Dr W N Adams Smith who had returned to his home in New Zealand.

The outcome of the elections was decisive and long-lasting. Effective from 1 June 1986, William (Bill) Schwartz representing Cyprus, and Mrs Peggy McGinley representing the Gulf, found themselves holding three positions: Co-Chairs of the House of Laity, one-year term; Lay Representatives (Cyprus and Gulf) of the Diocesan Standing Committee, three-year term; and Lay Representatives on the Provincial/ Central Synod, five-year term. They were eligible for re-election at the end of their terms, and indeed were successfully re-elected: Bill Schwartz until his ordination in 1993; and Mrs McGinley until her retirement in 2010. Interestingly, by that year both had been appointed as Honorary Canons of St Christopher's Cathedral, Peggy McGinley as a lay canon on 26 February 1997, and Bill Schwartz as a clerical canon on 6 February 2006.

During 1985 Bishop Harry Moore and his wife visited all the chaplaincies in the diocese at least once, except Aden. They flew to America to attend the General Convention of ECUSA, then to England where they attended a banquet at Buckingham Palace in honour of the Ruler of Qatar during his state visit to the UK. The thinking behind the invitation had been that the bishop's presence might help in efforts to obtain permission for an Anglican chaplain to reside in Qatar. Several more years were to pass before this happened.

Then, in November 1985, Bishop Moore received an unexpected invitation from the CMS in London offering him the position of General Secretary. He and Betty had been very happy in the diocese with no desire to move on. Yet, after much thought and collaborative discussion with others in the diocese, Bishop Moore resigned in January 1986, giving six months' notice. He later reflected that this "was probably the hardest decision I have ever been called on to make".[16] For the second time within three years, the See of Cyprus and the Gulf was vacant.

On 23 April 1986, the next significant event in the life of the diocese took place when, at St Helena's church in Larnaca, Major Gerald Green "with the greatest pleasure … received at the hand of the Right Reverend Harry Moore, Bishop in Cyprus and the Gulf"[17] an Episcopal Mandate and Declaration, effective on that day, proclaiming that:

> "St Christopher's Church, Bahrain, hitherto known as St Christopher's Pro-Cathedral, shall be known as St Christopher's Cathedral, Bahrain, our Cathedral in the Gulf. It is also our pleasure that the Chaplain of St Christopher's Cathedral, Bahrain, in future shall be titled the Provost of the Cathedral Church."[18]

At St Helena's church, Larnaca
Bishop Harry Moore handing his crosier and his Episcopal Mandate
to Major Gerald Green on 23 April 1986
Source: St Christopher's Cathedral archive

Major Green, churchwarden emeritus,[19] was in Cyprus to be one of the Bahrain chaplaincy's representatives at the 1986 Diocesan Synod which began on 24 April. As Bishop Moore's episcopate was drawing to a close, he had decided to present St Christopher's with a personal gift to mark his decision to elevate the church to full cathedral status. This was the crosier made in Cyprus by 48 Command Workshop, Royal Electrical and Mechanical Engineers, presented to the bishop on 6 November 1983 by the UN church of St Columba in Nicosia. On 23 April 1986 the bishop formally presented the crosier and the Mandate to Major Green.

A few weeks later, on 1 June 1986, a Service of Thanksgiving was held in St Christopher's Cathedral, during which Major Green presented the Mandate to the provost, the Very Reverend John Parkinson. He then made a second presentation. "It is my pleasure to pass to you this crosier", for the bishop, and his successors, to use whenever visiting their churches in the Gulf. "I am charged to place it in your hand, Very Reverend Sir, for safe keeping in this, St Christopher's Cathedral."[20] Even today, when not in use, the crosier's three sections are unscrewed and stored in the same silk-lined wooden box as when it travelled to Bahrain with Major Green as hand luggage. The "First Class" Gulf Air label is still tied to the handle.

Bishop Moore and his wife Betty attended their farewell party in Nicosia on 27 June 1983. Meanwhile, once again the Diocesan Standing Committee had found itself dealing with the Archbishop of Canterbury, this time assisted by his Adviser on Anglican Communion Affairs, Terry Waite. As soon as the bishop had resigned in January 1986, the process of appointing his successor began.

This time, the agreed procedure of the Diocesan Standing Committee, chaired by Cecil Griggs, was documented in seven points: to notify the Archbishop of Canterbury of the vacancy in the See of Cyprus and the Gulf; to establish consultation with him; to present a list of potential names to the Archbishop's representative after chaplaincies had been asked to submit any nominations to the Standing Committee; to then invite the Archbishop to comment on each name and to request relevant biographical information; on Wednesday 23 April 1986 the Standing

Committee would review all the information it had received; and on Friday 25 April 1986 would consult with the President Bishop. (By that date, the Most Reverend Samir Kafa'ity had succeeded Bishop Hassan Dehqani-Tafti.) Finally, the diocese's nomination would be presented to the Archbishop of Canterbury so that he might submit the name to the President Bishop for him to issue a mandate for consecration and installation in accordance with the constitution of the Central Synod of the ECJME.

The 1983 amendments to the Diocesan Constitution had clarified the process and ensured the democratic integrity of the next bishop's appointment. Even so, the Vacancy-in-See Committee - convened by the Very Reverend John Parkinson - had a difficult task. Four of the nine members were already familiar names: Mr George Meikle and Mr Cecil Griggs representing Cyprus, and Major Gerald Green and Mrs Peggy McGinley representing the Gulf. Bill Schwartz, then a member of the Diocesan Standing Committee and an elected alternate to represent Cyprus on the Vacancy in See Committee, recollects:

> "The next Bishop of the Diocese of Cyprus and the Gulf needed to be a man of vision and hope; with experience of the region; holding informed views concerning the interchange between Christian and Islamic culture in the development of the Gulf societies; a bishop who saw his role as an opportunity to build, strengthen, and nourish the work of the Anglican Church, not only in the Middle East, but the work of the [whole] Church".[21]

The Venerable John Brown, Archdeacon of Berkshire in the Diocese of Oxford, was discerned to be that person. The Archbishop of Canterbury, the Most Reverend Robert Runcie, recognised John Brown to be "a man of real spirituality who has great gifts of theological interpretation and exposition. … He has a real love for the Islamic world, having served in Jerusalem and Khartoum, writes and speaks Arabic fluently. …. Combines vision, warmth and humility - and a good sense of humour".[22]

On 3 July 1986, Archdeacon Brown having just arrived in France with his son Richard to start a bicycle tour, received a telephone call from his wife Rosemary:

"Lambeth Palace rang today. ... They wish to know if you are willing to go on a shortlist to be Bishop of Cyprus and the Gulf".[23] His response was that he would think about it during his bicycle tour. Twenty days later on 23 July he arrived at Lambeth Palace to meet Archbishop Runcie. As the interview drew to a close the archbishop said that he would be happy to confirm the nomination.

Archdeacon John Brown
Diocese of Cyprus & the Gulf archive

In November 1986, the Bishop-designate and his wife Rosemary arrived in Nicosia. Assisted by Provost Bryan Henry and his wife Christine they began to acquaint themselves with the diocesan offices and their new home, not a bishop's palace but "a very modern, rather luxurious three-bedroom flat on the first floor of an apartment block."[24] John Brown mused in his diary:

> "I am to be bishop of a diocese that, together with Europe and Alaska, is one of the largest in area in the world, within which are a few scattered parishes, many congregations, and a job description

that I can already see refers as much to politics and diplomacy as to ecclesiasticism. I do not think there can be any kind of training for this particular episcopal job. Clearly it is a 'hands-on' diocese and I shall have to create whatever infrastructure appears to me to be absolutely necessary to the work of God."[25]

The consecration of the Venerable John Brown on 10 January 1987, in St Paul's Cathedral, Nicosia, was a special occasion for more than the obvious reason: it was the first, and the only time so far, that the consecration of an Anglican bishop has taken place in Cyprus.

Among the visiting luminaries present were the Right Reverend Leonard Ashton CB and the Right Reverend Peter Coleman, Bishop of Crediton in Devon, then Chairman of the link arrangement between the dioceses of Exeter, and Cyprus and the Gulf. The preacher was the Right Reverend Patrick Rodger, Bishop of Oxford, under whom Archdeacon Brown had served since 1977. The Most Reverend Samir Kafa'ity, President Bishop of the ECJME presided at the service.

An added joy was the presence of His Beatitude Archbishop Chrysostomos, Head of the Greek Orthodox Church in Cyprus who "so warmly shared" in the consecration. Following these rites, the Right Reverend John Brown was enthroned as the third Bishop in Cyprus and the Gulf. On 3 February 1987, he began his first tour of the Gulf archdeaconry.

To Bahrain the bishop travelled with his wife Rosemary, the Very Reverend Bryan Henry and Mr Cecil Griggs, all to be present at his enthronement in St Christopher's Cathedral on 6 February. During that morning, before the ceremony, Bishop Brown was received by the Ruler, His Highness Shaikh Isa bin Salman Al Khalifa, at his palace in Riffa:

"What a joy it is to be with him. [Shaikh Isa] said, 'You are Christian; I am Muslim; we are brothers.' We spoke in Arabic and English - his English is perfect and idiomatic. ... He told me I was always welcome to visit him. It was a good and happy beginning."[26]

The bishop wrote in his journal that day: "So now all the ceremonies are over. The work begins! How long will the honeymoon period last?!"[27]

Barely at all, as it turned out. He had imposed upon himself a relentless fact-finding tour of the diocese before he addressed the Diocesan Synod due to take place in May 1987.

After leaving Bahrain, accompanied by the Reverend Ian Young, Assistant Chaplain in Bahrain, the bishop next arrived in Qatar. Although the Qatar chaplaincy was still formally attached to that of Abu Dhabi, it had been agreed in 1986 that it would greatly help Archdeacon Michael Mansbridge if Qatar could be looked after from Bahrain. The bishop observed that the arrangement was working well. He was met with nothing but kindness everywhere he visited, remarking that:

> "Ian has done a great job in bringing together people of very different shades of churchmanship and denomination. He has an important ministry to Asian Christians, especially those in the hotel where he stays every two weeks. …

> "This is because Qatar is one of the States in the Gulf that will not permit us to have a church building or a resident priest. I wonder if that will change? … We had a strong feeling of being in a truly basic Christian community, like the early church. The constant comment in Qatar is, Why, when England is so tolerant about opening new mosques, cannot the Qatar government be a little more open towards Christians?"[28]

In Abu Dhabi, where Archdeacon Mansbridge was based, the approach towards Christian churches was more relaxed. Yet challenges faced all those who were engaged in Anglican ministry throughout the emirate. While the number of British and American expatriates was in lower due to a recession, the expatriate Indian, Pakistani and Sri Lankan population was very large. Many were Anglican or came from the United Churches of South India, North India or Pakistan. Others belonged to the Mar Thoma Church and related quite easily to an Anglican bishop, which pleased Bishop Brown.

The Reverend Dennis Gurney was established ministering in Dubai and Sharjah. The bishop assessed him to be a straightforward Church of England vicar who, having been a farmer into his mid-thirties, stood no nonsense and appeared to be very good for the parish.

Bishop Brown privately disliked the use of the word chaplaincy in his diocese, even when overseas.[29] He sensed that the parish of Dubai and Sharjah would "take some watching", noting its long history of division and the perception by some locally that it had been established as a joint Anglican/Free Church or nondenominational venture.

> "For all my ecumenical thinking, that may make things difficult for me, and I think I shall have to work on this. ... Of course, there is no such thing as a Parson's Freehold overseas, and the insecurity for a clergyman not having a freehold office explains why the debate keeps on coming up in the Church of England. However, in this diocese not even the bishop has a freehold appointment, so we are all in the same boat."[30]

Hotel public rooms used as venues for Christian gatherings became a theme in the bishop's tour. On 27 February 1987 in the Sharjah Continental Hotel he had attended a fellowship breakfast after which he confirmed eleven people of the Church of Pakistan. It was a chaotic service but nevertheless the bishop enjoyed it.

During the next day he paid a fleeting visit to Ras al Khaimah where, also in a hotel, the Arab Christian manager and the mostly Filipino staff - Latin Catholics and Pentecostals - had gathered to receive the bishop's blessing. He recalled it as being "a very moving occasion performing this simple action, which one can easily do without thinking out the habit, but which means a great deal to people who only see their own priest about twice a year."[31]

That day, 28 February 1987, proved to be a watershed for the bishop and the young diocese. Early that morning he received a message to say that the Ruler of Sharjah, His Highness Shaikh Dr Sultan bin Muhammad Al Qasimi, would receive him later that day. The Shaikh had earned his doctoral degree from Exeter University and had endowed its Centre for Gulf Studies. He had also just returned from the Sudan where the Bishop had ministered many years earlier. They had things in common to talk about, including engaging in a long discourse about the People of the Book[32] coming together in an effort to create the conditions for peace.

A few days later with a different Ruler, the same topic arose. On 3 March, the bishop was granted a long-hoped-for audience with the Ruler of Ras al Khaimah, His Highness Shaikh Saqr bin Muhammad Al Qasimi. It was known that Shaikh Saqr did not hold particularly pro-Christian sentiments, such as his refusal to allow the Roman [Latin] Catholic Church to function in his emirate. As he did not speak English, the bishop found the opportunity to speak Arabic again very good for him, despite having become "rusty" in the language since leaving Jordan in 1956. He soon judged the small, elderly and seemingly frail Ruler to be indeed very tough; and that as a member of the great Qasimi tribe, like the Ruler of Sharjah, belonging to both "the desert and the sea", he had a great dignity about him.

> "Shaikh Saqr asked me if I was married and was evidently pleased with my reply. I didn't understand why until he asked me why Roman Catholic priests are not permitted to marry. I explained that this was a matter of discipline not of doctrine. The Shaikh expounded at length his theory that an unmarried priest is not in a position to counsel people with family problems. The conversation became quite animated and interesting. ...

> "We spoke about Christians being 'People of the Book' in the Qur'an, and the Shaikh launched into quite an impressive statement about our common heritage in Abraham and Moses. He did not fail to include the Jewish people, and he went on to remind me that Islam honours Jesus as a prophet and apostle and said that it is a pity that Christians could not go on towards an acknowledgment of Muhammad. I did not fail to make my own witness. Altogether it was quite an astonishing conversation. I am certainly the first ordained Christian the Shaikh has ever had a long theological discussion with."[33]

The Ruler told Bishop Brown that he would always be welcome in Ras al Khaimah and that he looked forward to seeing him again. The bishop noted that Shaikh Saqr's eldest son, also present, used the word 'sha:rik:in', meaning sharers or companions, and that therefore he had been accepted by the Ruler's family. The bishiop was very grateful to receive this privilege. "There has been much to thank God for today."[34]

Sunday 1 March 1987 was a busy day for the bishop in Dubai and Sharjah: celebrating at three Eucharists, presiding at a Family Service, and dedicating new buildings within the Holy Trinity complex. This included Trinity Hall, the work of Dennis Gurney who had established a rolling building programme to increase the number of premises to provide worship space for the thousands of Christians who filled the rooms to capacity each week, few of whom were Anglicans.

Holy Trinity, Dubai
Copyright: Penny Calder

By the end of March 1987 the bishop had visited Oman and Kuwait, and completed his first tour of the Gulf archdeaconry. While admitting that it had been long and tiring, he had deliberately seen the journey as a pilgrimage. Early in his episcopate he had visited all Anglican parishes in Cyprus, and during April and May visited them again. As it was possible to cross the United Nations Buffer Zone, the Green Line, through the Ledra Palace passport check points in Nicosia, the bishop had been able to visit church members in Kyrenia. Those who had survived the crisis in 1974 and remained in the north, and whose Kyrenia residences were registered in the Republic of Cyprus, were also able to travel to the south across the Green Line. This included Anglican clergy ministering at St Andrew's.

The bishop's explorations had prompted him to reflect that the diocese was too dependent upon handouts from generous people outside its fold who wished to be linked in some way. "Linking, or 'twinning', is in itself a good thing to develop Christian fellowship, but it should not chiefly be a financial relationship."[35] Already the dioceses of Oxford and Exeter had been very generous but, he mused, the money they send should be used to build up a capital fund and not used for day-to-day expenses. With these thoughts, and many others, four months into his episcopate on 7 May 1987, Bishop Brown delivered his first Presidential Address to the Diocesan Synod. Those listening were left in no doubt that they had heard a detailed manifesto, amounting to the bishop's master plan to consolidate and enhance existing diocesan structures, review its theological underpinning and the role of its clergy, and create new opportunities for its growth. The plan was projected to evolve during the next four or five years.

Already, the bishop and the Standing Committee had been concerned about the Diocesan Administrator's workload, especially as Cecil Griggs was a very hard-worked volunteer. He himself had suggested to Bishop Brown that having a cleric who could divide his time between the office and St Paul's Cathedral would be a good idea, and so resolve another debate: whether or not it was right that one person should carry the workload of the Provost of St Paul's, chaplain to the Nicosia parish, and Archdeacon in Cyprus, all at the same time. As a result, the Reverend John Burdett had been appointed to serve as Non-Stipendiary Assistant Priest at St Paul's, Nicosia, and as Stipendiary Assistant Diocesan Administrator. He arrived in June 1987 with his wife Margaret. Another new arrival in the diocesan office was a second secretary to assist Georgia Katsantonis. Her sister had recommended Amryl Panayiotou, a national of Trinidad and Tobago who was married to a Cypriot.

The diocesan office was to be computerised too. The initiator of this technological advance was Bill Schwartz, then a member of St Barnabas in Limassol and working with a Christian ministry helping to develop communication technology for use by Christians in the Middle East. Bishop Moore had recognised that this expertise could be useful to his diocese and so invited Bill to introduce computers to the diocesan staff. The purchase of an Apple Macintosh device was approved at Bishop Moore's final Diocesan Synod in 1986, installed by Bill in the following year. This was the first computer the diocese was to own. He also introduced email to the Diocesan Synod. He later recalled: "this had a transforming effect on the way in which the Diocese operated."[36]

Rather surprisingly, also in 1987, the Managing Trustees of the JEMT (Cyprus), in collaboration with the Cyprus Archdeaconry Board of Finance, announced their plan to buy two plots of land in Paphos on which to build an Anglican church in the name of St Margaret, and an associated complex. The Trustees, with St Antony's Church Council, were to launch an appeal to raise £250,000. Remarkably, given the lessons learned when the cost of redeveloping St Helena's site was miscalculated, a motion to receive the report of the JEMT (Cyprus) Trustees which included this project was unanimously carried.[37]

Marshalling his concern for theology and his wish to define clerical tasks clearly, the bishop highlighted the vital role of an archdeacon in the life of the diocese:

> "Historically, he [an archdeacon] is oculus episcopi (eye of the Bishop), which does not mean he is a spy! It means that he keeps the bishop briefed and fully informed of what is going on in the diocese, of the needs and opportunities that the bishop might otherwise miss. …That this role is important in a diocese as scattered as ours hardly needs explanation. Both archdeacons know that I am accessible to any priest or lay person who might wish to have access to me. If the matter is important, then the distances involved must not be a consideration." [38]

The bishop emphasised, too, that encouraging vocations to the ordained ministry was "very much part of what we must be about as a diocese". He set out how he would ensure that candidates were properly chosen and trained. In summary, a committee conduct a selection process and then recommend to the bishop that an applicant, or applicants, should go forward for training. He would discuss with each ordinand their appropriate course of Theological Education by Extension.

To assist with this, the bishop had appointed the Reverend Ian Young as the first Diocesan Director of Ordinands (DDO) in Cyprus and the Gulf. Already six potential ordinands had been identified, among them Derek Hearne in Kuwait, Duncan Harris the Missions to Seamen Lay Chaplain in Dubai, and Ian Thurston then teaching Religious Education at St Christopher's School in Bahrain.

To conclude his first presidential address, the bishop remarked that he had also begun to hold one or two other ideas together.

> "First, the bishop is pontifex, bridge-builder. I recognise this role within our inner diocesan life insofar as it is my earnest desire to draw together Christians of different denominations and awareness of God's activity. … Secondly, as part of the bridge-building task, I should place a high priority on relationships with the House of Islam. … Not only bridge-builder, but also servant. I reflect that I am here not to supervise the running of a well-oiled machine, but to follow my Master truly and be among you as one who serves."[39]

263

Before long he was travelling again, this time with Ian Young to visit and forge a link with the Southern Dioceses Ministerial Training Scheme (SDMTS) based at Salisbury Theological College in England. In September 1987, Derek Hearne,[40] Duncan Harris and Ian Thurston began training in their parishes using the SDMTS course.

Much had been achieved in the diocese that year, with plans being developed to realise the bishop's vision for its immediate future. Then, on 17 October 1987 in Muscat, he and his wife Rosemary received shock news from Cyprus that during the previous night Cecil Griggs had died in his sleep at the age of sixty-seven. Sadly, his widow Phaedra died after a short illness in early 1988. In tribute, the bishop said: "We all know how much Cecil meant to the diocese, and the great commitment he himself had to its welfare."[41] The legacy of Cecil Harry Griggs as a founding father of the diocese cannot be underestimated. A stained-glass window in St Paul's Cathedral, Nicosia, is dedicated to his memory.

The church of Ayia Kyriaki Chrysopolitissa, Kato Paphos, Cyprus,
located within an archaeological site

Copyright: Angela Murray

Chapter 12

THE DISRUPTIONS OF WAR

1988 - 1992

By early 1988, Bishop Brown's commitment to being pontifex/ bridge-builder was increasingly evident in diverse ways. For example, in Cyprus he had broadcast on the British Forces Network, and had visited all the Anglican parishes on different occasions. (He consistently refrained from using the term chaplaincies.) Generally speaking, the size of congregations was increasing, for two main reasons. The comparative safety of Cyprus had attracted many people to relocate from Lebanon which remained troubled by civil war. At St Barnabas in Limassol, where the Christian Arab population had grown considerably, the bishop hoped to form an Arabic-language service to serve their needs.

Many retired expatriates were living in Cyprus. Once again, the island had become a popular destination for holiday-makers. The bishop recognised that demand for pastoral ministry to both groups was both important and increasing. When on 24 January 1988 he licensed the Reverend John Godfrey with charge of the Anglican congregations in Limassol and Paphos he knew that this dual ministry to rapidly expanding towns far apart could not be sustained indefinitely.

In the old town of Kato Paphos, the church of Ayia Kyriaki Chrysopolitissa is a focal point within a much-visited archaeological site. Believed to have been built in circa 1500, the church later became the Greek Orthodox Cathedral of the town. One tradition says that St Paul was scourged in Paphos at a pillar near the church, hence it is also called "The Church by St Paul's Pillar". On 6 March 1988, the Anglican congregation relocated from the nearby small church of St Antony to Ayia Kyriaki, having accepted the Orthodox invitation to share use of the church with the Latins who were already using it. This can be traced to 17 January 1982, the Feast Day of Antony which that year had fallen on a Sunday. As the Orthodox community required use of St Antony's church for their vespers on that day, the Anglican congregation was allowed to hold its evening worship in Ayia Kyriaki. In 1987, the Latin Catholic priest, Father Mark Hurst, gained permission for his congregation to relocate their regular worship permanently from St Antony to Ayia Kyriaki Chrysopolitissa. The Anglicans received a similar invitation but declined thinking that the church was too large, and because they were contemplating building a church of their own. This was the proposed St Margaret's complex.

Later in March 1988, the bishop visited Iraq to support and encourage the small community of expatriates in Baghdad. Graham Spurgeon, a longstanding churchwarden at St George's, who was to leave Iraq in June that year, "had held the dwindling community of the church together in a wonderful way, and devoted a great deal of time and effort to it which is especially wonderful when one considers the tragic situation in which it is placed".[1] This was a reference to the Iran–Iraq War which had begun on 22 September 1980 when Iraq invaded Iran. Bishop Brown wrote in his diary on 21 March 1988: "Missiles exploding from time to time. On the road towards Basrah heavy tanks and artillery on the move. In every part signs of the terrible war, the genocide, that is going on."[2] (The conflict ended on 20 August 1988 when Iran accepted a UN-brokered ceasefire.) Despite this tragedy, Baghdad was a place in the diocese where the bishop could meet many other Church leaders from many of the ancient Eastern churches such as the Assyrians, the Armenians, and their Catholic (Uniate) counterparts, especially the Chaldeans, the largest single Church in Iraq.[3] He was also pleased that his two well-publicised visits to the Minister of Religious Affairs in Iraq had been most friendly and welcoming.

So far this year, the bishop's journeys had included visits to Kuwait, Bahrain and Ras al Khaimah where the Rulers had warmly greeted him. At the southern extremity of the archdeaconry, not without difficulty, he had managed to visit North Yemen. Aden was still in the grip of a Marxist government.

All this, and more, had formed the crux of his Presidential Address to the 1988 Diocesan Synod, an exposition of his theological thinking related to the diocese and a definition of Anglican vision:

> "For me, the vision originates in the belief that the Christian Church is meant to be much more than a loose federation of gathered congregations. In this important sense the Anglican Church is fundamentally different from, say, the Congregationalist or the Baptist Churches, and is aligned with the ancient Churches, Orthodox and Catholic, that keep firmly in their sights and in their thinking and in their practice, the universality of the historic episcopate and the Orders of bishops, priests and deacons. ... Bishops, priests and deacons are called by the whole Church, not simply by a local gathering. If we begin there, as Anglicans within the ancient tradition, we shall quickly see that the Anglican Church, like all Churches that are real Churches, is truly a Lay institution enabled by the bishops, priests and deacons. It is a world-wide fellowship."[4]

The bishop emphasised the need for everyone at Synod to keep these basic principles firmly in mind:

> "If we do not, we shall not find it easy to discover why we meet in this way at all, or how we justify the expense. ... Christians who go pale (or puce, depending on the temperament!) at the mention of the word Stewardship, should reflect that all I have said about the global vision of the divine has to do with what it means to be a Christian steward - that is, a steward of God's mysteries, which involves the sanctification or hallowing of all God's gifts to God's use."[5]

The extent to which the Diocese of Cyprus and the Gulf was indebted to the generosity of many friends outside its sphere was not in doubt. The appointment of the Reverend Ian Young as the diocese's first DDO was one example, and this had been made possible by friends in the Diocese of Oxford.

Cyprus, Iraq and the Gulf region were very much at the mercy of political narratives and economic trends. Therefore, the Diocesan

267

Standing Committee had decided to resurrect Bishop Leonard Ashton's attempt to create a Capital Endowment Fund. The aim was to raise one million pounds sterling as working capital, to be invested in a trust registered as a charity. Its income would be administered by trustees selected from within the diocese, and possibly some from outside. The Appeal was to be made principally to commercial interests and grant-making bodies. Two more years were to pass before the Declaration of Trust was signed on 5 September 1990 and the Appeal launched in the following month.

Since the death of Cecil Griggs in October 1987, the Reverend John Burdett had worked tirelessly in the diocesan office, bearing "the burden and heat of the day in more ways than one".[6] He had helped with a number of tasks, including assisting with legal matters. One problem, recalled by Bill Schwartz, then the Diocesan Assistant Treasurer, was that "Cecil's gentlemanly, informal style meant that it was difficult for those who had to carry on with his work. No-one even knew who the signatories to bank accounts were".[7]

During 1988, it was decided to abolish the Cyprus Archdeaconry Board of Finance (CABOF) and reconstitute it as a sub-committee of, and responsible to, the Diocesan Standing and Finance Committee. The members of the sub-committee were the bishop, the Archdeacon in Cyprus and five lay people representing the five Cyprus parishes/chaplaincies and elected by their parish councils. Furthermore, effective on 1 July 1989, the financial year was to run from 2 July to 30 June annually, to bring it into line with that of the Diocesan Board of Finance (DBF).

There was a change in the diocesan office too when, in November 1988, the assistant secretary Amryl Panayiotou began maternity leave. Anetta Stylianou, Georgia Katsantonis's sister-in-law, joined the office team to provide temporary assistance. However, when Amryl gave birth to twins, adding to her two older children, she chose to concentrate on caring for her family and resigned from her job. Anetta became a permanent member of staff, serving for the next thirty years in various roles and titles until February 2018. She then continued on a part-time basis as Secretary to the Jerusalem and East Mission Trust (Cyprus).

Anetta Stylianou
Source: personal collection, reproduced with permission

Significantly, too, in 1988 Bishop Brown decided to appoint Honorary Canons in the diocese. The new initiative had been suggested by the provosts and cathedral church councils of St Paul's in Nicosia and St Christopher's in Bahrain where there are no residentiary canons, apart from the provost. This is the case with almost all Anglican cathedrals outside England, Scotland and Wales. Instead of a chapter (college of clerics), governance of the two cathedrals in the Diocese of Cyprus and the Gulf is under the authority of each dean. (In 2001, following a name change in the Church of England, provosts became known as deans.) Each cathedral church council may include other licensed clergy, such as an assistant or associate priest and/or an assistant curate, and elected lay members.

On 5 June 1988, Bishop John Brown installed the diocese's first three honorary canons at St Christopher's Cathedral in Bahrain: the Venerable Michael Mansbridge, Archdeacon in the Gulf and chaplain of St Andrew in Abu Dhabi; the Reverend Ian Young, DDO and chaplain for Qatar (commuting from Bahrain); and the Venerable Alun Morris CBE, Archdeacon in Eastern Arabia and the Gulf (1962-1964) and chaplain in Bahrain (1954-1964). A few months later in Cyprus, on 5 February 1989, the bishop also installed two honorary canons at St Paul's Cathedral in Nicosia: the Reverend Arthur Rider MBE, retired, chaplain of St Andrew, Kyrenia (1980-1987); and the Reverend Peter

Delaney, vicar of All Hallows by the Tower in London, in recognition of his contribution to the work of the diocese. (On 9 July 1990, Fr Delaney was appointed as the Bishop in Cyprus and the Gulf's Commissary in the UK.[8]) Also on 5 February 1989, Bishop Brown honoured the Right Reverend Leonard Ashton CB, the diocese's first bishop, who had retired in 1983, by installing him as Episcopal Canon of St Paul's Cathedral.

The Reverend Canon Peter Delaney
Source: personal collection, reproduced with permission

Meanwhile, licensed Readers in Cyprus had met in October 1988 for a day in Nicosia which, it was hoped, would become an annual event. Eight potential Readers had begun training within the diocese, using the Course of Extension Studies provided by St John's College in Nottingham, in England.

During the spring of 1989 work began to raise awareness of the diocese internationally and so garner support for the proposed Appeal. Prominent on a single-page publicity document was the question: Why the Need For One Million Pounds Working Capital?

The answer was that the Diocese of Cyprus and the Gulf is not part of the Church of England and receives no financial help from it. In 1988 it had no endowments. All its funding came from two main sources: a few well-wishers, including churches in the UK and the USA; and those living in the diocese and served by it. The bishop was committed to growth, not retrenchment. Funds were needed to support that goal.

In Cyprus there were nine congregations, a combination of retired people, diplomats, those working for offshore companies, journalists, teachers, and their families. Only one Anglican congregation remained in Iraq, at St George's in Baghdad. In the Arabian peninsula there were thirty-two established congregations, predominantly nationals of the UK, USA, Pakistan, India, Sri Lanka, the Phillipines, South Korea and several African countries. A frequent misconception, even today, is that all expatriates living in affluent Gulf countries are well-off with residual income to spare. The reality is that many thousands are low-income migrant workers with onerous commitments to support dependants in their home countries. Of those who are Christians, many also support their churches at home.

271

In March 1989, the bishop spent a week in London with the link parish of All Hallows by the Tower to start planning his Appeal campaign. He was advised by those who understood the world of business that the only way for this to succeed was for him to 'sell' his vision for the diocese on a face-to-face level to busy people who are always being asked to give money. Two lunch parties were arranged, attended by senior people from the City of London's banking and business community, leaders of industry such as the senior executives of Shell, BP and British Aerospace, and church people. At both events the bishop presented a paper which articulated his vision. During that week he was made a member of the World Trade Centre movement, thereby gaining access to all the trade centres throughout the world, particularly those in Bahrain, Abu Dhabi and Dubai.

On 2 April 1989 Bishop Brown flew across the Atlantic Ocean for the first time to spend a week in the USA publicising the diocese and the Appeal, primarily in New York. The linchpin to his presentations was the paper which he had delivered in London, with the financial sums in dollars and the term "working capital" replaced with "endowment fund". Losing no time, on 3 April he visited the Reformed Church in America on Riverside, then St John the Divine Episcopal Cathedral to meet the "energetic" Very Reverend James Morton whom he had first met in Jerusalem when they were both installed as canons of St George's Cathedral. After a visit to Washington DC, the bishop introduced himself to the "nerve centre of the American Episcopal Church, generally called '815' (being 815 Second Avenue)".[9] St Bartholomew's in Park Avenue, linked with All Hallows by the Tower in London, extended a warm welcome and invited him to preach at a healing service. On 7 April the bishop wrote in his diary:

> "This has been a good week and I have made a lot of new friends, for myself and for the diocese. ... I now have an agenda of work, combining this trip with my earlier visit to London, which will last me out my time. It is a matter of speedily following up all the goodwill created and extending it in as many directions as possible."[10]

272

Almost three weeks later on 26 April 1989, the Anglican Primates convened in Cyprus for their first meeting since the 1988 Lambeth Conference. In the Greek Orthodox Church calendar that year, 28 April 1989 was Good Friday. Archbishop Chrysostomos I used that opportunity to welcome the Primates to the Church of Panayia (Our Lady) tis Pallouriotissa in Nicosia. Two days later, on Orthodox Easter Day, he invited the Archbishop of Canterbury, the Most Reverend Robert Runcie, to St John's Orthodox Cathedral in Nicosia for the reading of the Gospel in English, accompanied by Bishop Brown.

Archbishop Chrysostomos extended his hospitality still further. During the evening of 2 May he received the Primates at a private meeting during which he spoke earnestly of the Cyprus problem, expressing his feelings for his people, especially for the families of those who had been missing since 1974. He did not believe that the current round of talks between Georgios Vasos Vassiliou, President of the Republic of Cyprus, and Rauf Denktash, President of the Republic of Northern Cyprus, would lead anywhere, emphasising that "there was a strong need for the west, and especially Britain as a guarantor power, to do more than talk in sympathy".[11] Following this meeting, Archbishop Chrysostomos hosted a lavish garden reception to which he had invited some twelve hundred people, including anyone from the Anglican community who wished to attend. Indeed, many did attend, including a good number who travelled from Paphos and Limassol to be part of the occasion.

Ascension Day in the Anglican calendar fell on 4 May that year. Bishop Brown and Archbishop Runcie chose to celebrate this without fuss or publicity at St Andrew in Kyrenia. The Archbishop of Canterbury also wished to visit a long-standing friend, the elderly Reverend Evelyn Chavasse, retired and living nearby. Their journey did not start well. In Nicosia they were held up at the Green Line check-point by the Turkish authorities who wished to acknowledge the archbishop's presence. Bishop Brown insisted that this was a private visit to a very sick Anglican priest. In the end, the British High Commissioner intervened to facilitate "an unimpeded passage. It was a tricky hour."[12]

273

During the 1989 Diocesan Synod which convened in the following week, there was a unique reason to rejoice. Archdeacon Michael Mansbridge announced that two lay chaplains serving in the Diocese of Cyprus and the Gulf had been honoured by the President of the Missions to Seamen, HRH the Princess Royal.

In 1988, Mr David Pellatt, the Missions to Seamen Lay Chaplain in Bahrain, had been chosen as the first person to receive the President's Award which recognised outstanding service to seafarers. Mr Duncan Harris, Lay Chaplain in Dubai and due to be ordained on 26 May 1989, was now the second person to receive this new award.

There was more positive news, albeit lacking in detail. The bishop explained that during his visit to the USA one diocese in the Episcopal Church of the United States had expressed serious interest "in forging a personal link with Cyprus and the Gulf"[13]. It ltranspired that Bishop Brown had met the Right Reverend Terence (Terry) Kelshaw who, in

March 1989, had been consecrated as Bishop of the Episcopal Diocese of the Rio Grande. Already the two Englishmen were developing their idea to set up a companion diocese link.

On 24 May 1989 Bishop Brown was in Bahrain once more, on this occasion to dedicate the new Worship Centre adjacent to St Christopher's Cathedral. The two-storey building, formerly St Christopher's School, had been converted for use by other Christian groups who otherwise had no appropriate worship rooms available to them. This was a pastoral response to the Bahrain Government's intent to stop the illicit use of apartments and villas in residential areas as meeting venues for unlicensed Christian congregations.

Two days later, on 26 May 1989, a landmark service was held at the cathedral during which the bishop ordained Duncan Harris and Ian Thurston to the diaconate.

> "The importance of these ordinations for this Diocese cannot be over-emphasised. Starting in September 1987, they have completed a full course of training recognised by the Church of England through Salisbury Theological College in the United Kingdom. The high standard that I am insisting upon and which is being implemented by Canon Ian Young our Diocesan Director of Ordinands and Training will ensure that those ordained in this diocese will be received by the Church of England should they wish to return to serve there. We are indebted to the Diocese of Oxford, to All Hallows by the Tower and to the Missions to Seamen for making this vital work of training possible."[14]

The diversity of ministry in the Diocese of Cyprus and the Gulf was fast becoming one of its defining and unique features. One manifestation of this took place on 20 October 1989 when Bishop Brown licensed a Pakistani Presbyterian minister to serve Urdu-speaking congregations in Oman. He reflected:

> "It is extraordinary how so many of the non-Roman Catholic, non-Orthodox Asian Christians look to the Anglican bishop as the authoritative figure, as their bishop in fact; even those who belong to traditions that have theologically rejected bishops.

"This of course is something the Church of England does not at all understand, but it is crucially central to the life of an Anglican bishop anywhere in the eastern world. Here lies the genius of the Anglican Communion, that it can contain many traditions and even many stereotypes and prejudices."[15]

On 19 November 1989, the Very Reverend John Parkinson, Provost of St Christopher's Cathedral, attended his last service in Bahrain before relocating to minister elsewhere. The bishop presided, and during the service he confirmed one adult, the author of this book. As she knelt at the communion rail to receive the sacrament for the first time, John Parkinson unexpectedly stepped down from the sanctuary and knelt beside her, he to receive the sacrament for the last time as provost of the cathedral. That pastoral gesture is a cherished memory.

The start of the new decade was celebrated on 14 January 1990 when the Very Reverend Derek Taylor was installed as the new Provost of St Christopher's Cathedral. But 1990 was to be a year remembered later throughout the diocese for the disruptions of the first Gulf War.

St Christopher's Cathedral, 1990 - *Front, left to right:* Michael Rawlinson (cathedral warden), the Reverend Canon Ian Young, the Very Reverend Derek Taylor, the Right Reverend John Brown, the Venerable Michael Mansbridge, Major Gerald Green (Warden Emeritus)

Behind, left to right: the Reverend Paul Burt, the Reverend Ian Thurston, Roy Topping (Reader), and an unidentified church member

Diocese of Cyprus & the Gulf archive

Before that war dominated the scene, on 5 April in Cyprus, down in Kato Paphos, the controversial proposal to build an entire church complex was aired at a "difficult public meeting" chaired by the bishop. During this he tried to persuade the Anglican parishioners "to get their priorities right".[16] While a good number of them were determined to buy land on which to build a new church, the bishop wanted them to concentrate on using the "admirable" Greek Orthodox church of Ayia Kyriaki, already on loan to the diocese. By doing so, resources could be accrued to pay the stipend of a full-time priest. The bishop reminded the audience that it was a long way for the chaplain at St Barnabas to drive from Limassol every Sunday to take services in Paphos, and also during the week to undertake the growing workload of pastoral ministry. He wrote in his diary: "The saying of the day came from a non-churchgoer at the back: 'Who does that fellow in a purple vest think he is coming here and telling us what to do?'!"[17] In due course, the bishop did win the debate, but not in 1990.

In the southern extremity of the diocese, on 22 May 1990, the expected merger between the People's Democratic Republic of Yemen (South Yemen) and the Yemen Arab Republic (North Yemen) was formalised to create the Republic of Yemen. The Marxist regime in Aden had been ousted from power. Although it was still too early to forecast how and when an Anglican church might be restored in Yemen, at least cautious hope was now possible.

In dramatic contrast, on 2 August 1990 the Iraqi army invaded and occupied Kuwait, in effect turning a peaceful country into a prison camp. Many expatriates went into hiding in fear of being used as human shields. During the invasion the church of St Paul in Ahmadi was miraculously left unscathed. It is believed that this was because a Christian contingent in the Iraqi army took it upon themselves to guard the property. The Reverend Michael Jones was not so fortunate. While attempting to lead a convoy to freedom, he was taken hostage. Two days later he and his wife Jean had been due to start their annual leave. Instead, they became the "guests" of Saddam Hussain, detained in Baghdad, accommodated in a tent. Towards the end of September the bishop did manage to make a telephone call to Brian Pavamani, churchwarden at St George's, who had just returned from a service in the church. His good news was that Michael Jones had officiated in church, having been permitted to attend for one hour. The Iraqi authorities were to grant him this privilege every Sunday until he and Jean were released in mid-December 1990.

The Reverend Michael Jones (*far left*), Bishop John Brown and two Readers at the church of St Paul Ahmadi
Diocese of Cyprus & the Gulf archive

The invasion had been met with international condemnation. Immediately the UN Security Council imposed economic sanctions against Iraq. The first stage of the Gulf War was codenamed Operation Desert Shield. A coalition of nations formed the largest military alliance since the Second World War. Ground forces were based in Saudi Arabia. Bahrain International Airport became a fighter-bomber base for the RAF. The United States Air Force was also deployed in Bahrain, and extensively in other locations in Arabia. Among the military field hospitals erected, including provision to treat chemical warfare injuries, the British established a large tented facility on a site not far from Awali church in Bahrain. St Christopher's Cathedral in the heart of the capital was a host to all those seeking quiet reflection and pastoral comfort, including military personnel. Yet, all the while, it was somehow hoped that the weight of international pressure would force Iraq to withdraw from Kuwait without allied military intervention. Bishop Brown was more pragmatic. "It does look as if some kind of war is inevitable. How much of my diocese will go up in smoke?"[18]

During all this tension, meetings about the diocese's funding base had been taking place in London. On 5 September 1990, a Declaration of Trust was signed whereby six trustees were to establish a charitable fund in the UK to be called the Diocese of Cyprus and the Gulf Endowment Fund, thereafter known as the Foundation. This was a prelude to the launch of the Appeal in October. The bishop remarked:

> "It is arguable that this is a bad time to make an appeal for funds for the Middle East. I am going to argue that this is precisely the best time, since so much of the diocese is highlighted at present in the media. … The basis of my appeal is that it is of crucial importance to maintain support for Christians living as expatriates in the heartlands of Islam, not by maintaining existing parishes, which I believe should support themselves … but by supporting a travelling leader, the bishop, in his enabling, uniting and encouraging role, as well as assisting new work; for example in the Emirates, in Yemen, and eventually in Iraq."[19]

On 17 October 1990 the Appeal was launched at the World Trade Centre in London. The staff at All Hallows had done a tremendous job in setting up exhibition material illustrating aspects of the diocese. Around one hundred and sixty people attended, more than the most optimistic estimates. Derek Nimmo was one patron of the Appeal. With theatre interests in various places along the Arabian Gulf coast, he was particularly supportive and stayed throughout the launch. Pierre Salinger, the head of the Associated Press and former press secretary to President Kennedy was another welcome attendee. The presence of some dozen Church of England bishops greatly pleased Bishop Brown. However, with much displeasure he noted:

> "The oil companies had all been invited; they were notable by their absence and for the dreadful letters they had written, pleading the crisis and the uncertainty of their own future in the Middle East! And these are the employers whose staff we spend a lot of time pastoring."[20]

Bishop John Brown and Derek Nimmo
Diocese of Cyprus & the Gulf archive

In a letter to British newspapers, Bishop John contrasted the willingness of countries like Great Britain and the United States to act on UN resolutions condemning the invasion of Kuwait with their unwillingness to act on resolutions regarding Palestine and Cyprus. The reason, he speculated, was oil. His comments resulted in his being banned from visiting the areas of Cyprus under Turkish control. There was a backlash to this, recalled by Bill Schwartz: "Another John Brown, visiting northern Cyprus on holiday shortly afterwards, was imprisoned for two days by mistake. Much later, after 2003 when crossing the Green Line became possible, the ban on Bishop Brown was still found to be in place. This issue remains sensitive. The Church, and the diocese, have learned to tread carefully regarding it."[21]

By mid-December 1990 all the hostages in Iraq had been freed, including the Reverend Michael Jones and his wife Jean who returned safely to England. On 28 December the bishop set off from Cyprus to Baghdad, via Amman to collect a visa from the Iraqi Embassy there. His purpose was to assess the situation at St George's and once again offer pastoral support to the congregation. He learned that there were no more than thirty British people left in Iraq, fewer than a dozen

279

Americans, and a handful of European diplomats. The churchwardens and lay Reader had left. He assessed that "it is plain that the church will not, in the foreseeable future, be able to function as an organization. Within this framework of sadness we had a happy Eucharist. There were seven of us present and I kept on walking down to the west end so that we could have the organ played for the last time."[22] The bishop did what he could to secure the property against illegal entry and to safeguard its effects. He also took a number of files away with him for safekeeping.

The UN deadline of 15 January, the date by which Iraqi troops were required to leave Kuwait, was imminent. No-one really believed that Saddam Hussain would comply unconditionally. He ignored the deadline. And so it was that on 17 January 1991 an allied aerial and naval bombardment was launched on military installations in Iraq and Kuwait. The first Gulf War, codenamed Operation Desert Storm, lasted for six weeks. The ground assault to liberate Kuwait was launched on 24 February. Operation Desert Storm ended on 28 February 1991.

As far as it was possible under the circumstances, chaplaincy life in the diocese continued uninterrupted, except of course in Aden, Kuwait and Baghdad. In Cyprus significant changes had taken place during 1990. On 15 April the Reverend John Burdett and his wife had left the island, he having served as non-stipendiary priest at St Paul's Cathedral and as the Diocesan Administrator and Secretary since 1 June 1987. Since 1986 Bill Schwartz had been in post as Assistant Treasurer. After John's departure he became both Treasurer and Diocesan Secretary, serving in those roles until 1999.

At the end of November 1990, the Very Reverend Bryan Henry retired. This created vacancies for two positions: Provost of St Paul's Cathedral in Nicosia, and Archdeacon in Cyprus. By the end of the year, Bishop Brown concluded that the best way forward for coordinating the parishes in Cyprus on behalf of the diocese was to appoint a rural dean and therefore he suspended the Archdeaconry in Cyprus. This was an episcopal prerogative. With immediate effect, the Venerable Michael

Mansbridge, then Archdeacon in the Gulf and chaplain at St Andrew Abu Dhabi, became the sole archdeacon in the diocese. It was not until 8 September 1991 that the Very Reverend Patrick Blair was installed as the next Provost of St Paul's Cathedral in Nicosia, followed by his licensing on 6 October 1991 as Rural Dean in Cyprus.

Meanwhile, during the Iraqi military retreat from Kuwait, its forces had set fire to over seven hundred oil wells. The air was filled with a dense cloud of rank, black smoke. Ahmadi became virtually uninhabitable. Even as far south as Bahrain, Qatar and the east coast of Arabia, the normally blue sky became laden with dark toxic oil pollution. It took nine months for the fires to be controlled and in that time St Paul's was unusable for normal services. As most of the Western Christian community had fled from Kuwait or were in hiding, it was the Indian Christian community who rallied alongside the liberating allied troops to restore St Paul's church to a place of active worship. The first service to be held in the church after the war was conducted by Captain Pollard, chaplain of the Royal Regiment of Fusiliers. Seeing the destroyed east window, he asked his men to remove it and board up the open space.

281

Ironically, it was the bombardment by the allied air forces which caused the most damage to the church building. All the stained-glass windows were blown out by blasts. The Kuwait Oil Company replaced the broken windows and repaired the roof. Bishop Brown appointed David Dorrington as churchwarden and gave him the task of rebuilding the Anglican congregation. The first service in the church following its repair took place on Sunday 3 November 1991, attended by five people. By Christmas the congregation had swelled to eighty worshippers.

By this time, significant changes were evolving in the Qatar chaplaincy. As described earlier, in April 1986 at the request of Archdeacon Michael Mansbridge who was also chaplain in Abu Dhabi, the Reverend Canon Ian Young had started to commute from Bahrain to Qatar to take services in the Doha English Speaking School. At first this happened once a month, then later became twice a month. In late 1991, the British Ambassador in Qatar, Graham Boyce, himself a churchman, realised that the growth of the Anglican church in that country depended on the chaplain being resident. He informed the

Qatari government that he intended to take Canon Ian Young onto his staff as an attaché. The Qataris agreed as this would allow Canon Young to carry out his ministry under the protection of the British Embassy. In this way, the Qatari government would not be asked to issue a work permit to a priest which it would not do.

Canon Young moved to Doha in early January 1992 and remained on the staff of the British Embassy as attaché until he left in 2007. When the bishop and his wife Rosemary visited Doha between 17 and 20 January 1992, they judged the villa which Canon Young had rented to be an "admirable vicarage and meeting place".[23] Known as Church House, this became the discrete focal point of the evolving chaplaincy in Qatar. However, Canon Young recalls:

> "These were still difficult days in Qatar. I would receive phone calls asking why I was in the country and that I was not wanted. The lights on my garden wall were on occasion smashed. Muslims (expatriates, never Qatari) would arrive at the door asking for money and strange questions in the hope of being admitted to the house and see if it was a 'church'. Only the protection of the British Embassy got me through these days, knowing that as a 'diplomat' I would not be arrested."[24]

For the first time in two years Diocesan Synod convened on 31 January 1992. The Reverend Canon Peter Delaney had been invited to lead the devotions. In his address, the bishop explained to those who were new to synod that All Hallows by the Tower in London was the link parish in the UK for the Diocese of Cyprus and the Gulf and that Canon Delaney and his staff were always ready to host events connected with the diocese. In particular more recently, the crisis in Kuwait and the Gulf War had given the diocese a very high international profile, greatly helped by those at All Hallows. As a result, the diocese was now receiving many interested enquiries from all parts of the world. Also noteworthy to synod members, the Reverend Ian Thurston, whom the bishop had priested on 9 September 1990, left Bahrain after his final service there on 19 December 1990 to continue his ministry at All Hallows, serving as Assistant Curate.

Bishop Brown announced that a formal companion diocese link was now established with the Diocese of the Rio Grande in New Mexico. He explained that this system of twinning was a well-known part of American church life, and was usually expected to last no more than six years. He had visited Bishop Terence Kelshaw in New Mexico and invited him to be guest speaker at the 1993 Diocesan Synod. This new link was intended to encourage and increase the quality of spiritual formation in both dioceses. During the 1990-91 financial year, the Diocese of the Rio Grande had also donated $10,000 to Cyprus and the Gulf's diocesan funds.

This was especially appreciated since there was no doubt that the Gulf crisis and war had affected the launch of the Appeal quite seriously, made worse by the economic recession in the United Kingdom. In early 1990, $150,000 had been granted by the Proctor & Gamble Trust in Southern Ohio, given to the bishop to use at his sole discretion. Already in early 1992 the diocese was reaping benefit from accrued interest. That sum had been added to the original £75,000 approved by synod in 1989 to start the Appeal, this being the residual amount from the first attempt to build up the endowment launched by Bishop Leonard Ashton. Thus the total capital had increased to just over £200,000, far short of the target £1million pounds but not an inconsiderable figure.

In the mid-summer of 1992, the bishop embarked on what he described as a very important trip to the Yemen. Between 7 and 16 July he attended many meetings. The first was with the Minister of Religious Affairs who explained that a new law in the united Yemen decreed that all property which had been confiscated after the revolution in 1970 must be returned to the original owners. The bishop's immediate reply was that he would like one of the former Anglican churches in Aden to be returned. "The Minister thought this right and said he would have no objection to an Anglican priest working and living in Aden."[25]

On 8 July, Bishop Brown set off early from the British Embassy in Sana'a where he was staying, accompanied by an embassy official.

Their purpose was to visit the Grand Mufti of Yemen whose residence was an old traditional house standing tall in a narrow dusty lane, only just wide enough for the embassy 4-wheel-drive vehicle to pass along. Inside, the house was a blaze of colour, adorned with oriental carpets, carved wooden doors and stained-glass windows unique to Yemen, yet it all seemed very unostentatious. The bishop and his companion were welcomed in impeccable English by the Grand Mufti's son who escorted them to a traditional Arab *majlis*, a long room furnished with rugs on the floor and cushions lined up against the walls. Presently, a venerable-looking elderly gentleman, white bearded and with a warm, smiling face, entered to greet them. While squatting on the floor, usual pleasantries were exchanged and *gahwa* (coffee) was served. Then the serious conversation began. The Grand Mufti, Ahmad Muhammad Zabarah, was known to be a moderate Sunni of the Zaidi sect, and had travelled widely. He and the bishop spoke about Christian-Muslim relationships and how they might be improved.

> "The Grand Mufti was very helpful in suggesting how I should formally approach the government concerning the building or restoration of a church in Aden and the putting in of an Anglican priest. He said he would support any application I made with his own letters to the government. The embassy official who was with me asked the Grand Mufti if he would be interested in being invited to make a sponsored visit to the United Kingdom, and he was clearly delighted. I said I would arrange for him to have a meeting at Lambeth Palace and a tour."[26]

For a very different sort of meeting, on 11 July the bishop was hosted by the Canadian Occidental Oil Company, staying in their executive office suite which occupied the top two floors of the Mövenpick hotel in Aden. He had "quite a lot of work to do" with the company, indicating that he sought their logistical and financial support to set up a new chaplaincy in Aden. The bishop needed someone living in the city, preferably a layman to begin with, who would negotiate terms with the governor and the local departments for religious affairs, electricity and planning. He had Tom Hamblin in mind who, with his wife Edna, were ready to work anywhere they were needed in the area.

Christ Church in Aden, circa 1993
Diocese of Cyprus & the Gulf archive

Three days later, on 14 July, a worthwhile meeting took place with the deputy governor of Aden. A potential obstacle arose when he asked the bishop if he could provide the title deeds to the properties in which he was interested. This was a challenging request. The Crown Colony days were a long time ago and in the intervening period there had been civil wars and much disruption. Research was needed to try and find the title deeds.

Before leaving Aden on 16 July, the bishop was taken on a tour of the former Anglican church in Crater which had been used as a CID headquarters during the Marxist regime. During his visit he felt most uncomfortable. "I don't really want this one back; there are too many bad vibes."[27] He then had another look at the former Christ Church at Steamer Point (Tawahi) and found this to be a much better proposition. Although it was very dilapidated and restoration would cost a large sum, the bishop felt that it would be worth the effort to have a presence in Yemen once again, especially in Aden. Between 7 and 14 December 1992, when he returned for more negotiations, violence erupted in Sana'a, Hodeidah and Aden.

"There was plenty of gunfire and I was pleased to be in a 4-WD vehicle that could, if necessary, do U-turns over central reservations, Beirut-fashion. All this reminded me of my days in Jerusalem and Amman in the nineteen-fifties."[28]

Undeterred, the bishop had an excellent meeting with Dr Iriyani, the foreign minister. The tireless work of the British ambassador also enabled him to consolidate his position with commercial interests, especially Yemen Hunt oil company, Nabors drilling company, and Canadian Occidental, all of whom were likely to assist in the restoration work at Christ Church in Aden. The critical hurdle remained: permission to proceed was still anxiously awaited.

In Kuwait, the Remembrance Day Service on 11 November 1992 at St Paul Ahmadi had been an especially moving occasion. After the Gulf War, Mrs Colleen Williams had written to the British Ambassador to suggest raising funds in memory of the forty-seven British military personnel who had lost their lives during the invasion, occupation and liberation of the country. And so it was that the next of kin were present at the service as guests of the Kuwaiti government and the Gulf War Memorial Fund committee. The bishop dedicated a memorial plaque. General Sir Peter de la Billière read the names inscribed on it, and the families laid poppy wreaths at its base.

In Cyprus, the idea to build a church complex in Kato Paphos had been abandoned. During 1992 the bishop had approved the official formation of the Anglican Chaplaincy of Paphos. As he had urged in April 1990, funding was now available to pay the stipend of a full-time priest. The Reverend Canon Derek Gibbs was appointed and in December 1992 he was installed as the new chaplaincy's first incumbent.

After the disruptions of war, the diocese was now able to function more easily. Long-standing constraints in some chaplaincies remained unresolved, such as in Iraq, Qatar and the Yemen. Only time would answer the rhetorical question: for how long would peaceful conditions prevail in the Middle East?

Chapter 13

EVOLUTION

1993 - 1999

During the next seven years, an eclectic mix of opportunities defined the Diocese of Cyprus and the Gulf's expanding ministry and mission. Inevitably, some were easier to realise than others, and not all reached their full potential during that period. More than once setbacks stalled progress. Yet, when the twentieth century drew to a close, a number of significant new and inspired achievements had been woven into the diocese's narrative.

On 20 April 1993, the Grand Mufti of Yemen issued a fatwa, in writing, stating that Christ Church in Tawahi, Steamer Point, Aden, was restored to the Diocese of Cyprus and the Gulf. A quarter of a century had passed since the church had been used as a place of worship.

Christ Church in Aden, prior to restoration
Diocese of Cyprus & the Gulf archive

The bishop, with others in the diocese, created a plan to divide the building: half to be retained as a church, and half to be converted into a hostel for church workers working in the hinterland of Yemen, and where seafarers visiting the port could rest. It was hoped also to build a clinic in the grounds to serve the Adeni community, and to construct accommodation for medical staff. But first, planning permission was required. Those in decision-making positions were keen to help and orally agreed, but they were reluctant to provide written consent. With frustration, the bishop, Tom and Edna Hamblin, and others, had to wait until 1994 before receiving the go-ahead, in writing.

Meanwhile, in Cyprus, celebrations were held at St Paul's Cathedral in Nicosia. Firstly, 21 March 1993 was commemorated as the day on which, one century earlier, the cornerstone of the original St Paul's church was laid on the new site by Lady Sendall, wife of the then British High Commissioner. Moreover, in the autumn Her Majesty Queen Elizabeth II, Head of the Commonwealth, was in Cyprus to attend the Commonwealth of Nations Heads of Government conference.

19 October 1993: Bishop John Brown and HM Queen Elizabeth II
in the grounds of St Paul's Cathedral, Nicosia
Source: personal collection of Richard Brown, reproduced with permission

Her itinerary included a visit to the cathedral, during which on 19 October 1993 she marked its centenary year by unveiling and dedicating a memorial plaque.

The lives of Bill and Edith Schwartz, formerly of St Barnabas Limassol and since 1989 worshipping at St Paul's cathedral in Nicosia, took a new turn in 1993. Bill had undergone a period of discernment and training for ordained ministry. On 16 February he was deaconed by Bishop Brown at St Helena's in Larnaca, and on 2 August he was priested at All Hallows by the Tower in London, coinciding with the annual reunion of the Friends of the Diocese of Cyprus and the Gulf.

The Very Reverend and Venerable Dr Bill Schwartz, and his wife Edith,
at St Christopher's Cathedral in 2019
Personal collection, reproduced with permission

Another new development in their lives also began during the winter of 1993. They, together with two long-standing friends Jonathan and Lynda Warner - teachers at the Eastern Mediterranean University in Famagusta - found a way to restart regular worship in the old town. (When the Turkish army arrived in July 1974, the Anglican church of St Mark in the southern suburb of Varosha became inaccessible. The church was later demolished and Varosha remains deserted.) Bill recalls that although Jonathan and Lynda were not Anglicans, they appreciated the importance of a recognised "Church" and so helped to form the new group. It first met in the UN peacekeepers' chapel inside the Austrian UN contingent's compound located on the south side of the Salamis road, between Sakarya and the EMU campus. The host was the chapel's priest, a Nigerian. Unfortunately, when his tenure ended there was no way to sustain the arrangement, so for a while the group met in a restaurant.

The form of worship was interdenominational with an Anglican format offered once or twice a month. Bill drove from Nicosia to conduct services. At that time he was a non-stipendiary priest and also Diocesan Treasurer and Secretary.[1] The Reverend Philip Blair, an Anglican priest in early retirement who taught English at EMU, was happy to lead the group's evening prayer on alternate weeks. In 1995 the Reverend Michael Stokes became the incumbent at St Andrew's in Kyrenia. He too shared the ministry in Famagusta, driving there once a month to celebrate the Eucharist. Bill describes the hazards:

> "The roads in northern Cyprus were tedious and after dark somewhat dangerous because of the careless drivers. The drive from Nicosia to Famagusta was unpleasant, and a bit more than an hour in duration including going through the checkpoint. The drive from Kyrenia to Famagusta was also about an hour, but the road through the mountains was much more problematic. Narrow, winding, and with limited signage, the trip was almost always an adventure. After dark it was safer to drive back to Nicosia, and then over the main pass north to Kyrenia, adding about a half-hour to the trip."[2]

In 1996, the university gave permission for Christian services to be held in its Cultural Centre, the mediaeval Nestorian church of St George the Foreigner which had been converted to stage the drama department's productions. This was the first time that public Christian worship had been permitted in Famagusta since 1974. The congregation met at 5 pm on Sunday evenings during university term times, and afterwards shared fellowship at the nearby Moonwalker café, owned by a member of the congregation. Jonathan Warner recounts that "the other members comprised EMU teachers, spouses and their children; students (including three of the four Albanian students); a Turkish Cypriot who had become a Christian later in life; sometimes holidaymakers;

and curious visitors from Kyrenia. … Polish Catholics shared the Peace with English Evangelicals. Despite our differences in tradition, we were able to unite around the Gospel of Jesus Christ, and to worship Him."[3]

When the congregation decided that it needed some kind of legal status, with the support of the Reverend Michael Stokes it became informally linked with St Andrew's in Kyrenia, but not as an official church plant. This arrangement also enabled it to follow the Anglican lectionary and so maintain consistency in preaching. A church council of five members,[4] chaired by Jonathan Warner, organised the group's worship programme, sometimes leading it themselves and sometimes inviting a speaker when a visiting priest was unavailable. Once a week, the Revered Philip Blair and his wife Joanne hosted Bible study at their apartment. In due course, the congregation adopted the name of St Mark in continuity with the former Anglican church.

During the same period, south of the Green Line, an embryonic chaplaincy was formed in the south-east of the island. Initially, the primary aim was to serve holidaymakers to the area, usually between late March and the end of November. Unofficially the new venture was called the Chaplaincy of Ayia Napa and Protaras, although it was not registered as such. For the first three years priests who provided ministry were not licensed by the bishop. Instead, a succession of non-stipendiary locum priests visited from the UK, offering their services under the supervision of the Anglican rural dean in Cyprus, the Very Reverend Patrick Blair, also the Provost of St Paul's Cathedral in Nicosia.

In late April 1993, the Reverend John Peters was the first to arrive from England on a locum basis, funded by the Intercontinental Church Society (ICS) based in London. He acquainted himself with the MECC centre at the old monastery in Ayia Napa, and met the rural dean. With arrangements thus made, on Sunday, 2 May 1993, Anglican morning worship began in the gatehouse chapel of the monastery. John Peters recorded in his journal that worshippers were from various European countries, including many Irish Roman Catholics who asked first if the service was Catholic. Even when told that it was Anglican, they stayed for the first half. In Protaras the first service took place on 27 June, in the Sea View Conference Room at the Sunrise Beach Hotel.

The chaplain's journal entry for that day: "Congregation entirely comprised of Irish RCs! Still, all received Communion, and very grateful for the ministry offered."[5]

During his three-month stay in Cyprus, John Peters tirelessly promoted the new chaplaincy's services. He visited local hotels and holiday apartments, introduced himself to their managers and pinned up advertisement posters in the lobbies. Every Sunday morning the chaplain broadcast a three-minute "Pause for Thought" on Napa Radio. His immediate successors were George Jennings and Ian Watts who, during their equally short stays in Cyprus, energetically continued this pattern of worship and associated publicity.

At first, the "vicarage" was a small apartment at one end of Ayia Napa. Within a year, a larger apartment was rented some six miles/ten kilometres away, well sited in what the Rural Dean called "the Protaras tourist strip". This allowed the priest to have closer contact with visitors to the area and so increased numbers at the evening services at the Sunrise Beach Hotel. A small car was purchased for the chaplaincy, made possible by a special grant from the ICS. The Reverend Douglas Gibson served as a locum between March and April 1994. One week after arriving he wrote in the chaplain's journal: "Have contacted 66 hotels with posters, only 134 to go!"[6]

Nationals from Germany, Holland, Scandinavia and Switzerland often outnumbered British and Irish who attended worship, and so those familiar with Anglican liturgy were in the minority. From time to time Farsi-speaking Iranian Christians were present. Even when no translator was available they were pleased to be part of the congregation.

Continuity in the provision of ministry was the main issue. The Rural Dean in Cyprus remarked in his report for that year: "It would make a great difference to have chaplains staying longer, but they will be difficult to find as we cannot offer any stipend, and so rely on those who are pensioners or otherwise able to support themselves."[7] Fortunately, the ICS was able to continue with its financial support, at least for the time being. During the next few years, retired clergy living in the Diocese of Exeter provided locum ministry too.

On 1 June 1996, the Reverend Stuart Roger Broughton became the first locum chaplain in Ayia Napa and Protaras to be licensed by the bishop. This now allowed him to conduct marriages. On 28 July he was also granted permission by the bishop to minister anywhere in the diocese. While important in themselves, these legalities were in anticipation of the Rural Dean's retirement. The Very Reverend Patrick Blair and his wife Gillian left Cyprus on 30 September 1996. The bishop chose not to appoint a new Rural Dean in Cyprus. (At that time, the sole archdeacon in the diocese resided in Abu Dhabi.)

By now expatriate residents in south-east Cyprus had increased in numbers, including in Deryneia and Paralimni. This created demand for Anglican services to continue throughout the winter season at Ayia Napa monastery, which they did for the first time in 1997.

Ayia Napa monastery
Copyright: JPPhotography, Cyprus

Meanwhile, two contrasting developments had taken place in the diocese, the first also in Cyprus. On 15 February 1994, an application was submitted to register the Jerusalem and Middle East Trust (Cyprus) as a charity trust on the island. Just over a year later on 31 March 1995, the registration formalities were complete.

The background to this had begun twenty-one years earlier when, on 2 March 1973 in London, the Declaration of Trust to form the Jerusalem and the East Mission Trust (Cyprus) was signed and sealed by Sydney Charles Crowther-Smith, notary public. Ten days later on 12 March 1973, also in London, the managing trustees of the JEMT (Cyprus) met for the first time. The registration of the charity trust in Cyprus in 1995 meant that, more conveniently, a board of trustees who lived on the island became primarily responsible for the management of Anglican church property throughout Cyprus, though it continued to be owned by the Jerusalem and the East Mission Trust Limited registered in the United Kingdom.[8]

In Bahrain during October 1994, the Reverend Roy Topping departed after five-and-a-half years' service as the Seafarers Welfare Representative for the Bahrain International Seafarers Society (BISS). Having served as a Reader in the Bahrain chaplaincy, he had been deaconed at St Christopher's Cathedral by Bishop Brown on 4 October 1992, and on 1 August 1993 priested at St Michael Paternoster Royal in London. In the words of Michael J Borner, Chairman of BISS: "Roy has been through some turbulent times during his tour with BISS but always could be relied upon to give generous support and caring understanding to the seamen and their manifold problems. This service was recognised with his award of an MBE for outstanding performance during the Gulf War and his selection for the Missions to Seamen President's Award, presented to Roy by HRH the Princess Royal."[9]

This chronicle of events now reverts to the unfolding story at Christ Church in Aden. Repairs to the windows and pillars began in October 1993, completed in February 1994. By March 1994 planning consent had been received in writing so that the British building contractor, John Spracklen, could divide the church interior to create new facilities in one half of the property; and build a clinic and accommodation for medical staff in its grounds. Those in government departments whom the bishop visited were pleased with progress, and the locals in Aden expressed delight that the "English church" was making a comeback.

The roof repairs were completed on 1 May 1994. Then on 4 May a new drama began. For the next two months, ending on 7 July, a civil war was waged between pro-union forces in the north and socialist dissident separatists in the south. One outcome was another catastrophe for Christ Church. Vandals and lawless gangs looted and desecrated the church. Tom and Edna Hamblin lost many personal possessions when the church house was entered and burgled. The bishop wrote in his journal:

> "Of course, the army was far too strong for the rebels, and most of the Aden officials, with whom I have built up such good rapport, have fled or been killed. Aden airport is in a mess. John Spracklen's house, along with many others, has been ransacked and he and his wife have lost most of their personal possessions. … His building yard with the vehicles has been looted. All the work already completed on Christ Church has been destroyed, and much material stolen. I am determined that this setback will not destroy the vision I have long had for the re-establishment of Anglican work in Aden. There is no question of compensation for losses in a situation like this, we have to re-assess everything."[10]

295

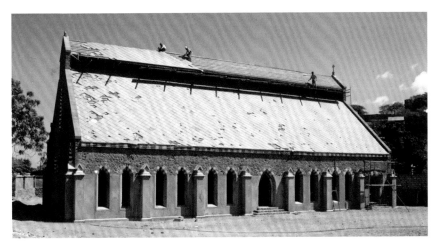

Christ Church during restoration in 1994, view from the south
Source: Merrill Morrow collection, Diocese of Cyprus & the Gulf archive

Bishop Brown and John Spracklen agreed that, given proper permission, they would concentrate on building the clinic and convert the back part of the church into accommodation for medical staff. They would restore the church later. Their view was that if the local authorities saw that they were committed to help the local poor Adeni community, who had minimal health facilities, then they would be more sympathetic to specific church requirements later on. Already the bishop had in mind agencies in Holland and Germany who were interested in sending medical supplies to Aden, including all that would be required by ante-natal and post-natal clinics. He did not think that it would be difficult to obtain medical staff. That said, the situation was a great disappointment to him personally: "I shall retire next summer and I had hoped that this project would have been completed, ready for me to dedicate it all before leaving. Never mind, the important thing is to get it moving as quickly as possible, and my successor can finish it off."[11]

Tom and Edna Hamblin
Diocese of Cyprus & the Gulf archive

In late August 1994 Tom and Edna Hamblin returned to Aden, not only to oversee building work, but also to restore Anglican worship in the city and so try to rebuild a new congregation. They promised to stay until the end of November that year when their deferred obligations in the Far East and New Zealand would call them away.

The bishop and Tom met with the new authorities in Aden, especially with those in the Religious Affairs department, and Tom had a meeting with the new governor. All were keen that the clinic building work should go ahead. Bishop Brown believed that as long as there was peace in the country, this need not be hindered further. Of course, funds were badly needed. The diocese had already spent US$150,000 on the project. During the civil war US$90,000 worth of that investment had been lost.

On 9 January 1995, the bishop wrote in his journal: "So my final year as Bishop of Cyprus and the Gulf begins. There is much to do, but I am not desperate to complete any particular project, especially since it definitely will be impossible to complete the Aden work."[12] During his final Diocesan Synod later that month, he remarked that the work in Aden "has given us, as a diocese, the opportunity to do something we are usually not in a position to do: that is, serve the local indigenous community."[13] Increasing goodwill was being shown to the diocese by member churches within the Anglican Communion and other agencies, including CMS, the Anglican Consultative Council, ECUSA, the Diocese of the Rio Grande, JMECA and, gratifyingly, by the rest of the province of the Episcopal Church in Jerusalem and the Middle East.

To progress work in Aden, the bishop had made a strategic plan. On 9 June 1995 in Oman, he priested the Reverend James (Jim) Wakerley at the church of The Good Shepherd in Ghala, and almost immediately licensed him to serve as the chaplain at Christ Church in Aden. In addition he was to have oversight of all the development work. The fact that Jim had been the administrator of the hospital in Sharjah, and more recently the chaplaincy administrator in Oman, gave the bishop confidence that the new chaplain had all the right skills for the job.

The clinic buildings were soon completed, ready to receive the medical equipment and supplies from Holland. Bishop Brown admitted that they could have been ready much earlier, in spite of the civil war, if he had been prepared to pay bribes. This he had refused to do. The same applied to medicines which he insisted should be imported duty free as they were to be used to treat Adeni people. Although he was sure that paying bribes, or permitting some of the medicines to be siphoned off, would create no problem, "we must resist this, and that means getting the government people to agree in writing that we can have medicine duty free. Getting anything in writing is always the problem here, and my guess is that it will be another year of hard graft by Jim Wakerley before we get close to opening the clinic properly."[14] His prediction was accurate.

On 26 July 1995 Bishop Brown left Cyprus for the last time. Five days later, on 31 July at All Hallows by the Tower in London, during the annual reunion of the Friends of the Diocese of Cyprus and the Gulf, the bishop priested the Reverend Peter Sewell. This was a memorable way formally to mark the end of his energetic episcopate.

The Vacancy-in-See committee was already hard at work, mindful that this was the first time the process of searching and consulting in the selection of the diocesan bishop was being conducted from within the diocese. The Archbishop of Canterbury was not directly involved. Instead, Archdeacon Michael Mansbridge led the process with his customary charm and wisdom. The committee received thirty-two nominations from all over the world. This was viewed as a tribute to Bishop Brown as more people now knew about Cyprus and the Gulf than in 1986. The committee selected the Right Reverend Clive Handford, Bishop of Warwick. He and his wife Jane were already well known to many in the diocese of Cyprus and the Gulf. As described in earlier chapters, between 1978 and 1983 Bishop Handford had preceded Michael Mansbridge as Archdeacon in the Gulf and chaplain of St Andrew in Abu Dhabi. Prior to that, for five years he had served as Dean of St George's Cathedral in Jerusalem, and briefly during 1967, until the Six-Day War intervened, he was chaplain at St George's church in Baghdad.

On 31 May 1996, at St Paul's Cathedral in Nicosia, the Right Reverend Clive Handford was enthroned as the fourth Bishop in Cyprus and the Gulf. "The cathedral was full to overflowing, with representatives from other Christian communities, including the Orthodox, Catholic, Maronite, Armenian and several Protestant groups, as well as national and community leaders. Among the highlights of the memorable service was the unexpected presentation by the Greek Orthodox Archbishop Chrysostomos of a beautiful pectoral cross to Bishop Clive, followed by the archbishop walking down the aisle arm-in-arm with our own President Bishop, the Most Reverend Samir Kafity from [the Diocese of] Jerusalem, a sight which was not missed by the local TV cameras!"[15] A few days later on 9 June 1996 Bishop Handford was enthroned in St Christopher's Cathedral, Bahrain. A new era in the diocese's life had formally begun.

At All Hallows in London on 20 November 1996, at a meeting of the Diocese of Cyprus and the Gulf Endowment Fund (known as the Foundation), it was announced that the Appeal Fund had exceeded £400,000. This figure was before the deduction of £10,000 which the trustees made as a twice-yearly contribution to the diocesan budget based on interest accrued. The bulk of the capital had been donated from the companion link Diocese of the Rio Grande and the Diocese of Cyprus and the Gulf itself. It was realised that unless another major appeal were to be made, the fund would not grow substantially in the future. At the Diocesan Synod in 1997, the Reverend Bill Schwartz reported that of those funds, US$50,000 had been transferred to Aden to complete the cost of building the clinic.

Meantime in 1996 the major thrust of prayer and effort had been the licensing of the clinic and the registration of the doctors. Jim Wakerley enthusiastically recorded:

"It is not possible to adequately express our thanks to all who have assisted in such a variety of ways to enable the Ras Morbat Clinic of Christ Church to become a legal entity. In Aden how grateful we are for the willing support of the Governor, the British Vice-consul, the Director and his deputy of the Ministry of Public Health and many others from various government departments and the local community. The person who put in the most leg work was our faithful PR Officer, Mansour Khan. For thirteen months we lived with the expectancy that the licence would come any day. The licence was issued on 9 September 1996. The registrations of our doctors soon followed. The opening day was 12 October 1996, a very special day for those associated with the chaplaincy."[16]

On that day Dr Harry Robertson arrived for a six-week visit. He was still remembered by many families in Aden, having previously practised from 1956 to 1963 at the Keith-Falconer Memorial Hospital in Sheikh Othman, a city district within the Aden Governorate. Dr Robertson proved to be a great help to Dr Malcolm Dunjey the inaugural medical director of the Ras Morbat Clinic, and to Thea Groeneveld the midwife. By the end of the first week, patients were queuing outside the gate at six o'clock in the morning ready for the clinic to open at eight.

Patients attending Ras Morbat Clinic
Diocese of Cyprus & the Gulf archive

Jim Wakerley told synod members that "although the clinic had occupied so much of our praying, giving, thinking, effort and dreaming, it must be recognised that this is by no means the total vision for Christ Church. There is our Community Centre. The size of the main church had allowed the building to be divided in half".[17]

The back of the original church now had a mezzanine floor which provided some accommodation and a large lounge upstairs. A church hall, kitchen, store and office were downstairs. Jim was also very grateful to the Reverend Dennis Gurney and friends in the chaplaincy of Dubai and Sharjah for their financial support and the provision they had made toward furnishings.

Of course, Christ Church itself was at the heart of all this activity. With joy, on 13 December 1996 Holy Communion was celebrated in the church after a break of twenty-six years. It was an emotional watershed, a time for thanksgiving but also cause to remember that the chaplaincy's ministry went far beyond liturgical services. In November 1996, the chaplain had been assigned a port pass, encouraged by the port commander who wished the chaplain to be freely able to visit seafarers on board the ships and offer ministry. Jim and Carol Wakerley were also working energetically among the many refugees staying in Yemen, and discovering new opportunities among expatriate groups in Sana'a, Taiz, Jibla, Saada. All of them had asked the chaplain to visit periodically to perform services.

10 October 1997, rededication of Christ Church, Aden
Left to right: Tom Hamblin, the Reverend Jim Wakerley,
Bishop Clive Handford, Archdeacon Michael Mansbridge
Diocese of Cyprus & the Gulf archive

With more rejoicing on 10 October 1997, Bishop Handford rededicated Christ Church, blessed the new hostel and other facilities in the compound, and officially opened the Ras Morbat Clinic. Bishop Brown will have proudly received news that, indeed, his successor had "finished off" the job he had begun.

The peninsula of Qatar projects north from the Arabian mainland into the Gulf. It is approximately 100 miles/160 kilometres in length. Its breadth varies, the average distance being about 45 miles/72 kilometres. Oil and gas dominate all economic activities in Qatar. The North Field is the largest single concentration of natural gas on earth. Like her sister Gulf states, Qatar depends heavily on an expatriate labour force. In 1996, the total population was just less than half a million, locals being outnumbered four to one by expatriates drawn mainly from the West, Asia and other Arab states, especially Egypt. The country's international sporting events were attracting world famous players and athletes. The new grass golf course was operational, ready to host the Masters tournament in 1997. The International Sailing Regatta was also drawing competitors from around the world. During 1996 several more US companies arrived in Qatar where the Amir, HH Shaikh Hamad bin Khalifa Al Thani, was slowly continuing to open the country. But there were restrictions. The Reverend Canon Ian Young explained:

> "It was especially noticed last year [1996] when Christmas trees and all reference to Christmas were ordered to be removed from shops and hotels. Church activities are being observed closely. … Church buildings are forbidden in Qatar, and the meeting of Christians for worship is not officially sanctioned, but we continue to pray that one day we may be given permission to erect a building for worship. However, Anglican services have been held regularly here since western expatriates came to work in the oil industry in the early 1950s and we remind ourselves that the Church is people and not simply a building so this lack of our own building does not deter us from worshipping the Lord."[18]

Most certainly, it did not. The main service was held on Sunday evenings in the Doha English Speaking School, made possible by the friendly support and cooperation of the headmaster. A Friday morning service, introduced during 1997, soon proved to be particularly popular with families. Sunday morning Eucharist and other worship events took place at the church house where the chaplain lived and had his office. Monthly Eucharists were held in Dukhan, the oil town situated about 50 miles/80 kilometres west of Doha on the west coast of the peninsula. Also during 1997 a new centre for worship was established at the home of Richard and Ann Harwood in the town of al Khor, a settlement in the north-east of the peninsula where many expatriate workers involved in the Ras Laffan gas project were housed. Canon Ian Young hoped that as more people were moved to this outpost, it would become a new growth point within the parish. The Sunday School was expanding and flourishing, led by Pamela Shield, among others. She was licensed as a Reader in April 1997.

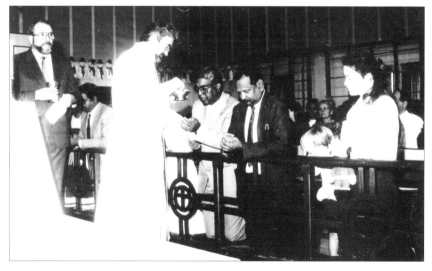

Holy Communion at the Doha English Speaking School,
celebrated by the Reverend Canon Ian Young
Diocese of Cyprus & the Gulf archive

In his report for the year, the chaplain recorded that the Anglican Church would find great difficulty in functioning in Qatar without the support of the wider community. Added to the facilities offered by the Doha English Speaking School, the British Embassy continued to sponsor the chaplain and support the parish in so many ways, as did the General Manager of the Ramada Hotel, numerous banks, British Aerospace and other commercial enterprises. The parish had come a long way since the 1950s when, almost alone, the Reverend Kenneth Jenkins had pioneered Anglican ministry in Qatar, spending much of his time living out of a suitcase as he journeyed from place to place in Qatar, in Abu Dhabi and beyond.

Nestling between the west of the Qatar peninsula and the east coast of Saudi Arabia lies the archipelago of Bahrain. The land area of the two largest islands is sometimes compared in overall size to that of the city-state of Singapore. By the mid-1990s, Bahrain's thriving economy was based on a diverse mix of oil, gas, aluminium and other industries, with the capital Manama host to international banking, insurance, hotel and restaurant sectors. Throughout the country, the retail phenomenon of shopping malls was booming, and more besides. As elsewhere in the Arabian Gulf nations, all this industrial and commercial activity boosted their economies. But there was, and remains, a dark side. In many Gulf countries, the high cost of living can cause debt and poverty among lower-income employees, local and expatriate, and migrant workers especially may in some instances be exploited by, for example, the withholding or non-payment of wages.

During the mid-1990s a group of Christian leaders in Bahrain - Anglican, Roman Catholic and Evangelical - thought about how they might help to relieve this situation and so came up with the idea of forming the Ecumenical Conference of Charity (ECC). Spearheaded by the Very Reverend Derek Taylor, the ECC was established in October 1996 as part of the social programme of St Christopher's Cathedral.

The founding documents, titled *Serving Together*, run to eighteen pages. The theme throughout is Christian Vocation of Service. The constitution and by-laws describe its function: to model a vision for the faith communities by challenging them to reflect in their own behaviour the mission of Jesus who cared for those who cannot help themselves; to actively help the poor through works of charity; through prayer and good works, to strive to meet the immediate needs of the poor but also to reduce or eliminate the cause of poverty; to be involved with special issues or pastoral needs which have broader ramifications, such as visits to those in hospitals and prisons, and facilitating repatriation. Membership is open to all Christian groups in Bahrain. Now, more than twenty years since its foundation, the work of the ECC remains as much in demand today as it did in 1996, still under the auspices of St Christopher's Cathedral.[19]

Similar problems are pervasive elsewhere in the Arabian Gulf region. Over the years Anglican chaplaincies have extended their programmes of social care in other ways, such as ministry in expatriate labour camps, particularly in the UAE. By the mid-1990s the Reverend Dennis Gurney, then senior chaplain of the Chaplaincy of Dubai and Sharjah with the Northern Emirates, had identified another problem:

> "Newcomers to the Emirates and our friends in Cyprus may wonder why the chaplaincy should involve itself so deeply in providing accommodation for so many different congregations to use some of our facilities every week.

> "In Dubai there are three legal appointed places for Christian worship: St Thomas, the Indian Orthodox Church; St Mary's, the Roman Catholic Church; and Holy Trinity, Anglican and allied churches. The Indian Orthodox and Roman Catholic churches will not allow any other Christian denominations to use their facilities. It is against the law, and a punishable offence, to hold regular Christian worship in places which are not authorised. In view of this, the Chaplaincy Council has had as a priority the provision of suitable and adequate facilities for Christians to worship in their own languages and according to their own tradition."[20]

Dennis Gurney called this a ministry of hospitality. While this was undoubtedly true, it required huge capital investment. Undaunted, he motivated others to help him pursue his mission.

On 4 October 1996, at Holy Trinity in Dubai, Bishop Clive Handford dedicated a new three-storey Community Hall able to seat twelve hundred on each of the three floors, therefore able to cope with fifteen thousand Christians who attended the Anglican Church compound each week. The bishop also dedicated the new Chaplaincy House, the caretaker's accommodation and two apartments. Dennis Gurney wrote: "This is part of the chaplaincy council's continuing determination to provide a secure, safe and legal place for as many Christians as possible to worship, have fellowship and be trained for Christian service."[21]

The Community Hall was brought into full use during March 1997 after mains electricity was eventually arranged. The latest development on the compound was a two-storey building housing a Christian Resource Centre, coffee bar and chaplaincy offices on the ground floor, and a spacious hall to accommodate over two hundred people on the first floor. This building was completed during August 1997.

In Sharjah, construction of the new church of St Martin had been constantly delayed. By January 1997 the final building permit had been granted. Work was expected to start very soon, and indeed it did. On 26 October that year, the bishop dedicated the new church. Dennis Gurney, with his usual exuberance, described the facilities as "magnificent, beautiful and supremely practical, and with five separate worship areas [they] will enable the chaplaincy to provide secure, safe and legal places for many other Christian fellowships".[22] Bishop Handford observed that the main chapel on the ground floor was large enough to hold approximately five hundred people, and there must have been at least that many on 26 October. It was a joyous occasion and everyone was impressed with the speed with which the building had been completed, eight months only. Upstairs, three small halls were designed to enable many other Christian fellowship groups to meet.

Meanwhile, on 22 June 1997, a new St Luke's Worship Centre began operating in the northern emirate of Ras al Khaimah. Although located on a large site, it offered only limited accommodation in buildings which were formerly a club. But in the chaplain's assessment, the site had great potential for development.

At St Christopher's Cathedral compound in Bahrain, a large building project was well under way. Over a period of several years and despite considerable renovation, the almost forty-year old church hall had reached the end of its useful life. After seeking expert opinion, the council decided in May 1996 to proceed with building a new complex and launched an appeal, led by the Provost, the Very Reverend Derek Taylor. Then some parishioners challenged the wisdom of spending so much money, projected to be almost one hundred thousand dinars. The project was put on hold. On 6 April 1997 Fr Derek Taylor retired, disappointed that the project had not started during his time in Bahrain.

In May 1997 a second vote was called for in the council on whether to renovate or to rebuild. The motion was passed 9-6 to ratify the rebuilding decision. The six dissenting members submitted their resignations in a joint letter, received by the council at its meeting on 30 June and forwarded to the bishop. Planning permission for the proposed community centre was obtained. The Very Reverend Keith Johnson, installed as the new provost on 8 October 1997, oversaw the building project's progress. In December, the church hall was demolished and in the New Year construction work began. On 1 October 1998, St Christopher's Community Centre was officially opened by the Assistant Under-Secretary for Social Affairs, Mr Sadiq Al Shehabi, and HE Ian Lewty, the British Ambassador. The inauguration, also attended by corporate sponsors and community representatives, was followed by a service of thanksgiving and dedication in the cathedral. The six dissenting church members had accepted the offer to be co-opted back onto the council. Harmony had been restored.

The complex comprises two meeting halls. The largest is dedicated to Canon Alun Morris, the second chaplain to serve at St Christopher's (1954-1964), and the founding father of St Christopher's School. The other hall serves as a coffee room and offers worship space for small Christian groups. The entire community centre, a third larger than the former building, is now used seven days a week for worship by many Christian groups who otherwise would have no legal place to meet, and on special occasions the centre provides facilities for other functions. Today, it is hard to visualise that the project's worth was ever in doubt.

307

In May 1997, the congregation of St Andrew in Abu Dhabi said goodbye to their chaplain, the Venerable Michael Mansbridge and his wife Fiona, after serving in the emirate for fourteen years. In addition to his ministry as chaplain in Abu Dhabi, Michael Mansbridge had been Archdeacon in the Gulf (1983-1990), and then in 1991 was appointed as archdeacon of the entire diocese. That position he still held, the difference now was that on 25 May 1997, at St Paul's Cathedral in Nicosia, Bishop Clive Handford collated and installed him as Provost. Instead of taking the title The Very Reverend, the Venerable Michael Mansbridge chose to retain that title.

25 May 1997, after the installation of the new Provost at St Paul's Cathedral, Nicosia
Left to right: the Reverend Canon Ian Young, Mrs Fiona Mansbridge,
Provost and Archdeacon Michael Mansbridge, Bishop Clive Handford, Mrs Jane Handford
Diocese of Cyprus & the Gulf archive

While this was a new beginning, there was closure in another respect. The diocesan companion link with the Diocese of the Rio Grande had run its course. The bishop reported to the 1999 Diocesan Synod that he had in mind the possibility of a link with an African diocese, an idea to be explored. For now, he had a more pressing concern, his frustration with the situation at St George's church in Baghdad. Although it had been vandalised, the building was thought to be structurally sound. A caretaker had been appointed to clean up the grounds and buildings and so show to the authorities that the diocese was still concerned about the property. The problem was that since December 1973, following the expulsion from Iraq of the Reverend Geoffrey Colin Davies, the Baghdad chaplaincy had been effectively in abeyance. Gaining permission for clergy to visit Iraq was difficult.

A breakthrough occurred in March 1999 when the Reverend Canon Andrew White, Director of International Ministry at Coventry Cathedral in England, was invited to visit Baghdad. With Bishop Handford's blessing he did so. Reporting back, Canon White spoke of the invitation from the Iraqi authorities for a group of churchmen to visit the city. A few weeks later the bishop, Canon Ian Young and five persons from the Church of England travelled to Iraq where they met senior government officials. They also saw something of the appalling suffering being endured by ordinary Iraqi people, raising acute questions about the wisdom and morality of applying indiscriminate sanctions.

309

When they arrived at St George's church they faced a depressing sight. There were no doors. All the furniture had been removed except for the base of the altar which was still intact. The font was standing by the door. With everyone helping, they were able to manhandle it back into its proper position. The caretaker, a member of the Chaldean Catholic Church, was living in the church hall with his wife and baby daughter. He explained that each Sunday he lit candles on what remained of the altar, and each evening he lit candles elsewhere to provide light in the church. Twice a day he played church music as loud as he could, feeling that by doing all this he was letting the local people know that the church was still in business. He had also developed good relations with the residents around the church, and with the security guards in the government offices nearby. Contractors had been called in to survey the building and basic repairs had been made to make it weatherproof and birdproof. On the Sunday morning before the bishop and his party left, he celebrated the Eucharist with a mixed group of about fifteen people. He later wrote:

"It was a very special occasion, not least for me since I had last celebrated the Eucharist at St George's Baghdad thirty-two years ago. It does seem possible that the church could be restored. That needs further thought and discussion with the relevant authorities in Baghdad to ensure that we would have some measure of security and assurance that we would be able to continue to use the church. There is no Anglican community there at present, nor one that would associate themselves with us. In the extremely depressed state of the country, there are very, very few foreigners at all. However, when sanctions are at least partially lifted there are very clearly commercial interests in the West and elsewhere who are just waiting to get in. There will then be a community to minister to, and I hope the church can be ready for that ministry. We shall have to proceed very sensitively in anything that we do with the restoration of the church, but I believe that is something which, now, we ought to seriously contemplate. ... I was able to get an assurance that I would be able to go back to Iraq whenever I wished, and I hope to test out that promise later in the year."[23]

On 31 August 1999 the Venerable Michael Mansbridge retired. In recognition of his outstanding service to the diocese, the bishop granted him the title Archdeacon Emeritus, and the title Canon Emeritus of both St Paul's Cathedral in Nicosia and St Christopher's Cathedral in Bahrain. On 7 November 1999, the Venerable Ian Young was collated as Archdeacon in Cyprus and the Gulf. He remained the chaplain in Qatar. The new provost at St Paul's Cathedral, the Very Reverend John Morley, was installed on 19 December. When the year 1999 ended the diocese had immeasurable cause to reflect on its journey so far with thanksgiving.

Chapter 14

STEADFAST THROUGH STIRRING TIMES

2000 - 2007

In anticipation of the year 2000, known as Y2K, many people feared that computer programs storing year values as two-digit figures, such as 99, would cause catastrophic failures. Commercial aircraft could be grounded. Banking systems, medical services and electricity supplies might fail, and so on. An extreme vision was that the turn of the century would cue apocalyptic upheaval on earth and throughout the universe. When 1 January 2000 arrived, none of the predicted calamities occurred.

This is not to say that transition to the new decade was without challenges. Divergence within the province of the Episcopal Church in Jerusalem and the Middle East was one example. The Diocese of Jerusalem had provoked ardent debate by proposing a scheme to re-establish an archbishopric in Jerusalem.[1] The other three dioceses in the province - Cyprus and the Gulf, Egypt and North Africa, and Iran - had resisted the proposal, content that the structure which had existed for more than twenty-four years had, by and large, served well, and could continue to do so. A motion to support this opinion had been proposed at the 1999 Diocesan Synod of Cyprus and the Gulf, and carried unanimously. But this was only one of the four possible diocesan voices, and not the end of the matter.

On face value, it might be asked: how did this debate relate to the Diocese of Cyprus and the Gulf? It will be recalled that the composition of the Episcopal Church in Jerusalem and the Middle East had been agreed in 1973 whereby a minimum of four dioceses was required (see page 148 of this book). These were to be: a reconfigured Diocese of Jerusalem, to include Palestine, Israel, Jordan, Lebanon and Syria; a revived Diocese of Egypt and North Africa to include Egypt, with

Algeria, Libya, Tunisia, Ethiopia, Somalia and Eritrea; the existing Diocese of Iran; and a new Diocese of Cyprus and the Gulf. This structure was codified in a new constitution and implemented with the inauguration of the new province on 6 January 1976. Should the Diocese of Jerusalem secede from this union, constitutional discord would be one inevitable outcome.

On 1 February 2000, the provincial Central Synod met at the Lordos Beach Hotel in Larnaca. Debate was divisive. On 8 February, the Diocesan Synod of Cyprus and the Gulf convened at the same hotel. Bishop Handford's impassioned remarks about the future of the province were unambiguous:

> "Friends, we came very close last week to its break-up. There were two or three points where we stood on that abyss. … I pray God we do not come to that, but we may. We must be prepared for the possibility while not at this time seeking it. … We must hang in there for the sake of many of our brothers and sisters who feel the pain much more than we do. …

> "There came to my mind, at the end of those meetings, words from the English mystical poet, William Blake, who in his *Songs of Innocence* wrote: 'Man was made for joy and woe, and when this we rightly know, through the world we safely go. Joy and woe are woven fine, a clothing for the soul divine.'[2] Who knows how, in the economy and the grace of God, joy and woe are being finely woven this past week in our province. I feel this, because I have been tied up with this Church for more than thirty years and have worked very much for this province. I cannot convey to you, I wish I could … the eager anticipation with which during last week I looked forward to this synod, because this diocese is joy. … Thank you for your support in words and in prayer for what we have been going through this past week, and what I guess we will go through."[3]

The Central Synod next met on 16 May 2000, this time in Cairo. After prolonged discussion it was agreed that a commission should be established to examine the future of the province. Cyprus and the

Gulf's representatives were Archdeacon Ian Young, and Ralph Williams who, being resident in Paphos and previously in Kuwait, had some knowledge of both archdeaconries. The commission first met on 13 December 2000. Surprisingly, the Bishop in Jerusalem said that it was "no longer his wish to press for the establishment of an archbishopric. … Nevertheless, the status of the Anglican Church in Jerusalem, and especially of its Bishop, in relation to the other Churches there, clearly remains a concern."[4] The commission persevered with its task.

The third millennium began on 1 January 2001. Four days later the Diocese of Cyprus and the Gulf celebrated the twenty-fifth anniversary of its formation on 5 January 1976. On that day, at St George's Cathedral in Jerusalem, the Right Reverend Leonard Ashton CB had been instituted as the new diocese's inaugural bishop. As events turned out, on 19 January 2001, two weeks after the silver jubilee of the diocese, Bishop Ashton died at the age of eighty-five. His funeral on 30 January, in the English town of Chesham where he was born and maintained a home throughout his adult life, happened to take place on the first day of the 2001 Diocesan Synod in Cyprus. In tribute to Bishop Ashton, Bishop Clive Handford told his audience:

> "We have much to celebrate and much for which to give thanks to God. When the diocese began, Bishop Leonard came as Assistant Bishop, finding his role not really understood and, in some quarters, scarcely welcomed. … It was a diocese set up without any resources or endowments, except the human resources within it, and a bishop of great faith and resilience, and great generosity because at the beginning he floated quite a bit of the diocese out of his own pocket."[5]

In Cyprus, he travelled around in a little Mini car appropriately purple in colour. His filing cabinet was a brown suitcase, and his office in Nicosia was whatever room he was able to live in, firstly in RAF quarters provided through his contacts, then at the Ledra Palace Hotel[6] and later in rented apartments.

313

"We have come a long way. ... What of the future? ... I would hope that we continue to remember that we are an Episcopal Anglican diocese. We have particular traditions, but we rejoice that people of other traditions come in and share fellowship and membership with us. If we are to serve the ecumenical cause of all the Churches we have to remember where we stand ... let us be true to our own tradition, remembering that if properly understood it is not something fixed and static but something dynamic, moving and developing. ... Let us not be ashamed in that, or we serve no one."[7]

For many years, the diocese's commitment to serving others had included assisting seafarers visiting ports in the diocese, or those stranded in them. Anglican chaplains in Larnaca, Limassol, Bahrain and in the UAE often ministered in a dual role: as a chaplain or assistant chaplain in a parish, and as a Missions to Seamen port chaplain. By the year 2000 it was felt that the charity's name was out of kilter with modern thinking, particularly a need to recognise gender equality. In July that year, after representations from the missions' chaplains and liaison bishops around the world, the charity's members voted to change the name to the Mission to Seafarers. On 4 April 2001 a service of blessing and rededication was held at Westminster Abbey in London, attended by the Mission to Seafarers President, HRH The Princess Royal.

The Reverend Canon Marvin Bamforth, Mission to Seafarers port chaplain in Limassol, 2007-2013; chaplain in Paphos, 1998-2006

Copyright: Angela Murray

The sanctuary at St Stephen's church, Stephanie village, near Tala
Copyright: Angela Murray

By now, two new initiatives were evolving in Cyprus. After much planning and prayer, the first church plant of the Anglican community in Paphos was inaugurated during a carol service on Christmas Eve 2000. The plant was intended as an outreach to the many English-speaking people who live in and around Stephanie village, a modern development between Paphos and the village of Tala. The rented premises were a taverna which had been converted for versatile use. The Reverend Marvin Bamforth, the Anglican chaplain in Paphos, recorded that nearly "one hundred folk gathered to celebrate and that the atmosphere was very special".[8] On 28 January 2001, the bishop dedicated the premises in the name of St Stephen and so "put the seal on what promised to be an exciting phase of local Anglican life".[9]

Before long a second church plant of the Paphos Anglican community was formed in Polis, a small town facing Chrysochous Bay on the north-west coast of Cyprus, and on the edge of the Akamas peninsula, a nature reserve. Jack Harding, who had lived in Cyprus for many years, was aware that a place of worship for the Christian migrant workers living in the Polis area was needed.

The Reverend Marvin Bamforth consulted with friends in the Greek Orthodox Church of Cyprus and permission was granted for Anglicans and Latin Catholics to share use of the little Greek Orthodox church of St Nicholas. In June 2001 a small group of Anglicans first met to worship in the church. Congregation members were mostly Sri Lankan, with one or two British residents, usually about ten in total. When Polis began to develop and the regular Anglican congregation swelled to about fifteen, the church of St Nicholas became too small. A vacant furniture store in nearby Prodromi was rented and suitably converted to be a church building. On 23 April 2006 Bishop Clive Handford dedicated the church in the name of St Luke.

3 November 2000 - Bishop Clive Handford prepares to lay the foundation stone for
Christ Church Jebel Ali, with the Reverend Canon Dennis Gurney (on the right)
Reproduced with permission of Christ Church

On 3 November 2000 in the emirate of Dubai, the bishop had laid the foundation stone for Christ Church in Jebel Ali (Hill of Ali[10]) in what was then relatively undeveloped desert south of Dubai itself. This was being built to serve the spiritual needs of those working or living in the rapidly expanding areas of the Jebel Ali Free Zone, Jebel Ali industrial area, Dubai Marina and Jumeira. When Bishop Handford consecrated Christ Church on 8 March 2002 he declared it as "a truly wonderful occasion with clergy representation from other Gulf chaplaincies, also from the Mar Thoma Church, the Church of Pakistan and the Church of South India". Some nine hundred people filled the church. Its interior design is a combination of light-coloured wood with alternating gold and blue stained-glass windows, creating a sense of spacious calm and peace. On 13 December 2002 the Reverend Jim Wakerley was licensed as the first chaplain of Christ Church Jebel Ali.

The Archbishop of Canterbury, the Most Reverend and Right Honourable Dr George Carey, arrived in Bahrain on 1 November 2001. He was the second head of a world Church to visit the nation - the Ecumenical Patriarch of Constantinople[11] had visited a few months earlier. Dr Carey, Mrs Eileen Carey, and the Reverend Canon Dr Herman Browne,[12] the Archbishop's Senior Advisor on Anglican Communion Affairs, were greeted in Bahrain by the Minister of Justice and Islamic Affairs, HE Shaikh Abdulla bin Khalid bin Ali Al Khalifa, and by Bishop Clive Handford who was already in the country.

317

2 November 2001 - The Archbishop of Canterbury, the Most Reverend Dr George Carey; the Reverend Canon Dr Herman Browne; and the Right Reverend Azad Marshall, visiting bishop from the Church of Pakistan, about to process into St Christopher's Cathedral, Bahrain

Diocese of Cyprus & the Gulf archive

"Hours after His Grace landed, British Ambassador Peter Ford hosted a 100-guest garden reception at the British Embassy. People witnessed what one parishioner called the 'down-to-earthness' of one of the Church's most important spokesmen in the world."[13] The next morning at St Christopher's Cathedral, the archbishop presided at a family service which included baptisms and confirmations. On 3 November 2001, he toured St Christopher's School and conducted a service attended by several hundred students. Later, he and the bishop had an audience with the Amir, HH Shaikh Hamad bin Isa Al Khalifa; and in the afternoon, before some four hundred members of Bahrain's community, Dr Carey delivered a significant lecture at Bait Al Qur'an (House of the Qur'an)[14].

> "The theme of my address 'How Far Can We Travel Together?' must be seen in the context of the events that have occurred since September 11.[15] … Christians and Muslims, whether we like it or not, are on a journey together and we live in a world where different faiths jostle side by side. We are able to choose to walk together in harmony or to jockey for position and so add to the chaos and troubles of our world by treating one another as enemies rather than neighbours who should be friends. In my view, interfaith dialogue is not an option but a necessity - neither is it an impossibility - but we must acknowledge that the answer to the question 'how far can we travel together?' cannot be answered at the outset of the journey. It is something we shall only discover as we set out boldly on the way."

The archbishop and his party then flew to Qatar, where he became the first head of a world Church to visit the country. In Bishop Handford's words, this was a breakthrough for the Anglican chaplaincy. "In a sense the church has only ever been semi-officially there. Archdeacon Ian [Young] does not go about in a clerical collar. We never go through the airport, he or I or anybody, dressed in clerical dress. Yet, when we arrived from Bahrain, the archbishop and I descended from the plane in purple cassocks and were met by government representatives. The government put cars at our disposal for the whole of the visit. We were given a very clear indication that we shall have a church building in Qatar before long."[16]

Dr Carey presided at a Eucharist held in the gymnasium of the Doha English Speaking School. Five hundred people attended, with many having to stand. Of those, eight people representing six nationalities were confirmed by the archbishop. During a separate simple ceremony, he blessed an inscribed stone. The wording reads: "This stone commemorates the visit to Qatar of the Archbishop of Canterbury, the Most Reverend and Right Honourable Dr George Leonard Carey 3-5 November 2001". The stone is now mounted on the left-side wall just inside the Anglican Centre.

Not only were his visits to Bahrain and Qatar hailed as a great honour for the diocese, but also the hospitality offered by both governments indicated their desire to encourage interfaith relationships. Described later, a seminar hosted by Qatar in April 2003 is a noteworthy example.

Cyprus is host to the two Sovereign Base Areas (SBAs)[17] created as a British Overseas Territory in 1960 when Cyprus achieved independence from the United Kingdom and became a republic. On 27 October 1960, the Archbishop in Jerusalem, the Most Reverend Angus Campbell MacInnes, conducted the service which celebrated the laying of the foundation stone of the garrison church in Dhekelia (within the Eastern Sovereign Base Area). It was consecrated in the name of St George on 11 March 1962 and rededicated in the name of St Barnabas in 2005. The church has a long association with the Diocese of Cyprus and the Gulf. For example, signatures of its successive bishops appear in the service registers. Between 1960 and the mid-1970s Sunday evening services at St Helena's were led by the Forces chaplain based at Dhekelia. He was on call at other times. His telephone number at the rectory was painted on a board outside St Helena's.

Memorably, in January 2002, St George's church hosted the Diocesan Synod's evening Eucharist. Just a ten-minute drive from the Lordos Beach Hotel, the distinctive building is one of the largest non-Orthodox churches in Cyprus, set on a hill inside the garrison's main entrance and visible for some distance along the main road.

The imposing interior is high, wide, with a long nave leading to the altar set before a strikingly unembellished and sensitively-lit arched alcove. Stained-glass windows along the north and south walls honour regiments who have served at the garrison. For most people who were present at that Synod Eucharist, it was a rare if not unique opportunity to worship in this church which "continues to serve the whole military and civilian population of Dhekelia as an ecumenical centre shared by all denominations of the Christian Church".[18]

An eclectic mix of other landmark events took place in 2002. In Bahrain, on 14 February, a hereditary monarchy was declared by HH Shaikh Hamad bin Isa Al Khalifa who proclaimed himself king. A new constitution was promulgated. From 1783 until 1971, the Bahraini monarch had held the title *Hakim* (Ruler). After the nation became an independent sovereign state in 1971, HH Shaikh Isa bin Salman Al Khalifa (Shaikh Hamad's father), chose the title Amir (Commander or Prince). He died of a heart attack on 6 March 1999, less than a month after attending the funeral of King Hussein of Jordan. It has been said that Bahrain's constitutional monarchy is based on the Jordanian model.

With respect to provincial affairs, on 22 February 2002, Bishop Clive Handford was elected by the Central Synod to serve for a five-year term as President Bishop. He was the first diocesan of Cyprus and the Gulf to hold that office, and the first President Bishop to have a European nationality. That said, his long association with the Middle East had begun many years earlier when, in January 1956, Clive Handford went to Jordan as a young British national serviceman. "While there, I recall meeting a deacon at the church, John Brown, who eventually became Bishop in Cyprus and the Gulf".

Meanwhile, in Damascus on 12 July 2001, the commission which had been discerning the future of the province presented its proposals to the standing committee of the Central Synod. In summary, "the Diocese of Jerusalem should have a unique independent status within the worldwide Anglican Communion … a special status be given to the Bishop in Jerusalem to reflect the importance of his position as representative of the Anglican Communion in the Mother City of our faith"[19]; and the three remaining dioceses of Egypt, Iran, and Cyprus and the Gulf, should be reconstituted as the Province of the Middle East. These proposals were forwarded to the Anglican Consultative Council (ACC) and its President, the Archbishop of Canterbury, for their consideration. On 18 June 2002, Bishop Handford reported that during his conversations with the ACC and those at Lambeth Palace "it was clear that both bodies showed little enthusiasm and support for the proposals"[20]. Indeed, they were not presented to the ACC when it met during September 2002 in Hong Kong[21].

Dr George Carey retired at the end of October. His successor, the Most Reverend Rowan Douglas Williams, Bishop of Monmouth and Archbishop of Wales, was elected on 2 December 2002. By now it seemed likely that the structure of the Episcopal Church in Jerusalem and the Middle East would stay unchanged, and so it transpired.

An imaginative presentation by Tom Hornsby, an ecclesiastical architect of considerable repute, was an inspiring highlight of the 2003 Diocesan Synod. Archdeacon Ian Young had met Tom in London and persuaded him take up the challenge to design the proposed Anglican church in Qatar. Tom's starting point was that any guest who arrives in a church should be welcomed. It should be a place of accessibility, gathering, transition, preparation, even paradise; a place for contemplation, and for encounter. There should be a sense of participation.

The phrase *solvitur ambulando* is often ascribed to St Augustine, meaning that "things are resolved by walking up and down". For example, the inclusion of a labyrinth[22] in a church design offers a means of walking as a devotional activity. Of course, a church should have points of focus, such as the altar, the font, places of transition and celebration. It was too early to say what the final design of the Anglican church in Qatar would be. Tom's conceptual visuals were a fine start.

More tangibly, part two of his presentation was an illustrated overview of the approved plans to restore St Andrew's church in Kyrenia, and a virtual tour using colour transparencies to show the ambitious engineering work in progress. In 1977 the east end of the church was demolished after the wet clay beneath its foundations began to subside and slide down the hillside, taking part of the building with it. A nearby road and government regulations meant that the only way to stabilise the site and restore the church was to dig out the collapsed area and create a basement hall as the foundation to the new extension. CY£100,000 was required to complete this work. At that time, St Andrew's could seat seventy people. With the extension, the capacity would double. For the duration of the works, the Reverend Anthony Fletcher and St Andrew's congregation had been offered use of the Cheshire Home[23] in Kyrenia.

Synod Quiet Morning, 30 January 2003: Bishop Clive Handford with Abbot Symeon and a fellow monk at St George's monastery, Troulli, near Larnaca
Diocese of Cyprus & the Gulf archive

During that synod, Bishop Handford reminded his listeners that "we live in stirring times. We are in the prayers of many people". This reality check was a reference to the envisaged invasion of Iraq. The consensus was that a letter should be drafted and approved to be sent to the Anglican Communion News Service, the chaplaincies of the diocese, the President of the USA, the Prime Minister of the UK and the Secretary-General of the UN. The text read:

"The Synod of the Diocese of Cyprus and the Gulf, representing the Anglican Churches within the region, can find no theological and humanitarian justification for the proposed invasion of Iraq. We strongly disagree that war is the solution to the present stance of the Iraqi regime or to the suffering of the Iraqi people. The Diocese of Cyprus and the Gulf encourages people of all faiths to work together for lasting peace and justice for Iraq."

While most people believed that a war was inevitable, the letter was a gesture of solidarity and heartfelt protest. After all, another war might destroy any hope of restoring the Anglican chaplaincy in Baghdad. Since the mid 1970s it had not functioned in any meaningful way and remained without an incumbent chaplain.

On 19 March 2003 a coalition led by the USA invaded Iraq to depose President Saddam Hussain Abd Al Majid Al Tikriti. Based on intelligence reports, later proved to be erroneous, the American president, George W Bush, and the British prime minister, Tony Blair, alleged that the Iraqi president possessed weapons of mass destruction and had links with the Al Qaeda terrorist organisation. On 9 April 2003 Saddam Hussain was deposed and went into hiding. It was not until 13 December 2003 that he was captured.[24]

During July that year, the bishop and the archdeacon visited Baghdad. They sensed a general feeling of lawlessness which was breeding insecurity and fear. Robberies in the streets, cars being held up and the abductions of individuals, particularly of young women, were common. Widespread bomb attacks, especially suicide bombings, targeted coalition forces, Iraqi civilians and Iraqi police. There were, however, some improvements including the reinstatement of some electricity supplies and the provision of safe drinking water. Hospitals were functioning more fully. Local medical staff were being trained again and more schools had re-opened. The Coventry Cathedral Ministry of Reconciliation had been officially invited by the American/British military to play a role in the reconstruction of Iraq. This project was headed by the Reverend Canon Andrew White, a familiar visitor to Baghdad before the war who, with two other colleagues, now visited the city twice a month.

323

After the 2003 war, St George's church was looted and vandalised again. Only three years earlier had it been possible to complete repairs to the desecration caused after the Gulf War in 1991. Extraordinarily, although a safe had been smashed open, it was a mystery that a silver cross had been left behind. During the 2004 Diocesan Synod, the bishop reported that the recent damage had been repaired, making it possible for a service to be held at St George's every Sunday. Approximately two hundred people attended. All but ten were Iraqi Christians living in the surrounding area and unable to attend their own churches. A Sunday School was functioning again too, providing for one hundred children. The church services were being conducted by the senior American Episcopal military chaplain, Padre Frank Wismer, his colleagues, and Canon Andrew White. They were based in the heavily fortified Green Zone, the HQ of the Coalition Provisional Authority,[25] where foreign military personnel and civilians lived and worshipped. The Green Zone was the former government centre of the now deposed Ba'ath party.

Bishop Clive recorded thanks to Christopher Segar, the Senior British Diplomat in Iraq, for all the work he had done and continued to do for the Anglican church in Baghdad. Due to the volatile situation, re-establishment of the Anglican chaplaincy in Baghdad was put on hold for eighteen months. Nevertheless, the 2004 Diocesan Synod passed a motion without dissent approving CYP£200,000 expenditure towards that goal. How that would be represented in the diocesan budget was not discussed.

Meanwhile, at the invitation of the Amir of Qatar, HH Shaikh Hamad bin Khalifa Al Thani, the second seminar in the Building Bridges[26] series of interfaith dialogues took place between 7 and 9 April 2003. This seminar, titled *Scriptures in Dialogue*, was attended by fifteen Christian and fifteen Muslim scholars from near and far, including the Reverend Canon Dr Kenneth Bailey who, from 1990-1991, had been Ecumenical Theologian-in-Residence at St Paul's Cathedral in Nicosia. The Archbishop of Canterbury, Dr Rowan Williams, was in the chair.

In his opening address, he stressed that the latest conflict in Iraq, now into its fourth week, highlighted the urgent need for people of different faiths to listen to each other.

Archdeacon Ian Young made the most of the archbishop's stay by arranging for him to celebrate the Eucharist at the Doha English Speaking School, and bless a cross-shaped foundation stone for the intended Anglican church. The stone is now displayed above the entrance to the Church of the Epiphany, at the top of the grand staircase - with its cascading water feature - leading from the main entrance of the Anglican Centre.

Also in April 2003, there was cause for cautious optimism in Cyprus. For the first time in twenty-nine years certain crossings were opened in the Green Line which divided the island, a decision made by the northern administration to ease restrictions. Correspondents reported scenes of excitement and confusion as the first residents, from the north and the south, went through the Ledra Palace checkpoint in Nicosia. "But while these steps were expected to go some way to ease the tension and the economic imbalance between the two communities, there were no signs that the key political issues of territory and sovereignty were any closer to being resolved."[27]

St Andrew's church, Kyrenia
Copyright: Angela Murray

325

On 30 November 2003, the bishop rededicated the renovated and expanded church of St Andrew in Kyrenia. This celebration prepared the way for the next landmark event in the life of the diocese. During the morning of Thursday 5 February 2004, two coaches left the Lordos Beach Hotel on the south coast of Cyprus to transport more than one hundred synod members over the Kyrenia mountain range and down to the old harbour town on the north coast. This was the first time that St Andrew's congregation had been able to host a synod Eucharist, and it was the first year that a synod Eucharist could be held north of the Green Line. Indelible poignant emotions were felt by many. It was a truly memorable day.

A few months later, on 1 May 2004, the Republic of Cyprus became a member of the European Union. Those living in the south of the island became less Middle Eastern and more European in outlook. This was much less evident in the northern area which, for example, continued to attract many non-European students, especially from African nations. Those enrolled at the Eastern Mediterranean University formed the majority of the Anglican congregation in Famagusta which, even today, is characterised as a largely student chaplaincy.

In September 2003, Maggie Le-Roy arrived in Cyprus where some years previously she had trained in the discipline of spiritual direction. She was now waiting to renew her visa so that she could return to Lebanon where, for ten years, she had served with Youth for Christ.[28] The Dean of St Paul's Cathedral, the Very Reverend Steve Collis, asked her: should the visa for Lebanon not be renewed, would she stay in Cyprus and fulfill Bishop Clive's dream to establish a retreat house in the diocese? The visa was not renewed, so in February 2004 Maggie started working part-time for the diocese as Retreats Facilitator, initially financially supported through the organisation Interserve.[29]

Part of Maggie's new ministry involved organising day retreats in the Troodos mountains at St George in the Forest, in other churches on the island, and in private houses. As this initial workload was not huge

Maggie also worked part-time with St Paul's Cathedral to form Chill, a youth group for teenagers, aged fourteen to eighteen, and became a team member of a new ministry called The Place, an outreach to international college students, most of whom were Pakistanis, Indians, Nepalis, Chinese and Africans. After two years the retreats ministry had grown to the point that Maggie needed to devote herself full-time to the task and so handed over leadership of Chill and ended her involvement with the international student work.

In September 2005 a new phase in Maggie's sphere of ministry began. Wendy and David Foulger, who attended St Paul's, were living in Kapedes village, some 18 miles/30 km south from Nicosia. They came to know that the owner of an attractive traditional house in the village, who was due to move to a property that she was renovating, would be prepared to let the old house to the diocese. Its situation made it an ideal proposition as a retreat venue. The secluded house is reached off a narrow cobbled street, a short walk from the village square where cars can be parked, near the Macheras National Forest Park. In September 2006 a rental contract was agreed. Much preparation was helped by Judy Cannan who, on 7 September, arrived in Cyprus as a volunteer assistant retreats facilitator.[30] Anetta Stylianou, a member of the diocesan staff, had suggested that the retreat house should be called Katafiyio, "a place of refuge". On 13 September 2006 it was officially opened by the bishop. Archdeacon Ian Young and Dean Steve Collis were present, as were Maggie and Judy, and some thirty friends and supporters.

327

Katafiyio retreat house
Copyright: Retreats Ministry, reproduced with permission

Katafiyio comprises two bedrooms with a study/art-room between them. Downstairs there is a large sitting room, a bathroom and kitchen, and a room thought to have previously housed animals. The portico faces a courtyard garden planted with a variety of trees: walnut, apricot, pomegranate, lemon and pomelo. A grapevine and a Virginia creeper grow up the walls of the house. A pair of wooden doors set in the high boundary wall form the entrance to the courtyard. Just inside, a small building thought to have been a dairy is now a prayer room.

The retreats ministry offers diverse opportunities to suit the needs of groups and individuals such as partners in mission, aid organisations, those in secular employment or retirees - in fact anyone who seeks rest from busy ness, a closer connection with God and discernment for direction in life. The ministry extends to the Gulf archdeaconry where Maggie Le-Roy also leads retreats. Christ Church Aden is one example.

After October 1997, when the bishop rededicated Christ Church and opened Ras Morbat medical clinic within its compound, chaplaincy life in Aden began to thrive and its outreach to the community soon expanded. From 6 November 1998 to March 2001, the Reverend Roger Bruggink, an RCA minister with the bishop's permission to officiate, together with his wife Adilee, worked hard to enable this progress. The clinic's main purpose was to serve the local low-income population, offer basic health education, and provide pre and post-natal care. All this continued undisturbed until 1 January 2001. Early that morning a bomb exploded just outside the church, destroying a large section of the perimeter wall, dislodging cabinets in the kitchen, and shattering glass on that side of the church, and in nearby shops and houses. The Brugginks, the only two people on site at the time, were not injured. Undaunted, they literally picked up the pieces and, with help, ensured that the clinic continued to function.

After they left in March 2001, the Reverend Canon Benjamin Chase and his wife Bobbie arrived to offer locum ministry. Before his retirement, Ben had given distinguished service in the Canterbury Group.

Between September 2001 and June 2003, the Reverend Colin Noyce and his wife Irene served in Aden. In October 2002 an eye clinic was established on the church compound. This had been a gradual process, partly the result of visiting doctors who helped out at the general clinic with specialist eye care; and after a donation of surgical equipment. This had been received in 1999 from the Christoffel-Blindenmission (CBM), a German-based mission founded in 1908 to support people without sight, regardless of nationality, gender or religion. In 2000, the British Council had donated an electricity generator.

By 2004 very good and dedicated teams were running the Aden clinics and church. Mansour Khan was, and remains, an invaluable member of the administration staff. Most of the medical staff were Yemeni and Muslim. The maintenance staff were largely Ethiopian and Christian. A Cuban eye surgeon, also a Christian and employed by the Yemeni military, visited the eye clinic twice a week: first to perform the more complex eye operations, and then during the next morning to follow up with the patients. His visits were free of charge on the understanding that he also treated Yemeni military personnel at the clinic. Showing their concern for the security of the clinics, and in appreciation of the medical care they provided, Yemeni authorities insisted on placing a guard outside the property 24 hours a day. The clinics employed their own 24/7 security guard to monitor the compound internally.

Between November 2003 and August 2005, several Anglican priests offered locum ministry for a few months each. Most were familiar faces: the Reverend Canon Dennis Gurney OBE (a former senior chaplain in Dubai), the Reverend Jim Wakerley, and Ben and Bobbie Chase once again. In 2004, the Reverend Peter Crooks with his wife Nancy spent two months in Aden. They returned in September 2005 and stayed for three years. Peter had three roles: chaplain, director of the Ras Morbat clinics, and port chaplain on behalf of the Mission to Seafarers. Nancy administered the church compound.

In 2007, during a typical day, between fifty and seventy-five patients visited the general clinic, seventy percent of whom were women. Over seven hundred eye operations were performed. Forty per cent of the patients came from Aden, the rest from elsewhere in Yemen. Each was charged US$50 for their operation, although the price was negotiable. The eye clinic also offered outreach to deprived areas, such as the city of Mocha and the island of Socotra, 236 miles/380 km off Yemen's southern coast. In total, twenty thousand patients were seen in both clinics in 2007. Almost all of the staff were Yemeni.

Ministry of the Word at Christ Church, Aden, led by the Reverend Peter Crooks
Reproduced with Father Peter's permission

The church also maintained five guest rooms with a capacity for fifteen guests, each charged Yemeni Riyals 2000 / US$10 per night, and hosted small conferences and retreats. The combined income helped to offset the annual maintenance costs of the clinics and the church.

Peter Crooks also tried to devote at least two mornings every week to visiting ships and ministering to seafarers. The Aden Port Authority had issued him with a pass, especially helpful during an emergency. An example occurred in 2006 when twenty-two Nigerian seafarers were abandoned in Aden without pay. For several months they were given refuge at Christ Church. On one day during that episode, the first officer of a container ship warmly greeted Peter on board. After hearing about the Nigerians' plight, he pulled out his wallet and gave him a handful of dollar notes. "'For their food', he explained, adding simply, 'I was once without money in the port of Rotterdam and the Mission helped me'."[31]

The companion link between the Diocese of Cyprus and the Gulf and the Diocese of Exeter had been established in 1983. Cyprus and the Gulf supplied Exeter with several thousand hand-made palm crosses every year. Exeter supplied locum priests when the need arose. Bishop Handford recalled that in conversations between himself and Bishop Michael Langrish of Exeter "it emerged that we were both thinking of establishing an additional link. I suggested that we explore the possibility of a joint, three-way, partnership. Two dioceses were suggested, one in Brazil and the other being Thika. Overwhelmingly we voted for Thika".[32] Their idea was to offer each diocese a different kind of link, but not to supersede those that existed.

The Diocese of Thika, part of the Anglican Church of Kenya, had been established on 1 July 1998; on 31 January 1999, its first bishop, the Right Reverend Dr Gideon Githiga, had been consecrated. On 24 July 2005, a tripartite Companions in Mission Covenant was signed by Bishop Handford, Bishop Langrish and Bishop Githiga. At the 2006 Synod of the Diocese of Cyprus and the Gulf, Bishop Githiga presented an address titled "Getting to Know One Another".[33]

He described the Diocese of Thika as lying in an agricultural region, not far from Mount Kenya. The population was predominantly Kikuyu, the largest ethnic group in Kenya of which there are forty-two. Three languages were used for worship, English, Swahili and Kikuyu, depending on what a particular congregation preferred. On the downside, poverty was prevalent, and so was AIDS,[34] with the result that many children were HIV-positive and/or orphans. The link continues to provide prayerful support.

For the chaplaincy of Qatar, the year 2005 was one of mixed fortunes. Happily, on 10 May in Doha, a long-awaited "Contract for Lease of State Private Property"[35] was signed. During October 2005 the Archbishop of Canterbury hosted a reception at Lambeth Palace to mark the launch of the UK fundraising appeal for the project, namely the construction of the Anglican Centre, and within it the Church of the Epiphany. Already there was considerable worldwide interest. On 12 December 2005 "a truly memorable and unforgettable event took place" when the authorities officially handed a large plot of land to the Christian community for the building of five church complexes. A government representative cut a blue ribbon to open the site. Planning permission had been granted by the Qatari government for the Anglican Centre, and without any alterations to the submitted inspirational design.

Then, later in December 2005, the sad news was received that Tom Hornsby, the London-based architect of the project, had died. Months earlier he had been diagnosed with terminal cancer. The funeral took place on 22 December 2005 at St Mary's Church in Islington. Tom's business partner, Roger Molyneux, with David Gillespie, a Doha-based architect, took over Tom's brief. Ground-breaking at the site of the Anglican Centre was scheduled for February 2006.

Also early in 2006, transition took place in south-east Cyprus. Since May 1999, the Reverend Robin Brookes and his wife Valerie (Val) had ministered to the congregations which met in the gatehouse chapel of the Ayia Napa monastery, and in a hotel at Protaras. After certain crossing points were opened in the Green Line during 2003, Robin and Val also began to minister to the congregation of St Mark's in Famagusta, it having chosen the name of the former Anglican church in the town. Robin led services and, with Val, led Bible study. Before long they felt called to do more, and so in January 2006 they relocated to Famagusta.

In March 2006, the Reverend Michael Crawford arrived in Ayia Napa. Then, in June 2007, the new Orthodox bishop in the area asked the Anglicans to cease using the gatehouse chapel at the monastery. The Scandinavian Church in Ayia Napa offered use of its premises, and so in September 2007 the Anglican congregation in south-east Cyprus adopted this church building as its sole place of worship.

Anglican worship in the cloisters of Ayia Napa monastery
Copyright: Stuart Plowman

In 2006 Diocesan Synod was faced with an alarming prospect: a chronic diocesan budget deficit augured insolvency, unless remedial action was taken immediately. A deficit of U$160,000 had been recorded for the previous financial year with no prospect of any immediate improvement. There were several reasons. Many employers in the Gulf archdeaconry were making staff redundant, and reducing pay and benefits for the remainder. In Cyprus, congregation members were mostly retirees living on fixed incomes. The cost of living was rising throughout the diocese, and inflation was also pushing up the running costs. At the same time, contributions to the diocese from the chaplaincies were not increasing, and in some cases were falling. Significant budget deficits were the result.

After a tense debate, synod passed a motion *nem con* that a task force, approved by the diocesan standing committee, should be formed.

Its scope[36] was to review the finances and procedures of the diocese, identify opportunities for improvement, explain in detail the trends leading to the current financial deficit and recommend a funding strategy for the next three years. The task force team members[37] were consultants selected for their combined management, banking, accounting and auditing expertise. The coordinator was John Banfield. The study team was asked to report to the standing committee within three months. The final report was presented in May 2006.

Essentially, the diocese required contributions from all its chaplaincies to be increased by US$100,000 a year to US$350,000 to fully fund its commitments. This would equate to about ten percent of their combined 2005 gross income. The task force also recommended that the diocese and the chaplaincy in Yemen should identify an organisation with relevant fundraising experience to help assess the potential support for the Ras Morbat clinics in Aden. Current deficits were expected to eliminate the diocese's cash reserves. Those could be partly restored in 2007 and 2008 if the new level of required parish contributions was introduced in 2007. A report with these recommendations was circulated to the chaplaincies.

While the standing committee waited for feedback, other important changes were taking place. Archdeacon Ian Young had already declared his wish to move on from Qatar and discern a new stage in his ministry. To ensure a smooth succession, the bishop, having on 1 May 2006 appointed Ian as archdeacon emeritus, named the Very Reverend Steve Collis, Dean of St Paul's Cathedral, as Archdeacon in Cyprus; and the Very Reverend Alan Hayday, Dean of St Christopher's Cathedral, as Archdeacon in the Gulf. In January 2007 Ian Young left Qatar, although he officially remained chaplain there until 30 April. The bishop thanked Ian for being "a very real presence in all sorts of ways in this diocese over many years [since 1984] … and a very devoted and effective parish priest in Qatar. He will be remembered very much there for that."[38]

Bishop Handford was also due to retire at the end of April 2007, following his seventieth birthday during that month. The first day of the 2007 Diocesan Synod was 29 January. During an open forum the future of the diocese was discussed. Should its structure remain the same, and if it were to be changed, should the bishop's successor be appointed for a transitional period, say two years? One option was that the Cyprus archdeaconry could join the Diocese of Europe, and that the Gulf archdeaconry could be integrated within another diocese in the province. After vigorous and anxious debate, there was agreement by acclamation that Cyprus and the Gulf in its present configuration should not break apart. "There was a distinct and powerful sense of unity, and a desire for continuity."[39] Although Bishop Handford did not attend the forum, he was greatly relieved when told the outcome.

With more peace of mind than might otherwise have been possible, he and his wife Jane retired at the end of April 2007 after many years of service within the province. Those in Cyprus and the Gulf who had shared part of that journey with them could reflect that, with grace, diplomacy and great determination, Bishop Handford had steered the diocese through "stirring times",[40] and celebrated many of its joys too.

335

Bishop Clive Handford and his wife Jane, at home in Yorkshire, UK
Copyright: Angela Murray

By May of 2007 it had become clear that diocesan finances were not improving. John Banfield who had coordinated the work of the finance task force in 2006 was co-opted on to the standing committee as an advisor, later to be appointed Honorary Director of Finance. When Michalakis Patsalides retired in October 2007, having served for more than two decades as the diocese's accountant, the preparation of diocesan accounts was outsourced to PricewaterhouseCoopers.

In December 2007 David Hardacre retired having served as the Diocesan Treasurer and Diocesan Secretary since 1999. Some of his diocesan administrative responsibilities were transferred to the Very Reverend Steve Collis, also Archdeacon in Cyprus. These changes allowed John Banfield to oversee the diocese's accounts from his home in the UK. During 2007 the Jerusalem and the Middle East Church Association (JMECA) committed to an increase in its level of support. The Foundation, previously the Endowment Fund, reinstated its contributions to the diocese and agreed to cover the cost of refurbishing the bishop's residence. Importantly, contributions from chaplaincies were belatedly beginning to increase thereby reflecting the proposals made in the task force report. The combined effect of all these changes was expected be a modest budget surplus in 2008.

Bishop Michael Lewis and his wife Julia, October 2019
Personal collection, reproduced with permission

Meanwhile, the Vacancy-in-See committee had met several times and considered twenty-seven nominations for the bishopric. The Right Reverend Michael Lewis, Bishop of Middleton in the Diocese of Manchester, was appointed to be the fifth Bishop in Cyprus and the Gulf. On 24 November 2007 he was enthroned at St Paul's Cathedral in Nicosia, and on 1 December at St Christopher's Cathedral in Bahrain. Bishop Michael and his wife Julia had embarked on a fresh chapter of their lives and a new era in the history of the diocese had begun.

Chapter 15

TOWARDS MATURITY

2008 - 2015

Within two months of his enthronement at St Paul's in Nicosia Bishop Michael Lewis had visited all of the chaplaincies in Cyprus and most of those in the Gulf region, including a visit to the Mission to Seafarers centre in Dubai. On 29 January 2008, sixty-six days into his new episcopate, he declared that "there are several modes for a presidential address by a bishop at his diocesan synod. In a diocese like ours, one mode which cannot, and should not, be avoided is travelogue."[1] Its purpose is "partly to proclaim and savour the diversity of the diocese, and also inspire us to Christian solidarity in that diversity". Another mode for a presidential address, he suggested, is to highlight one or more big issues. "In Cyprus and the Gulf, let alone in our Province of Jerusalem and the Middle East, we are not short of them."[2] The bishop highlighted three:

> "Firstly, if ever a grasp of and a willingness to work at both world and regional politics were called for, it's here, and not just for the bishop. … I am talking about responsibly knowing, critically listening, and fervently praying about tragedies and sorrows of nations and peoples, castes, classes, and ethnic groups less known, or less attended to by the international media; and about the economics and the sociology that both feed into and flow from the politics.

> "Secondly, the opportunity presented in a very large part of our diocese by the proximity of significant numbers of Christians to their Muslim-majority neighbours is just that: an opportunity, and not just for the bishop. …

> "Thirdly, the great Eastern stream of Orthodox Christianity is virtually nowhere closer to our part of the Western stream than

here, in both parts of our diocese, and yet sometimes it seems as though a gulf in understanding exists, abetted by uncertainty as to how we might converse and share with one another."[3]

A perennial concern about cashflow was another big issue. At that same Diocesan Synod, John Banfield reported another budget deficit in the financial year 2006/7. He also explained the organisational and financial changes made during 2007. Based on these he was able to forecast a modest surplus for 2007/8, the first in four years. Two other significant changes were proposed to synod, and approved: the diocese's accounting currency should be changed from the US dollar to the euro, and the financial year July to June should be the calendar year January to December. At last the financial outlook was looking moderately encouraging, but with two cautions. Chaplaincy contributions had to achieve the levels suggested in the task force report, and there was a need to rebuild the cash reserves of the diocese from the very low level which had resulted from three years of budget deficits.

In his first presidential address the bishop also emphasised the need for a diocesan programme, saying that he worked best collaboratively and intended to do that with colleagues. More widely, he would test and check the ideas he was formulating. As a start the bishop had asked himself, and now asked his audience: "Are we able to be confident in our diversity as a diocese and above all to enjoy what we do and who we are, as one Body? I sense yes, and that our unusual mix makes many of us rather proud. Not only do we need to communicate that to one another in an unforced way; the rest of Anglicanism ... needs to hear it too."[4]

During the next few years, manifestations of that diversity were to be expressed in countless ways and in many places, particularly in the Gulf archdeaconry. On 28 September 2008, in Doha, a ceremony was held on the site where the Anglican Centre was to stand and the Church of the Epiphany within it. This commemorated the start of physical construction, to be overseen by the Reverend Canon Bill Schwartz. He had been installed as chaplain in Qatar on 7 December 2007, having served the Canterbury Group for almost eight years. On 1 June 2009 he would additionally become Archdeacon in the Gulf following the retirement and departure from Bahrain of his predecessor, the Very Reverend Alan Hayday, who had also served as the Dean of St Christopher's Cathedral for almost seven years.

It so happened that on the same day, in Iraq, Bishop Lewis admitted and licensed Faiz Basheer Jerjes as Lector at St George's church in Baghdad. Faiz was born, raised and educated in the city. Having studied theology at the Armenian Catholic Seminary in the Lebanon from 1975 to 1980, Faiz had joined the ministry team at St George's in 2006. He and Canon Andrew White had the idea of building a new educational facility. They recognised a need to provide Iraqi children with a safe environment where they could study out of harm's way. During the 1930s and until the Second World War a small school had existed on the compound of St George's. By the 1980s the vacant schoolhouse was being used to store broken furniture.[5] In June 2009, building work began on two classrooms, initially to accommodate twenty kindergarten-age children, plus accommodation for the priest and his family, and a flat for the bishop and his wife, and others, during their visits. On 11 July 2010 Faiz Jerjes became the first Iraqi Anglican to be ordained to the diaconate. In October 2011, the Anglican School of the Redeemer, *Al Fadi*, was officially named by Father Faiz and the Governor of Baghdad.

339

The Archbishop of Canterbury, the Most Reverend Dr Rowan Williams, welcoming the Reverend Faiz Jerjes at Lambeth Palace, London, in March 2012

Diocese of Cyprus & the Gulf archive

On 11 September 2011 Deacon Faiz had been priested in "a jubilant liturgy".[6] The bishop, the two archdeacons,[7] and Canon Andrew White laid hands on Father Faiz. They were surrounded by clergy of the Chaldean and Latin rites and the Ancient Church of the East, Emmanuel Dabbaghian, archbishop of the Armenian Catholics, among them. As the final procession left the church, women ululated with delight and a sheep was slaughtered in celebration.

In distressing contrast, the Kingdom of Bahrain had become a focus of international concern and media attention three days after the 2011 Diocesan Synod ended. On Monday 14 February anti-government protesters, led by the largely Shia Bahraini opposition political groups, occupied the Pearl Roundabout in the centre of the capital, Manama. This protest, and others which escalated across the country, had been inspired by the events of the Arab Spring, a series of anti-government uprisings and armed rebellions that had spread across North Africa and the Middle East during the previous year. In Bahrain, 17 February 2011 became known locally as Bloody Thursday.

The next day, the Friday morning family service at St Christopher's Cathedral did take place. A stark difference was that the usual congregation of some one hundred was depleted to nine, including the dean and his wife. The author of this book was present. The Very Reverend Christopher Butt placed a circle of chairs in the sanctuary to create a sense of unity and support and prayerfully thanked those present for making the effort to negotiate their way through police checkpoints and navigate around protesters' impromptu roadblocks. Burning car tyres and felled palm trees became the norm. Many expatriate dependants had left the island and others were planning to do the same, uncertain about their safety. The dean, anticipating being asked what he and his wife Tricia planned to do, reassured the other anxious seven around them that they were staying.

After a month, the Bahraini government suppressed the revolt with the support of the Gulf Cooperation Council and its military arm, the Peninsula Shield Force. On 14 March 2011 a thousand troops from Saudi Arabia and five hundred from the UAE entered Bahrain to assist in the operation. A day later King Hamad declared martial law and a three-month state of emergency. The Pearl Roundabout was cleared of protesters and the iconic monument at its centre was demolished. By early June many of the expatriates who had left Bahrain were returning. The night curfew was lifted. Friday and Sunday congregations at St Christopher's began to increase again, and the ordination of the first candidate in the diocese to be priested by Bishop Lewis, planned to take place in St Christopher's Cathedral on 11 June 2011, went ahead. It was a special event for other reasons and they are described later in this chapter.

In the United Arab Emirates significant events had been taking place. On 27 November 2009, in Ras al Khaimah, the bishop had blessed the site and laid the foundation stone for a new church of St Luke. This was to be erected at al Jazeera al Hamrah, some 19 miles/30 km away from the existing Worship Centre, an unassuming group of portacabins. Just over two years later, on what had been empty stony desert, the largest church so far[8] in the Diocese of Cyprus and the Gulf was ready for use, able to seat a thousand people. An adjacent block of worship halls, a chapel, and a home for the priest and his family were complete too, all overseen by the chaplain, the Reverend Nelson Fernandez. On 9 March 2012 the bishop consecrated the church.

St Luke's church, Ras al Khaimah
Copyright: Angela Murray

In accordance with custom and before the clerical procession entered he rapped his crosier on the main entrance doors. "They swung open to admit the people. There was a bit of a stampede up the nave to get to the front seats, but when everyone had found a place, the crucifer led Bishop Michael and all the clergy to the sanctuary for a solemn Eucharist and blessing."[9]

Al Ain, the traditional heartland of the ruling family in the emirate of Abu Dhabi, lies some 112 miles /180 kilometres due south of Ras al Khaimah, and 170 km/105 east of Abu Dhabi city where St Andrew's church is located. Between the mid-1990s and April 2010, its successive chaplains - Archdeacon Michael Mansbridge, the Reverend Tom Goode, the Reverend Stephen Collis, and the Reverend Clive Windebank - had led the fledgeling al Ain Anglican Community. It met at St Mary's, al Ain's Roman Catholic church. After the Reverend Andrew Thompson became chaplain of St Andrew's in September 2010 he arranged for the small Anglican congregation in al Ain to worship in a room at the Oasis Hospital. During 2012, with the bishop's approval, the al Ain Anglican Community chose the name St Thomas. In that year permission was given for the congregation to worship in the chapel within the new municipal crematorium[10] at al Foah, and it began to do so. Soon after news of this appeared on the internet, however, permission was withdrawn, and instead in 2014 the congregation's place of worship became a large room offered by a local golf club.

Buildings and congregations are one manifestation of church life; another is ministry to wider groups and communities beyond church walls. In October 2011, while accompanying her husband the bishop on a visit to Dubai, Mrs Julia Lewis documented her witness of an affecting situation which sadly was not unusual. "There are men and women in most churches in the Gulf who give up their time to visit and try to improve the lives of many of the poor migrant workers who have left families and homes in their desire for paid work. In some cases, the suffering they endure is hard to believe."[11] One of the groups that visited such workers was led by Lalitha, wife of the Reverend Ernest Victor, chaplain of St Martin's in Sharjah. During three evenings of each week her group called on migrant workers. Julia Lewis accompanied them during one such visit.

> "The journey was long and frustrating though the Dubai rush-hour traffic. There were many alley ways and narrow turns. The last few yards were made on foot to what looked like the doors of a refrigeration unit. We entered a courtyard about two inches deep in rainwater. We picked up our skirts and paddled across to a very small room. In this there were six sets of bunk beds, a refrigerator, one locker and a vegetable basket."[12]

> "The room housed twelve women and one man, as well as a variety of insect life. Each woman had all her possessions within the confines of her bunk, including electric fires and fans. To gain some privacy the women had draped towels around where their pillows were. Very touchingly most bunks were decorated with crucifixes or Sacred Hearts. About thirty maids gathered in this crowded but bare room and I was asked to speak to them. All I could think of to talk about was that, however bad things get, there is a reason, although it may take a very long time to find it. I started to read Psalm 42. During the translation, many maids recognising it pulled out their Bibles and began to read in unison in their own languages. … My admiration for these women was immense as they strived to support their families who were all so far away."[13]

Julia was so moved by the experience that she sent an account of her visit to the council of the Dubai, Sharjah and the Northern Emirates Chaplaincy, highlighting the problems endured by housemaids, particularly untreated medical conditions. As a result, a female doctor volunteered her time to go on the trips. The required medicines were purchased by St Martin's church. This was not the end of the story. After Julia and the bishop arrived in Baghdad, she spoke during a Mothers' Union service at St George's church. A collection was taken. At another service, in the American embassy, she spoke again and more money was donated. The next stop was Bahrain. There the bishop and Julia went to the Manama souq, where she haggled with shopkeepers until they found one who understood what she was trying to do: supply each poor migrant women with a pashmina, a large shawl made with fine-woven cashmere wool, to be used for privacy or to wear when the weather was cold.

> "This kind man allowed me to buy forty beautiful pashminas, all in different colours. I gave these to Dean Christopher Butt who wrapped and posted them to the Reverend Ernest Victor in Sharjah. His wife Lalitha took them to the poor maids and gave them out at Christmas time. … The fact that so many people had contributed to this outreach, from the struggling women at St George's to the wealthy Americans in the embassy in Baghdad, the Dean of St Christopher's Cathedral, the chaplain's wife in Sharjah, the female visitors and translators from St Martin's, to the minibus driver and the souq shopkeeper, just shows how good and generous people are. I feel enormously privileged to be part of the Diocese of Cyprus and the Gulf."[14]

One feature of these years was an openness to providing, under the authority of the Bishop in Cyprus and the Gulf, Anglican worship in languages other than English if there was scope and staffing to do so. In 2009 Bishop Azad Marshall, previously visiting bishop for congregations of the Church of Pakistan in the Gulf, was licensed by Bishop Michael Lewis as honorary assistant bishop in the diocese. His mother-tongue was Urdu and so it was that Urdu-language Anglican worship became a feature of diocesan life in, for example, Kuwait.

It was in Kuwait too that on 11 January 2009 the inaugural Eucharist for a formalised Mandarin-language congregation, hitherto lay-led with oversight from the Anglican chaplain of St Paul Ahmadi, was celebrated by the Reverend Canon Siow Chai Pin, the first Anglican Chinese priest to serve in the diocese. Unfortunately ill health compelled him to return to Singapore in August that year. But the congregation continued to meet, until on 6 January 2017 Ms Zhu Peijin, a member of the congregation, was deaconed by the bishop. She was ordained priest at St Paul's on

27 January 2018 continuing to minister to the thriving Mandarin-language Anglican congregation as well as assisting in English-language worship.

Tamil-language[15] Anglican congregations also evolved. On 2 March 2011 in the parish of Qatar, in a temporary building on the site where the Anglican Centre was under construction, the inaugural Eucharist of a Tamil-language congregation was celebrated by the Reverend Jebaraj Devasagayam. In Bahrain on 20 April 2014 the Reverend Stephen Thanapaul presided at a similar inaugural Tamil-language Eucharist at St Christopher's Cathedral. The congregation, starting with twenty or so members, would develop to consist of around eighty adults and children meeting every Friday evening as one of the language streams of the cathedral parish.

From autumn 2013 Igbo-language[16] worship became a feature of the life of the Church of the Epiphany in Doha, Qatar, led by the Reverend Samuel Ugwuneri; and there too, on 15 May 2015, Father Jebaraj Devasagayam began leading worship in Marathi.[17]

The public ministry of women had been another area of development. In 1986 the Central Synod of the province, responding to the fact that there were female priests, who had been ordained elsewhere in the Anglican Communion and now for one reason or another found themselves subsequent to their ordination living in the Diocese of Cyprus and the Gulf, agreed that the bishop of that diocese might license them for non-stipendiary ministry (NSM). Successive bishops had then granted Permission to Officiate (PTO) to several such women.

In January 2010, however, at a meeting of the province's House of Bishops, Bishop Michael Lewis, backed by his diocesan synod, sought his episcopal colleagues' views on his intention to move a resolution in Central Synod that would, if passed, give provincial consent to his being able, within Cyprus and the Gulf alone, to ordain to the priesthood suitably tested and trained women. When Central Synod met between 9 and 10 November that year in the Jordanian capital Amman, he proposed a motion, seconded by the Bishop in Jerusalem, the Right Reverend Suheil Dawani:

"That this Synod shall be content that the Bishop in Cyprus and the Gulf, after he has consulted his Diocesan Synod, may exercise his judgment and discretion in ordaining suitable candidates whether male or female to the priesthood, and in discerning suitable candidates whether male or female for appointment to licensed chaplaincies in his diocese."[18]

The motion was passed with one abstention. This paved the way for a landmark event: on 5 June 2011 at St Christopher's Cathedral in Bahrain the Reverend Catherine Dawkins became the first woman to be ordained priest within the Diocese of Cyprus and the Gulf and therefore within the province of the Episcopal Church in Jerusalem and the Middle East.

5 June 2011 - Ordination of the Reverend Catherine Dawkins at
St Christopher's Cathedral, Bahrain
Copyright: Angela Murray

Catherine's association with the diocese had begun in the late summer of 2009 when she joined her husband, the Reverend Nigel Dawkins, who in July that year had been appointed chaplain at Christ Church in Aden and port chaplain for the Mission to Seafarers. She had earlier had formation and ministerial training at Ridley Hall, Cambridge, in the UK. On 15 January 2010, at Christ Church, the bishop ordained her to the diaconate and appointed her as assistant chaplain in the Yemen.

During the spring of 2011, however, civil disobedience and political disruption broke out in the country. As a result Nigel and Catherine decided to leave Aden. Nevertheless, between their arrival in Aden in 2009 and their departure in March 2011 the husband and wife team brought the finances of the Aden Project into good order and had consolidated outside sources to fund seventy-five percent of the two clinics' needs. At Diocesan Synod in 2012 John Banfield, Honorary Director of Finance, commended them for this work. He also stressed that the turmoil in the Yemen meant that the diocese's activity and presence in Aden now needed more, not less, support than before.

Other important developments were under way. On 18 December 2010 the Venerable Dr John Holdsworth was installed as chaplain at St Helena's in Larnaca and collated as both Archdeacon in Cyprus and Executive Archdeacon of the diocese. As the recent former principal of a theological college, St Michael's at Llandaff in Wales, Archdeacon Holdsworth brought very significant expertise in the area of vocation and ministry. When, a month or two later, the Reverend Andrew Thompson, at that time Diocesan Director of Ordinands, presented his report to Diocesan Synod in 2011, he was certain that the executive archdeacon's arrival was boding well for the development of theological education in the diocese. "With his formidable experience and ability in this field, there is foreseeable improvement in a number of areas."[19]

Within a year, Archdeacon Holdsworth had introduced "a new pathway in vocational training", a six-module course called Exploring Faith. It was to serve the purposes of focused learning in the diocese, including the formation of future clergy and Readers. Its advantages were that it had a practical base and was underwritten by a university. Credits gained were recognised by other academic institutions worldwide. As time went on, Church Learning Groups were set up in a variety of locations across the diocese so that groups of learners could engage with the course. For those on the way towards authorised public ministry, Exploring Faith was to remain the default route.

The formation of a body to advise on the assessment and selection of candidates in whom a possible vocation towards such public ministry had been discerned was a priority for the executive archdeacon. His view was that "in a maturing, developing and growing diocese" a Bishops' Advisory Panel was essential. During 2012 a panel of assessors or selectors was established. In the chair was the Very Reverend Christopher Butt. Elizabeth George, then a Reader-in-training under his supervision, was appointed as secretary.

By 2013, two people had completed the full cycle of discernment, selection, training and ordination under Bishop Michael Lewis's oversight. The first was the Reverend Faiz Jerjes whose ordination has already been described. The second was Joanne Henderson. On 28 September 2012 she was ordained deacon at St Andrew's in Abu Dhabi, and on 27 September 2013, the Reverend Jo Henderson was priested at St Christopher's Cathedral, Bahrain. She continued to serve her curacy at St Andrew's.

Around this time the bishop convened a group of people as the Ministry Forum, to think imaginatively about the way forward for vocation and ministry. In 2014 the Forum recommended that there should be a single DDO for the diocese, not one for each archdeaconry. The bishop asked Dr Holdsworth to fill the role. Other suggestions were that vocations advisers should be appointed in each archdeaconry to work closely with the DDO, and that a Theological Educators Group should be formed, its members nominated by the bishop. This met for the first time between 24 and 26 March 2014, at St Paul's in Kuwait.

27 June 2015 - The Venerable Dr John Holdsworth at Llandaff Cathedral, Wales, on the occasion of Deacon Kent Middleton's ordination

Diocese of Cyprus & the Gulf archive

Ministerial training and support is always expensive. In order that its costs might be clearly seen by the diocese, a separate budget line was established. This gave some security of continuity to ordinands whose training was in progress, at that time there were: in Cyprus, Christine Goldsmith at St Barnabas Limassol and Geoffrey Graham at St Helena Larnaca; and in the Gulf, Jon Lavelle from St Andrew Abu Dhabi, and Kent Middleton from Christ Church Jebel Ali.

In 2013 most unwelcome events affected the life of the diocese. As part of the after-effects of the world economic crisis of the preceding years, banks in Cyprus had been found to be compromised as a result of exposure to overleveraged property companies and in particular through involvement with the debt crisis in Greece. The government's bond credit rating was downgraded to junk status. On 25 March 2013 a €10 billion international bailout by the Eurogroup,[20] the European Commission, the European Central Bank, and the International Monetary Fund was announced. The deal was that Cyprus would agree to close its second-largest bank, the Laiki or Popular Bank, and impose a one-off levy on all uninsured deposits in the Republic and possibly around forty-eight percent of uninsured deposits in the island's largest commercial bank, the Bank of Cyprus. Thus in April 2013 bank deposits above €100,000 incurred a forty-eight percent "haircut".

Immense distress was caused for many Cypriots and also for expatriates, especially those who relied on investments to fund their retirement. Without warning, the Bank of Cyprus also froze €103k of the Diocese of Cyprus and the Gulf's investments and deposits. Immediately the executive archdeacon prepared a legal challenge on behalf of the diocese and in November 2013 a court ruling judged that the Diocese of Cyprus and the Gulf should be treated as a charity rather than a commercial business. The "haircut" was reduced to €41,000, paid over in the same month in exchange for Bank of Cyprus equity shares.

For some time the bishop had been keen to appoint an Honorary Diocesan Chancellor as his legal adviser and point of reference. In

2013 he named Mr Stanley Hooper to assume that role. Mr Hooper, a barrister of Gray's Inn, London, had served as High Court Registrar and Diocesan Registrar in Botswana. In England he had been one of Her Majesty's coroners for South Yorkshire and Chair of Humberside Police Authority Standards Committee. In 2008 he and his wife Sue had retired to live above Pissouri Bay between Limassol and Paphos. After his appointment the Chancellor began work on drafts of a possible code of canon law for the province of the Episcopal Church in Jerusalem and the Middle East and its dioceses.

Stanley and Sue Hooper were among several residents of the Pissouri area who felt the need for Anglican worship in the village, which, though in the parish of Limassol, was some distance from the church of St Barnabas. With the agreement of the bishop and the chaplain, the Reverend Canon Derek Smith, a Pissouri Anglican Group began to worship in the municipal room beneath the local amphitheatre. On 12 May 2013 the bishop dedicated the congregation, effectively a church plant of the parish of Limassol, in the name of St Lazarus.

A notable event earlier that year took place in the north-east of the island when a Synod Eucharist was celebrated in Famagusta. This was the second occasion, after the Eucharist at St Andrew Kyrenia in 2004 described in the previous chapter, on which such an occasion had taken place in the northern areas. In 2008 the congregation meeting under the name of St Mark Famagusta had relocated from the church of St George the Foreigner, otherwise known as the Nestorian church, in the walled city of Famagusta. The new place of worship was the Orthodox chapel of Little St George on the Salamis road. Later, the adjoining halls became available for Sunday school and other activities. In October that year the Reverend Zinkoo Han arrived from South Korea with his wife Hyeonshil and their two children and was licensed by the bishop to serve as assistant chaplain at St Mark's.

When the Reverend Robin Brookes and his wife Val retired in 2010, Zinkoo became the chaplain. He developed a close rapport with the predominantly African students who made up most of his congregation, all of whom attended the adjacent Eastern Mediterranean University. Several other groups also used Little St George's, all student-led and of a non-Anglican and largely Pentecostal nature. The Reverend Zinkoo Han recalled that "although cooperation with these churches was not easy, most of the time we had good relationships with them". St Mark's, led by a Korean priest while very Nigerian in feel and flavour at most services, was typified by energetic worship featuring full-throated singing and enthusiastic prayer. At the same time Zinkoo was careful to provide authentic Anglican Eucharistic structure every Sunday morning.

The Reverend Zinkoo Han and his family wearing Korean national dress, and St Mark's congregation, Famagusta, celebrating a festive event
Copyright: St Mark's church

351

He also nurtured the existing twinned relationship between St Mark's and St George's in Baghdad. On 19 February 2012, the Sunday following that year's Diocesan Synod, the three representatives from St George's participated in St Mark's morning service and mingled with worshippers afterwards. Father Faiz Jerjes preached in Arabic, his churchwarden Dawlat Abouna beside him to translate into English. St Mark's youth band accompanied the hymns. Following the service Nawal, Father Faiz's wife, distributed small gifts to the youngest members of the congregation - games and puzzles with a Christian theme - and presented a clerical stole to Zinkoo which had been made by the Mothers' Union branch at St George's of which Nawal was president. It was a memorable occasion.

Not far from Famagusta but south of the Green Line, interesting developments took place in the years 2012 and 2013. In the first of those years, with the consent of the chaplain in Ayia Napa, the Reverend Simon Holloway, and with the bishop's knowledge, a group of church members formed a new congregation in nearby Deryneia. Led by Readers Peter Day and Bill Garrett, the group met for the first time in the very small Orthodox Chapel of St Helena and St Constantine on the edge of the village. Soon it was realised that the building was simply too small for Sunday gatherings. On 1 March 2013 the bishop led an inaugural act of worship in slightly larger premises, a converted shop on Ammochostos Avenue, formerly Famagusta Road, in the centre of Deryneia. The nascent congregation, by now about thirty, chose the name St John the Evangelist and the bishop agreed to it.

On 21 April 2013 the Anglican congregation in Ayia Napa chose the name Christ Church.[21] Its sole place of worship remained the Scandinavian Church which, in October 2011, had moved from its first site, an adapted wooden restaurant, to larger accommodation in a converted bank on Nissi Avenue. The Anglican congregations in south-east Cyprus, Christ Church and St John the Evangelist, continued to have access to the tiny chapel of St Helena and St Constantine on suitable occasions and small weddings were sometimes celebrated there.

A new arrival in the diocese during October 2013 was the Reverend Canon Paul Maybury, who came from the Diocese of Bradford. On 1 December 2013 he was licensed by the bishop as mission priest across south-east Cyprus, with particular responsibility for guiding and nurturing the congregation of St John the Evangelist.

He was also licensed to the half-time post of Spirituality Coordinator. In this role he worked with the Retreats Facilitator, Maggie Le-Roy, alongside the Spirituality Development Team. That team, constituted in 2012 as a network, comprised members from across diocese and began to set the agenda for activities and initiatives in the field of spirituality. Examples included exploring the possibilities of pilgrimage ministry, especially in Cyprus; developing resources for occasional liturgical use; promoting the practice of spiritual direction; generally providing a forum for the exchange of ideas in the field of spirituality; and supporting the retreats ministry. The team expressed a desire to meet three times a year but, recognising the need for budgetary constraint, settled for twice.

A craft workshop setting in the courtyard garden of Katafiyio retreat house
Copyright: Sarah Maybury

In the Gulf archdeaconry in 2013, a church plant in the emirate of Dubai came to fruition. The impetus was a conversation in November 2012 between the Reverend Canon Stephen Wright, chaplain at Christ Church Jebel Ali, and Charlotte Lloyd-Evans. Charlie had been in Dubai for a year and had become very involved in the life of the school which her children attended. Now she felt the call to withdraw from some of those commitments to dedicate more time to the church and her role as a Reader.

For some time Steve Wright had felt a strong desire to start a church group in the area of Dubai called Academic City. Attempts he had made to contact schools and other venues to identify a suitable meeting place had not been successful. As Charlie Lloyd-Evans had good relationships with her children's school, Steve Wright asked her two things: would she be prepared to commit herself to planting a new church and would she be prepared to approach the school which her children attended about this? After prayer and discussion with her family she agreed.

"What followed over the next few weeks were repeated incidents of God stepping out before us and dealing with any barriers before we even got to them. Firstly, it was my approach to the head teacher of the school. I expected to have to convince him into this idea of allowing a church to meet on school premises. ... However, after less than a minute's conversation explaining our request, he put his hand out and said 'it's yours'. The process of putting a contract in place, with a minimal rent, was quick and hassle free. The planning team was assembled, and I remember being concerned about the issue of provision for children. Looking around the planning team there did not appear to be an obvious candidate for taking on the responsibility for this and it was a central element of my prayers for this new church."[22]

After the planning group met for prayer at the new location in the school on 26 January, worshippers at what was initially called Christ Church Academic City celebrated the first service there on the Feast of Candlemas, 2 February 2013.

In Qatar, the new Anglican Centre began functioning in July of the same year prior to its official opening on 21 September. Its two-storey design allowed large and small groups to worship simultaneously in multiple worship spaces of differing sizes. Michael Cole, the Centre's first general manager, wrote on the diocesan website that the building "provides a warm welcome for many Anglican/Protestant/Evangelical Christians to address both their spiritual and community needs". Soon there were to be around fifteen thousand Christians of all sorts using the various rooms and halls of the Centre for worship on any given weekend.

A compact hexagonal chapel on the ground floor seats about forty together with another thirty in the balcony. Other than the main church space, the chapel is the only area in the compound furnished with pews. Subsequently it was often chosen for intimate wedding ceremonies. Elsewhere on the same level a full-immersion baptismal font designed on early-Christian lines is the centrepiece of a dignified internal courtyard. A grand staircase at the entrance to the Centre, with a cascading water feature, leads up to the second floor.

It is on the upper floor that the "extraordinarily impressive" Church of the Epiphany, as the bishop described it, sits at the heart of the Anglican Centre. From the Living Water[23] stone font water constantly flows. Above the altar, the painted Epiphany Star reredos by Mark Cazalet is a striking work of art and focus of devotion. The Epiphany can accommodate up to six hundred and fifty people, together with a large choir around the organ on the balcony.

The church of the Epiphany in Doha, Qatar
Copyright: Angela Murray

On the morning of 29 September 2013, as a preliminary to the consecration of the church, an engraved commemorative stone was fixed to the wall on the right-hand side of the Anglican Centre's entrance. Glue was ceremonially applied to its reverse by Bishop Michael Lewis, his predecessor Bishop Clive Handford, Archdeacon Bill Schwartz, and Archdeacon Emeritus Ian Young. During that evening Bishop Michael Lewis presided at the rites of consecration. The celebratory Eucharist, attended by several hundred people - parishioners, serving and retired clergy, and guests and friends of the diocese - set the seal on a day that had been hoped and prayed for over many years.

The Middle East is typically portrayed and imagined as a region fraught with violence and political disharmony. Sadly, such a description fits the Yemen, and its southern coastal city of Aden endures frequent disruption. During one period of relative calm in 2013, the Reverend Peter Crooks and his wife Nancy were serving at Christ Church and the Ras Morbat clinics once again. Their letter to *The Olive Branch* magazine published that summer paints a vivid picture.

> "We managed on this visit to swim at least once a week at Elephant Bay, mostly in the late afternoon when it was cooler. … We drove ourselves to the beach and to other places in town, something we'd not felt it wise to do on our other recent visits. We usually returned home after swimming at dusk, often forgetting until too late, and after we had sounded our horn or rung the gate bell for entry to the courtyard, that whoever was on guard duty would then be at prayer. If the young guards resented this interruption they never showed it and quickly appeared. … With the opening affirmations of the Muslim call to prayer - 'God is great … and there is no god but God' - Christians would surely readily concur.

> "Every working day at the clinics begins with prayer in the church. There, the Christian members of staff, now just six, meet for fifteen or twenty minutes before the clinics open, something respected and appreciated by our Muslim colleagues, some of whom are not shy to ask if we might remember them, their families or their friends in our prayers. Then, on Thursday afternoons, the Ethiopian congregation comes to worship - about thirty in all, men, women and children. All are refugees. Some, like Gashu and Elyas, who are on our staff and greatly valued, have made Yemen their home. … Relatively few of the congregation have regular jobs, but all come smartly-dressed to worship, many appearing an hour or more before the service begins, and some an hour afterwards! Those who come early kneel or prostrate themselves to pray. The church is filled with fervent murmurings, sighs and the occasional sudden outburst of praise. With these, the voice of prayer is never silent, 'nor dies the strain of praise'[24]."[25]

Gashu with young patients at the Ras Morbat clinic
Copyright: the Reverend Peter Crooks

Christ Church Aden and its medical work have been a unique and highly valued ministry that has gained solid respect within the country: "a work of faith and a labour of love. Its scope is broad but there is much to suggest that its effectiveness is deep and enduring."[26] The holistic ministry also offered "a striking example of constructive and harmonious working together of Christians and Muslims in the service of the weak and disadvantaged. This witness is manifest through the clinics, the church, hospitality facilities, mission to seafarers and work with refugees."

In October 2008 the bishop established a Council of Reference for Christ Church Aden. Alongside him, the two archdeacons, John Banfield, the Reverend Peter Crooks, and Mrs Nancy Crooks were among its founding members. In 2014 the Council decided to close the general clinic to avoid competing with a newly opened government polyclinic just two hundred metres away. Resources were now to be concentrated on continuing and enhancing provision of eye treatment. The government and nearby commercial clinics welcomed this proposal. Arrangements were made for redundant staff from the general clinic, while the staffing of the eye clinic was increased to allow for the work to expand, for instance through outreach in Mocha and in UNHCR refugee camps.

357

The bishop had begun his Presidential Address to the 2014 Diocesan Synod with these words: "So how are we doing? When I say 'we' I mean the parishes, chaplaincies, and ministries that together make the diocese." To answer his question he focused on five diocesan priorities.

The first was presence and witness. Buildings and compounds, he said, were a visible token of commitment to stay for the long haul. For instance, St Martin's church in Sharjah, already a much used complex, had been "transformed by a huge extension" which the bishop had dedicated on 22 June 2013.

Extension at St Martin church, Sharjah
Copyright: St Martin's

Soon, on 2 March 2014, he was to dedicate an extension to the church of St Barnabas Limassol. He applauded the local decision that this small historic church, "regularly bursting at the seams with worshippers, [should] carefully craft additional space for worship while respecting the integrity of the building".[27]

Another example of presence and witness was the work of the Mission to Seafarers which was going from strength to strength throughout the diocese, blessed by high-quality appointments of chaplains, and by committed volunteers and staff. In 2013, as part of the charity's restructuring, the Reverend Dr Paul Burt[28] had been appointed Regional Director for the Gulf and South Asia, based in Dubai. "One challenge … beyond keeping up the momentum is to remember why we are doing what we are doing."[29] The diocese was not in the building industry or property development, nor in the rental or heritage business, nor even or only a charitable association. "We are in and of the Kingdom of God."

The bishop's second priority was a strong base of thoughtful, educated, and active laity and clergy. He emphasised that everyone in the diocese ought to be committed to learning and exploration in the Faith. Next came the creation of a much stronger support network. The Endowment Fund was now known as the Cyprus and the Gulf Foundation. Previous high hopes for the diocese's endowment had not come to fruition, through circumstances entirely beyond its control. Bishop Brown's effort to launch an appeal in 1990 had coincided with the lead-up to the First Gulf War and confidence had been dented. "A continuing question is whether, and how, to make another attempt at diocesan endowment."[30]

Serious encounter with Islam was the fourth priority. The bishop found some existing examples around the diocese and in surrounding regions to be definitely encouraging and sometimes humbling. But he did long for more widespread involvement of lay people in opportunities for encounter, dialogue and study.

The fifth priority was evangelism, and how to do it in the context of the region. The bishop believed that "we should realise that our presence and church life can be genuinely evangelistic, exactly where we are in every single country of this diocese without exception. To be evangelical is to believe that News is Good. ... I link evangelism, and our appetite for it, with my earlier plea for refreshing exploration of the Christian faith as disciples".[31]

"So, how are we doing? ... We are not to be our own judges. Here we should sit under scripture, which is a primary record and a spelling out of the gospel of the Word himself. ... Life in the Diocese of Cyprus and the Gulf is sometimes extraordinarily challenging but for myself immeasurably rewarding. Anyway, it is where God has put us. Let us rejoice in it."[32]

Since its formation in 1978, the core activity of the Association of the Friends of the Diocese of Cyprus and the Gulf has been prayer and fellowship. The annual occasion in London, almost always at the start of August, is the AGM and Celebration Eucharist at All Hallows by the Tower, serving for many as a reunion for those who once lived and worked in the diocese. It is the main event, to which all have a standing invitation. At the 2012 AGM Mrs Mary Banfield retired, having worked devotedly as secretary of the Friends from 1991, and for a number of those years as treasurer. She was succeeded by Mrs Sally Milner. The task of editing *The Olive Branch*, the Association's publication, had been taken on by Julia Lewis. An expanded content and stylish format with colour photographs ensured that the magazine continued to promote its original aims: to foster communications between chaplaincies in Cyprus and those in Gulf countries, and to sustain the interest of those who had lived in the diocese and others associated with it.

The first Spring Gathering of the Friends had taken place in late April 1999, held at Pilgrim Hall, a Christian hotel and conference centre set in the heart of the East Sussex countryside. It was run by Michael and Maggie Lee who many Friends remembered from their time spent in Cyprus. The gathering in April 2010 was the last to take place at Pilgrim Hall. Instead, the Spring Gathering in 2011 met at Glenfall Retreat House and Conference Centre, set in wooded countryside near the spa town of Cheltenham in Gloucestershire.

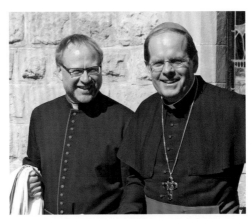

Canon Robert Jones and Bishop Michael Lewis
Diocese of Cyprus & the Gulf archive

Some fifty Friends together with the bishop and his wife attended the two-day event. Canon Robert Jones of the Diocese of Worcester, a regular guest at Diocesan Synod, led devotions and bible study sessions. The spring gatherings took place at Glenfall House for three years. In July 2013, however, it closed, owing to the same economic pressures faced by some other retreat facilities. Not all such places ceased to function. Launde Abbey is an elegant Christian Retreat House and Conference Centre set in parkland on the borders of Leicestershire and Rutland. The twelfth-century chapel inside the abbey is part of the original Augustinian priory. Launde was the venue for the Spring Gathering in 2014 and continued as such in the years that followed.

Launde Abbey
Copyright: the Very Reverend Christopher Butt

At the AGM in August that year, Ron and Bernice Maitland joined the Friends' committee and set about organising a new event. The aim was to offer a reunion location easier to reach for those living in the north of England and in Scotland. The first Northern Gathering was held in York on 22 October 2014, centred on the Bar Convent, believed to be the oldest active open-order convent in England. It is situated just outside York's old city walls, near the railway station and the town centre. The occasion included a Eucharist in the convent's chapel, lunch, and a visit. Not surprisingly it was to York Minister.

In 2014, in order to strengthen financial administration in the diocese, the standing committee decided to bring day-to-day accounting back in-house once more. In April Mrs Evangelia Georgakaki was appointed as Finance Officer. She assisted the executive archdeacon in establishing the diocese as a legal entity in the republic of Cyprus. It was formally incorporated on 3 April 2015 as The Anglican Church (Cyprus) Limited. Although its principal purpose was to provide Anglican clerics and parishes within the Republic of Cyprus with greater legal security, its Articles of Association also gave the diocese a legal identity and a more assured standing in that country.

In south-east Cyprus, the Orthodox Church as well as civil authorities responded favourably to an approach made during 2014 by the Reverend Canon Paul Maybury seeking permission and goodwill for the growing congregation of St John the Evangelist to worship in the Orthodox church of St Phanourios. Situated in the grounds of Deryneia cemetery, it had been privately built early in the twenty-first century by a Cypriot in memory of his mother. Only one Orthodox service was held in the church each year, though it was always open for prayer. On 15 March 2015, Bishop Michael Lewis dedicated the congregation of St John the Evangelist during the first Anglican service to take place in the church, in the presence of the Mayor of Deryneia and representatives of the local Orthodox church committee. St Phanourios thus became St John's spiritual home.

Later in the year, on 8 October, the bishop rededicated the impressively refurbished church of St Andrew in Abu Dhabi, and on 24 October 2015, he dedicated the church plant of Christ Church Jebel Ali in the name of St Catherine, then worshipping in Academic City. It was later to move to a venue in Silicon Oasis.

As 2015 drew to a close, St Paul's cathedral in Nicosia saw the installation of a circular labyrinth in a quiet area of the garden, instigated by Maggie Le-Roy and the Retreats Ministry, with the permission of the Very Reverend Jeremy Crocker and the cathedral council. The labyrinth is laid out in four segments, each a reminder of the four dioceses of the province of the Episcopal Church in Jerusalem and the Middle East. It provides a place to walk or be still, to pray and simply be.

Chapter 16

LOOKING AROUND, LOOKING FORWARDS

2016 - 2019

On 5 January 2016 the Diocese of Cyprus and the Gulf reached a milestone anniversary. Bishop Michael Lewis remarked:

> "As we celebrate forty years on from 1976 when we were founded, we are called as Christians to look in two other directions: around us, and forwards. … In Iraq, it hardly needs saying how tough life has been for Christians. … Now IS[1], Da'esh, has taken Mosul and the Christian heartlands of the biblical Plain of Nineveh, and the Christians there have been torn from their roots and possessions in towns and villages that long predate Islam. … In Baghdad, St George's continues to be open to anyone who wants to enter and longs for what it offers: a holy place, worship, a welcome, food, assistance, the clinic, the school, dependable love." [2]

In the Yemen, Christians were lying low. Church buildings had been damaged and "previously unapologetic public worship"[3] had to go underground at least for a while. The chaplain in Aden, the Reverend Velvet John, and his wife, the Reverend Janet Vijayakumary, had been compelled to leave in February 2015 during the worst of the fighting and were not able to return. "But the church building and the words Christ Church on the compound gate still stand as a witness."[4] The work of the clinic, the diocese's defining ministry of service in that city, was suspended, but only for a matter of a few months. By September 2015 it had resumed. The staff continued to do what they had always done, in what the bishop described as "the most difficult circumstances imaginable. They are all Muslims and almost all young women. They, and the extraordinary man [Mansour Khan] who is our general manager and administrator, a devout Muslim, to whom Christ Church and the Ras Morbat clinic are very dear, are committed to the ethos that Christ Church has always stood for: look around; look forward."[5]

In Limassol, the Reverend Christine Goldsmith, curate at St Barnabas, was doing just that. Her ministry included visits to the Kofinou refugee camp near Larnaca. During the weeks before Diocesan Synod in 2016 she launched an appeal to chaplaincies in the Gulf archdeaconry for donations of books in Arabic and Farsi, puzzles and games, to help relieve the boredom of camp life. The response was extraordinary. In Bahrain, for example, a feature in the *Gulf Weekly* generated vast donations of books and games. Footballs were given by the Arsenal Soccer School Bahrain and the Bahrain Rugby Football Club. Representatives travelling to synod transported many of these in their luggage, and hundreds more kilos of books were carried by Gulf Air which donated the excess baggage costs.

After the synod, on 5 February 2016, a group visited Kofinou. Horrific stories were heard of how families had become refugees, usually after violence, and of unscrupulous traffickers. All spoke about handing over their life savings for either promises of safe transport or buying space on a leaky boat to escape from war. There was joy too. Visitors witnessed the delight of children as they delved into the treasure troves of boxes filled with books, especially when they found familiar stories such as tales about Aladdin and Cinderella.

Within the diocese, new ways of communicating were evolving. On 12 June 2012 a Blue Skies Thinking Day had taken place at St Andrew's Centre in Abu Dhabi, the first meeting of a communications team convened by Archdeacon John Holdsworth. Almost a year later, on 1 May 2013, he launched scene@cypgulf, the first issue of what has become the diocese's regular electronic newsletter. This was followed in February 2014 by the first edition of scene@synod. During 2016 Archdeacon Bill Schwartz spearheaded the rebranding and redesign of the diocese's website, generously assisted by Niall Brennan, a parishioner living in Qatar, who donated the time and expertise of his company to undertake the task.

The Spirituality Development Team made much use of Skype, another modern telecommunications tool. Group audio and video calls, along with face-to-face meetings, had enabled this ministry to grow in partnership with churches and clergy. Early in 2016 the team reviewed itself and agreed to a new name, the Barnabas Team, from the reference at Acts 4:36 to Barnabas, whose name means "Son of Encouragement", encouragement in things of the Spirit being the team's rationale.

St Barnabas, the patron saint of Cyprus, was especially in the mind of Harry Ching, at that time Reader and Lay Chaplain in St Mark's student chaplaincy, Famagusta. Barnabas's tomb lies near the monastery that bears his name, a short drive from St Mark's in the ancient necropolis of the ruined city of Salamis. In April 2016 Harry embarked on a pilgrimage to follow the footsteps of Barnabas and Paul, who together walked from Salamis to Paphos (Acts 3:5-13). Harry's walk took six days. Each day he covered about 18.5 miles/30 kilometres. Members of his parish accompanied him for the first two days; others from St Helena Larnaca and St Barnabas Limassol hosted him during the middle stages; and a small group from Paphos joined him at Yeroskipou to walk the final leg to the church of Ayia Kyriaki Chrysopolitissa in Kato Paphos where a short service was held at the nearby St Paul's Pillar. There, according to tradition, St Paul was tied and scourged. Harry recalled:

> "The week after the pilgrimage I was on crutches and paid several visits to the physio! I still wonder how St Paul managed his mission over two thousand years ago, with only tracks to follow and no roads. It was the pain and stress from the pilgrimage that allowed me to understand the courage and strength of the Apostles to bring the Good News to the people of their time."[6]

Significant clerical appointments were made in the Gulf archdeaconry, not least in the group of churches making up the chaplaincy of Dubai, Sharjah and the Northern Emirates, where there had been certain differences of opinion and clashes of personality.

Among the new clergy in post were the Reverend Tim Heaney who in June 2012 had arrived at Holy Trinity in Dubai from the Diocese of Truro, and in January 2015 was licensed by the bishop as chaplain at Christ Church Jebel Ali. The Reverend Drew Schmotzer, formerly domestic chaplain to Bishop Mouneer Anis of Egypt and subsequently priest in Algiers, was licensed at St Martin Sharjah in February 2016. The Reverend Jon Lavelle, curate at St Christopher's

Cathedral in Bahrain, moved to Ras al Khaimah where, at St Luke's on 22 April 2016, he was licensed as chaplain, also to serve the church of St Nicholas in Fujairah. Finally on 11 September the bishop licensed the Reverend Harrison Chinnakumar as the new chaplain for Holy Trinity Dubai. For the previous four years he had served at St Paul's in Kuwait, with particular responsibility for the Urdu-language congregation that Bishop Azad Marshall had been unable to visit and to which it had proved impossible to appoint a Pakistani passport-holder.

Meanwhile, in Cyprus, the bishop had identified a new opportunity. On 14 September 2016 he convened Cyprus's first Social Outreach Forum, held in Nicosia's sector of the UN Buffer Zone at the Home or House of Cooperation[7] opposite the old Ledra Palace Hotel. While the forum met under the aegis of the Anglican diocese, the bishop's concept was that any agency or individual involved in matters of social concern, whether explicitly Christian or not, could pool experiences and share best practices for the common good of all living on the island. It became an annual event.

During 2015 the three Anglican congregations in south-east Cyprus - Christ Church Ayia Napa, St John the Evangelist Deryneia, and St Mark Famagusta - agreed to coalesce as a new parish to be called Ammochostos, the Greek equivalent of Famagusta. The bishop wrote that "Father Gabriel Amat, who is that rare bird, a Catalan Anglican from Barcelona"[8] arrived on 1 July 2015 to minister alongside Canon Paul Maybury and Harry Ching. Both left Cyprus in 2016, Paul Maybury in August to be Canon Precentor of Bradford Cathedral in England; and in September the Reverend Harry Ching, a deacon since 25 June, to be assistant curate at Christ Church Jebel Ali. Justin Arnott, a Reader at St Paul's in Nicosia who was himself on the route to ordination, succeeded Harry at St Mark's for a short period. The parish of Ammochostos became a legal entity on 7 March 2017, and on 25 March the Reverend Martin Phillips-Last was licensed as its full-time stipendiary parish priest, serving and overseeing all its congregations.

Diocesan ministerial training entered a new phase on 14 September 2017. At Queen's College Faculty of Theology in Newfoundland, the provost Dr Richard Singleton and the Venerable Dr John Holdsworth on behalf of the Diocese of Cyprus and the Gulf signed a Memorandum of Understanding. Thus a training partnership was launched which would ensure delivery and accreditation of the Exploring Faith course, already in its fifth year as the diocese's normative training pathway. The Reverend Christine Goldsmith and the Reverend Geoffrey Graham became Cyprus and the Gulf's first graduates of the Queen's College BTh in Discipleship and Ministry degree programme. On 11 June 2018, at St Paul's Cathedral in Nicosia, they were presented with their degrees by Dr Singleton.

In September 2017, also in Nicosia, Dr Helen Perry had joined the diocesan staff as Administration Officer. Mrs Anetta Stylianou officially retired from that role at the 2018 Diocesan Synod, although she continued to serve as secretary to the JEMT (Cyprus). At St Luke Ras al Khaimah on 14 April 2018 the Reverend Kent Middleton moved from a curacy at the cathedral in Nicosia to be licensed to succeed the Reverend Jon Lavelle[9] following the latter's appointment to a church in his home town Buffalo, New York. On Michaelmas Day that year, the bishop was in Baghdad again where at St George's he officially opened two new developments: first a three-storey building to be the principal structure of the Anglican School of the Redeemer, Al Fadi; and immediately afterwards together with Patriarch Louis-Raphael Sako, head of the Chaldean Catholic Church and doyen of Iraq's religious leaders, the relocated Hope Resource Centre, an ecumenical facility for all Christian traditions.

During 2019 the life and ministry of the diocese continued apace. In March the Reverend Tim Heaney of Christ Church Jebel Ali returned to the UK. On 25 April the Very Reverend Christopher Butt retired, succeeded as Dean of St Christopher's Cathedral in Bahrain by the Very Reverend and Venerable Dr Bill Schwartz who was installed on 1 June. He remained Archdeacon in the Gulf. The Venerable Dr John Holdsworth retired at the end of July, followed on 7 September by the Venerable Christopher Futcher who was installed as Archdeacon in Cyprus and chaplain at St Helena Larnaca. Ordinations continued to take place, further clergy appointments were made and four new honorary canons were appointed, all listed in Part Three of this book. A long-discussed reconfiguration of the Dubai, Sharjah and the Northern Emirates chaplaincy was implemented in July 2019. Four new parishes were formed: Dubai (Holy Trinity); Jebel Ali (Christ Church) with Academic City (St Catherine); Sharjah (St Martin); and Ras al Khaimah (St Luke) with Fujairah (St Nicholas). New projects were started or contemplated, even if their fruition would be likely to be some way off. For example, a proposal was under consideration to revive a Mission to Seafarers' presence in two ports within the diocese: Basrah in Iraq and Aden in Yemen.

On 17 November 2019 Bishop Michael Lewis began a new phase in his ministry when he officially became President Bishop and Primate of the Province of Jerusalem and the Middle East, bearing the honorary title Archbishop.[10] A celebratory Eucharist was held at St Andrew's in Abu Dhabi to mark the occasion. Like Bishop Clive Handford before him, who had also served as President Bishop, he retained his principal role as Bishop of the Diocese of Cyprus and the Gulf while holding primatial office. When "looking around us, and forwards" in November 2019, he wrote:

> "The Middle East, together with the Eastern Mediterranean, remains a region of volatility and uncertainty, even while some oases of stability and calm quietly abide. The Anglican Diocese of Cyprus and the Gulf's first vocation has been and must continue to be present, attentive, gracious, and imaginative in all the varied countries and all the diverse peoples it tries to serve, offering authentic worship and ecumenical generosity, despite sometimes feeling itself to be fragile and beleaguered. It has unrivalled opportunities to commend Christ in season and out of season, not least by loving service and by the evidence of Christian lives faithfully lived. Long may it flourish as a sign of God's Kingdom on earth."[11]

PART THREE

CHRONOLOGIES

BISHOPS

in Cyprus and the Gulf

1976-1983 - The Right Reverend Leonard Ashton CB

b 27 June 1915, d 19 January 2001

1942 deaconed; 1943 priested

1942-1945, Curate, St Cuthbert and St Mary, Cheadle, Diocese of Chester

1945-1973, RAF service: 1945-1962, Chaplain (with the relative rank of Squadron Leader, later rising to Wing Commander); 1962-1965, Assistant Chaplain-in-Chief; 1965-1969, Chaplain, St Clement Danes (the Central Church of the RAF on the Strand in London); 1969-1973, Chaplain-in-Chief, RAF (promoted to the relative rank of Air Vice-Marshal) and Archdeacon for the RAF in the Church of England; 1973, retired from the RAF

1974, 22 January, consecrated at St Clement Danes Church

1974-1976, Assistant Bishop, Diocese of Jerusalem

1976, 5 January, invested as the first Bishop in Cyprus and the Gulf at the Collegiate Church of St George the Martyr, Jerusalem

1967-1983, Honorary Chaplain to HM Queen Elizabeth II

1983, 3 July, final service at St Paul's Cathedral, Nicosia

1983, July, retired from full-time ministry and returned to the UK

1983-2001, Honorary Assistant Bishop, Diocese of Oxford

1983-1986 -The Right Reverend Henry (Harry) Moore

b 2 November 1923

1952 deaconed; 1953 priested

1952-1956, Diocese of Manchester: 1952-1954, Curate at St Luke, Farnworth; 1954-1956, Curate at St Leonard, Middleton

1957-1959, Church Mission Society (CMS) Chaplain, Khuzistan Oil Fields, Diocese of Iran

1960-1974, Diocese of Manchester: 1960-1963, Rector at St Margaret, Burnage, 1963-1974, Rector at St Leonard, Middleton

1974-1980, Home Secretary to the CMS, England

1980-1983, Deputy General Secretary and Executive Secretary, CMS

1983, 29 September (Michaelmas Day), consecrated at Winchester Cathedral

1983, 1 November, enthroned at St Paul's Cathedral, Nicosia

1983, 20 November, enthroned at St Christopher's Pro-Cathedral, Bahrain

1985, November, invited to be appointed General Secretary of the CMS

1986, January, resigned his See; remained in post until his successor was announced

1986, 27 June, attended a farewell party in Nicosia

1986, July, returned to the UK and service with the CMS

1990, retired from full-time ministry

1990-1994, Honorary Assistant Bishop, Diocese of Durham

1994 - , PTO, Diocese of Hereford

1987-1995 -The Right Reverend John Brown

b 13 July 1930, d 23 October 2011

1955, deaconed at the Collegiate Church of St George the Martyr, Jerusalem; began curacy as Chaplain to Amman and East Jordan, Diocese of Jerusalem

1956, priested at St George's, Jerusalem; left Jordan due to the Suez Crisis

1957-1960, Senior Curate, St Mary the Virgin, Reading, Diocese of Oxford

1960-1964, taught Arabic to ordinands in Omdurman, South Sudan; Chaplain at Khartoum Cathedral when required

1964-1986, Diocese of Oxford: 1964-1969, Vicar, St Michael & All Angels, Stewkley; 1969-1973, Vicar, St Luke, Maidenhead; 1973-1977, Vicar, Holy Trinity, Bracknell, and Rural Dean of Sonning; 1978-1986, Archdeacon of Berkshire

1987, 10 January, consecrated and enthroned at St Paul's Cathedral, Nicosia

1987, 6 February, enthroned at St Christopher's Cathedral, Bahrain

1995, 26 July, retired from full-time ministry and returned in the UK

1995-2011, Honorary Assistant Bishop, Diocese of Lincoln

1996-2007 - The Right Reverend Clive Handford CMG

b 17 April 1937

1963 deaconed; 1964 priested

Sept 1963-Sept 1966, Curate, St Peter and St Paul, Mansfield, Diocese of Southwell

Sept-Dec 1966, staff member, Collegiate Church of St George the Martyr, Jerusalem

6 Jan 1967-June 1967, Chaplain, Mesopotanian Memorial Church of St George the Martyr, Baghdad; left when the Iraq cut diplomatic relations with the UK, USA and West Germany due to the Six Day Arab-Israeli War

Sept 1967-early Jan 1973, Chaplain to English-speaking congregations in Beirut

1973 (for the year), Research Fellow and staff member, St Augustine's College in Canterbury (Kings College, University of London)

1974-1978, Dean, Cathedral Church of St George the Martyr, Jerusalem

1978-1983, Chaplain, St Andrew, Abu Dhabi; Archdeacon in the Gulf, Diocese of Cyprus and the Gulf

1983-1990, Diocese of Southwell: Feb 1983 - July 1984, Vicar of Kneesall, Laxton and Wellow, Rural Dean of Tuxford and Norwell, and Bishop's Ecumenical Chaplain; 1984-1990, Archdeacon of Nottingham

1990, 6 December (St Nicholas Day), consecrated at Westminster Abbey, London

1990-1996, Bishop of Warwick, Diocese of Coventry

1996, 31 May, enthroned at St Paul's Cathedral, Nicosia

1996, 9 June, enthroned at St Christopher's Cathedral, Bahrain

2002-2007, Primate of the Episcopal Church in Jerusalem & the Middle East

2007, 30 April, retired from full-time ministry; returned to the UK

2007-2014, Honorary Assistant Bishop, Diocese of Ripon and Leeds, and since 2014, Honorary Assistant Bishop in the new Diocese of Leeds

2007- The Right Reverend Michael Lewis

b 8 June 1953

1978 deaconed; 1979 priested

1978-1991, Diocese of Southwark: 1978-1980, Curate, Christ the King, Salfords; 1980-1984, Chaplain, Thames Polytechnic; 1984-1991, Vicar, St Mary, Welling

1991-1999, Diocese of Worcester: 1991-1999, Team Rector of Worcester SE; and 1993-1999, Rural Dean of Worcester East

1999, 7 December (Feast of St Ambrose), consecrated at York Minster

1999-2007, Bishop of Middleton, Diocese of Manchester

2007, 24 November, enthroned at St Paul's Cathedral, Nicosia, Cyprus

2007, 1 December, enthroned at St Christopher's Cathedral, Bahrain

2017, 17 May, elected by the Central Synod of the Episcopal Church in Jerusalem & the Middle East to serve as Primate beginning in November 2019

ARCHDEACONS

in Cyprus and the Gulf since 1899

Archdeacons appointed as Honorary Canons of either/both diocesan cathedrals are indicated with an asterisk * - see related chronology

It is normal to omit the title Canon after the titles The Very Reverend and The Venerable

The Very Reverend (Provost or Dean) takes precedence over The Venerable (Archdeacon) when the two roles apply to the same person

DIOCESE OF JERUSALEM

1899 - 1901	**The Venerable Josiah Spencer** the first Archdeacon in Cyprus Chaplain, St Paul, Nicosia, 1879-1901 *(Between 1878 and 1887 Anglican canonical oversight in Cyprus was vested in the Bishop of Gibraltar)*
1901 - 1927	**The Venerable Beresford Potter** Archdeacon in Cyprus, 1901-1927; and Archdeacon in Syria, 1915-1921 Chaplain, St Paul, Nicosia, 1902-1905

The following eight priests served as Archdeacon in Cyprus, and Chaplain at St Paul, Nicosia

Sept 1927 - June 1931	**The Venerable Harold Buxton**
July 1931 - Sept 1937	*No record of an Archdeacon in Cyprus*
Sept 1937 - Jan 1948	**The Venerable Malcolm Maxwell**
Sept 1949 - 1955	**The Venerable Donald Norwood Goldie**
1955 - 1958	**The Venerable Arthur W Adeney**
1958 - 1960	**The Venerable W Kenneth Blackburn**
1960 - 1963	**The Venerable William Benjamin Farrer**
1964 - 1967	**The Venerable Peter J Chandler**
1967 - May 1975	**The Venerable John (Jack) Nicholls**
May 1975 - May 1978	*No Archdeacon in Cyprus was appointed*

374

1940s - 1957	*Archdeacons serving in the Diocese of Jerusalem visited Arabia from time to time*
1950-1957	**The Venerable Cyril Victor Roberts** Archdeacon in Iraq and Eastern Arabia Chaplain, St George's, Baghdad (1946-1957)
1962 - 1964	**The Venerable Gwilyn Alun Morris CBE** * Archdeacon in Eastern Arabia and the Gulf Chaplain, St Christopher, Bahrain, 1954-1964
Dec 1970 - Jan 1976	**The Venerable Ralph Lindley CBE** the first Archdeacon in the Gulf, Chaplain, St Andrew, Abu Dhabi; and in Qatar

DIOCESE OF CYPRUS & THE GULF

Jan 1976 - May 1978	**The Venerable Ralph Lindley CBE** Archdeacon in the Gulf Chaplain, St Andrew, Abu Dhabi; and of Qatar
1978 - Aug 1980	**The Venerable Douglas Northridge** Archdeacon in Cyprus Chaplain, St Paul's Church, Nicosia - *died after a heart attack while on holiday in the UK*
1978 - 1983	**The Venerable Clive Handford** Archdeacon in the Gulf Chaplain, St Andrew, Abu Dhabi, and Qatar *see also Primates, and Bishops*
1981 - 1990	**The Very Reverend Bryan Henry** Archdeacon in Cyprus Provost, St Paul's Cathedral, Nicosia
1983 - 1990	**The Venerable Michael Mansbridge** * Archdeacon in the Gulf Chaplain, St Andrew, Abu Dhabi; and Qatar until 1986
1991 - 2006	*The roles and titles of the two archdeacons were combined*
1991 - 1999	**The Venerable Michael Mansbridge** * Archdeacon in Cyprus and the Gulf Chaplain, St Andrew, Abu Dhabi, until 1997 Provost, St Paul's Cathedral, Nicosia, 1997-1999 *chose to retain the title The Venerable*

375

1999 - April 2006	**The Venerable Dr Ian Young MBE** * Archdeacon in Cyprus and the Gulf Chaplain, Qatar, 1986-2006
2006 - 2009	**The Very Reverend Stephen Collis** * Archdeacon in Cyprus Dean, St Paul's Cathedral, Nicosia, 2002-2009
Aug 2009 - Dec 2010	*No Archdeacon in Cyprus was appointed*
May 2006 - May 2009	**The Very Reverend Alan Hayday** * Archdeacon in the Gulf Dean, St Christopher's Cathedral, Bahrain, 2002-2009
June 2009 -	**The Venerable Dr William Schwartz OBE** * Archdeacon in the Gulf Senior Chaplain, The Epiphany, Qatar, 2007-2014 Dean, St Christopher's Cathedral, 2019 - *with the title The Very Reverend*
Dec 2010 - July 2019	**The Venerable Dr John Holdsworth** * Executive Archdeacon, Diocese of Cyprus and the Gulf, and Director of Ministry Archdeacon in Cyprus Chaplain, St Helena, Larnaca
7 Sept 2019 -	**The Venerable Christopher Futcher** Archdeacon in Cyprus Chaplain, St Helena, Larnaca

PROVOSTS & DEANS

*   *See chronology: Archdeacons*

**   *See chronologies: Archdeacons; & Canons of the Two Cathedrals*

***   *See chronology: Canons of the Two Cathedrals*

\#   *Honorary Prebendary of Exeter Cathedral, England*

- *It is normal to omit the title Canon after the title The Very Reverend*

- *Following a name-change in the Church of England, since 2001 Provosts have been styled as Deans*

THE CATHEDRAL CHURCH OF ST PAUL
Nicosia, Cyprus

15 May 1981	*Rehallowed as the Diocesan Cathedral*
1981 - 1990	The Very Reverend Bryan Henry *
1991 - 1996	The Very Reverend Patrick Blair also Rural Dean in Cyprus
1997 - 1999	The Very Reverend Michael Mansbridge **
1999 - 2001	The Very Reverend John Morley
2002 - 2009	The Very Reverend Stephen Collis **
2009 - 2014	The Very Reverend John Tyrrell CD
2015 -	The Very Reverend Jeremy Crocker

THE CATHEDRAL CHURCH OF ST CHRISTOPHER
Manama, Bahrain

2 May 1982	*Rehallowed as the Pro-Cathedral of the Gulf*
23 April 1986	*The Pro-Cathedral was granted full cathedral status by episcopal mandate*
1986 - 1989	The Very Reverend John Parkinson MBE \#
1990 - 1997	The Very Reverend Derek Taylor
1997 - 2001	The Very Reverend Keith Johnson
2002 - 2009	The Very Reverend Alan Hayday **
2009 - 2019	The Very Reverend Christopher Butt ***
2019 -	The Very Reverend Dr William Schwartz OBE **

CANONS OF THE TWO CATHEDRALS

in Cyprus and Bahrain

- Within England, Scotland and Wales a Cathedral Chapter (the governing body of the Cathedral) usually comprises the Dean, residentiary canons and lay members.

- In almost all Anglican cathedrals outside England, Scotland and Wales, including those in the Diocese of Cyprus and the Gulf, there are no residentiary canons, apart from the Dean. Instead, governance is under the authority of the Dean and the Cathedral Church Council which may include other licensed clergy (such an assistant or associate priest and/or an assistant curate) and elected lay members.

- Within the Diocese of Cyprus and the Gulf, honorary canons may be senior priests who are based in chaplaincies/parishes, or were until their retirement. Among them have been priests whose ministry includes service to the Missions to Seamen, since 2000 known as the Mission to Seafarers.

- Other honorary canons are priests who, although not stipendiary incumbents in the diocese, have made significant contributions to its work, such as an Ecumenical Canon Theologian, commissaries to the bishop who are based in a country outside the diocese, and an Honorary Canon appointed for his Anglican Communion and ecumenical experience.

- Since 1997, lay canons have been appointed who have a been honoured for specific service to both chaplaincy/parish life and the diocese's affairs.

Abbreviations:

+Leonard	The Right Reverend Leonard Ashton
+John	The Right Reverend John Brown
+Clive	The Right Reverend Clive Handford, 1997 - 2002
	The Most Reverend Clive Handford, 2002 - 2007
+Michael	The Right Reverend Michael Lewis

THE CATHEDRAL CHURCH OF ST PAUL
Nicosia, Cyprus

The Venerable Michael Mansbridge (d 17 Jan 2014) - Chaplain, St Andrew, Abu Dhabi, 1983-1997; Archdeacon in the Gulf, 1983-1990; installed by +John as a Canon of St Christopher's Cathedral, 5 June 1988; installed by +John at St Paul's Cathedral, Nicosia, as Archdeacon of Cyprus and the Gulf, 8 Sept 1991, and on the same day installed as a Canon of the cathedral; Provost, St Paul's Cathedral, 1997-1999; upon retirement, 31 Aug 1999, granted the title Archdeacon Emeritus by +Clive, and granted the titles Canon Emeritus of St Paul's Cathedral, Nicosia, and St Christopher's Cathedral, Bahrain

The Venerable Dr Ian Young MBE - Assistant Chaplain, St Christopher's Cathedral, Bahrain, 1984-1986; Chaplain, Qatar, 1986-2007 (visited from Bahrain until Dec 1991); Diocesan Director of Ordinands and Training, 1988-1999; installed by +John as a Canon, St Christopher's Cathedral, 5 June 1988; Gulf Liaison Officer for the Middle East Council of Churches, 1987-1989; installed by +Clive as an Honorary Canon, St Paul's Cathedral, Nicosia, 7 Nov 1999; on the same day collated as Archdeacon in Cyprus and the Gulf, served until 30 Apr 2006; Provincial Secretary, Episcopal Church in Jerusalem and the Middle East, 2002-2006; granted the titles Archdeacon Emeritus, and Canon Emeritus of St Christopher's Cathedral, 1 May 2006

The Right Reverend Leonard Ashton CB (d 19 Jan 2001) - Assistant Chaplain-in-Chief, RAF, 1962-1965; Chaplain, St Clement Danes, RAF Church, London, 1965 - 1969; Chaplain-in-Chief of the (British) Royal Air Force, and Archdeacon for the RAF in the Church of England, 1969-1973; consecrated at St Clement Danes Church, Central Church of the RAF, London, 22 Jan 1974; Assistant Bishop, Diocese of Jerusalem, 1974-1976; installed as an Episcopal Canon of St George's Cathedral, Jerusalem, 6 Jan 1976; inaugural Bishop, Diocese of Cyprus and the Gulf, 1976-1983; installed by +John as Episcopal Canon of St Paul's Cathedral, Nicosia, 5 Feb 1989

The Venerable Peter Delaney MBE - Precentor and Residentiary Canon, Southwark Cathedral, London, 1973-1977; Vicar, All Hallows by the Tower, London, 1977-2004; appointed Prebendary, St Paul's Cathedral, London, 1995; installed by +John as an Honorary Canon, St Paul's Cathedral, Nicosia, 5 Feb 1989; appointed by +John as his Commissary in the UK, 9 July 1990 and similarly by +Clive, 1996-2007; Archdeacon of London, 1999-2009; Priest-in-Charge, St Stephen Walbrook, City of London, 2004-2014

The Reverend Canon Arthur Rider MBE (d 26 Aug 2005) - Chaplain, St Andrew, Kyrenia, 1980-1987; installed by +John as an Honorary Canon, St Paul's Cathedral, Nicosia, 5 Feb 1989

The Reverend Canon Dr Kenneth Bailey (d 23 May 2016) - raised in Egypt, then moved to the USA for higher education; ordained in the Presbyterian Church; a distinguished New Testament theologian and Arabist, taught at the Ecumenical Institute for Theological Research in Tantur, Israel, and in Lebanon; relocated to Cyprus in 1990 to continue his research; installed by +John as Ecumenical Canon Theologian-in-Residence of St Paul's Cathedral, Nicosia, 8 Sept 1991; retired to New Wilmington, Pennsylvania, in 1995

The Reverend Canon Michael Jones (d 9 Dec 2014) - Chaplain at St Paul Ahmadi, Kuwait, 1983-1990; held hostage in Baghdad after the invasion of Kuwait; returned to the UK in 1991; Chaplain, St Barnabas Limassol, Cyprus, 1996 -2003; Port Chaplain, Mission to Seafarers in Cyprus, 1996-2003; installed by +Clive as an Honorary Canon of St Paul's Cathedral, Nicosia, 6 Jan 2001; upon retirement appointed Canon Emeritus by +Clive in 2003

The Venerable Jonathan Gough - joined the Royal Army Chaplains Department, 1989; left the regular army to serve as Ecumenical Secretary to the Archbishop of Canterbury, 2001-2005; returned to regular military service in 2005; appointed Canon of Gibraltar Cathedral, Europe, Feb 2005; appointed for his Anglican Communion and ecumenical experience by +Clive as an Honorary Canon of St Paul's Cathedral, Nicosia, 28 May 2006; Regional Senior Chaplain for Yorkshire and the North East, 2011-2014; Assistant Chaplain General at Army HQ Regional Command, Aldershot, 2014-2018; installed as Archdeacon of Richmond and Craven, Diocese of Leeds, 10 March 2019

The Reverend Canon Stephen Collis - Chaplain, St Andrew, Abu Dhabi, 2000-2002; Dean, St Paul's Cathedral, Nicosia, 2002-2009; Archdeacon in Cyprus 2006-2009; appointed by +Michael as an Honorary Canon of St Paul's Cathedral, Nicosia, 1 Aug 2009

The Reverend Canon Paul Burt - Curate in Edinburgh, 1984-1988; Associate Priest, St Christopher's Cathedral, Bahrain, 1988-1990; Rector, Holy Trinity, Melrose, Scotland, 1990-1999; Housemaster, Winchester College Quiristers and Head of Religious Studies, Pilgrims' School, Winchester, 2000-2004; Chaplain, King's College School, Cambridge; 2004-2006; Senior Chaplain, Winchester College, 2006-2012; Chaplain, Mission to Seafarers, Dubai and the UAE, Sept 2012-April 2013, then Regional Director, Gulf and South Asia, April 2013-Oct 2018; installed by +Michael as an Honorary Canon, St Paul's Cathedral, 6 May 2018

The **Reverend Canon Brian Elliott** - ordained in 1975; commissioned into the Royal Army Chaplains Department in 1977; served in the UK, Germany and other theatres including in Cyprus - Episkopi (twice), Dhekelia and with the United Nations in Nicosia; retired from the regular British Army in 2009 as a Deputy Assistant Chaplain-General having compiled a standard reference on Remembrance Liturgy 'They Shall Grow Not Old' (Canterbury Press); married into a Nicosia Anglo-Cypriot family; since 2009 has PTO within the Diocese of Cyprus and the Gulf; a part time chaplain to the UN; part-time Officiating Chaplain to the (British) Forces; installed by +Michael as an Honorary Canon of St Paul's Cathedral, 6 May 2018

The **Very Reverend Bertrand Olivier** - a French national who, prior to ordination in 1996, pursued a career in international public relations and communications consultancies in London; Vicar, St Barnabas, Southfields, Southwark, 2000-2005; Vicar, All Hallows by the Tower, London, 2005-Feb 2018; Commissary to +Michael in the UK, Feb 2014-Feb 2018; elected member of the General Synod of the Church of England, 2015-2018; Dean of Montreal and Rector of Christ Church Cathedral, Montreal, Canada, since 12 March 2018; installed by +Michael as an Honorary Canon of St Paul's Cathedral, Nicosia, 6 May 2018

381

The **Venerable Dr John Ivor Holdsworth** - deaconed in St Woolos Cathedral Newport, Wales, 1973; priested, 1974; served a curacy in Newport, then Parish Priest in the Swansea Valley at Abercrave, and later in Gorseinon; Principal of the Church in Wales Theological College, Cardiff, 1997-2003; Dean of the Faculty of Theology, Cardiff University, 2001-3, Archdeacon of St David's, Diocese of Cardiff, 2003-2010; in the Diocese of C&G, Executive Archdeacon, Archdeacon in Cyprus, Chaplain of St Helena's, Larnaca, Dec 2010 - July 2019; Visiting Professor at Glyndwr University, 2012-2018; in April 2019, awarded an honorary DD degree by Queens College Newfoundland, Canada, in recognition of his contribution to ministerial training; author, television broadcaster, teacher and external examiner; TAVR Army Chaplain; since retirement in July 2019, Honorary Director of Ministry, Diocese of C&G; installed by +Michael as Canon Theologian, St Paul's Nicosia, 3 Nov 2019

The **Reverend Canon Faiz Basheer Jerjes** - raised and educated in Baghdad, Iraq; studied theology at the Armenian Catholic Seminary in the Lebanon, 1975-1980; joined the ministry team at St George's Baghdad, 2006; admitted and licensed by +Michael as Lector, 1 June 2009; deaconed on 11 July 2010, priested on 11 Sept 2011; also in 2011 graduated from the Babylon College of Philosophy and Theology/Babylon Institute, and appointed curate at

St George's; installed as parish priest on 4 Jan 2015, and authorised by +Michael to manage all matters, spiritual and temporal (including management of property, finances, and representation to the Iraqi government) on behalf of the Anglican Church in Iraq; in March 2018, a founder of the Massarat Foundation for confronting hate speech in Iraq; and in 2019, received a national award for his outstanding role in reconciliation between different religions and sects in Iraq; since 2014, both in Iraq and elsewhere, has participated in conferences and seminars on reconciliation in Iraq; installed by +Michael as an Honorary Canon, St Paul's Nicosia, 3 Nov 2019

THE CATHEDRAL CHURCH OF ST CHRISTOPHER
Manama, Bahrain

The Venerable Michael Mansbridge (d 17 Jan 2014) - Chaplain, St Andrew, Abu Dhabi, 1983-1997; Archdeacon in the Gulf, 1983-1990; installed by +John as a Canon of St Christopher's Cathedral, 5 June 1988; installed by +John at St Paul's Cathedral, Nicosia, as Archdeacon of Cyprus and the Gulf, 8 Sept 1991, and on the same day installed as a Canon of the cathedral; Provost, St Paul's Cathedral, 1997-1999; upon retirement, 31 Aug 1999, granted the title Archdeacon Emeritus by +Clive, and granted the titles Canon Emeritus of St Paul's Cathedral, Nicosia, and St Christopher's Cathedral, Bahrain

The Venerable Dr Ian Young MBE - Assistant Chaplain, St Christopher's Cathedral, Bahrain, 1984-1986; Chaplain, Qatar, 1986-2007 (visited from Bahrain until Dec 1991); Diocesan Director of Ordinands and Training, 1988-2003; installed by +John as a Canon, St Christopher's Cathedral, 5 June 1988; Gulf Liaison Officer for the Middle East Council of Churches, 1987-1989; installed by +Clive as an Honorary Canon, St Paul's Cathedral, Nicosia, 7 Nov 1999; on the same day collated as Archdeacon in Cyprus and the Gulf, served until 30 Apr 2006; Provincial Secretary, Episcopal Church in Jerusalem and the Middle East, 2002-2006; granted the titles Archdeacon Emeritus, and Canon Emeritus of St Christopher's Cathedral, 1 May 2006

The Venerable Alun Morris CBE (d 26 Aug 2000) - a Chaplain to the British Forces, 1942-1946; Chaplain, Palestine Police Force, 1946-1948; Minister, St Michael's, North Hull, UK, 1948-1954; Chaplain, St Christopher's Church, 1954-1964; during the first few years of this ministry regularly served congregations in Qatar, Dubai and Abu Dhabi; appointed as an Honorary Canon, St George's Collegiate Church, Jerusalem, 1960; a founding father of

St Christopher's School, Bahrain, opened on the church compound at Easter 1961; Archdeacon, Eastern Arabia and the Gulf, 1962-1964; retained his canonry as the Archbishop in Jerusalem's Chaplain/Secretary for Pilgrimages to the Holy Land, 1965-1967; installed by +John as an Honorary Canon, St Christopher's Cathedral, 5 June 1988

Canon Margaret (Peggy) McGinley - Canterbury Group member; Lay Member, Provincial Synod, Episcopal Church in Jerusalem and the Middle East, 1986 -1996; Chairman (Gulf), House of Laity of the Diocesan Synod, 1986-2010; Lay Member (Gulf), Diocesan Standing Committee, 1986-2010; appointed Reader by +John, 25 March 1987; installed by +Clive as an Honorary Lay Canon, St Christopher's Cathedral, 26 Feb 1997

The Reverend Canon Dennis Gurney OBE - Senior Chaplain of Dubai, Sharjah and the Northern Emirates, 1984-2001; installed by +Clive as an Honorary Canon, St Christopher's Cathedral, 25 March 1998; granted the title Canon Emeritus upon retirement, 1 July 2001; locum Chaplain, Christ Church, Aden, Yemen, Nov 2003 - Feb 2004, and in other diocesan chaplaincies

The Reverend Canon Benjamin Chase - Rector, Canterbury Group, Oct 1988 - June 1999; installed by +Clive as an Honorary Canon, St Christopher's Cathedral, 2 May 2000; Chaplain, Christ Church, Aden, March-Sept 2001, May-Aug 2005; Anglican Priest, Protestant Church in Oman, 2006-2007

The Very Reverend Dr William Schwartz OBE - licensed as Reader by +Leonard, 1982; Chairman (Cyprus), House of Laity of the Diocesan Synod, 1986-1993; Lay Member (Cyprus), Diocesan Standing Committee, 1986-1993; Diocesan Assistant Treasurer, 1986-1990; Lay Member, Central Synod of the Episcopal Church in Jerusalem and the Middle East, 1986-1993; ordained deacon, 16 Feb 1993; ordained priest, 2 Aug 1993; NSM Assistant Curate, St Andrew, Kyrenia, 1993-1995; Diocesan Secretary/Treasurer, 1990-1999, with NSM licence for the diocese, 1995-1999; Rector, Canterbury Group, 1999-2007; installed by +Clive as an Honorary Canon, St Christopher's Cathedral, 6 Feb 2006; Senior Chaplain, Epiphany, Qatar, 2007-2014; Provincial Treasurer, 2007-2017; Archdeacon in the Gulf, and *ex officio* member of Diocesan Standing Committee and Bishop's Council since 1 June 2009; Dean of St Christopher's Cathedral, installed 1 June 2019

The Reverend Canon Alan Hayday - ordained in 1969; served in the Diocese of Lincoln, finally as Team Rector, Brumby Team, Scunthorpe, 1986-2002; appointed Honorary Canon of Lincoln Cathedral, 17 Nov 2000 and Canon Emeritus of Lincoln, 2002; Dean of St Christopher's Cathedral, 2002-2009;

Diocesan Director of Ordinands (Gulf), 2003-2009; Archdeacon in the Gulf, 1 May 2006 - 31 May 2009; upon retirement appointed by +Michael as an Honorary Canon, St Christopher's Cathedral, 1 June 2009

Canon John Banfield - appointed Chairman Mobil Oil Co Ltd, London, in 1994, and Vice President Mobil Europe in 1996; retired from Mobil, 2001; appointed Non-Executive Director, Surrey Oaklands National Health Service (NHS) Trust, 2002, and Chairman, Surrey and Borders Partnership NHS Trust, 2005; retired from the NHS, 2011; co-opted onto the Diocesan Standing and Finance Committee, 2007; Hon Diocesan Director of Finance, 2007-present; later assumed a broader executive portfolio, including membership of the council for Christ Church and the Ras Morbat Clinic Aden; installed by +Michael as an Honorary Lay Canon, St Christopher's Cathedral, 4 Dec 2011

The Reverend Canon Andrew Thompson MBE - Chaplain, St Paul, Ahmadi, Kuwait, 2006-2010; Diocesan Director of Ordinands (Gulf), 2009-2014; Senior Chaplain, St Andrew, Abu Dhabi since Aug 2010; installed by +Michael as an Honorary Canon, St Christopher's Cathedral, 4 Dec 2011

The Reverend Canon Stephen Thanapaul - ordained in 1992; Bishop's Chaplain to +Jason Dharmaraj, Diocese of Tirunelveli, Church of South India, 1993 -1998; Associate Editor, *Narpothagam,* Tirunelveli Diocesan Magazine, 1993-1998; training at Seamen's Church Institute of New York and New Jersey, 1998 - 1999; Parish Priest, Shunmugapuram, Tuticorin, Tamil Nadu, 1999-2002; Chaplain to Truck Drivers, 1999 - 2002; Chaplain, Mission to Seafarers, Tuticorin Seafarers' Centre, Tamil Nadu, 2002-2009; Assistant Priest, St Christopher's Cathedral, and Port Chaplain, Mission to Seafarers in Bahrain, 12 Feb 2009 - present; pioneered the St Christopher's Cathedral Tamil Congregation in April 2014; installed by +Michael as an Honorary Canon, St Christopher's Cathedral, 23 Feb 2018

The Reverend Canon Jebaraj Devasagayam - entered ministry in 1978 as a cross-cultural missionary, licensed in the Church of North India to serve in the Diocese of Kolapur; pursued three areas of ministry, often overlapping: church ministry, theological teaching, and publishing-writing for theological publishing houses in India (including the Theological Research and Communication Institute, the Theological Book Trust and the Association for Theological Education by Extension); Assistant Chaplain, Church of the Epiphany, Doha, Qatar 2010 - present; pioneered the Epiphany Tamil Congregation, 2011; and the Epiphany Marathi Congregation, 2014; installed by +Michael as an Honorary Canon, St Christopher's Cathedral, 23 Feb 2018

Canon Angela Murray MBE - assisted in BBC radio and television production in London, 1965-1970 / 1973-1978; graduate of Birmingham University (1973) and Cranfield University (1983); since 1981 has evolved her vocation as an historian and published author; member of St Christopher's Cathedral, 1988-2019, and of the Bahrain Anglican Church Council, 1993-2019; Lay Member (Gulf), Diocesan Standing Committee and Bishop's Council, 2013-2019; since 1991 has led community, charity and diocesan projects; author of this history of the Diocese of C&G; installed by +Michael as an Honorary Lay Canon, St Christopher's Cathedral, 23 Feb 2018

The Reverend Canon Christopher Butt - deaconed in the Diocese of Ely in 1979; priested in 1980; Assistant Curate, St Barnabas Cambridge, 1979-82; Chaplain, St John's Cathedral and Priest-in-charge Emmanuel Church, Hong Kong, 1982-89; Rector, St Martin's, Windermere,1989-98; Team Rector, Parish of South Gillingham, Kent, 1998-2009; Dean, St Christopher's Cathedral, Bahrain, 2009-2019; clergy member of the Bishop's Council and the Diocesan Standing Committee, 2013-19; Chair, House of Clergy, 2013-19; Chair of Selectors for the Bishop's Advisory Panel, 2012-2018; installed by +Michael as an Honorary Canon, St Christopher's Cathedral, 25 Oct 2019

The Reverend Canon Harrison Chinnakumar - entered ministry in 1986 as a cross-cultural missionary, serving the Tribal Belt in India; graduated from the Union Biblical Seminary, Pune, India, then moved to pastoral ministry, initially at All Saints Cathedral, Nagpur, Church of North India; moved to the Church of South India, Bangalore, 2005; between 2005-2011 pursued higher theological studies; Chaplain at St Paul's, Kuwait, 2012-2016; since 2016, Chaplain at Holy Trinity Dubai; appointed by +Michael as an Honorary Canon, St Christopher's Cathedral, June 2019

385

ORDINATIONS

Diocese of Cyprus and the Gulf

by Bishop Leonard Ashton

The Reverend Clive Windebank
> 1978, 10 September: deaconed at St Paul, Nicosia, Cyprus
> 1979, 25 March: priested at St Paul, Ahmadi, Kuwait

The Reverend Samuel Masih
> 1981, in March, deaconed at the Church of the Magi, Salalah, Oman

by Bishop Harry Moore

The Reverend Geoffrey Brookes
> 1985, 24 November: deaconed at St Christopher's Cathedral, Bahrain
> 1986, 23 March: priested at St Christopher's Cathedral, Bahrain

by Bishop John Brown

Three priests (marked *) were ordained to serve as Missions to Seamen chaplains in the Diocese of C&G with dual roles as associate chaplains/parish priests.

In 2000 the charity was renamed the Mission to Seafarers.

The Reverend Ian Thurston
> 1989, 26 May: deaconed at St Christopher's Cathedral, Bahrain
> 1990, 6 August: priested at All Hallows-by-the Tower, London - *coinciding with the annual reunion of the Friends of the Diocese of Cyprus and the Gulf*

The Reverend Duncan Harris *
> 1989, 26 May: deaconed at St Christopher's Cathedral, Bahrain
> 1990, 4 August: priested at St Michael Paternoster Royal, City of London - *to serve as a Missions to Seamen chaplain in the diocese*

The Reverend Dr John Chesworth
> 1992, 2 October: deaconed at the Church of The Good Shepherd, Ghala, Oman
> 1993, 2 August: priested at All Hallows-by-the Tower, London - *coinciding with the annual reunion of the Friends of the Diocese of Cyprus and the Gulf*

The Reverend Roy Topping MBE *

1992, 4 October: deaconed at St Christopher's Cathedral, Bahrain
1993, 1 August: priested at St Michael Paternoster Royal, City of London -
to serve as a Missions to Seamen chaplain in Bahrain

The Very Reverend Dr William Schwartz OBE

1993, 16 February: deaconed at St Helena's Church, Larnaca, Cyprus
1993, 2 August: priested at All-Hallows-by-the-Tower, London -
coinciding with the annual reunion of the Friends of the Diocese of Cyprus and the Gulf

The Reverend Victor Salve *

1994, 23 November: deaconed at St Christopher's Cathedral, Bahrain
1995, 5 July: priested at St Christopher's Cathedral, Bahrain - *to serve as Chaplain to the Mission to Seamen, Bahrain*

The Reverend James Wakerley

1994, 30 September: deaconed at the Church of The Good Shepherd, Ghala, Oman
1995, 9 June: priested at the Church of The Good Shepherd in Ghala, Oman

The Reverend Peter Sewell

1994, 30 September: deaconed at the Church of The Good Shepherd, Ghala, Oman
1995, 31 July: priested at All-Hallows-by-the-Tower, London -
coinciding with the annual reunion of the Friends of the Diocese of Cyprus and the Gulf

The Reverend Ernest Victor

1995, 9 June: deaconed at the Church of The Good Shepherd in Ghala, Oman

by Bishop Clive Handford

The Reverend Ernest Victor

1996, 11 October: priested at the Church of The Good Shepherd in Ghala, Oman

The Reverend Daniel Borkowski

1998, 11 June: deaconed at St Christopher's Cathedral, Bahrain
1998, 3 December: priested at St Christopher's Cathedral, Bahrain

The Reverend Michael Loader

2005, 2 October: deaconed at St Paul's Cathedral, Nicosia, Cyprus

The Reverend Susan Place

2005, 2 October: deaconed at St Paul's Cathedral, Nicosia, Cyprus *by Bishop Michael Lewis*

In November 2010, a resolution of the Central Synod of the Episcopal Church in Jerusalem and the Middle East (held in Amman, Jordan) allowed the Bishop in Cyprus and the Gulf to ordain women to the priesthood within the diocese.

Bishop Michael Lewis had proposed the motion: "that this Synod shall be content that the Bishop in Cyprus and the Gulf, after he has consulted his Diocesan Synod, may exercise his judgment and discretion in ordaining suitable candidates whether male or female to the priesthood, and in discerning suitable candidates whether male or female for appointment to licensed chaplaincies in his diocese". The motion was passed with one abstention.

The Reverend Catherine Dawkins
2010, 15 January: deaconed at Christ Church, Aden, Yemen
2011, 5 June: priested at St Christopher's Cathedral, Bahrain - *the first woman to be ordained priest within the Diocese of Cyprus and the Gulf, and also within the Province of the Episcopal Church in Jerusalem and the Middle East*

The Reverend Lawrence Hilditch
2010, 2 July: deaconed at St Paul's Cathedral, Nicosia, Cyprus
2011, 19 June: priested St Paul's Cathedral, Nicosia, Cyprus

The Reverend Dr Michael Ellis
2010, 2 July: deaconed at St Paul's Cathedral, Nicosia, Cyprus
2011, 19 June: priested St Paul's Cathedral, Nicosia, Cyprus

The Reverend Faiz Jirjees
2010, 11 July: deaconed at St George, Baghdad, Iraq - *the first Iraqi Anglican ordinand*
2011, 11 September: priested at St George, Baghdad, Iraq

The Reverend Joanne Henderson
2012, 28 September: deaconed at St Andrew, Abu Dhabi
2013, 27 September: priested at St Christopher's Cathedral, Bahrain

The Reverend Jon Lavelle
2014, 13 September: deaconed at St Christopher's Cathedral, Bahrain
2015, 5 September: priested at St Christopher's Cathedral, Bahrain

The Reverend Kent Middleton Obl CR
2015, 27 June: deaconed at Llandaff Cathedral, Wales, UK - *by the Most Reverend Barry Morgan, Archbishop of Wales and Bishop of Llandaff, on behalf of Bishop Michael Lewis*
2016, 25 June: priested at St Paul's Cathedral, Nicosia, Cyprus

The Reverend Christine Goldsmith
    2015, 27 June: deaconed at St Paul's Cathedral, Nicosia, Cyprus
    2016, 25 June: priested at St Paul's Cathedral, Nicosia, Cyprus

The Reverend Geoffrey Graham
    2015, 27 June: deaconed at St Paul's Cathedral, Nicosia, Cyprus
    2016, 25 June: priested at St Paul's Cathedral, Nicosia, Cyprus

The Reverend Hin Lai (Harry) Ching
    2016, 25 June: deaconed at St Paul's Cathedral, Nicosia, Cyprus
    2017, 23 September: priested at Christ Church Jebel Ali, UAE

The Reverend Zhu Peijin
    2017, 6 January: deaconed at St Paul, Ahmadi, Kuwait
    2018, 27 January: priested at St Paul, Ahmadi, Kuwait

The Reverend Charlotte Lloyd-Evans
    2017, 23 September: deaconed at Christ Church Jebel Ali, UAE
    2018, 15 September: priested at St Andrew, Abu Dhabi, UAE

The Reverend Navina Thompson
    2018, 20 April: deaconed at St Andrew, Abu Dhabi, UAE
    2019, 4 May: priested at St Paul's Cathedral, Nicosia, Cyprus

The Reverend Justin Arnott
    2018, 7 July: deaconed at St Paul's Cathedral, Nicosia, Cyprus
    2019, 21 September: priested at St Paul's Cathedral, Nicosia, Cyprus

The Reverend Peter Day
    2018, 7 July: deaconed at St Paul's Cathedral, Nicosia, Cyprus
    2019, 21 September: priested at St Paul's Cathedral, Nicosia, Cyprus

READERS

- *Place of licensing is the name of the church stated*

- *Those admitted to the office of Reader are licensed to serve within the diocese. In practice, Reader ministries are usually specific to the chaplaincies stated*

3 Sept 1973   **Stanley Edward McGinley**
Canterbury Group
appointed as a Reader; awarded the Jerusalem Cross by the Most Revd George Appleton, Archbishop in Jerusalem; 25 Sept 1987 re-licensed by +John

Licensed by Bishop Leonard Ashton

25/26 Feb 1977   *At the Diocesan Synod (Gulf) Archdeacon Ralph Lindley named nine readers already licensed by the bishop.*

It is assumed licensing took place after 5 Jan 1976 and before 25/26 Feb 1977, hence 1976/7

1976/7   **Peter D Hipwell**
St Andrew, Abu Dhabi chaplaincy

1976/7   **John P Egan**
Lada Jeanne Hardwick
Terry Edwin Orr
Canterbury Group

1976/7   **John Gordon Samuels**
St Barnabas, Limassol chaplaincy

1976/7   **Mervyn Sawyer**
St Antony, Paphos, within Limassol chaplaincy

1976/7   **Antony F G Foulger**
Holy Trinity, Dubai, and to serve in Ras al Khaimah

1976/7   **Dr Philip Horniblow**
Place of licensing not known; to serve congregations in Oman

1977   **Ernest Noble**
St Christopher, and Awali Church, Bahrain chaplaincy

1977/8   **Clive Windebank**
St Paul Ahmadi, Kuwait chaplaincy
10 Sept 1978 deaconed; 25 March 1979 priested

By 1982	**James D Thornton**
	Kevin Williams
	St Christopher, and Awali Church, Bahrain chaplaincy

1982	**William Schwartz**
	St Barnabas, Limassol chaplaincy
	16 Feb 1993 deaconed; 2 Aug 1993 priested

12/15 May 1983	*By this Diocesan Synod more Readers had been licensed by Bishop Leonard Ashton. His report states the total number serving in the diocese.*
	Cyprus 7: Kyrenia, Larnaca, Nicosia and Paphos, 1 in each; Limassol 3
	Gulf 17: Dubai, Kuwait, Qatar, 1 in each; Bahrain, Oman, 2 in each; Abu Dhabi 3; Canterbury Group 7

1983	**Arthur Simmonds**
	St Andrew, Abu Dhabi chaplaincy
	Philip Bourne
	St Helena, Larnaca chaplaincy
	Dr W N Adams-Smith
	St Paul Ahmadi, Kuwait chaplaincy
	Hugh Haile
	St Andrew, Kyrenia chaplaincy
	Michael Rigby
	St Christopher, and Awali Church, Bahrain chaplaincy

Licensed by Bishop Harry Moore

| 1984, 8 July | **Joyce Napper** |
| | St Helena, Larnaca chaplaincy |

| 1986, April | **Ian Thurston** - *licensing day not known* |
| | St Christopher, Bahrain chaplaincy |

Licensed by Bishop John Brown

| 1987, 9 Feb | **David Pellatt** |
| | St Christopher, and Lay Chaplain to Missions to Seamen, Bahrain chaplaincy |

| 1987, 25 March | **Margaret (Peggy) McGinley** |
| | Canterbury Group |

By 1990	**Roy Topping** - *licensing date not known*
	St Christopher, and Lay Chaplain to Missions to Seamen, Bahrain chaplaincy
	4 Oct 1992 deaconed; 1 Aug 1993 priested

391

Licensed by Bishop Clive Handford

1996, 30 June	**Oriole Hart** **Barbara Vaughan** St Paul Ahmadi, Kuwait chaplaincy
1997, April	**Paul Joseph** **Pamela Shield** Gymnasium of Doha English Speaking School, *venue before Epiphany consecration on 29 Sept 2013*, Qatar chaplaincy
1998, 25 Oct	**Deirdre Baker** **Margaret Hobbs** **Angela Pursey** St Paul's Cathedral, Nicosia chaplaincy, and to serve other chaplaincies in Cyprus as needed
	Edith Schwartz St Paul's Cathedral, as above 1999-2007 Canterbury Group; 2007-2019 Qatar chaplaincy; April 2019 - , Bahrain Chaplaincy
1998, 29 Nov	**Alan Hill** St Paul Ahmadi, Kuwait chaplaincy
1998, 27 Dec	**Brenda Read** St Paul's Cathedral, Nicosia chaplaincy, and to serve other chaplaincies in Cyprus as needed
1999, 15 Aug	**Michael Thomas Procter** St Barnabas, Limassol chaplaincy
2000, 22 Oct	**Albion Winslow Land** St Paul's Cathedral, Nicosia chaplaincy
2001, 12 May	**Richard Harwood** licensed at Khor out-station, Qatar chaplaincy to develop ministry at Khor, 50 miles/80 kms north of Doha
2001, 13 May	**Tricia Boerse** Gymnasium of Doha English Speaking School, *venue before Epiphany consecration on 29 Sept 2013*, Qatar chaplaincy
2003, 5 March	**Margaret Yearsley** St Barnabas, Limassol chaplaincy
2003, 22 June	**John Smith** Ayia Kyriaki, Paphos chaplaincy
2004, 2 May	**Colin John Anthony Johns** **Trevor Sait** - Diocesan Synod Sacristan, 2005-2018

Barbara Ann Sen
Ayia Kyriaki, Paphos chaplaincy

2004, 10 Dec **Robin Tems**
Canterbury Group

2005, 10 April **Christopher Howsam**
Ayia Kyriaki, Paphos chaplaincy

2005, 26 June **Wendy Foulger**
St Paul's Cathedral, Nicosia chaplaincy; to serve at churches
in the British SBAs and at St Columba, the UN church in the
Buffer Zone, with permission to officiate the sacrament

2005, 2 Dec **Bruce William Goodwin**
to serve the Protestant Church in Oman

2007, 1 Feb **Joanne Henderson**
licensed at St Helena, Larnaca, to serve at St Andrew, Abu
Dhabi chaplaincy
28 Sept 2012 deaconed, 27 Sept 2013 priested;

2007, 18 March **Stuart Plowman**
licensed at the Scandinavian Church, Ayia Napa, to serve the
South-East Cyprus chaplaincy

Licensed by Bishop Michael Lewis

2008, 2 March **Avinash Madhukar Awhad**
Sibella Laing
Jasmine Weeks
Shaun Weeks
St Paul, Ahmadi, Kuwait chaplaincy

2008, 14 Sept Licensed at Ayia Kyriaki, to serve Paphos chaplaincy:
Allan Hodgson
Kenneth Wiseman
14 July 2013 licensed as Lay Chaplain, Mission to Seafarers

2008, 12 Oct **Valerie Brookes**
Church of St George Exorinos (the Foreigner), Famagusta, to
serve at St Mark, chaplaincy of South-East Cyprus

2009, 10 May **Geoffrey Richard Adams**
Peter Edward Jones
Canterbury Group

2010, 9 May **Ann Bailey**
10 Feb 2005 recognised by +Clive with PTO and on 10 April
2005 publicly celebrated at Ayia Kyriaki to serve Paphos
chaplaincy; 9 May 2010 confirmed as an Anglican and licensed
by +Michael for Reader ministry in Paphos chaplaincy

2011, 2 July	**Sally Milner** **Talita van der Westhuizen** **Alan Dempster** St Paul Ahmadi, Kuwait chaplaincy
2011, 13 Oct	**Jared Wade Fontenot** St Andrew, to serve at St Thomas, al Ain, Abu Dhabi chaplaincy
2011, 14 Oct	**Thomas Pape** St Andrew, Abu Dhabi chaplaincy
2012, 29 Jan	Licensed at St Barnabas, Limassol: **William Garrett** to serve South-East Cyprus /Ammochostos chaplaincy
	Peter Day to serve South-East Cyprus /Ammochostos chaplaincy *7 July 2018 deaconed; 21 Sept 2019 priested*
	Christine Goldsmith to serve Limassol chaplaincy, including St Lazarus, Pissouri *27 June 2015 deaconed; 25 June 2016 priested*
	Alan Ward to serve Paphos chaplaincy
2012, 24 Feb	**Deborah Fitch** **Elizabeth Marie Norton** Gymnasium of Doha English Speaking School, *venue before Epiphany consecration on 29 Sept 2013,* Qatar chaplaincy
2012, 1 June	**Charlotte Lloyd-Evans** licensed at Holy Trinity, Dubai, to serve DSNE chaplaincy *23 Sept 2017 deaconed; 15 Sept 2018 priested*
2013, 18 Jan	**Ashok Vase** licensed at Christ Church, Jebel Ali, to serve DSNE chaplaincy
2013, 15 March	**Vivien Buckle** **Patricia Butt** **Elizabeth George** **Simon Phillips** St Christopher's Cathedral, Bahrain chaplaincy
2013, 7 July	**Justin Arnott** St Paul's Cathedral, Nicosia chaplaincy; 1 Nov 2016 licence renewed to serve as Reader and Lay Chaplain, St Mark, Famagusta *7 July 2018 deaconed, 21 Sept 2019 priested*

394

2014, 29 June	**Geoffrey Graham** St Helena, Larnaca chaplaincy 27 June 2015 deaconed, 25 June 2016 priested
2014, 7 Sept	**Harry Ching** St Mark, Famagusta, to serve as Reader and Lay Chaplain *25 June 2016 deaconed, 23 Sept 2017 priested*
2014, 26 Sept	**Wendy Roderick** St Thomas, al Ain, Abu Dhabi chaplaincy
2015, 25 June	**William Grundy** St Paul's Cathedral, to serve Nicosia chaplaincy
2017, 14 Nov	Licensed at St Paul's Cathedral, Nicosia: **Raymond Elliott** to serve Paphos chaplaincy **Kevin Moore** to serve Ammochostos chaplaincy at Christ Church, Ayia Napa
2019, 18 Jan	**Dr Angel Afolabi** St Christopher, and to serve at Awali Church, Bahrain

PRIESTS WITH PERMISSION TO OFFICIATE

- *This alphabetical list names priests known to have been granted Permission to Officiate (PTO) in the diocese since its formation on 5 January 1976.*

- *Several names are also listed in the Anglican Ministry chronology, such as those priests who served/are serving with PTO in specific circumstances: before being licensed as an incumbent; leaders of non-English language Anglican congregations; during long interregnums; and ordained spouses accompanying their chaplain/parish priest husbands.*

Amat, The Reverend Gabriel
Backhouse, The Reverend Colin
Boultbee, The Reverend Michael
Brimacombe, The Reverend Keith
Broughton, The Reverend Stuart Roger
Brow, The Reverend Robert Charles
Brown, The Reverend Martin
Bruggink, The Reverend Roger Allen (RCA Minister)
Burrow, The Reverend Ron
Calder, The Reverend Canon Ian
Chapman, The Reverend Deborah
Chase, The Reverend Peter
Chase, The Reverend Canon Benjamin
Crawford, The Reverend Michael
Daniel, The Reverend Rajinder
Denny-Dimitriou, The Reverend Julia
Devasagayam, The Reverend Jebaraj
Elliott, The Reverend Canon Brian
Ellis, The Reverend Dr Michael
Graham, The Reverend Michael
Gurney, The Reverend Canon Dennis, OBE
Hamblin, The Reverend Derek
Hastings, The Reverend David
Hilditch, The Reverend Lawrence
Hill, The Reverend Geoffrey

Iroka, The Reverend Canon Pius
Jervis, The Reverend William Edward
Jeynes, The Reverend Tony
Kang, The Reverend Heejin (Methodist)
Lee, The Reverend Robert David
McGirr, The Reverend Canon Eric
McHugh, The Reverend Brian
Mauntel, The Reverend Christina (Evangelical Lutheran)
Morgan, The Reverend Marian
Morrell, The Reverend John
Nichols, The Reverend Christopher
Nicholson, The Reverend Ian
Nisbet, The Reverend Gillian
Ore, The Reverend Canon Michael Bamidele Olarewaju
Pearson, The Reverend J Norris
Pearson, The Reverend Michael (Church of Pakistan)
Pillai, The Reverend Arul Raj Kovil
Place, The Reverend Susan
Price, The Reverend Roderick
Rasiah, The Reverend Kingsley Douglas
Sadiq, The Reverend Daniel
Salvage, The Reverend Patrick
Schwartz, The Very Reverend and Venerable Dr William, OBE
Shier, The Reverend Pamela
Thompson, The Reverend Canon Andrew, MBE
Toombs, The Reverend Ian
Tyrrell, The Reverend Carol, RN BSN
Ugwuneri, The Reverend Canon Samuel
Vijayakumary, The Reverend Janet
Ward, The Reverend Stephen (Methodist)
Wash, The Reverend John
Watkins, The Reverend Dr Michael Morris
Watters, The Reverend Kay
Windebank, The Reverend Clive
Yates, The Reverend Ros

EVOLUTION OF DIOCESAN STRUCTURES

relating to Anglican canonical oversight in
Cyprus, Iraq and the Arabian Gulf region

1839 - 1978

1839	Establishment of Aden Settlement
	Pastoral care of the British garrison and civil community in Aden devolves upon chaplains of the Indian Ecclesiastical Establishment, primarily those serving in the Anglican Diocese of Bombay, itself formed in 1837
1841	Formation of the Diocese of Jerusalem as an Anglican/Lutheran joint venture under the auspices of Queen Victoria (Great Britain) and King Frederick William IV (Prussia), also referred to as the Anglo-Prussian Union
1842	Formation of the Anglican Diocese of Gibraltar
1877	Formation of the Anglican Diocese of Lahore to include Delhi, East Punjab, Kashmir, and what is now Pakistan, with some responsibility for the south-eastern areas of Arabia including Dubai and Muscat
1878	British military chaplains first arrive in Cyprus; at the request of the Bishop of Gibraltar, they also serve the few Anglican civilians living on the island
1879	The first Anglican chaplain arrives to serve in Cyprus, under the oversight of the Bishop of Gibraltar, then the Rt Revd Charles Sandford
1881	Following the death of Bishop Joseph Barclay, 3rd Bishop in Jerusalem, a successor is not named for some years
1886	The Anglo-Prussian Union is dissolved
1887	Reconstitution of the Diocese of Jerusalem as a solely Anglican entity; appointment of the Rt Revd George Francis Popham Blyth as 4th Bishop in Jerusalem
	Despite his initial resistance, the Bishop of Gibraltar agrees with the Bishop in Jerusalem's suggestion that for practical reasons Anglican oversight in Cyprus should be transferred to the charge of Jerusalem

1937   April: Anglican oversight in Aden passes from the Diocese of Bombay to that of the Sudan

1957   8 July: the Anglican Diocese of Jerusalem becomes one of five dioceses within a newly constituted Archbishopric of Jerusalem, extra-provincial and under the metropolitical authority of the Archbishop of Canterbury; Cyprus, Iraq and almost the entire Arabian peninsula remain under the canonical authority of the Bishop in Jerusalem

        The Rt Revd Angus Campbell MacInnes takes office as 8th Bishop in Jerusalem; the Archbishop of Canterbury invests Bishop MacInnes with the title Archbishop in Jerusalem and Metropolitan; the Bishop in Jerusalem retains Anglican oversight in Cyprus, Iraq and most of the Arabian peninsula

1975   The entire area of the Sudan becomes a separate Province, hence Anglican canonical oversight in North and South Yemen passes from the Bishop of the Diocese of the Sudan to the Bishop of the Diocese of Egypt

1976   5 January: Jerusalem - inauguration of the Diocese of Cyprus and the Gulf at St George's Cathedral; the institution of the Rt Revd Leonard Ashton CB as the 1st Bishop in Cyprus and the Gulf

        The geographical area of the Diocese of Cyprus and the Gulf: Cyprus, Iraq, Bahrain, the Arabian peninsula (except south-west Arabia and the two Yemeni republics), Das island in Abu Dhabi emirate and Masira island off the east coast of Oman

        6 January: Jerusalem - inauguration of the province of the Episcopal Church in Jerusalem and the Middle East (ECJME) comprising four dioceses: the new Diocese of Cyprus and the Gulf; the pre-existing Dioceses of Egypt and North Africa with the Horn of Africa; and Iran; together with a reconfigured Diocese of Jerusalem (including Lebanon, Syria, Jordan and Palestine)

1978   November: Central Synod of the ECJME confirms that Anglican oversight in south-west Arabia, and the two Yemeni republics including the four islands of the Socotra archipelago, should be transferred from the Diocese of Egypt and North Africa with the Horn of Africa to the Diocese of Cyprus and the Gulf

ANGLICAN CHAPLAINCIES & CHURCHES

in Cyprus, Iraq and the Arabian Gulf region
formations, dedications and consecrations

1863 - 2019

1863	Yemen, Aden - construction of Christ Church at Steamer Point, Tawahi
1864	10 Jan: Yemen, Aden - consecration of Christ Church by the Rt Revd John Harding, Bishop of Bombay
1879	Cyprus - formation of the Limassol and Nicosia chaplaincies
1886	27 April: Cyprus, Nicosia - consecration of the church of St Paul by the Rt Revd Charles Sandford, Bishop of Gibraltar
1896	23 April: Cyprus, Nicosia – reconsecration of the rebuilt church of St Paul on a new site by the Rt Revd George Francis Popham Blyth, Bishop in Jerusalem
1906	Cyprus, Larnaca - construction of an "English" church named St Helen
1907	25 Dec: Cyprus, Larnaca - inaugural service at St Helen's
1913	Cyprus, Kyrenia - construction of a building for Anglican worship, later named St Andrew, marking the formation of the Kyrenia chaplaincy
1915	31 Oct: Cyprus, Limassol - dedication of St Barnabas church by the Revd Canon Frank Newham, chaplain at St Paul's Nicosia, and the Revd Edward Herbert Taylor, Forces Chaplain at the British Garrison in Polemidia, Limassol
1917	Iraq, Basrah, Ashar - the British army builds the church of St Peter
1922	Iraq - British forces depart; St Peter's now under the care of a civil chaplaincy of Basrah and the Persian Gulf; Baghdad, formation of a civil chaplaincy; the Iraqi government grants use of a former Turkish gatehouse at the city's south gate as a church
1928	27 Oct: Cyprus, Troodos - HE Sir Ronald Storrs, Governor of Cyprus, dedicates the foundation stone for the church of St George in the Forest
1931	3 June: Cyprus, Troodos - consecration of St George in the Forest by the Rt Revd Rennie MacInnes, 5th Bishop in Jerusalem
1936	10 Feb: Iraq, Baghdad - laying of the foundation stone for the Mesopotamian Memorial Church of St George the Martyr by Lt Col J Ramsay Tainsh CBE VD

1937	6 March: Iraq, Baghdad - dedication of the Mesopotamian Memorial Church of St George the Martyr by the Rt Revd George Francis Graham Brown, 6th Bishop in Jerusalem
1947	Nov: Iraq, Kirkuk - dedication of a building as the Church of the Wise Men by the Rt Revd Weston Henry Stewart, 7th Bishop in Jerusalem
1948	Kuwait, Ahmadi - formation of an Anglican chaplaincy
1952	Bahrain - construction of St Christopher's church
1953	13 March: Bahrain - consecration of St Christopher's by the Rt Revd Weston Henry Stewart, 7th Bishop in Jerusalem
1956	16 Nov: Kuwait, Ahmadi - consecration of St Paul's church by the Rt Revd Weston Henry Stewart
1960	Qatar, the Trucial States, Muscat and Oman - formation of a chaplaincy bearing that name
1968	15 Feb: Abu Dhabi - dedication of St Andrew's church by the Most Revd Angus Campbell MacInnes, 1st Archbishop in Jerusalem
1970	5 April - division of the chaplaincy of Qatar, the Trucial States, Muscat and Oman to become: the chaplaincy of Dubai and Sharjah, also serving Muscat and Oman; and the chaplaincy of Abu Dhabi and Qatar
	6 Dec: Dubai - dedication of Holy Trinity Church by the Most Revd George Appleton, Bishop in Jerusalem, Archbishop in Jerusalem
1973	Dec: Iraq - expulsion of the Reverend Colin Davies; Anglican ministry in Iraq falls into abeyance due to political circumstances
1975	12 Oct: Oman - dedication of the new Protestant Church building in Ruwi by the Vicar-General in Jerusalem, the Rt Revd and Rt Hon Dr Robert Stopford
1976	5 Jan: Jerusalem - inauguration of the Diocese of Cyprus and the Gulf at Evensong in St George's Cathedral
	18 April, Easter Sunday: Cyprus, Paphos - inaugural Eucharist at St Antony, a small church no longer in use for Orthodox worship
1977	UAE, Abu Dhabi - the government of Abu Dhabi informs the Anglican and Roman Catholic church councils that, for development purposes, it requires the land occupied on the corniche by its churches
1978	Oman - implementation of the Protestant Church in Oman, a new chaplaincy bearing that name; its leadership is shared between an Anglican chaplain and a Reformed Church of America (RCA) pastor
	Nov: Cyprus, Larnaca - demolition of the old church of St Helen

401

1980	6 Jan: Cyprus, Larnaca - Bishop Leonard Ashton dedicates the new church of St Helena; dedicates the new chaplaincy of Larnaca
	24 March: Cyprus, Paphos - St Antony's congregation adopts a constitution which allows the formation of a separate parish from Limassol, known as the Anglican Church of Paphos - *see also 1992*
	Oman, Salalah - Bishop Leonard Ashton and the local Roman Catholic bishop jointly dedicate the Church of the Magi
1981	15 May: Cyprus, Nicosia - Bishop Leonard Ashton rehallows St Paul's as the diocesan cathedral
1982	24 April: Abu Dhabi - the Most Revd and Rt Hon Stuart Blanch, Archbishop of York, lays the foundation stone for the new church of St Andrew
	1 May: Bahrain - the Archbishop of York rehallows St Christopher's as the Pro-Cathedral of the Gulf
1983	28 - 29 Nov: Abu Dhabi - dedication of the new St Andrew's Centre by Bishop Harry Moore
1984	15 Jan: UAE, Abu Dhabi - inaugural service in the new church of St Andrew
1985	UAE, Ras al Khaimah - at a family home in the al Nakheel area, the Revd Dennis Gurney starts Anglican worship as a church plant of the chaplaincy of Dubai and Sharjah; informally, the chaplaincy name evolves to be Dubai, Sharjah and the Northern Emirates (DSNE)
1986	23 April: Bahrain - St Christopher's Pro-Cathedral is granted full cathedral status by episcopal mandate
	April: the Reverend Ian Young takes over ministry in Qatar by commuting once a month from Bahrain to Doha; formation of the chaplaincy of Abu Dhabi, and the chaplaincy of Qatar
1988	March: Cyprus, Paphos - the Anglican congregation permanently relocates from the church of St Antony to Ayia Kyraki Chrysopolitissa
1989	Nov: Oman, Ghala - Bishop John Brown consecrates the chapel of the Good Shepherd
	UAE, Dubai - rebuilding of Holy Trinity church to double its size; construction of additional worship halls
1992	Cyprus - official formation of the Anglican chaplaincy of Paphos
1993	20 April: Yemen - the Grand Mufti of Yemen, Ahmad Muhammad Zabara, issues a fatwa to Bishop John Brown allowing Christ Church in Tawahi, Steamer Point, Aden, to be restored to the Diocese of C&G

1993	Easter: Cyprus, Ayia Napa - Anglican worship, a morning service, is held for the first time in the old monastery gatehouse chapel
	27 June: Cyprus, Protaras - similarly, an Anglican service is held for the first time in the Sea View Conference Room at the Sunrise Beach Hotel
	Dec: Cyprus, Famagusta - interdenominational worship begins, led by staff members at the Eastern Mediterranean University, with an Anglican format offered once or twice a month by a visiting chaplain from Kyrenia or Nicosia
1996	1 June: Cyprus - Bishop Clive Handford licenses an Anglican priest to serve in the chaplaincy of Ayia Napa and Protaras, *de facto* marking its formation date
	4 Oct: Dubai, Holy Trinity - the bishop dedicates a new three-storey Community Hall able to seat a total of 3,600 people
1997	10 Oct: Yemen, Aden - Bishop Clive Handford dedicates the refurbished Christ Church; and also formally opens the Ras Morbat Clinic
	26 Oct: Sharjah - dedication of the new church of St Martin
2000	24 Dec: Cyprus, Tala, St Stephanie village - inaugural Anglican worship takes place in rented premises, a converted taverna
2001	28 Jan: Cyprus, Tala - Bishop Clive Handford dedicates the new congregation in the name of St Stephen, a plant of the Paphos chaplaincy
2002	8 March: Dubai - the bishop consecrates Christ Church, Jebel Ali
	Cyprus, Polis - granting of permission for Anglicans and Latin Catholics to share use of the Orthodox church of St Nicholas for worship
2003	15 June: Cyprus, Limassol - Bishop Clive Handford dedicates an extension to the west end of St Barnabas church
	30 Nov: Cyprus, Kyrenia - the bishop rededicates the renovated and extended church of St Andrew
2006	23 April: Cyprus, Prodromi - following relocation from Polis to new premises, a converted furniture store, the bishop dedicates the second church plant of the Anglican Church of Paphos in the name of St Luke
2007	Sept: Cyprus - the congregations in Ayia Napa and Protaras start using the Scandinavian Church in Ayia Napa as their sole place of worship
2008	Cyprus, Famagusta - the congregation of St Mark relocates to the Orthodox chapel of Little St George on the Salamis road
2009	27 Nov: UAE, Ras al Khaimah - laying of the foundation stone for St Luke's church at al Jazeera al Hamrah

403

2012	9 March: Ras al Khaimah emirate - consecration of the new church of St Luke by Bishop Michael Lewis
	Oct: Cyprus, Deryneia - the new congregation of St John the Evangelist first meets in the Orthodox chapel of St Helena and St Constantine
	Abu Dhabi emirate - the al Ain Anglican community chooses the name St Thomas, with the bishop's approval
2013	2 Feb: Dubai emirate, Dubai Academic City - a church plant of Christ Church Jebel Ali, meets for the first time - *see also 2015, 24 Oct*
	21 April: Cyprus - the Anglican congregation in Ayia Napa chooses the name Christ Church
	12 May: Cyprus, Pissouri - dedication by Bishop Michael Lewis of St Lazarus, a church plant of St Barnabas Limassol
	22 June: UAE, Sharjah - dedication of an extension to St Martin's church
	21 Sept: Qatar, Doha - official opening of the Anglican Centre
	29 Sept: Qatar, Doha - consecration of the Church of the Epiphany by Bishop Michael Lewis
2014	Cyprus, Deryneia - Orthodox and civil authorities grant permission for Anglicans to worship in the church of St Phanourios
	2 March: Cyprus - Bishop Michael Lewis dedicates an extension to St Barnabas church, Limassol
2015	15 March: Cyprus, Deryneia - the inaugural Anglican service in St Phanourios church, and the dedication of the congregation in the name of St John the Evangelist by Bishop Michael Lewis
	24 Oct: Dubai Academic City - the bishop dedicates the congregation of St Catherine, a church plant of Christ Church Jebel Ali
2017	7 March: Cyprus - formalisation of Ammochostos chaplaincy to include three pre-existing churches: Christ Church Ayia Napa; St John the Evangelist Deryneia; and St Mark Famagusta
2019	1 July: UAE - reconfiguration of the Dubai, Sharjah and the Northern Emirates (DSNE) chaplaincy to become four chaplaincies/parishes: Dubai (Holy Trinity); Jebel Ali (Christ Church) with Academic City (St Catherine); Sharjah (St Martin); and Ras al Khaimah (St Luke) with Fujairah (St Nicholas)

ANGLICAN MINISTRY

in Cyprus, Iraq and the Arabian Gulf region

1878 - 2019

LISTING PROTOCOL

ANGLICAN CHAPLAINS / PARISH PRIESTS in ascending date order under:

- **Region**
- **Country name**
- **Town or village**
- **Church name**

THE VERY REVEREND (Provost/Dean) takes precedence over
    THE VENERABLE (Archdeacon) when the roles apply to the same person

ASSOCIATE / ASSISTANT PRIESTS AND ASSISTANT CURATES
    titles are identified

CHAPLAINS SERVING THE MISSIONS TO SEAMEN / MISSION TO SEAFARERS
    and ministries which include a dual role as an associate chaplain/parish priest.
    See the Glossary for changes in the charity's name since its formation in 1856

PRIESTS with PTO (Permission to Officiate)
    such as: before being licensed as an incumbent; leaders of non-English
    language Anglican congregations; serving in long interregnums; and ordained
    spouses of their chaplain/parish priest

LAY CHAPLAINS
    relevant to a specific context

INDEX OF LOCATIONS - ANGLICAN MINISTRY

- *The evolution of diocesan structures and chaplaincy names are not identified in this chronology - see the previous two chronologies*

- *The start date of ministry is the licensing date, unless otherwise stated*

406

CYPRUS

FAMAGUSTA

St Mark

Prior to 1946	*Anglican chaplains visited from Nicosia*
1946 - 1954	**The Reverend Wilfred T S Castle** also travelled to St Barnabas, Limassol to provide ministry, 1946-1954; and to Larnaca, 1946-1947
1954 - July 1974	*Chaplains visited from Nicosia, Limassol and Larnaca; ministry in Famagusta fell into abeyance*
1993 - 1999	*Interdenominational worship began on the Eastern Mediterranean University campus, led by staff members; an Anglican format was offered once or twice a month, served by a visiting chaplain from Kyrenia or Nicosia*
1996	*Worship transferred to the old city of Famagusta in the EMU's Cultural Centre, the church of St George Exorinos converted into a theatre*
May 1999 - 31 Oct 2010	**The Reverend Robin Brookes** visited from Ayia Napa, 1999-2006; moved to Famagusta in March 2006; *see also South-East Cyprus, Ayia Napa, 1999-2006*
2008	*Worship relocated to the chapel of St George on the Salamis Road*
13 Oct 2008 - 27 July 2014	**The Reverend Zinkoo Han** Assistant Chaplain
7 Sept 2014 - 24 June 2016	**Mr Hin Lai (Harry) Ching** Reader and Lay Chaplain
25 June 2016 - 18 Sept 2016	**The Reverend Hin Lai (Harry) Ching** Assistant Curate; *see also UAE, Dubai, Jebel Ali, Christ Church, 19 Sept 2016 - 31 Oct 2019*
1 Nov 2016 - March 2018	**Mr Justin Arnott** Reader and Lay Chaplain *see also Cyprus, Nicosia, St Paul, 7 July 2018 -*
20 Apr 2018 - 16 June 2019	**The Reverend Navina Thompson** Assistant Curate
17 June 2019 -	**The Reverend Peter Day** Assistant Curate; *see also South-East Cyprus, Deryneia, St John the Evangelist*

KYRENIA
St Andrew

1913 - 1938	*Readers led regular worship; Anglican chaplains visited occasionally from Nicosia*
1935 - 1936	**The Reverend A Williams**
1938 - 1946	**The Reverend Canon Frank Newham** *see also Cyprus, Nicosia, St Paul, 1926*
1946 - 1971	*Readers led regular worship; Anglican chaplains visited occasionally from Nicosia, as did British and Canadian Forces' chaplains*
1971 - 1977	**The Reverend W P Basil Pitt OBE**
1977 - 1979	**The Reverend Evelyn Chavasse DSO, OBE** **The Reverend Sir Patrick Ferguson-Davie Bt** shared ministry as honorary chaplains
Jan 1980 - 1987	**The Reverend Canon Arthur W Rider MBE**
1987	**The Reverend Canon Peter Collins**
15 May 1988 - Spring 1992	**The Reverend Daniel Pope**
Nov 1992 - Feb 1995	**The Reverend John Kemp**
Feb 1993 - Feb 1995	**The Reverend William Schwartz** NSM Assistant Curate *see also Canterbury Group 1999-2007, Qatar 2007-2014, Bahrain 2019 - ; Archdeacons; Provosts & Deans*
1995 - Jan 2000	**The Reverend Michael Stokes**
Apr 2000 - 2004	**The Reverend Anthony Fletcher**
1 Nov 2004 - 15 Feb 2007	**The Reverend Tony Jeynes** licensed 11 Nov 2004; *see also Paphos 2007-2009; and Priests with PTO*
1 Sept 2007 - 24 Oct 2010	**The Reverend Michael Houston**
29 Jan 2011 - 23 March 2013	**The Reverend Richard Frost**
12 Apr 2014 - 4 August 2018	**The Reverend Wendy Hough**
August 2018 -	**The Reverend Michael Graham** retired with PTO

LARNACA

1878	**The Reverend David Nickerson** British military chaplain; at the request of Bishop Charles Sandford (Gibraltar) served the few English civilians in Cyprus
1879 - 1899	**The Reverend Josiah Spencer** relocated to reside in Nicosia later in 1879; continued to serve Larnaca, *see also Cyprus, Nicosia, St Paul*

408

1899 - 1901	**The Venerable Josiah Spencer** also Archdeacon in Cyprus
St Helen	*Built in 1907*
1907 - 1945	*Anglican chaplains from Nicosia and Limassol, and British military chaplains, ministered once or twice a year*
1946 - 1947	**The Reverend Wilfred T S Castle** lived in Famagusta, also ministered in Larnaca
1948 - 1960	*Ministry as for 1907-1945*
1960 - circa 1976	*British military chaplains based at the garrison in Dhekelia provided Sunday evening ministry*
Nov 1978	*The church of St Helen was demolished*
St Helena	
6 Jan 1980	*The new church of St Helena was dedicated; the chaplaincy of Larnaca was inaugurated*
6 Jan 1980 - Dec 1982	**The Reverend Idwal Brian Bessant** with extended responsibility as Diocesan Chaplain to visit unstaffed congregations in the Gulf, such as in Baghdad and Sana'a
15 June 1983 - Oct 1991	**The Reverend Colin E Holbrook** with extended responsibility, as above
9 Feb - March 1992	**The Reverend Ronald Goodchild**
10 May - June 1992	**The Reverend David White**
2 Feb 1992 - Jan 1997	**The Reverend Duncan Harris**
9 Nov 1997 - Feb 2001	**The Reverend Paul Faint** both also Port Chaplain, Missions to Seamen/ Mission to Seafarers, Cyprus
1 Apr 2001 - May 2002	**The Reverend Derek Hamblin** *see also UAE, Ras al Khaimah, St Luke, 23 Feb 2003 - 2004*
2 June 2002 - Apr 2005	**The Reverend Daniel Borkowski**
7 Aug 2005 - summer 2006	**The Reverend David Hastings** served as long-term locum priests
14 Sept 2006 - Jun 2009	**The Reverend Douglas Cockbill**
18 Dec 2010 - July 2019	**The Venerable Dr John Holdsworth** also Archdeacon in Cyprus; Executive Archdeacon, Diocese of C&G, and Director of Ministry
13 Jan 2013 - June 2015	**The Reverend Sean Semple** Associate Priest

409

27 June 2015 -	**The Reverend Geoffrey Graham** Assistant Curate, 27 June 2015 - 24 June 2016 Assistant Priest, 25 June 2016 - 7 July 2018 Associate Priest, 8 July 2018 -
7 Sept 2019 -	**The Venerable Christopher Futcher** also Archdeacon in Cyprus
7 Sept 2019 -	**The Reverend Anne Futcher** NSM Assistant Priest also the archdeaconry's social concern officer

LIMASSOL

St Barnabas

1879	**The Reverend Dr Hunter Finlay**
1879 - 1881	**The Reverend Avidis Garboushian**
1881 - 1916	*Military chaplains serving at Polemidia garrison and at Troodos summer camp also ministered to Anglican civilians in Limassol:*
1881-1886	**The Reverend Ronald Fisher McLeod**
1886-1888	**The Reverend John Hackett**
1888-1892	**The Reverend Walter Hebden Milner**
1893-1895	**The Reverend John Hackett**
1899-March 1906	**The Reverend Arthur Clement Buss**
1905-1906	**The Reverend Edwin Watts**
Jan 1908 - 26 Apr 1909	**The Reverend D J Hunt**
1909 - 24 June 1916	**The Reverend Edward Herbert Taylor**
1927 - 1928	**The Reverend Alexander Sutherland Lindsay**
1928 - 1933	**The Reverend Henry Baldwin Fulford Eales**
1946 - 1954	**The Reverend Wilfred T S Castle** served Limassol from Famagusta until completion of St Barnabas vicarage in 1952; also ministered in Larnaca, 1946-1947
1950s - 1974	*Limassol chaplaincy included responsibility for Famagusta, Larnaca, Paphos and adjacent districts; ministry to the mining community at Limni near Polis; and during the summer at St George in the Forest, Troodos*
Dec 1954 - May 1976	**The Reverend Canon Hubert S Matthews** retired in 1974; continued to serve until the formation of the Diocese of Cyprus and the Gulf on 5 Jan 1976; attended the first Diocesan Synod (Cyprus) in May 1976
1976 - 1978	**The Reverend Walter Frederick Gunn**
1978 - 1982	**The Reverend Charles Buckmaster**

1982	**The Reverend Colin Chapman** long-term locum
1 Jan 1983 - 14 Sept 1986	**The Reverend Desmond Sheppard MBE** final service 14 Sept 1986; funeral 24 Sept 1986 *see also Kuwait, Dec 1978 -1983*
1 Feb 1987 - 31 Dec 1987	**The Reverend Canon George E Beechey** long-term locum
24 Jan 1988 - 31 May 1992	**The Reverend John Godfrey**
20 Sept 1992 - 6 Feb 1994	**The Reverend Canon Peter Campbell Moore** repatriated to the USA after suffering a stroke
2 June 1994 - 23 Apr 1995	**The Very Reverend Samuel W Reede**
28 Apr 1995 - 3 Sept 1995	**The Reverend W Lumley**
9 Sept 1995 - 23 Feb 1996	**The Very Reverend Samuel W Reede** long-term locums
1 July 1996 - 30 Sept 2003	**The Reverend Canon Michael Jones** also Port Chaplain, Mission to Seafarers, Limassol, 2001-2003; *see also Kuwait, 1983-1990*
19 Oct 2003 - 11 Sept 2005	**The Reverend Colin M Noyce** also Port Chaplain, Mission to Seafarers, Limassol; *see also Yemen, Sept 2001 - June 2003*
1 Jan 2006 - 31 March 2009	**The Reverend Roderick (Rod) Price** Priest with PTO, 1 Jan - Apr 2006; licensed 23 Apr 2006; retired 31 March 2009 *see also Priests with PTO, 2009*
9 Aug 2009 - 31 July 2017	**The Reverend Canon Derek Smith** first service 9 Aug; licensed 9 Sep 2009
27 June 2015 - 30 Dec 2018	**The Reverend Christine Goldsmith** Assistant Curate, 27 June 2015 -24 June 2016 Assistant Priest, 25 June 2016 - 14 July 2018 Associate Priest, 15 July 2018 - 30 Dec 2018
5 May 2018 -	**The Reverend Canon Dr Andrew Mayes TSSF** also Diocesan Spirituality Adviser

Mission to Seafarers

23 Apr 2007 - July 2013	**The Reverend Canon Marvin Bamforth** Port Chaplain, Mission to Seafarers, Limassol; *see also Cyprus, Paphos, 1998-2006*
14 July 2013 -	**Mr Kenneth Wiseman** Reader; and Lay Chaplain, Mission to Seafarers, Cyprus

PISSOURI: St Lazarus

2010 -	*Ministry as Limassol, St Barnabas*

411

NICOSIA
St Paul's Church

1879 - 1899	**The Reverend Josiah Spencer** also served Larnaca
1899 - 1901	**The Venerable Josiah Spencer** also Archdeacon in Cyprus; continued to serve Larnaca
1901 - 1905	**The Venerable Beresford Potter** also Archdeacon in Cyprus, 1901-1927; Archdeacon in Syria, 1915-1921
29 Sept 1905 - 12 July 1907	**The Reverend Samuel Cooke Collis Smith**
20 Oct 1907 - 22 Oct 1908	**The Reverend F Llewellyn Edwards**
25 Oct 1908 - 1925	**The Reverend Henry Smale**
1920s - July 1974	*Archdeacons in Cyprus ministered monthly to* *the copper mining communities in the north at* *Skouriotissa and in the north-west at Limni;* *pastoral responsibility for Lefka, Myrtou and* *adjacent districts; the Bishop in Jerusalem also* *made periodic visits*
Jan 1926 - 13 May 1926	**The Reverend F Llewellyn Edwards**
June 1926 - 7 Nov 1926	**The Reverend Canon Frank D Newham** also Director of Education in Cyprus, 1900-1930; *see also Cyprus, Kyrenia, St Andrew, 1938-1946*
6 Mar 1927 - 7 Jun 1927	**The Reverend Alfred Huddle**
30 Sept 1927 - 18 June 1931	**The Venerable Harold Buxton** also Archdeacon in Cyprus
27 Sept 1931 - 29 Sept 1937	**The Reverend Thomas S B F de Chaumont**
30 Sept 1937 - 25 Jan 1948	**The Venerable Malcolm Maxwell** also Archdeacon in Cyprus, from 17 March 1938
25 Sept 1949 - 1955	**The Venerable Donald Norwood Goldie** also Archdeacon in Cyprus
1955 - 1958	**The Venerable Arthur W Adeney** also Archdeacon in Cyprus *see also Iraq, Basrah, Nov 1938 - early 1941*
1958 - 1960	**The Venerable W Kenneth Blackburn** also Archdeacon in Cyprus
1960 - 1963	**The Venerable William Benjamin Farrer** also Archdeacon in Cyprus; *see also Iraq,* *Baghdad, 1957-1960*
1963	**The Reverend Albert Keene**
1964 - 1967	**The Venerable Peter J Chandler** also Archdeacon in Cyprus

1967 - May 1975	**The Venerable John (Jack) Nicholls** also Archdeacon in Cyprus
Oct 1973 - July 1974	*Due to low attendance at the copper mining* *communities in Skouriotissa and Limni, services* *held only on special occasions, and at Christmas* *and Easter; no ministry after July 1974*
18 Jan 1976 - 1977	**The Reverend Peter Cowen**
May 1975 - May 1978	*Bishop Ashton did not to appoint an Archdeacon* *in Cyprus during this period*
1 May 1978 - 15 Aug 1980	**The Venerable Douglas Northridge** also Archdeacon in Cyprus; died after a heart attack while in the UK

St Paul's Cathedral

25 June 1981 - 25 Nov 1990	**The Very Reverend Bryan Henry** Provost; Archdeacon in Cyprus 1981-1990
24 June 1984 - 7 June 1987	**The Reverend Howell (Howie) Sasser** NSM Assistant Priest
1 June 1987 - 15 Apr 1990	**The Reverend John Burdett** NSM Assistant Priest and Diocesan Administrator/Secretary (stipendiary)
8 Sept 1991 - 29 Sept 1996	**The Very Reverend Patrick Blair** Provost, licensed and installed 8 Sept 1991; licensed as Rural Dean of Cyprus 6 Oct 1991
25 May 1997 - 31 Aug 1999	**The Venerable Michael Mansbridge** Provost, Archdeacon in the Diocese 1991-1999; (retained the title The Venerable during his tenure as Provost); retired, 31 Aug 1999; *see also* *UAE, Abu Dhabi, St Andrew, 1983-1997*
19 Dec 1999 - 25 Dec 2001	**The Very Reverend John Morley** Provost, 1999-2001; Dean 2001
19 Dec 2002 - 3 Aug 2009	**The Very Reverend Stephen Collis** Dean; Archdeacon in Cyprus 2006-2009; *see also UAE, Abu Dhabi, 2000-2002*
2 Oct 2005 - 26 May 2012	**The Reverend Michael Loader** Assistant Chaplain
2 Oct 2005 - 2 Jan 2009	**The Reverend Susan Place** Assistant Chaplain *see also Priests with PTO*
21 Nov 2009 - June 2014	**The Very Reverend John Tyrrell CD** Dean

413

7 Dec 2009 - June 2014	**The Reverend Carol Tyrrell RN BSN** Deacon with PTO 7 Dec 2009 - 7 Feb 2011 Assistant Curate 7 Feb 2011 - June 2014
24 May 2015 -	**The Very Reverend Jeremy Crocker** Dean
25 June 2016 - 13 Apr 2018	**The Reverend Kent John W L Middleton, Obl CR** Assistant Curate; *see also UAE, Ras al Khaimah,* *St Luke, and Fujairah, St Nicholas, Apr 2018 -*
7 July 2018 -	**The Reverend Justin Arnott** Assistant Curate; *see also Cyprus, Famagusta,* *St Mark, Nov 2016 - March 2018*

PAPHOS

1976	*The Anglican Church of Paphos was formed*
1979	*Bishop Ashton permitted the Anglican Church of* *Paphos to be unofficially known as a chaplaincy*

St Antony

1976 - 1988	*Ministry as Cyprus, Limassol*

Ayia Kyriaki Chrysopolitissa

|---|---|
1988 - 1992	*Ministry as Cyprus, Limassol*
1992	*The Anglican Chaplaincy of Paphos was formed* *officially, and the first resident chaplain appointed*
Dec 1992 - 28 Sept 1994	**The Reverend Canon Derek Gibbs** resigned to join the Latin Church
3 Apr 1995 - Dec 1997	**The Reverend Roy Kilford**
14 Sept 1998 - 2006	**The Reverend Canon Marvin Bamforth** *see also Cyprus, Limassol;* *Mission to Seafarers, 23 Apr 2007 - July 2013*
10 Sept 2002 - Feb 2004	**The Reverend R Keith Henshall** Associate Chaplain; licenced 25 Sept 2002
27 Feb 2007 - 31 Dec 2009	**The Reverend Tony Jeynes** *see also Cyprus, Kyrenia, 2004-2007; and Priests* *with PTO*
29 Sept 2009 - 15 Nov 2012	**The Reverend Andrew Notere**
2 July 2010 - 26 Aug 2012	**The Reverend Dr Michael Ellis** Assistant Curate; *see also Priests with PTO*
18 Jan 2014 - 10 May 2015	**The Reverend Nicholas (Nic) Denny-Dimitriou**
18 Jan 2014 - 10 May 2015	**The Reverend Julia Denny-Dimitriou** Priest with PTO

414

16 March 2014 - 22 May 2016	**The Reverend Andrew Symonds** House for Duty Associate Priest, with particular responsibility for marriage ministry
4 March 2016 - March 2019	**The Reverend Canon Robert Anthony Stidolph** House for Duty Associate Priest, as above
18 Sept 2016 -	**The Reverend Andrew Burtt**

POLIS

| June 2001 | *A church plant of the Paphos chaplaincy began to worship in the Orthodox church of St Nicholas*
Ministry as for Paphos, Ayia Kyriaki |

PRODROMI: St Luke

| 2006 - | *The congregation in Polis moved to new premises, a converted furniture store in Prodromi* |
| 23 April 2006 | *Bishop Clive Handford dedicated the church building in the name of St Stephen*

Ministry as for Paphos, Ayia Kyriaki |

TALA: St Stephen

| 24 Dec 2000 | *The first church plant of the Paphos chaplaincy was inaugurated during a carol service held in rented premises, a converted tavern* |
| 28 Jan 2001 | *Bishop Clive Handford dedicated the church building in the name of St Stephen*
Ministry as for Paphos, Ayia Kyriaki |

SOUTH-EAST CYPRUS

AYIA NAPA & PROTARAS

2 May 1993	*Anglican worship in Ayia Napa began in the gatehouse chapel at the old monastery*
27 June 1993	*Anglican worship in Protaras began at the Sunrise Beach Hotel* *Locum clergy served under the supervision of the Rural Dean in Cyprus, the Very Reverend Patrick Blair, until his retirement in Sept 1996*
2 May - 18 July 1993	**The Reverend John Peters**
26 Aug - 26 Oct 1993	**The Reverend George Jennings**
11 Nov - 12 Dec 1993	**The Reverend Ian Watts**
19 Mar - 19 Apr 1994	**The Reverend Douglas Gibson**
20 Apr - 1 July 1994	**The Reverend Jim Ledger**
1 July - 13 Sept 1994	**The Reverend Geoff Houghton**

13 Sept - 19 Dec 1994	**The Reverend Keith Thomson**
30 Mar - 16 May 1995	**The Reverend Douglas Gibson**
17 May - 12 July 1995	**The Reverend George Jennings**
28 July - 10 Aug 1995	**The Reverend John Taylor**
30 Aug - 28 Oct 1995	**The Reverend John Dennett**
2 Nov - 28 Dec 1995	**The Reverend George Jennings**
5 Mar - 27 Dec 1996	**The Reverend Stuart Roger Broughton** licensed 1 June 1996; granted PTO in the diocese, 28 July 1996
1996-2007	*Clergy licences referred to the Chaplaincy of Ayia Napa and Protaras*
4 Jan - Dec 1997	**The Reverend Dr Michael M Watkins** licensed with responsibility for Ayia Napa and Protaras 2 Feb 1997; *see also 31 Mar - 27 Sept 1998; and Priests with PTO*
14 Jan - 29 Mar 1998	**The Reverend Denis Hutchings**
31 Mar - 27 Sept 1998	**The Reverend Dr Michael M Watkins** *see also 4 Jan - Dec 1997, and Priests with PTO*
11 Nov - 6 Jan 1999	**The Reverend Fred Preston**
24 Mar - 9 May 1999	**The Reverend Michael Boultbee**
30 May 1999 - 1 Jan 2006	**The Reverend Robin Brookes** *see also South-East Cyprus chaplaincy, Famagusta, St Mark, 2006-2010*
5 March 2006 - 26 Dec 2010	**The Reverend Michael Crawford** Parish Priest, Ayia Napa; *see also Priests with PTO*

AYIA NAPA

June 2007	*The Orthodox bishop in the area asked the Anglican congregation in South-East Cyprus to cease using the gatehouse chapel at the monastery*
Sept 2007	*The congregation adopted the Scandinavian Church in Ayia Napa as its sole place of worship*

Christ Church

21 April 2013	*The Anglican congregation in Ayia Napa chose the name Christ Church*
2 Oct 2011 - 31 Aug 2014	**The Reverend Simon Holloway** Chaplain; *see also South-East Cyprus, Ayia Napa, Christ Church, 2013-2014*
1 Dec 2013 - Aug 2016	**The Reverend Canon Paul Maybury** Mission Priest; Diocesan Spirituality Co-ordinator; *see also, Deryneia, St John the Evangelist*

1 July 2015 - Oct 2017	**The Reverend Gabriel Amat** Priest with PTO
25 Mar 2017 -	**The Reverend Martin Phillips-Last** Chaplain; and Parish Priest (Ammochostos)
7 Mar 2017	*The Anglican chaplaincy/parish of Ammochostos* *was formed to include three pre-existing churches:* *Christ Church, Ayia Napa; St John the Evangelist,* *Deryneia; and St Mark, Famagusta*

DERYNEIA:
St John the Evangelist

Oct 2012	*The congregation met for the first time*
1 Dec 2013 - 6 July 2018	*Ministry as for Ayia Napa, Christ Church*
7 July 2018 -	**The Reverend Peter Day** Assistant Curate *see also Famagusta, St Mark, 17 June 2019 -*

TROODOS

St George in the Forest

1931 - 1980	*Ministry as Limassol, St Barnabas*
1980 -	*Ministry as Nicosia, St Paul's*

417

IRAQ

BAGHDAD

1922 - 1924	**The Reverend Frank Thomas Ford**
1924 - 1926	**The Reverend Thomas Herbert Jacques**
1928 - 1930	**The Reverend Frederick Arundel Rogers**
1930 - 1932	**The Reverend Hylton I'Brook Smith**
1932 - 1934	**The Reverend David Colin Dunlop**
1934-1935	**The Reverend Alfred Cohen Karmouche** CMJ Missionary
1935 - 1936	**The Reverend John Charles Fortescue-Thomas**

Mesopotamian Memorial
Church of St George the Martyr

1937 - 1939	**The Reverend Richard Armit Lowry**
1940 - 1946	**The Reverend Charles A Roach**
1946 - 1957	**The Venerable Cyril Victor Roberts** also Archdeacon in Iraq and Eastern Arabia 1950-1957

23 Jan 1958 - 1960	**The Reverend William Benjamin Farrer** instituted 7 Feb 1958; *see also Cyprus, Nicosia, 1960-1963*
1961 - 1964	**The Reverend John Robert de Chazal** also served Kirkuk
1965 - 1966	**The Reverend Alfred Walter Heath Cooke** also served Basrah and Fao
6 Jan - June 1967	**The Reverend Clive Handford** departed when British diplomatic relations with Iraq were severed due to the Six-Day War (5-10 June); *see also UAE, Abu Dhabi, 1978-1983; Bishops 1996-2007; Primates 2002-2007*
1968 - Dec 1973	**The Reverend Geoffrey Colin Davies** also served Basrah and Fao; expelled from Iraq
1973 - 2005	*No resident Anglican chaplain due to the political context*
1 Aug 2005 - 4 Jan 2015	**The Reverend Canon Andrew Paul B White** licensed as Priest in the diocese with particular responsibilities in Iraq; designated Vicar Emeritus, 4 Jan 2015
11 July 2010 -	**The Reverend Canon Faiz Jirjees (also Jerjes)** Assistant Curate, 11 July 2010 - 10 Sept 2011 Assistant Priest, 11 Sept 2011 - 3 Sept 2015 Chaplain, 4 Sept 2015

BASRAH

ASHAR: St Peter

1917 - 1922	*Military chaplains served at the garrison church*
1922	*British forces departed, leaving the church under the care of a civil chaplaincy*
1922	**The Reverend Cyril Wallis Carter**
1931 - 1934	**The Reverend Jasper Vallack Westlake**
1934 - 1936	**The Reverend Guy Edward Salter Bullock**
1936 - 1938	**The Reverend Francis William Bowyer** also ministered in Bahrain up to six times a year
Nov 1938 - early 1941	**The Reverend Arthur W Adeney** *see also Cyprus, Nicosia, 1955-8*
Dec 1941 - Dec 1942	**The Venerable Weston Henry Stewart** Acting Chaplain; Archdeacon in Palestine, Syria and Transjordan, 1928-1942 *see also Kirkuk, Iraq Petroleum Company chaplaincy, 1940-1941*

418

1944 - 1947	**The Reverend David Denton White** also Port Chaplain, Missions to Seamen, Basrah
1947 - early 1950	**The Reverend Edward J B Matchett** also Port Chaplain, Missions to Seamen, Basrah; and Hon RAF Chaplain serving Basrah, Bahrain and Sharjah, 1948-1950
1950 - 1952	**The Reverend Norman Ashby** also Port Chaplain, Missions to Seamen, Basrah, 1950-1; continued to serve at St Peter until early 1952; periodically visited Bahrain
Feb 1952 - 1954	**The Reverend Ronald Jack Gale** licensed 10 March 1952
Dec 1954 - Apr 1957	**The Reverend Peter Anthony Lawson Howell**
1957 - May 1960	**The Reverend Canon Haydn Parry MC** also Port Chaplain, Missions to Seamen, Basrah; *see also UAE, Dubai,* *Holy Trinity, 1971-1972*
1961 - 1963	**The Reverend Harold Marcus Wilson**
1965 - 1973	*Ministry as Baghdad*

KIRKUK - IRAQ PETROLEUM COMPANY chaplaincy
and out-stations along the pipeline

BABA GURGUR

1940 - 1941	**The Venerable Weston Henry Stewart** Acting Chaplain; Archdeacon in Palestine, Syria and Transjordan, 1928-1942; *see also Iraq,* *Basrah, 1941-1942*
	Served pipeline pumping station townlets located *at intervals of about 70 miles/112 km between* *Kirkuk and Haditha*
1941 - 1949	*If no IPC chaplain was resident, chaplains from* *Baghdad and Basrah offered ministry, and also to* *the pipeline pumping station townlets*

Church of the Wise Men

Nov 1947	*Bishop Weston Henry Stewart dedicated a* *temporary church building*
1 Dec 1949 - 1960	**The Reverend Canon Bernard Hall Coombs** **Wilson** Senior Anglican Chaplain in IPC
1960 - 1973	*Ministry as Baghdad*

THE GULF REGION

BAHRAIN

Awali church

1937 - 1946	*Ministry as Iraq, Baghdad*
1947-1951	*Ministry as Iraq, Basrah*
1951 -	*Ministry as Bahrain, St Christopher's Church/ Cathedral*

MANAMA:
St Christopher's Church

1951 - 1953	**The Reverend Robert C Rickells**
1954 - 1964	**The Venerable Gwilyn Alun Morris** also Archdeacon in Eastern Arabia and the Gulf, 1962-1964; *see also Canons of the Two Cathedrals*
1963	**The Reverend Richard Matthews** Assistant Curate; *see also UAE, Abu Dhabi, St Andrew, 1963-1967*
Dec 1964 -Jan 1967	**The Reverend Harold James Figg Edgington**
19 Mar 1967 - April 1969	**The Reverend Thomas Robinson**
24 Dec 1969 - 30 Sept 1975	**The Reverend Canon John B D (Shane) Cotter**
21 Oct 1975 - early July 1979	**The Reverend Barry J Simmons**
17 Oct 1979 - 30 July 1983	**The Reverend Michael Roemmele** late 1981 set up Missions to Seamen presence in Bahrain, appointed as its Hon Chaplain
2 May 1982	*St Christopher's Church rehallowed as the Pro-Cathedral in the Gulf by the Archbishop of York*
23 Oct 1983 - 22 Apr 1986	**The Reverend Canon John Parkinson** also Hon Chaplain, Missions to Seamen, Bahrain; *see also entry under St Christopher's Cathedral*
2 Sept 1984 - 22 Apr 1986	**The Reverend Ian Young** Assistant Priest, *see also entry under St Christopher's Cathedral, 23 Apr 1986 -*
24 Nov 1985 -31 Jan 1988	**The Reverend Geoffrey Brookes** Assistant Curate

St Christopher's Cathedral

23 Apr 1986	*Granted full cathedral status by episcopal mandate, signed by Bishop Harry Moore*
23 Apr 1986 - 19 Nov 1989	**The Very Reverend John Parkinson MBE** Provost; also Hon Chaplain, Missions to Seamen, Bahrain

23 Apr 1986 - 4 June 1988	**The Reverend Ian Young** Assistant Priest; see also Qatar, 1986-2007
5 June 1988 - 10 Dec 1991	**The Reverend Canon Ian Young** appointed Hon Canon of St Christopher's Cathedral 5 June 1988; *see also Qatar, 1986-2007;* *Archdeacons*
1988 - 1990	**The Reverend Paul Burt** Associate Priest, CMS Mission Partner; *see also* *UAE, Dubai, Mission to Seafarers, 2012 - Mar 2018*
26 May 1989 - 19 Dec 1990	**The Reverend Ian Thurston** NSM Deacon; priested, 9 Sept 1990
14 Jan 1990 - 6 Apr 1997	**The Very Reverend Derek Taylor** Provost
4 Oct 1992 - 4 Oct 1994	**The Reverend Roy Topping MBE** Assistant Priest; also BISS Seamens' Welfare Representative
23 Nov 1994 - 28 Dec 2008	**The Reverend Vijayanand Victor Salve** Assistant Priest BISS Seamens' Welfare Representative, Oct 1994- Sept 1997; part-time administrator, St Christopher's Cathedral 1992-2002; and for BISS, 1992-2005; appointed as chaplain to Missions to Seamen, Bahrain, Oct 1997
9 Sept 1997 - 2 May 2002	**The Very Reverend Keith Johnson** installed 8 October 1997 Provost 1997-2001; Dean 2001 - 2 May 2002; *see also Kuwait, 1969-1973*
17 July 2001 - 27 July 2002	**The Reverend Thomas Frizzell Jr** Associate Priest 17 July 2001 - 2 May 2002; Priest-in-Charge 3 May - 27 July 2002
1 Nov 2002 - 31 May 2009	**The Very Reverend Alan Hayday** Dean installed 14 Nov 2002; Archdeacon in the Gulf, 1 May 2006 - 31 May 2009
12 Feb 2009 -	**The Reverend Canon Stephen Thanapaul** Assistant Priest licensed at Synod in Cyprus 12 Feb 2009; first service in Bahrain 22 Feb 2009; Port Chaplain, Mission to Seafarers, Bahrain; responsible for St Christopher's Cathedral Tamil-language congregation, inaugural Eucharist 20 Apr 2014

421

18 Oct 2009 - 25 April 2019	**The Very Reverend Christopher Butt** Dean; Chair of the Bishop's Advisory Panel for Ministry, Jan 2013 - Oct 2018
13 Sept 2014 - Apr 2016	**The Reverend Jon Lavelle** Assistant Curate 13 Sept 2014 - 4 Sept 2015 Assistant Priest 5 Sept 2015 - Apr 2016 *see also UAE, Ras al Khaimah, St Luke, and* *Fujairah, St Nicholas, Apr 2016 - Apr 2018*
26 April 2019 -	**The Very Reverend Dr William Schwartz OBE** Dean; installed on 1 June 2019; Archdeacon in the Gulf, June 2009 - ; *see also Cyprus, Kyrenia, 1993-1995; Canterbury* *Group 1999-2007; Qatar, 2007-2014*

CANTERBURY GROUP

Formed around 1952, the Canterbury Group gives a name to Anglican/Episcopal ministry and worship in an area of the Diocese of Cyprus and the Gulf where publicised Christian worship is not currently permitted.

For this reason, although the Canterbury Group is a chaplaincy/parish within the diocese, its geographical context is not identified and titles of its leaders are omitted.

1976 - 1978	**Hugh Cartwright**
1979 - 1983	**Ronald Blount**
1983 - July 1983	**Paul Lawson**
1983/4 - Dec 1987	**John Langfeldt**
1983/4 - mid-1988	**Richard C Nevius**
Oct 1988 - June 1999	**Benjamin O Chase**
1992	**Ms Lada Hardwick**
June 1998 - Feb 2002	**Daniel Borkowski**
Aug 1999 - Sept 2007	**William Schwartz**
Dec 2004 - early 2007	**Jeff Mead**
Feb 2008 - May 2013	**Walter Schilling**
Feb 2008 - Jan 2014	**John (Rocki) Proffit**
Feb 2014 -	**Charles (Chuck) Reischman**

KUWAIT

1948	*Ministry as Iraq, Basrah, St Peter*
1949 - 1955	**The Reverend Raymond Pearson**

AHMADI: St Paul

1955 - 1962	**The Reverend Thomas Richard Ashton**
1962 - 1966	**The Reverend Harvey Roydon Phillips**

1966 - 1969	**The Reverend John Andrew Douglas Legg**
1969 - 1973	**The Reverend Keith Johnson** *see also Bahrain, 1997-2002*
1973 - 1975	**The Reverend John Pragnell**
1975 - 15 Apr 1978	**The Reverend Percy Desmond Kingston** known as "Pat", collapsed and died in the vicarage garden on Saturday 15 Apr 1978
Oct 1978 - 1983	**The Reverend Desmond Sheppard MBE** *see also Cyprus, Limassol, 1983-1986*
1979 - July 1983	**The Reverend Clive Windebank** NSM Assistant Chaplain, employed by the Kuwait Oil Company; *see also UAE, Abu Dhabi,* *St Andrew, 2003-2010; and Priests with PTO*
1983 - 2 Aug 1990	**The Reverend Michael Jones** taken hostage after Iraq's invasion of Kuwait and transferred to Baghdad; *see also Cyprus,* *Limassol, 1996-2003*
3 Mar 1992 - Feb 1993	**The Reverend Ralph Martin**
6 Dec 1992 - 17 Nov 2000	**The Reverend Dr Adetola (Tola) Roberts**
29 May 1999 - June 2003	**The Reverend Canon Stephen Wright** *see also UAE, Dubai, Jebel Ali, Christ Church,* *2004-2014*
1 Jan 2004 - 2006	**The Reverend Christopher Edgar**
1 Mar 2005 - 27 June 2010	**The Reverend Andrew Thompson** Priest with PTO, 1 Mar 2005 - Mar 2006; Priest with PTO, 1 Apr 2006 - 30 Sept 2006; licensed as Chaplain 1 Oct 2006; *see also UAE, Abu Dhabi, 2010*
11 Jan - 23 Aug 2009	**The Reverend Canon Siow Chai Pin** Assistant Priest, licensed 12 Feb 2009, the first Anglican Chinese priest to serve in the diocese, responsible for the Mandarin-language congregation; left Kuwait due to ill health
7 Feb 2011 - 14 Aug 2011	**The Reverend Keith John Brimacombe** *see also Priests with PTO*
25 Apr 2012 - 28 Aug 2016	**The Reverend Harrison Chinnakumar** licensed 11 May 2012; also responsible for the Urdu-language congregation as Bishop Azad Marshall could not obtain a visit visa; *see also* *UAE, Dubai, Holy Trinity, 2016*

423

6 Jan 2017 -	**The Reverend Zhu Peijin** Assistant Curate, 6 Jan 2017 - 26 Jan 2018 Assistant Priest, 27 Jan 2018 - ; responsible for the Mandarin-language congregation
5 May 2017 -	**The Reverend Canon Dr Michael Mbona** Senior Chaplain

OMAN

Feb - May 1891	**The Rt Reverend Thomas Valpy French**
1893 - 1978	*Pastors from the Reformed Church in America* *(RCA) served in Oman*
1976 - 1978	The Reverend Dr Harvey Staal - *in Salalah* The Reverend Rodney Koopmans - *in Ruwi*

Protestant Church in Oman (PCO)

1978	*Joint ministry implemented* **Anglican** *clergy in* **bold type**
1978 - Sept 1980	**The Reverend Alan Gates**
1978 - 1981	The Reverend Rodney Koopmans (RCA)
1980 - 1982	**The Reverend John Hall**
1981 - 1986	The Reverend Richard Westra (RCA)
1982 - 1984	**The Reverend David Lloyd**
1984 - 1986	**The Reverend Richard Boulter**
1986 - 1989	The Reverend Roger Bruggink (RCA) *see also Yemen, 6 Nov 1998-Mar 2001*
1987 - 1989	**The Reverend Ray Skinner**
1989 - 1991	The Reverend John Hubers (RCA)
1989 - 1990	**The Reverend Jane Kieller** *Non-Stipendiary Deacon*
1990 - 1995	**The Reverend Robert Fieldson**
1992, Sept	The Reverend Harvey Staal (RCA)
1992 - 1994	The Reverend Chuck Johnson (RCA)
1994 - 2000	The Reverend Martin Weitz (RCA)
1995, May - Aug	The Reverend Don Lenderink (RCA)
1995 - 1999	**The Reverend Gerard Storey**
1996 - Sept 2004	**The Reverend Ernest Victor** Priest-in-Charge in Sohar; ministered in labour camps, and isolated communities of nurses and teachers in the hinterland; *see also UAE, Sharjah,* *St Martin, Oct 2004 - June 2013*

2000 - 2001	**The Reverend John Aldis**
2000 - 2001	The Reverend Chuck Johnson (RCA)
2002 - 2003	The Reverend Willis Jones (RCA)
2003 - 2005	The Reverend Steve Rheingans (RCA)
2004 - 2006	**The Reverend Michael Clarkson**
2006 - 2008	The Reverend Edward Schreur (RCA)
2006 - 2007	**The Reverend Canon Benjamin Chase**
2009 - 2011	The Reverend Jack Buteyn (RCA)
2011 - 2013	The Reverend Dr Barry Dawson (RCA)
2012 -	**The Reverend Christopher Howitz**
2013 - 2014	The Reverend Jack Buteyn (RCA)
2014 - late 2017	The Reverend Ken Bradsell (RCA)
Aug 2018	The Reverend Joshua Bode (RCA)

QATAR

April 1951 - 1958	**The Reverend Kenneth Jenkins**
1 Sept 1958 - 31 Jan 1962	**The Reverend John Howells**
1963 - 1986	*Ministry as UAE, Abu Dhabi, St Andrew*
4 Aug 1986 - 4 June 1988	**The Reverend Ian Young** licensed 4 Aug 1986, effective 31 Aug 1986; re-licensed Chaplain in Qatar and licensed DDO, 1 Oct 1987; *see also Bahrain, 1986-1991*
5 June 1988 - 6 Nov 1999	**The Reverend Canon Ian Young** appointed Hon Canon of St Christopher's Cathedral 5 June 1988; having become resident in Qatar in 1992, re-licensed as Chaplain in Qatar and DDO, 19 Jan 1992
7 Nov 1999 - 30 Apr 2007	**The Venerable Ian Young** also Archdeacon in Cyprus and the Gulf, 7 Nov 1999 - 30 Apr 2006; appointed Archdeacon Emeritus 1 May 2006; departed end of Jan 2007 (officially chaplain in Qatar until end Apr 2007) *see also Bahrain, 1984-1986;*
7 Dec 2007 - 31 Dec 2014	**The Venerable Dr William Schwartz OBE** Senior Chaplain, Qatar; Archdeacon in the Gulf, 2009 - ; *see also Cyprus, Kyrenia, 1993-1995; Canterbury Group 1999-2007; Bahrain, 2019 - ; Provosts & Deans*
31 Dec 2010 -	**The Reverend Canon Jebaraj Devasagayam** Priest with PTO, 31 Dec 2010 - 8 Feb 2011; Assistant Chaplain, licensed 7 Feb 2011;

425

responsible for the Epiphany Tamil- language congregation, inaugural Eucharist 2 Mar 2011; and the Epiphany Marathi- language congregation, inaugural Eucharist 15 May 2015

DOHA:

Church of the Epiphany *Consecrated on 29 September 2013*

1 May 2015 - 18 Jan 2019 **The Reverend Paul Davies**

22 Nov 2019 - **The Reverend Canon Paul-Gordon Chandler**

UNITED ARAB EMIRATES (UAE)

ABU DHABI

ABU DHABI CITY:
St Andrew

26 Apr 1963 - 15 Jan 1967 **The Reverend Richard T Matthews**

16 Jan 1967 - 1 June 1969 **The Reverend Canon David Elliot**

Chaplains ministered at the oil installation on Das Island; at Ruwais town west of Abu Dhabi; and during periodic visits in Qatar until 1986

4 Dec 1970 - 1 May 1978 **The Venerable Ralph A Lindley CBE**
installed 7 Dec 1970, also Archdeacon in the Gulf

1 Oct 1978 - 20 Feb 1983 **The Venerable Clive Handford**
also Archdeacon in the Gulf;
see also Iraq, Baghdad, 1967;
Bishops, 1996-2007, Primates, 2002-2007

29 June 1983 - 14 May 1997 **The Venerable Michael Mansbridge**
also Archdeacon in the Gulf 1983-1990;
Archdeacon in Cyprus and the Gulf
1991-1999 (moved to Nicosia to be Provost);
see also Cyprus, Nicosia, 1997-1999; Canons of the Two Cathedrals

1 June 1996 - 27 Feb 1998 **The Reverend Peter Benge**
Associate Priest

26 Nov 1997 - 28 Oct 2000 **The Reverend Anthony Thomas R Goode**
licensed 9 Dec 1997

1 Dec 2000 - 28 Nov 2002 **The Reverend Stephen Collis**
see also Cyprus, Nicosia, 2002-2009, Canons of the Two Cathedrals

28 Feb 2003 - 30 Apr 2010	**The Reverend Clive Windebank** licensed 19 Mar 2003; departed from Abu Dhabi 8 May 2010; *see also Kuwait, 1979-1983, and* *Priests with PTO*
1 Sept 2010 -	**The Reverend Canon Andrew Thompson MBE** licensed 19 Sept 2010; *see also Kuwait, 2005-* *2010; and Canons of the Two Cathedrals*
28 Sept 2012 - Sept 2016	**The Reverend Joanne Henderson** Assistant Curate, 28 Sept 2012 - 26 Sept 2013 Assistant Priest, 27 Sept 2013 - Sept 2016
Feb 2006 -	**The Reverend Gillian Nisbet** Full-time NSM with PTO, Feb 2006 - 19 Sept 2013; Assistant Priest, 20 Sept 2013 - Mar 2016 Associate Priest, Mar 2016 -
17 June 2019 -	**The Reverend Navina Thompson** Diocesan NSM

AL AIN: St Thomas

Late 1990s - 2011	*Ministry as Abu Dhabi city, St Andrew*
From 1 Sept 2011	**The Reverend Canon Eric McGirr** Priest with PTO
11 Feb 2013 - 7 Nov 2014	**The Reverend Robert David Lee** Priest with PTO, to serve at St Andrew, and at St Thomas, al Ain, 11 Feb - 19 Sept 2013; Assistant Priest, 20 Sept 2013 - 7 Nov 2014
Nov 2014 - Oct 2015	*Ministry as Abu Dhabi city, St Andrew*
9 Oct 2015 - July 2016	**The Reverend Christopher Mann**
Aug 2016 - early Sept 2017	*Ministry as Abu Dhabi city, St Andrew*
23 Sept 2017 -	**The Reverend Charlotte Lloyd-Evans** Assistant Curate; appointed diocesan Warden of Readers, Oct 2018

DUBAI

BUR DUBAI:
Holy Trinity

1969 - 1971	**The Reverend Kenneth Ridgewell**
1971 - 1972	**The Reverend Canon Haydn Parry MC** *see also Iraq, Basrah, 1957 - May 1960*
1972 - 1978	**The Reverend Philip Sturdy** also Port Chaplain, Missions to Seamen in Dubai

Nov 1978 - 1981	**The Reverend John Paxton** also Port Chaplain, Missions to Seamen, Dubai and Sharjah; in 1981 stayed with the Missions to Seamen when port expansion in the UAE made a joint ministry impractical
1981 - 1984	**The Reverend Philip Saywell**
1984 - 2001	**The Reverend Canon Dennis Gurney OBE** *see also Yemen, 2003-2004*
2001 - 2002	**The Reverend Peter Roberts**
1 May 2004 - 2010	**The Reverend John Weir**
16 Oct 2011 - 8 June 2015	**The Reverend Dr Ruwan Palapathwala**
16 Oct 2011 - Mar 2012	**The Reverend Catherine Dawkins** NSM Assistant Priest
1 June 2012 - Dec 2014	**The Reverend Timothy Heaney** Associate Chaplain; *see also UAE, Dubai, Jebel Ali, Christ Church, 2015 - March 2019*
11 Sept 2016 -	**The Reverend Canon Harrison Chinnakumar** *see also Kuwait, 2012-2016*

DUBAI ACADEMIC CITY /

SILICON OASIS:
St Catherine

Feb 2013 -	*Ministry as UAE, Dubai, Jebel Ali, Christ Church*

JEBEL ALI: Christ Church

13 Dec 2002 - Dec 2003	**The Reverend James Burton Wakerley** *see also Yemen, Aug 1995 - Jan 1998; UAE, Ras al Khaimah, St Luke, 1999 - Dec 2002*
Jan 2004 - 31 Dec 2014	**The Reverend Canon Stephen Wright** licensed 1 Feb 2004; *see also Kuwait, 1999-2003*
1 Jan 2015 - 17 Mar 2019	**The Reverend Timothy Heaney** *see also UAE, Dubai, Holy Trinity, June 2012- 2015*
19 Sept 2016 - 31 Oct 2019	**The Reverend Hin Lai (Harry) Ching** Assistant Curate
15 Nov 2019 -	**The Reverend James Young**

DUBAI and UAE PORTS:
Missions to Seamen

1972 - 1978	**The Reverend Philip Sturdy** Port Chaplain; *see also UAE, Dubai, Holy Trinity, 1972-1978*

11 Sept 1976	*Dubai International Seafarers' Centre opened*
1978 - 1981	**The Reverend John Paxton** Port Chaplain; *see also UAE, Dubai, Holy Trinity,* *1978-1981*
1981	*Due to UAE port expansion the joint ministry* *between the Missions to Seamen and the* *chaplaincy of Dubai and Sharjah deemed no* *longer viable*
May 1981 - 1984	**The Reverend Ernest Arnold**
26 May 1989 - Dec 1991	**The Reverend Duncan Harris** *see also Larnaca, Feb 1992 - Jan 1997*
July 1992 - 31 Aug 2001	**The Reverend Trevor Hearn** Ports Chaplain
Mission to Seafarers	*The charity's name since July 2000*
Jan 2002 - May 2011	**The Reverend Stephen Miller** Senior Chaplain, Dubai & UAE Ports
1 Feb 2007 - July 2008	**Mr Stephen Traynor** Lay Chaplain; licensed at St Helena, Larnaca, Synod Eucharist, 1 Feb 2007
1 July 2011 - May 2012	**The Reverend Nigel Dawkins** *see also Yemen, 2009-2011*
Sept 2012 - Oct 2018	**The Reverend Canon Dr Paul Burt** Chaplain, Sept 2012 - Apr 2013; Regional Director, Gulf and South Asia, Apr 2013 - Oct 2018; *see also Bahrain, 1988-1990*
1 Sept 2014 -	**The Reverend Nelson Fernandez** Ports Chaplain; *see also UAE, Ras al Khaimah,* *St Luke, 2006-2014*
10 Nov 2018 -	**The Reverend Canon Andrew Bowerman** Senior Chaplain, Dubai & UAE Ports; and Regional Director, Middle East and South Asia

FUJAIRAH

St Nicholas

1985 - 2009	*Ministry as UAE, Dubai, Holy Trinity*
28 Nov 2009 - 2012	**The Reverend Peter Chase** Part-time chaplain; part-time chaplain, East Coast, Mission to Seafarers, UAE
19 Jan 2013 - 12 Dec 2014	**The Reverend Andrew Tucker**
22 Apr 2016 -	*Ministry as UAE, Ras al Khaimah, St Luke*

RAS al KHAIMAH
St Luke

1985 - 1999	*Ministry as UAE, Dubai, Holy Trinity*
11 Dec 1999 - Dec 2002	**The Reverend James Burton Wakerley** Associate Priest with responsibilities in Ras al Khaimah and Umm al Quwain; *see also Yemen, 1995-1998; UAE, Dubai, Jebel Ali, Christ Church, 2002-2003*
23 Feb 2003 - 2004	**The Reverend Derek Hamblin** Associate Priest; with responsibilities also in Umm al Quwain; *see also Cyprus, Larnaca, St Helena, 2001-2002*
2004 - 2006	**The Reverend Gilbert John Linden**
1 July 2006 - 31 Aug 2014	**The Reverend Nelson Fernandez** locum ministry, 1 July 2006 - June 2007; licensed 17 Oct 2007; part-time chaplain to Fujairah until June 2009; *see also UAE, Dubai, Mission to Seafarers, 1 Sept 2014 -*
22 Apr 2016 - Apr 2018	**The Reverend Jon Lavelle** *see also UAE, Fujairah, St Luke, 2016-2018; Bahrain, 2014-2016*
14 Apr 2018 -	**The Reverend Kent Middleton, Obl CR** *see also UAE, Fujairah, St Luke, 2018 - ; Cyprus, Nicosia, St Paul, 2016-2018*

SHARJAH
St Martin

1969 - 1989	*Ministry as UAE, Dubai, Holy Trinity*
11 Feb 1990 - 1992	**The Reverend Michael Darby**
1993 - 31 Jan 1997	**The Reverend Brian Bradley** Associate Priest
19 Feb 1997 - 2003	**The Reverend Bill Atkins** Assistant Priest
Sept 2003 - Dec 2003	**The Reverend Stephen Wright** interim ministry; *see also Kuwait, May 1999 - June 2003; UAE, Dubai, Jebel Ali, Christ Church, Jan 2004 - Dec 2014*
5 Oct 2004 - 18 June 2013	**The Reverend Ernest Victor** *see also Oman, 1996-2004*

20 Sept 2013 - 25 July 2014	**The Reverend John Chapman**
20 Sept 2013 - 25 July 2014	**The Reverend Deborah Chapman** Priest with PTO
26 Feb 2016 -	**The Reverend Drew Schmotzer**

YEMEN

ADEN: Christ Church

20 Apr 1993	*The Grand Mufti of Yemen, Ahmad Muhammad Zabara, issued a fatwa to Bishop John Brown to restore Christ Church to the diocese*
Mar 1993 - Apr 1994, and Aug - Nov 1994	**Mr Tom Hamblin** Reader absent from Yemen during the May-July 1994 civil war; *see also Yemen, 1998*
Aug 1995 - 24 Jan 1998	**The Reverend James Wakerley** *also UAE, Ras al Khaimah, St Luke, 1999-2002;* *Dubai, Jebel Ali, Christ Church, 2002-2003;* *Yemen, 2004*
Oct 1996 - mid 1997	**The Reverend Dr Malcolm Dunjey** inaugural Medical Director of Ras Morbat; licensed to offer ministry, 13 Jan 1997; left Aden due to ill health
Jan - Sept 1998	**Mr Tom Hamblin** Reader; *see also Yemen, 1993-1994*
6 Nov 1998 - Mar 2001	**The Reverend Roger Bruggink** RCA Pastor with PTO *see also Oman, 1986-1989*
Mar - Sept 2001	**The Reverend Canon Benjamin Chase** locum ministry; *see also Yemen, May - Aug 2005;* *Oman (PCO), 2006-2007; Cantebury Group,* *1988 -1999*
Sept 2001 - June 2003	**The Reverend Colin Noyce** also Port Chaplain, Mission to Seafarers, *see also Cyprus, Limassol, 2003-2005*
Nov 2003 - Feb 2004	**The Reverend Canon Dennis Gurney OBE** locum ministry; *see also, UAE, Dubai, 1984-2001*
Apr-May 2004	**The Reverend Peter Crooks** locum ministry; *see also Yemen, 2005-2008;* *and 2011-2013*

431

June - Sept 2004	**The Reverend James Wakerley** locum ministry; *see also Yemen, 1995-1998;* *UAE, Ras al Khaimah, St Luke, 1999-2002; UAE,* *Dubai, Jebel Ali, Christ Church, 2002-2003*
May - Aug 2005	**The Reverend Canon Benjamin Chase** locum ministry; *see also Yemen, 2001;* *Oman, 2006-2007*
Sept 2005 - Nov 2008	**The Reverend Peter Crooks** also Port Chaplain, Mission to Seafarers; Director of the Ras Morbat clinics; *see also Yemen, 2004; 2011-2013*
Jan - Feb 2009	**Mr David Judson** layman with permission to lead worship
Feb - Apr 2009	**The Reverend Paul Hunt** locum ministry
3 July 2009 - Mar 2011	**The Reverend Nigel Dawkins** also Port Chaplain, Mission to Seafarers, *see also UAE, Dubai, Mission to Seafarers,* *2011-2012*
15 Jan 2010 - Mar 2011	**The Reverend Catherine Mary Dawkins** Deacon and Assistant Chaplain *see also UAE, Dubai, Holy Trinity, 2011-2012*
Mar - Aug 2011	**Mr Roy Facey** layman with permission to lead worship
Aug 2011 - Dec 2013	**The Reverend Peter Crooks MBE** also Port Chaplain, Mission to Seafarers; Director of the Ras Morbat clinics; *see also Yemen, 2004; 2005-2008*
Nov 2014 - Feb 2015	**The Reverend T Velvet John** returned to India due to civil war in Yemen
13 Dec 2014 - Feb 2015	**The Reverend Janet Vijayakumary** PTO; wife of Fr Velvet John, also returned to India due to civil war in Yemen
Feb 2015 -	*Ras Morbat clinic continued to function fully*

PART FOUR

APPENDICES

ABBREVIATIONS & ACRONYMS

ACC	Anglican Consultative Council
ACCL	Anglican Church (Cyprus) Limited
ACCM	Advisory Council for the Church's Ministry
ADMA	Abu Dhabi Marine Areas Limited
ADPC	Abu Dhabi Petroleum Company
AIOC	Anglo Iranian Oil Company
APOC	Anglo Persian Oil Company
ARAMCO	Arabian American Oil Company
BAPCO	Bahrain Petroleum Company
BISS	Bahrain International Seafarers Society
BP	British Petroleum
Bt	Baronet
C&CCS	Colonial and Continental Church Society (now the ICS)
C&G	Cyprus and the Gulf
CABF	Cyprus Archdeaconry Board of Finance
CASOC	California Arabian Standard Oil Company
CB	Companion of the Order of the Bath (British honour)
CBE	Commander of the Order of the British Empire (British honour)
CD	Canadian (Armed Forces) Decoration
CDBF	Central Diocesan Board of Finance
CID	Criminal Investigation Department
CMG	Companion of the Order of St Michael and St George (British honour)
CMJ	Church Mission to Jews
CMS	Church Missionary Society (now, Church Mission Society)
DBF (Cyprus)	Diocesan Board of Finance (Cyprus)
DBF (Gulf)	Diocesan Board of Finance (Gulf)
D/C&G	Diocese of Cyprus and the Gulf
DC	(Washington) District of Columbia
DD	Doctor of Divinity
DDO	Diocesan Director of Ordinands
DISC	Dubai International Seafarers Centre
Dr	Doctor
DSNE	(Chaplaincy of) Dubai, Sharjah and the Northern Emirates
ECC	Ecumenical Conference of Charity
ECJME	Episcopal Church in Jerusalem and the Middle East

ECUSA	Episcopal Church of the United States of America (now known as TEC - The Episcopal Church)
EMU	Eastern Mediterranean University
EOKA	*Ethniki Organosis Kyprion Agoniston* (literal translation: National Organisation of Cypriot Fighters)
FCO	(British) Foreign and Commonwealth Office
Fr	Father
FRGS	Fellow of the Royal Geographical Society
GABF	Gulf Archdeaconry Board of Finance
GCC	Gulf Cooperation Council
GFO	Good Friday Offering
Hon	Honorary / Honourable
HRH	His / Her Royal Highness
Ibid	in the same source, used to refer to a book, page or passage previously cited; abbreviation of Latin *ibidem*
ICS	Intercontinental Church Society
IPC	Iraq Petroleum Company
IPCC	Iraqi Protestant Church Committee
J&EM	Jerusalem and the East Mission
JEMT	Jerusalem and the East Mission Trust Limited
JEMT (Cyprus)	Jerusalem and the East Mission Trust (Cyprus)
JMECA	Jerusalem and the Middle East Church Association
KBE	Knight Commander of the Most Excellent Order of the British Empire
KCB	Knight Commander of the Most Honourable Order of the Bath (British honour)
KCVO	Knight Commander of the Royal Victorian Order (British honour)
KOC	Kuwait Oil Company
LMA	London Metropolitan Archives
Lt Col	Lieutenant Colonel
MBE	Member of the Order of the British Empire (British honour)
MECC	Middle East Council of Churches
MECO	Middle East Christian Outreach
MFA	Ministry of Foreign Affairs
MV	Motor Vessel
MVO	Member of the Royal Victorian Order (British honour)
NATO	North Atlantic Treaty Organisation
NEC	National Evangelical Church
NEDC	Near East Development Corporation
NGO	Non-Government Organisation

NSM	Non-Stipendiary Minister/Ministry
OAPEC	Organisation of Arab Petroleum Exporting Countries
OBE	Officer of the Order of the British Empire (British honour)
Obl CR	Oblate of the Community of the Resurrection
OPEC	Organisation of Petroleum Exporting Countries
PC	Privy Council / Privy Councillor
PCO	Protestant Church in Oman
PDQ	Petroleum Development (Qatar) Limited
PDRY	People's Democratic Republic of Yemen
PDTC	Petroleum Development Trucial Coast
PNCC	Palestine Native Church Council
PTO	Permission to Officiate
PwC	PricewaterhouseCoopers
RAF	(British) Royal Air Force
RCA	(Dutch) Reformed Church in America
Revd	Reverend
RN BSN	Registered Nurse / Bachelor of Science in Nursing
Rt	Right
Rt Hon	Right Honourable
SBA	(British) Sovereign Base Area
SBAA	(British) Sovereign Base Areas Administration
SDMTS	Southern Dioceses Ministerial Training Scheme (based at Salisbury Theological College, England)
SOCAL	Standard Oil Company of California
SPG	Society for the Propagation of the Gospel in Foreign Parts (see also USPG)
TEC	The Episcopal Church (in the USA)
TPC	Turkish Petroleum Company
TSSF	Tertiary of the Society of St Francis
UAE	United Arab Emirates
UN	United Nations
UNSCOP	United Nations Special Commission on Palestine
USPG	United Society for the Propagation of the Gospel (now United Society Partners in the Gospel)
VD	Volunteer Officers' Decoration (British military decoration)
VE	Victory in Europe
Ven	Venerable
WCC	World Council of Churches
YAR	Yemen Arab Republic

GLOSSARY

Abbreviation: Diocese of C&G = Diocese of Cyprus and the Gulf

Anglican	denoting or relating to the Church of England and any Church worldwide that is in communion with the Archbishop of Canterbury; a participant in any member Church of the Anglican Communion
Anglican Church (Cyprus) Limited, The	registered/incorporated as a Limited Liability Company on 3 April 2015 to provide Anglican clerics and parishes within the Republic of Cyprus with greater legal security
Anglican Communion, The	the worldwide family of autonomous national or regional Anglican Churches together with six extra-provincial Churches and dioceses, all of which are normatively in communion and reciprocal relationship with the Archbishop of Canterbury, the Anglican Communion's spiritual head; the third largest Christian body in the world, after the Roman Catholic and Orthodox churches
Arabian Mission, The	an American Protestant organisation launched as The Arabian Mission in 1889, adopted by the Reformed Church in America in 1894 and formally dissolved in 1973; in particular it ministered in Basrah (southern Iraq), Kuwait, the islands of Bahrain and Muscat (now the capital of Oman)
archbishop	bishop of the highest rank; *see also* primate, and Most Reverend
archbishopric	the area over which an archbishop has authority; also, the title of the office of archbishop
archdeacon	a senior cleric to whom a bishop delegates certain responsibilities; *see also* Venerable
assistant curate	*see* curate
Barnabas Team, The	a network within the Diocese of C&G to discern, encourage, and support spiritual development and to enrich discipleship

438

bishop	a senior member of the Christian clergy, typically in charge of a diocese and empowered to confer holy orders; *see also* Archbishop, President Bishop
bishopric	the area over which a diocesan bishop has authority; also, the title of the office of bishop
Canon Law	a body of laws and regulations with ecclesiastical authority for the governance of a Christian organisation or Church and its members
Canterbury Group, The	the name in use from circa 1952 to denote the Anglican / Episcopal ministry and worship in areas of the Gulf region where publicised Christian worship is not permitted
cathedral	a church building in which a bishop has his official seat; from the Latin *cathedra* (chair)
chaplain	in the Diocese of C&G the term has frequently been used for what would elsewhere be called parish priest, or incumbent, or rector, or vicar
chrism	a consecrated oil used for anointing in Christian rites
Church Missionary Society, The	founded in 1799 as a British mission society working with the Anglican Communion and Protestant Christians around the world; in 1995 the name was changed to the Church Mission Society
Church Mission to Jews, The	as known in the 1930's, founded in 1809 as the London Society for Promoting Christianity Amongst the evangelical Anglicans
church planting	the practice of establishing a core of Christian worshippers in a new location with the intention that they may develop into a thriving congregation
collate	appoint a member of the clergy (for example, an archdeacon) to a benefice or office
College of Arms, The	the official heraldic authority for England, Wales, Northern Ireland and much of the Commonwealth, also known as the College of Heralds
commissary	a person to whom some responsibility or role is delegated by a senior authority; in the Diocese of C&G, the bishop's commissary in England has normally been the Vicar of All Hallows by the Tower, London

Commonwealth of Nations, The	normally known as the Commonwealth, an intergovernmental organisation of fifty-three member states, nearly all former territories of the British Empire
Community of the Resurrection, The	an Anglican religious community for men based in Mirfield, West Yorkshire, England
companion diocese	a diocese of the Anglican Communion formally linked in friendship with one or more others in a different province or provinces
curate	originally and still formally, the incumbent or priest-in-charge of a parish / chaplaincy, sharing the "cure" or care of souls with the bishop; in ordinary usage, the same as Assistant Curate
deacon	in Anglican, Roman Catholic and Orthodox churches, an ordained minister of an order conferred prior to that of priest, though some may remain deacons permanently
dean	a senior member of clergy in charge of a cathedral and its property; see provost, and Very Reverend
diocese	a geographical area whose churches and congregations are under the authority and administration of a bishop
disestablish	disengage a Church from state support and privileged status
ecumenical	involving relations between two or more Christian Churches, and/or Christian denominations
Ecumenical Conference of Charity, The	a social and charitable activity undertaken jointly by Christians of various Churches to respond to need and poverty irrespective of religious affiliation or belief; the ECC in Bahrain is registered under the auspices of St Christopher's Cathedral
emeritus	a former holder of an office having retired, but entitled by appointment to retain the title; from the Latin emereri, "to serve out one's term"
Endowment Fund	see Foundation
Episcopal (Church)	a designation for certain member churches of the Anglican Communion, such as The Episcopal Church (in the USA), the Scottish Episcopal Church, and the Episcopal Church in Jerusalem and the Middle East

440

Episcopal Church (in the USA), The	formerly known as the Episcopal Church in the United States of America (ECUSA), The Episcopal Church (TEC) is a member Church of the worldwide Anglican Communion
Evangelical	a Christian of any Church or denomination who places particular emphasis on, among other things, the primacy of holy scripture and personal salvation
evangelical	of or according to the teaching of the Gospel or the Christian religion, derived from the Greek *euangelion*: gospel or good news
fatwa	an authoritative legal opinion given by an acknowledged Islamic authority
Foundation, The	short form for The Diocese of Cyprus and the Gulf Foundation (formerly the Diocese of Cyprus and the Gulf Endowment Fund), established in 1990 by a Trust Deed as a UK charity (registered number 1000307); its aims are to advance the Christian religion according to the doctrines and principles of the Central Synod of the Episcopal Church in Jerusalem and the Middle East by the extension of the work, ministry and public worship throughout the diocese and such other purposes connected with the Church as the trustees may determine
Garter King of Arms	also known as Garter Principal King of Arms, the senior Officer of the College of Arms in the UK
Good Friday Offering	a special collection taken on Good Friday in most parishes of The Episcopal Church (USA) and The Anglican Church of Australia, always designated for the four dioceses of the Episcopal Church in Jerusalem and the Middle East
Gospeller	reader of the Gospel in a service of Holy Communion
Grand Mufti	the highest official of religious law in a Sunni or Ibadi Muslim country; "the senior expounder", for example the Grand Mufti of Yemen; *see also* mufti
Green Line	the demilitarised buffer zone in Cyprus, patrolled by the UN, extending for 112 miles/180 km
High Commissioner	the UK uses the term High Commissioner for its ambassadors to Commonwealth nations, such as Cyprus; *see also* Commonwealth of Nations

441

JEMT (Cyprus)	a board of Trustees in Cyprus responsible for the management of Anglican church property owned by The Jerusalem and the East Mission Trust Ltd
Jerusalem and the East Mission, The	a fund/charity established by Bishop George Francis Popham Blyth in 1888 for the maintenance and development of the diocese; the charity's jurisdiction also stretched from Syria to Egypt, and later Sudan and Iran; *see also* Jerusalem and the East Mission Trust Limited, and the Jerusalem and the Middle East Church Association
Jerusalem and the East Mission Trust Limited, The	formed by the Jerusalem and the East Mission and registered on 27 Dec 1929 as a non-profit limited company in the UK to hold title to land and to administer charitable trusts set up to help support Anglican presence in the Middle East and elsewhere
Jerusalem and the Middle East Church Association, The	instituted on 6 January 1976 to coincide with the inauguration of the Episcopal Church in Jerusalem and the Middle East, by decision of the council of the Jerusalem and the East Mission, which thus constituted the Jerusalem and the Middle East Church Association (JMECA) as a UK-based limited company and charity; today JMECA acts as a link with the Church of England to help serve the four self-governing dioceses which together form the Province of the ECJME; the Directors of the Jerusalem and the East Mission Trust form the Standing Committee of JMECA
Lambeth Conference	a normally decennial assembly of bishops of the Anglican Communion, convened by the Archbishop of Canterbury, the first such conference met in London at Lambeth Palace on 24 Sept 1867
Mar Thoma Church	otherwise known as the Mar Thoma Malankara Syrian Church, found principally in or deriving from the Indian State of Kerala, in full communion with the Churches of the Anglican Communion; one of the Churches tracing their origin to the Apostle Thomas
metropolitan	originally, a bishop of the Christian Church who resided in the chief city, or metropolis, of a civil province of the Roman Empire and, for

442

	ecclesiastical purposes, administered a territorial area coextensive with a civil province; in modern times also sometimes the archbishop or primate of a whole Church or Province
Mission to Seafarers	founded in 1856 as the Mission to Seamen Afloat at Home and Abroad; renamed in 1858 as the Missions to Seamen, and in 2000 as the Mission to Seafarers; a charity of the Anglican Communion, funded by voluntary donations, now serving 1.3 million merchant seafarers of all ranks, nationalities and beliefs; it offers support and emergency help to crews visiting 250 ports world-wide, to those stranded in them, and cares for victims of piracy
Most Reverend, The	the title given to an archbishop or presiding / president bishop within each of the Anglican Communion's provinces
mufti	an Islamic scholar and jurist who interprets Islamic law, qualified to give fatwas, *see also* fatwa
Nestorian Church	a Church within the Syriac tradition of Eastern Christianity, known as the Church of the East
Nissen hut	a tunnel-shaped military hut made of corrugated steel, with a cement floor, named after its inventor P N Nissen (1871-1930), a British engineer
oblate	a person who, while normally not resident in the core community of a monastery, convent, or Order, lives by its rules and is dedicated to its purposes; *see also* Community of the Resurrection
Orthodox Church	denotes either the Byzantine or Greek Orthodox family of Eastern Churches and any one of its constituent Churches such as the Church of Cyprus; or the Oriental Orthodox family of Eastern Churches and any one of its constituent Churches such as the Armenian Orthodox Church, the Coptic Orthodox Church, the Ethiopian Orthodox Church and the Syrian Orthodox Church
People of the Book	an Islamic term, *ahl al kitab*, referring principally to Jews and Christians
prebendary	an alternative title in some cathedrals for an honorary canon

443

President Bishop	the title used by the Primate of the Episcopal Church in Jerusalem and the Middle East
priest	a member of the Christian clergy of any of the episcopal churches who, under a bishop's authority, may preside at the eucharist and pronounce absolution and blessing
primate	within the Anglican Communion, the chief archbishop or bishop within each of its provinces
pro-cathedral	a parish church temporarily serving as a cathedral, such as St Christopher's Pro-Cathedral in Bahrain, 1982-1986
province	an autonomous national or regional member Church of the Anglican Communion, such as the Episcopal Church in Jerusalem and the Middle East
provost	former alternative term for dean, the head of an Anglican cathedral chapter; *see also* dean, and Very Reverend
rehallow	resanctify, reconsecrate
Reader	a lay person who has been selected, trained, admitted and licensed by the bishop of a diocese to preach, teach and lead worship in a pastoral context
Right Reverend, The	the title given to an Anglican/Episcopal bishop
See	the diocese of a bishop or the place within it where his/her cathedral is sited; Latin *sedes* (a seat)
Society for the Propagation of the Gospel in Foreign Parts	a Church of England missionary organisation, founded in 1701 to send Anglican clergymen and religious literature to Britain's colonies now the United Society Partners in the Gospel
tertiary	an associate in the Third Order of a Christian monastic organisation
United Thank Offering	a ministry of the Episcopal Church in the USA that solicits offerings to support innovative mission and ministry projects throughout ECUSA (now TEC) and the provinces of the Anglican Communion
Venerable, The	the title given to an Anglican/Episcopal archdeacon
Very Reverend, The	the title given to a dean or provost of an Anglican/Episcopal cathedral

BIBLIOGRAPHY

ARCHIVES
See **Notes & Sources for document references**

academia.edu - St John Simpson, *The Reverend Ralph Norman Sharp: A Short Appreciation*, undated, pdf format
Anglican Communion, anglicancommunion.org
Chaplaincy archives, Anglican Diocese of Cyprus and the Gulf:
    Bahrain: St Christopher's Cathedral
    Cyprus: Christ Church, Ayia Napa
    Cyprus: Paphos chaplaincy
    Cyprus: St Andrew, Kyrenia
    Cyprus: St Barnabas, Limassol
    Cyprus: St Helena, Larnaca
    Cyprus: St Paul's Cathedral, Nicosia
    Iraq: St George, Baghdad
    Kuwait: St Paul, Ahmadi, Kuwait
    UAE: Holy Trinity, Dubai
    UAE: St Andrew, Abu Dhabi
Church archive, SBA Dhekelia, Cyprus, St George's vestry
Church archives, UK:
    All Hallows by the Tower, London
    Exeter Cathedral
    Winchester Cathedral (*See* Hampshire Record Office)
Church archives, USA:
    Episcopal Church, episcopalarchives.org
    Reformed Church in America, rca.org
Cyprus Press and Information Office
Diocese of Cyprus and the Gulf, admin@cypgulf.org
Diocese of Jerusalem archive, j-diocese.org
Gale Digital Collections, www.gdc.gale.com
Hampshire Record Office: Hampshire Archives and Local Studies, hants.gov.uk
Jerusalem and the Middle East Church Association, jmeca.org.uk
Libraries:
    British Library, bl.uk
    India Office Library, IOR/R/15/2/1823 - Bahrain Church File
    Lambeth Palace Library, lambethpalacelibrary.org.uk
    Wellcome Library, London, wellcomelibrary.org
London Metropolitan Archives, cityoflondon.gov.uk
Middle East Centre Archive, St Antony's College, Oxford, sant.ox.ac.uk

Mission to Seafarers, London, missiontoseafarers.org
Museum of Army Chaplaincy, chaplains-museum.co.uk
Oil company archives:
    Bahrain Petroleum Company (BAPCO)
    British Petroleum (BP)
    Kuwait Oil Company (KOC)
Royal Collection Trust, rct.uk/collection

BOOKS

BIRKS, Revd Herbert, *The Life and Correspondence of Thomas Valpy French, First Bishop of Lahore,* Vol II, John Murray, London, 1895

BROWN, John, *Mainly Uphill: A Bishop's Journey*, privately published by Richard Brown, UK, 2012

CHRISTOFIDES, Felicity, *A Small But Suitable Church: The Early Years of the Anglican Church in Cyprus 1878-1901*, published by the author, Nicosia, 2014

CLARK, Victoria, *Dancing On The Heads Of Snakes*, Yale University Press, New Haven and London, 2010

CLARKE, Angela, *Bahrain Oil and Development 1929-1989*, Immel Publishing, London, 1991

CLARKE, Angela, *Through the Changing Scenes of Life 1893-1993*, published by The American Mission Hospital Society, Bahrain, 1993

COLLINS, P C, *A Short History of St Andrew's English Church, Kyrenia, Cyprus, 1913-1988*, digital recreation of a booklet written by J K Luard in 1973, produced by St Andrew's Church Kyrenia, 1988

CROOKS, Peter, *Yemen, Heartbreak and Hope*, published by the author, 2013

DODD, Charles, *The First Hundred Years: St Barnabas' Anglican Church - A Brief History of the Church in Limassol*, published by St Barnabas church, Limassol, Cyprus, 2015

GARDINER, Ian, *In the Service of the Sultan: A First Hand Account of the Dhofar Insurgency*, Pen & Sword Military, Barnsley, UK, 2008

HEARD-BEY, Frauke, *From Trucial States to United Arab Emirates*, Longman Group, UK, 1982

HENDERSON, Edward, *A History of St Andrew's Church, Abu Dhabi*, 1984

HENDERSON, Edward, *This Strange Eventful History, Memoirs of Earlier Days in the UAE and the Sultanate of Oman*, Motivate Publishing, 1993, London, Dubai and Abu Dhabi (first published in 1988 by Quartet Books Ltd, UK)

HOLLAND, Robert, *Britain and the Revolt in Cyprus 1954-59*, Oxford University Press, London, 1998

Holy Trinity Church 1969-2009: Forty Glorious Years, published by Holy Trinity Church, Dubai, 2009

HUNTER, Captain F M, *An Account of The British Settlement of Aden in Arabia*, Trübner & Co, London, 1877 (A Facsimile of the Original from Gale, Cengage Learning and the British Library)

JARMAN, Robert, *Cathedral of the Gulf: The History of St Christopher's and The Anglican Church in Bahrain*, published in Bahrain by The Anglican and Episcopal Church of Bahrain, 1990

MARKIDES, Diana, *Sendall in Cyprus 1892-1898: A Governor in Bondage*, Moufflon Publications Ltd, Nicosia, Cyprus, 2014

MORGAN, Tabitha, *Sweet and Bitter Island: A History of the British in Cyprus*, I B Tauris & Co Ltd., London & New York, 2010

REDDAWAY, John, *Odi et Amo, Vignettes of an Affair with Cyprus*, K Rustem & Brother, London, 1990

SCUDDER III, Lewis R, *The Arabian Mission's Story: In Search of Abraham's Other Son*, The Historical Series of the Reformed Church in America No 30, William B Eerdmans Publishing Co., Grand Rapids, Michigan, USA, 1998

SKINNER, Raymond Frederick, *Christians in Oman*, Tower Press, 1996

THOMPSON, Andrew, *Christianity in the UAE: Culture and Heritage*, Motivate Publishing, Abu Dhabi, Dubai & London, 2011

THOMPSON, Andrew, *The Christian Church in Kuwait: Religious Freedom in the Gulf*, Saeed and Sameer, Kuwait, 2010

WATERFIELD, Gordon, *Sultans of Aden*, Stacey International, London, 2002

WIBLINGER, Hans-Ulrich, *Kyrenia: A Harbour Town of Cyprus*, Vividus-Reisen, Germany, 2016

WORRALL, James, *State Building and Counter Insurgency in Oman: Political, Military and Diplomatic Relations at the End of Empire*, I B Tauris & Co, 2014

YERGIN, Daniel, *The Prize: The Epic Quest for Oil, Money and Power*, Simon & Schuster, 1991

ZWEMER, S M, *Arabia: The Cradle of Islam*, published by Fleming H Revell Company, New York, Chicago, Toronto, 1900

MAGAZINES, NEWSPAPERS & PERIODICALS

Bible Lands, magazine of the Jerusalem and the Middle East Church Association, jmeca.org.uk

Bulletin of All Hallows by the Tower with St Dunstan in the East, allhallowsbythetower.org.uk

GEO ExPro Geoscience magazine, geoexpro.com/magazine

Journal of the Royal Army Chaplains' Department (UK), Vol XIX, March 1964,

The Bahrain Anglican News, former magazine of St Christopher's Cathedral, Bahrain, stchcathedral.org.bh

The Olive Branch, magazine of The Association of Friends of the Diocese of Cyprus and the Gulf, UK, friends@cypgulf.org

The Owl, a weekly newspaper and review published in Cyprus 1888-1902

Theological Journal of the Christian Study Centre, Rawalpindi, Pakistan

NOTES & SOURCES

Chapter 1 - ANGLICAN PIONEERS IN CYPRUS, 1878 -1973

1   Repository: Lambeth Palace Library
    Proceedings of the Lambeth Conference 1878, 2-4 July, Order No LC7, Anglican chaplains and chaplaincies abroad (folios 213-53)
    Proceedings of the Lambeth Conference 1878, 22-24 July, Order No LC9, Anglican chaplains and chaplaincies abroad (folios 22-52, 194-9)

2   Christofides, Felicity, *A Small but Suitable Church: The Early Years of the Anglican Church in Cyprus 1878-1901,* published by the author, Nicosia, Cyprus, 2014, p 27, plus note 45: The Rt Revd Charles W Sandford, Bishop of Gibraltar at Project Canterbury, *Pastoral Letter to Clergy and Laity 1878*

3   Wiblinger, Hans-Ulrich, *Kyrenia: A Harbour Town of Cyprus,* Vividus-Reisen, Germany, 2016, p 90

4   Morgan, Tabitha, *Sweet and Bitter Island: A History of the British in Cyprus,* I B Tauris & Co Ltd., London & New York, 2010, p 2

5   Ibid, p 259, note 2 - A visitor to Cyprus claimed that the redundant coal boxes, filled with water, were placed around Government House for use as fire extinguishers: Baker, Samuel, *Cyprus as I Saw It in 1879,* Ch 9, p 194 (Project Gutenberg Etext no. 3656, 1 January 2003)

6   Morgan, p 2

7   Christofides, pp 40 and 48

8   Morgan, p 4

9   Christofides, pp 40-1, plus note 112: The Rt Revd Charles W Sandford, *Pastoral Letter to Clergy and Laity 1879*

10 Ibid, p 42, plus note 118: Knight, H J C, *The Diocese of Gibraltar*

11 Ibid, p 31, plus note 66: see copy in D/C&G archive Nicosia. The original is at Lambeth Palace Library, London. Ref Tait 242 folios 221-4

12 Ibid, p 72, plus notes 278 and 279:
    278 - The Rt Revd Charles W Sandford, Bishop of Gibraltar at Project Canterbury, *Pastoral Letter to Clergy and Laity 1879*
    279 - Anglican Diocesan and Cathedral Archives, Nicosia

13 Ibid, p 21, plus note 17: the Rt Revd Charles W Sandford, *Pastoral Letter to Clergy and Laity 1879*

14 Ibid, p 23, plus note 37: Knight, H J C, *The Diocese of Gibraltar,* p 2

15 Ibid, pp 23-24, plus note 38: the Rt Revd Charles W Sandford, *Pastoral Letter to Clergy and Laity 1878*

16 Ibid, p 64, plus note 221: *1879 Annual Report for C&CCS,* Vol IX 1876-1880, p 157, at LMA Archives CLC/005/MS15718/009

17 Ibid, p 64

18 Ibid, p 65, note 233: *1879 Annual Report for the C&CCS (See* note 16)

19 Ibid

20 Ibid, p 66, plus note 238: Meeting, 20 March 1879, *General Committee Book of C&CCS,* LMA Archives CLC/005/MS15674/004

21 Ibid, plus note 243: MS2913, Lambeth Palace Library

22 Ibid, p 64, plus note 224: correspondence with the Bishop of London at Lambeth Palace Library

23 Ibid, p 66, plus note 242: *Letter from F W Warren to the Bishops of London and Gibraltar,* 18 June 1879, Lambeth Palace Library

24 Ibid, p 50: the unhealthy site of Camp Ciftlik Pasha was abandoned in Nov 1878 in favour of Camp Mathiati, a provisional cantonment, 17 miles/27 km south-west of Nicosia in the foothills of the Macheras mountains

25 Ibid, p 68

26 Ibid, p 72

27 Wiblinger, p 19

28 Christofides, pp 84-87

29 Ibid, p 130

30 Ibid

31 Markides, Diana, *Sendall in Cyprus 1892-1898: A Governor in Bondage,* Moufflon Publications Ltd, Nicosia, Cyprus, 2014, p 20

32 Wiblinger, p 96

33 Christofides, p 174

34 The marriages of five daughters of the Ven Josiah and Mrs Bessie Spencer are recorded at St Paul's Church, Nicosia:
Mary, 4 May 1905 (Archived Item D001, RB&M, Entry 33)
Beatrice, 30 May 1908 (Archived Item D001, RB&M Entry 37)
Alice, 5 April 1910 (Archived Item D001, RB&M, Entry 41)
Florence, 27 April 1912 (Archived Item D001, RB&M, Entry 45)
Ida, 12 January 1915 (Archived Item D001, RB&M, Entry 48)

35 Wiblinger, p 124

36 Collins, P C, *A Short History of St Andrew's English Church, Kyrenia, Cyprus, 1913-1988,* p 2, D/C&G archive, Nicosia; also "St Andrew's Church Kyrenia", *Bible Lands,* No 12, Vol XVIII, Autumn 1973, p 144

37 Letter to *The Times,* 4 February 1919

38 MECA: Jerusalem and the East Mission, *Bible Lands,* Vol 7, Jan 1920

39 Morgan, pp 96-97

40 Ibid, p 103

41 "St George's in the Forest, Troodos, Cyprus", T S B F de Chaumont, *Bible Lands,* No 151, Vol IX, Jan 1937, pp 809-810

42 Ibid, p 809

43 EOKA – *Ethniki Organosis Kyprion Agoniston* (literal translation: National Organisation of Cypriot Fighters)

44 Morgan, p 218

45 The correct styling for the "Anglican Archdeacon in Nicosia" is "Archdeacon in Cyprus". During the negotiations, 1995-1960, three Archdeacons in Cyprus held office: 1949-1955, the Ven Donald Goldie; 1955-1958, the Ven Arthur W Adeney; 1958-1960, the Ven W Kenneth Blackburn

46 Morgan, p 219, note 34: Reddaway, John, *Odi et Amo, Vignettes of an Affair with Cyprus,* K Rustem & Brother, London, 1990, p 56

47 Morgan, p 219

48 Morgan, p 218, note 31: Holland, *Britain and the Revolt in Cyprus 1954-59,* p 85

49 Morgan, p 207

50 Ibid, p 251

51 Ibid, p 252, note 36: Holland, *Britain and the Revolt in Cyprus 1954-59,* p 317

52 Morgan, p 252, plus note 38: in 1959 the Greek Cypriot electorate was 238,000

53 Diocese of C&G, Minutes, 1st Diocesan Synod (Cyprus), 26 May 1976, p 1

Chapter 2 - VENTURING INTO ADEN & MUSCAT, 1839-1970

1   The Trucial Coast, also known as the Trucial States, Trucial Oman, and the Trucial Shaikhdoms, were tribal confederations bordering much of the south-east coast of the Arabian peninsula; known, too, as the Pirate Coast when raiders began to harass shipping, thus in 1853 the ruling shaikhs signed a treaty with Great Britain agreeing to a perpetual maritime truce, hence the term "trucial".

2   The co-founders of the Arabian Mission were three of Professor John G Lansing's students at the Theological Seminary of the Dutch Reformed Church in America in New Brunswick, USA: James Cantine, Philip T Phelps and Samuel Zwemer.

3   Hunter, Captain F M (compiler), *An Account of the British Settlement of Aden in Arabia,* Trübner & Co, London, 1877; later reproduced as a facsimile of the original by Gale Digital Collections and the British Library, p165

4   Clark, Victoria, *Dancing on the Heads of Snakes,* Yale University Press Publications, USA, 2010, p 30

5   Waterfield, Gordon, *Sultans of Aden,* Stacey International, UK, 2002, p 39

6   A silver dollar coin embossed with a bust of Empress Maria Theresa of Austria and the date 1780

7   Clark, p 31

8   Aden was the only area in Yemen under full British sovereignty; together with some offshore islands, it was known as Aden Settlement (1839–1932), Aden Province (1932-1937), Aden Colony (1937-1963) and reconstituted as the State of Aden (1963-1967) within the new Federation of South Arabia; this became the People's Republic of South Yemen on 30 Nov 1967, marking the end of British rule.

9   Hunter, p 26

10 Marshall, the Revd G S, "Christ Church, Steamer Point, Aden 1863-1963", *Journal of the Royal Army Chaplains' Department,* Vol XIX March 1964, p 9

11 Ibid

12 Hunter, p 147

13 Ibid

14 Ibid

15 Marshall, p 9

16 Hunter, p 168

17 Ibid, p 147

18 Ibid, p 27

19 Ibid, p 26

20 India Office Record, IOR_L_PS_12_1477_0001, 1933, P Z 5312, p 7

21 IOR_L_PS_12_1477_0001, 1936, P Z 3617, pp 5-6

22 Marshall, pp 9-10

23 The Revd Peter Crooks, and his wife Nancy, served at Christ Church, Aden: April-May 2004; Sept 2005-Nov 2008; Aug 2011-Dec 2013

24 Clark, p 88, note 65, quoting from: Paget, Julian, *Last Post: Aden 1964-1967,* Faber & Faber, London, 1969, p 255

25 Crooks, Peter, *Yemen, Heartbreak and Hope,* pp 30-31

26 Related in an email by Thanos Petouris, 29 March 2018

27 Brown, John, *Mainly Uphill,* p 268

28 The province of the Episcopal Church in Jerusalem and the Middle East, inaugurated on 6 Jan 1976

29 Stacey, Vivienne, "Thomas Valpy French, First Bishop of Lahore, *Al-Mushir* [the Counselor]", *Theological Journal of the Christian Study Centre,* Rawalpindi, Pakistan (1981/2), p 71

30 Ibid, p 44

31 Ibid, p 97

32 Ibid, p 76, the Cathedral Church of the Resurrection was consecrated on the Feast of the conversion of St Paul, 25 January 1887

33 Zwemer, S M, *Arabia: The Cradle of Islam,* published by Fleming H Revell Company, New York, Chicago, Toronto, 1900, pp 329-330

34 Ibid, p 330

35 Ibid, pp 346-7

36 Stacey, p 113

37 Swiss cottage tents are portable shelters widely used for camping and trekking

38 Historically, a caravanserai is an inn with a central courtyard for travellers in the desert regions of Asia and North Africa

39 Zwemer, pp 348-9

40 Birks, Revd Herbert, *The Life and Correspondence of Thomas Valpy French, First Bishop of Lahore,* Vol II, John Murray, London, 1895, p 371

41 Ibid, p 370

42 Ibid, p 371

43 Ibid, p 372

44 Ibid, p 375

45 Ibid, p 376

46 Ibid, p 386

47 Zwemer, pp 349-350

48 Birks, pp 390-1

49 Ibid, p 397

50 Ibid

51 Ibid, p 401

52 Ibid, pp 403-4

53 Scudder, Lewis R III, *The Arabian Mission's Story: In Search of Abraham's Other Son,* The Historical Series of the Reformed Church in America No 30, William B Eerdmans Publishing, Grand Rapids, Michigan, 1998, p 169

54 Bait An Noor means "house of light" in Arabic. This naming of the worship hall evokes images of Jesus as the light of the world.

451

Chapter 3 - FOOTPRINTS IN IRAQ, 1842-1973

1 Archibald Campbell Tait, 1811-1882, Archbishop of Canterbury 1868-1882

2 Riley, A, *Narrative of a Visit to the Assyrian Christians in Kurdistan* undertaken at the request of the Archbishop of Canterbury in the autumn of 1884, p 1, anglicanhistory.org/england/riley/narrative 1884.html

3 Keen, Rosemary. "Church Missionary Society Archive", Adam Matthew Publications, 29 Jan 2017

4 Persian was in accepted use at this time. It was not until later in the twentieth century that the Arabian Gulf became the official term used by the countries bordering the Gulf's western coastline

5 *See* Notes & Sources, Ch 2, Venturing into Aden & Muscat, note 1

6 Dunlop, D C, "A Church for Baghdad", *Bible Lands*, No 138, Vol VIII, Oct 1933, p 408

7 Yergin, Daniel, *The Prize: The Epic Quest for Oil, Money and Power*, Simon & Schuster, London, 1991, p 204

8 Dunlop, D C, "A Church for Baghdad", *Bible Lands*, No 138, Vol VIII, Oct 1933, p 407

9 Ibid, pp 407-408

10 Ibid, p 407

11 Ibid, pp 407-408

12 Ibid, p 408

13 St John's College was founded as the London College of Divinity in 1863 by the Revd Alfred Peache and his sister, Kezia, to provide an evangelical theological education to ordinands who could not go to university.

14 Letter from Bishop Graham Brown to the Archbishop of Canterbury, 6 July 1933, pp 1-2, File: Iraq, Baghdad, St George's, 1938-1948 / 1973-1974, Bishop's office, D/C&G

15 English translation of an article in *Alwehda* newspaper, 15 Jan 1935, p 1, file source as note 14

16 Postscript to a letter from the Revd Charles John Fortescue-Thomas to Bishop Graham Brown, 24 April 1935, p 2, file source as note 14

17 Later became the Rt Revd William Wilson Cash DSO, OBE, DD, Bishop of Worcester, 1941-1955

18 Letter from General Secretary, Rev Preb. W Wilson Cash DD, Church Mission Society, to Bishop Graham Brown, 17 May 1935, p 1, file source as note 14

19 From Bishop Graham Brown's letter to the Archbishop of Canterbury, "The Iraqi Protestant Congregation, Baghdad", 25 June 1935, p 5, file source as note 14

20 Ibid

21 Ibid

22 Letter titled "The British Chaplaincy, Baghdad", to Bishop Graham Brown from (Revd) J C Fortescue-Thomas, 27 May 1935, p 2, file source as note 14

23 Extract from same letter as Note 19, pp 6-7

24 The Jerusalem and the East Mission was a fund/charity established by Bishop George Francis Popham Blyth in 1888 for the maintenance and development of the

Diocese of Jerusalem, and on 6 Jan 1976 it was reconstituted as the Jerusalem and the Middle East Church Association. No 1, Vol 1 of the charity's quarterly paper *Bible Lands* was published in July 1899.

25 "Mesopotamia Memorial Church in Baghdad", *Bible Lands*, No 149, Vol IX, July 1936, p 748

26 "Mesopotamia Memorial Church, Baghdad", *Bible Lands,* No 152, Vol IX, April 1937, p 846

27 "The Bishop's Letter, *Bible Lands*, No 152, Vol IX, April 1937, p 824

28 "St Peters, Basra", F. W. B (the Revd Francis William Bowyer), *Bible Lands*, No 164, Vol X April 1940, p 1155-6

29 Ibid

30 "The Pipe-line", *Bible Lands*, No 166, Vol X, Oct 1940, pp 1175-6

31 Ibid, p 1176

32 "The Bishop's Last Week", *Bible Lands*, No 175, Vol X, Jan 1943, p 1326

33 "The Times' Obituary Notice", reprinted from *The Times* of Wed, 25 Nov 1942, *Bible Lands*, No 175, Vol X, January 1943, p 1320

34 White, D Denton, "The Basrah and Persian Gulf Chaplaincy", *Bible Lands*, No 8, Vol XI, Oct 1945, p 63

35 Bahrein, the official spelling until the end of 1952 when the government announced its preferred spelling: Bahrain

36 White, D Denton, "The Basrah and Persian Gulf Chaplaincy", *Bible Lands*, No. 8, Vol XI, October 1945, pp 62-63

453

37 The "flying angel" symbol first featured on the Missions to Seamen flag. In July 2000 the organisation's members voted to change the name to the Mission to Seafarers, since when the flying angel symbol has been modernised. The flag is recognised by seafarers at the Mission's clubs and centres around the world, representing a welcome, friendship and help from people they can trust.

38 Letter from the bishop to all Anglian Clergy, Weston, Bishop in Jerusalem, *Bible Lands*, No 17, Vol XI, Jan 1948, p 163

39 Registers of Services, Iraq, archived at All Hallows by the Tower, London, ref CG/19/A5

40 Letter from N M Jenkins, Hon Sec St Peter's Church Association, Basrah, to Bishop Stewart, 29 Jan 1957, File: Iraq, Basra, 1957-1974, Bishop's office, D/C&G

41 Letter from Bishop Weston Henry Stewart to C.W.W., "St Peter's Church, Basrah", 11 Feb 1957, p 1, same File source as note 40

42 Ibid

43 "The Bishop's Letter", *Bible Lands*, No. 14, Vol XIII, April 1957, p 203

44 Ibid, p 201

45 "The Archbishop's Report - Iraq and the Gulf", *Bible Lands,* No 7, Vol XVI, Summer 1965, p 7

46 Email from Bishop Clive Handford to the author, Dec 2018

47 Ibid

48 Letter from the Revd Colin Davies to J B Wilson, 13 Dec 1969, File: Basra - Iraq 1957-1974, Bishop's office, D/C&G

49 Email from Bishop Clive Handford to the author, Dec 2018

Chapter 4 - NEW ERAS IN BAHRAIN & KUWAIT, 1932-1975

1   The Arabian Gulf, or the Gulf, refers to the body of water between the east coast of the Arabian peninsula and the coast of Iran, including the Strait of Hormuz. The Arabian Gulf is the official name used by member countries of the Gulf Co-operation Council (GCC), formed in 1981. The Persian Gulf, the historical name, is used by Iran and some other countries. Historically, the name appears in old documents, books and on maps.

2   Following distinguished service in World War I, Frank Holmes was granted the title of honorary Major and thereafter used the title in his civilian life.

3   Clarke, Angela, *Bahrain Oil and Development 1929-1989*, Immel Publishing, London, 1991, pp 51-52

4   Ibid, p 123

5   Jebel Ad Dukhan, a small range rising to 402 feet/122.4 m in the centre of Bahrain island

6   Until 1940, CASOC existed, in effect, as a legal entity only while the practical development of the Saudi Arabian oilfield was conducted by SOCAL. On 31 Jan 1944 CASOC ceased to exist when the name was formally changed to the Arabian American Oil Company (ARAMCO).

7   *See* Note 1

8   Jarman, Robert L, *Cathedral of the Gulf: The History of St Christopher's and The Anglican Church in Bahrain*, St Christopher's Cathedral, Bahrain, 1990, p 13

9   Ibid, p 14

10 Simpson, St John, *The Reverend Ralph Norman Sharp: A Short Appreciation*, undated, pdf format, academia.edu, p 2

11 California Texas Oil Company Limited (CALTEX) was incorporated on 30 June 1936 as a subsidiary of the Bahrain Petroleum Company Limited (BAPCO).

12 Jarman, p 31

13 Morris, Alun, "Letter to Mr Yandell", 30 Jan 1981, D/C&G archive, p 2
William F Yandell was Peoples Warden at St Christopher's church, 1978-1979

14 Ibid, p 3

15 Ibid, p 6

16 Ibid, p 5

17 Thompson, Andrew, *The Christian Church in Kuwait, Religious Freedom in the Gulf*, Saeed & Sameer, Kuwait, 2010, p 69

18 Ashton, Richard, "Dedication of St Paul's Church, Ahmadi", *Bible Lands*, No 13, Vol XIII, Jan 1957, p 189

19 Thompson, pp 81-82

20 Ashton, same ref as note 18

21 Ibid, p 190

22 Ibid

23 Ibid

24 The Revd Andrew Thompson: chaplain at St Paul, Kuwait, 2005-2010; senior chaplain at St Andrew, Abu Dhabi, since Sept 2010; appointed an Honorary Canon of St Christopher's Cathedral, Bahrain, 4 Dec 2011

25 Thompson, *The Christian Church in Kuwait, Religious Freedom in the Gulf*, p 84

26 The Revd Keith Johnson, chaplain at St Paul, Kuwait, 1969-1973; the Very Revd Keith Johnson, Dean of St Christopher's Cathedral, Bahrain, 1997-2002

27 The Revd Clive Windebank, NSM Assistant Chaplain at St Paul, Kuwait, 1979-1983; chaplain at St Andrew, Abu Dhabi, 28 Feb 2003 - 30 Apr 2010

28 Email from the Revd Clive Windebank to the author

Chapter 5 - OPPORTUNITIES IN EASTERN ARABIA, 1954-1972

1 Bishop Stewart, "The Bishop's Letter", *Bible Lands*, No 3, Vol XIII, July 1954, p 1

2 "The Archdeaconry in Iraq and Eastern Arabia: Visits to Kirkuk and Qatar", *Bible Lands*, No 3, Vol XIII, July 1954, p 31

3 Ibid, p 33

4 Jenkins, Kenneth, "Qatar Chaplaincy", *Bible Lands*, No 10, Vol XIII, April 1956, p 147

5 Ibid

6 Morris, Alun, "Letter to Mr Yandell", 30 Jan 1981, D/C&G archive, p 4

7 Ibid

8 The Revd Gwilyn Alun Morris, Chaplain to the Forces 1942-1946, was familiar with military life. He was mentioned in dispatches in 1945.

9 Morris, p 4

10 Ibid

11 Ibid, p 7

12 Henderson, Edward, *A History of St Andrew's Church*, 1984, p 4, also Thompson, Andrew, *Christianity in the UAE: Culture and Heritage*, Motivate Publishing, 2011, p 97

13 Thompson, Andrew, *Christianity in the UAE*, p 97

14 Elliott, David, "The Dedication of St Andrew's Church", Abu Dhabi, Bible Lands, No 2, Vol XVII, Spring 1968, p 49

15 Archbishop Campbell MacInnes, "Visit to the Gulf: Abu Dhabi", *Bible Lands*, Spring 1968, No 2, Vol XVII, p 39

16 Foulger, Tony, "Letter to the Revd John Weir", *Holy Trinity Church 1969-2009*, published by Holy Trinity Church, 2009, p 109

17 Thompson, Andrew, *Christianity in the UAE*, p 117

18 Ridgewell, The Revd Kenneth, "Holy Trinity Church, Dubai", *Bible Lands*, No 2, Vol XVIII, Spring 1971, p 43

19 Ibid, pp 43-44

20 Parry, Haydn, "Dubai: A Record of 20 Weeks", *Bible Lands*, No 7, Vol XVIII, Summer 1972, p 195

21 Ibid, p 196

22 Yergin, Daniel, *The Prize: The Epic Quest for Oil, Money and Power*, Simon & Schuster, 1991, p 565

23 Worrall, James, *State Building and Counter Insurgency in Oman: Political, Military and Diplomatic Relations at the End of Empire*, I B Tauris & Co, 2014, p 292

24 Gardiner, Ian, *In the Service of the Sultan: A First-Hand Account of the Dhofar Insurgency*, Pen & Sword Military, Barnsley, South Yorkshire, UK, 2008, p 24

25 Archdeacon Lindley, "The Gulf, 1971", *Bible Lands*, No 2, Vol XVIII, Spring 1971, p 38

Chapter 6 - PRELUDE, 1943-1973

1. Potter, the Venerable Beresford, "The Right Reverend George Francis Popham Blyth, In Memoriam", *Bible Lands*, No 63, Vol IV, Jan 1915, pp 224-225

2. Transjordan - the Latin prefix means "across" or beyond, so Transjordan is the land on the other side, to the east of the River Jordan. From 1921-1946 this region was the British-controlled Emirate of Transjordan; 1946-1949 the Hashemite Kingdom of Transjordan and since 1949 the Hashemite Kingdom of Jordan.

3. The Revd Canon Charles Thorley Bridgeman was American Education Chaplain to the Bishop in Jerusalem from 1924 and Hon Canon of St George's Cathedral from 1929. He is not listed in Crockford's Clerical Directory after 1947.

4. Bridgeman, Charles T, "The Office of Anglican Bishop in Jerusalem", *Bible Lands*, No 175, Vol X, January 1943, pp 1327-8

5. MacInnes, Bishop Campbell, "Bishop Weston Henry Stewart", *Bible Lands*, No 8, Vol XVII, Autumn 1969, p 248

6. Ibid, p 250

7. Ibid, pp 250-1

8. Ibid

9. *majma* (plural *majma'at*) - the root word means convention, assembly, congregation, therefore can mean any gathering of people, and in formal usage when the gathering has organisational intent. *See also* note 28. The Arab church uses this term for their formal gatherings.

   mujamma - a convention hall or other place for large gatherings

   yom al jumaa - Friday, the day of gathering (for prayer)

10. See note 2

11. "The Bishop's Letter", *Bible Lands*, No 14, Vol XIII, April 1957, p 201

12. Bishop Samuel Gobat, second Anglican Bishop in Jerusalem, was the founder of a school in Jerusalem which took his name, and the great-grandfather of Mrs Campbell MacInnes, herself a qualified doctor.

13. "General Statement - The Anglican Communion in Jerusalem and the Middle East," *Bible Lands*, No 1, Vol XIV, July 1957, pp 8-9

14. "The Majma", *Bible Lands*, No 2, Vol XIV, Oct 1957, p 23

15. Ibid

16. Emails between Bishop Michael Lewis and the author

17. Emails between Bishop Clive Handford and the author

18. "Entry into the Cathedral", *Bible Lands*, No 6, Vol XVII, Spring 1969, p 173

19. Adkins, H, "The Enthronement Ceremony", *Bible Lands*, No 6, Vol XVII, Spring 1969, p 175

20. Appleton, the Most Revd George, "Address to the Annual Meeting of the Jerusalem and the East Mission", *Bible Lands*, No 11, Vol XVII, Summer 1970, p 329

21. The Reverend Samir Kafa'ity, later: Archdeacon (without geographical reference), 1974-1984; 12th Bishop in Jerusalem, 1984-1998; 2nd President Bishop of the Episcopal Church of Jerusalem and the Middle East (ECJME), 1986-1996

    The Reverend Clive Handford, later: Archdeacon in the Gulf, 1978-1983; 4th Bishop in 1996-2007; 5th President Bishop, ECJME, 2002-2007

22 Emails between Bishop Clive Handford and the author

23 Ibid

24 Ibid

25 The Archbishop's Report, *Bible Lands*, No 11, Vol XVIII, Summer 1973, pp 305-6

26 "A Constitution for the Island Council of the Episcopal Church in Cyprus, promulgated by the Archbishop in Jerusalem as Diocesan", 8 March 1972, D/C&G archive

27 Archbishop in Jerusalem, "Address to the Jerusalem and the East Mission", *Bible Lands*, No 7, Vol XVIII, Summer 1972, p 178

28 The need for two majmas, (plural *majma'at*), the other being in Jordan, was the division of the community consequent upon the foundation of the State of Israel in 1948. *See also* note 9

29 Email correspondence between Bishop Clive Handford and the author

30 Archbishop Appleton's Letter, *Bible Lands*, No 10, Vol XVIII, Spring 1973, p 283

31 General Synod of the Church of England voted overwhelmingly in July 1972 to retire archbishops, bishops, and most of its clergy at the age of seventy

32 Archbishop George Appleton's Sermon, *Bible Lands*, No 12, Vol XVIII, Autumn 1973, p 135

33 OPEC - Organisation of Petroleum Exporting Countries, formed in Sept 1960 with headquarters in Vienna, Austria, the founder members being Iran, Iraq, Kuwait, Saudi Arabia and Venezuela

34 Clarke, Angela, *Bahrain Oil and Development 1929-1989*, Immel Publishing, London, 1991, p 277

35 OAPEC - Organisation of Arab Petroleum Exporting Countries, formed on 9 Jan 1968 with its HQ in Kuwait, the nine members being Algeria, Bahrain, Iraq, Kuwait, Libya, Qatar, Saudi Arabia, Syria and the United Arab Emirates

36 Stop press Announcement issued by the Archbishop of Canterbury, 30 Nov 1973, *Bible Lands*, No 12, Vol XVIII, Autumn 1973, penultimate page (not numbered)

Chapter 7 - TRAUMA & TRANSITION, 1974-1975

1 "The New Assistant Bishop", *Bible Lands*, No 1, Vol XIX, New Year/Spring 1974, p 6

2 Ibid

3 Ibid, p 7

4 The Canterbury Group - a name given to Anglican/Episcopal ministry and worship in an area of the former Archbishopric of Jerusalem, now in the Diocese of C&G, where publicised Christian worship is not currently permitted; although the Canterbury Group is a chaplaincy/parish within the diocese, its geographical context and the titles of its leaders are not identified

5 "A letter from Bishop Ashton, May 1974, c/o Royal Air Force, Nicosia, Cyprus", *Bible Lands*, No 2, Vol XIX, Summer 1974, p 37

6 "Recollections" by the Rt Revd Leonard Ashton CB, *The Olive Branch*, No 9, March 1997, p 2

7 The Jerusalem and the East Mission Trust (Cyprus) is a charitable trust and not a limited company. The Declaration of Trust was signed and sealed on 2 March 1973

457

in London by Notary Public, Sydney Charles Crowther-Smith, and received on 12 March 1973 at the first meeting of the JEMT (Cyprus) Managing Trustees

8   "A letter from Bishop Ashton, May 1974, c/o Royal Air Force, Nicosia, Cyprus", *Bible Lands*, No 2, Vol XIX, Summer 1974, p 38

9   "George Appleton's Farewell Letter", *Bible Lands*, No 1, Vol XIX, New Year/Spring 1974, pp 3-4

10 St Augustine's College, in Canterbury, Kent, United Kingdom, located within the precincts of St Augustine's Abbey close to Canterbury Cathedral, served first as a missionary college of the Church of England (1848-1947); the Central College of the Anglican Communion (1952-1967); and was used by King's College, London, for a fourth year of pastoral theological training for its ordinands (1969-1976)

11 "George Appleton's Farewell Letter", *Bible Lands*, No 1, Vol XIX, New Year/Spring 1974, p 4

12 "A letter from Bishop Ashton, May 1974, c/o Royal Air Force, Nicosia, Cyprus", *Bible Lands*, No 2, Vol XIX, Summer 1974, pp 38-39

13 A letter from the Vicar-General, March, 1974, *Bible Lands*, No 1, Vol XIX, New Year/Spring 1974, p 5

14 Emails between Bishop Clive Handford and the author

15 "A letter from Bishop Ashton, May 1974, c/o Royal Air Force, Nicosia, Cyprus", *Bible Lands*, No 2, Vol XIX, Summer 1974, p 40

16 Ibid, pp 40-41

17 Letter from I McCluney, Chargé d'Affaires, British Embassy, Baghdad to Bishop Ashton, 17 April 1974, File: Iraq, Baghdad, St George's, 1933-1974, Bishop's Office, D/C&G

18 Ibid

19 Ibid

20 Letter from Bishop Ashton to Ian McCluney Esq, 23 April 1974, File: Iraq, Baghdad, St George's, 1933-1974, Bishop's Office, D/C&G

21 As from 1975, Sir Stephen Olver KBE, CMG

22 Minute 74/45 of a meeting of St Paul's Parish Council, 18 June 1974, St Paul's Cathedral archive, Nicosia

23 Ibid

24 Letter dated 25 Nov 1975, to JEMT (Cyprus) from the Vice-Presidency and Ministry of Defence of the Turkish Federated State of Cyprus, signed by the Acting Director-General Ismail Karagözlü, refers to "the Turkish Peace-keeping Operation of July-August 1974", D/C&G archive

25 Letter from Bishop Ashton to Canon Marcus Stephens, at All Saints, Beiurt, 1 Aug 1974, File: Iraq, Baghdad, St George's, 1933-1974, Bishop's Office, D/C&G

26 "Recollections" by the Rt Revd Leonard Ashton CB, *The Olive Branch*, No 9, March 1997, p 2

27 "A letter from Bishop Ashton, Jerusalem, 2nd September 1974", *Bible Lands*, No 3, Vol XIX, Autumn 1974, pp 54-55

28 Ibid, p 56

29 Ashton, Leonard, "A Visit to Kyrenia", *Bible Lands*, No 4, Vol XIX, New Year 1975, pp 84-86

30 Sermon, preached on 13 January 1976 by Bishop Robert Stopford, *Bible Lands*, No 1, Vol XX, New Year 1976, p 11

31 "The Archbishop of Canterbury's Sermon", *Bible Lands*, No 4, Vol XIX, New Year 1975, pp 90-91

32 Email correspondence between Bishop Clive Handford and the author

33 "A Letter from the Vicar-General, Robert Stopford", *Bible Lands*, No 6, Vol XIX, Summer 1975, p 122

34 Anglican Church property throughout the Middle East was also owned - and much still is - by the Church Missionary Society (CMS), the Colonial and Continental Church Society (C&CCS) now the Intercontinental Church Society (ICS), the United Society for the Propagation of the Gospel (USPG), and the (British) Foreign and Commonwealth Office (FCO)

35 "A New Partnership in the Middle East", *Bible Lands*, No 6, Vol XIX, Summer 1975, pp 124-136

36 Big Nine - official Missionary Societies of the Church of England at that time

37 "A New Partnership in the Middle East", *Bible Lands*, No 6, Vol XIX, Summer 1975, p 130

38 Ibid

39 Emails between Archdeacon Bill Schwartz and the author

40 Letter from the Revd David Penman to Bishop Ashton, 12 Aug 1975, File: Iraq, Baghdad, St George's, 1933-1974, Bishop's Office, D/C&G

41 Letter from Bishop Ashton to Bishop Hassan Dehqani-Tafti, 19 June 1975, File: Iraq, Baghdad, St George's, 1933-1974, Bishop's Office, D/C&G

42 Letter from Bishop Ashton to Bishop John R Satterthwaite, 19 June 1975 File: Iraq, Baghdad, St George's, 1933-1974, Bishop's Office, D/C&G

43 The Reverend David Penman was leaving Beirut, after a decade of missionary work in Pakistan and the Middle East; in 1982 he became a bishop coadjutor in the Diocese of Melbourne, and in 1984 he was appointed as the Archbishop of Melbourne; on 24 July 1989 he suffered a heart attack and died, aged fifty-three.

44 Letter from Bishop Ashton to the Revd D H Palmer, 24 Nov 1975, File: Iraq, Baghdad, St George's, 1933-1974, Bishop's Office, D/C&G

45 "A Letter from the Vicar-General", *Bible Lands*, No 7, Vol XIX, Autumn 1975, pp 138-9

46 Philip Horniblow and Harvey Staal, "The Protestant Church in Oman", Annual Report, 29 Feb 1976, p 2, D/C&G archive

Chapter 8 - THE INAUGURAL YEAR, 1976

1 *Bible Lands,* No 1, Vol XX, New Year, 1976, back cover

2 Habiby, the Revd Samir J, "Middle East Central Synod Inaugurated, Bishops Installed", Episcopal News Service, 6 January 1976, p 1, Digital Archives of the Episcopal Church, www.episcopalarchives.org

3 "The Episcopal Church in Jerusalem and the Middle East", a report by the Vicar-General, *Bible Lands*, No 1, Vol XX, New Year, 1976, p 4

4 Habiby, p 1

5 Sermon, Bishop Robert Stopford, *Bible Lands*, No1, Vol XX, New Year 1976, p 11

6   Ibid, pp 10-11

7   Ibid, p 8

8   Cardinal Leo Joseph Suenens, a Belgian prelate of the Roman Catholic Church, Archbishop of Mechelen-Brussel, 1961-1979; elevated to the cardinalate in 1962

9   Sermon, Bishop Robert Stopford, *Bible Lands*, No1, Vol XX, New Year 1976, pp 12-13

10 "St Paul's Church Newsletter", Dec 1975, St Paul's Cathedral archive, Nicosia

11 "St Paul's Church Newsletter", June 1975, St Paul's Cathedral archive, Nicosia

12 House for Duty - an arrangement whereby a priest may live in a church house in exchange for carrying out certain duties in a chaplaincy/parish, but without receiving a stipend. This may suit a priest receiving a pension (church or otherwise) such as retired military personnel, or a self-supporting priest who receives an income in another way.

13 Letter from Bishop Ashton to Air Marshal Sir John Aiken, KCB, RAF, 26 Jan 1976, D/C&G archive

14 Inventory provided by the RAF to St Antony's Church, D/C&G archive

15 The Revd Canon Hubert Matthews retired in 1974 but served until the formation of the Diocese of Cyprus and the Gulf on 5 Jan 1976 and attended the first Diocesan Synod (Cyprus) in May 1976

16 "An Ecumenical Gesture in Cyprus", *Bible Lands*, No 2, Vol XX, Spring 1976, pp 44-45

17 William Douglas Caröe, born 1 Sept 1857 in England, the youngest son of Anders Kruuse Caröe, Danish Consul in Liverpool, and Jane Kirkpatrick Green; prominent as a British ecclesiastical architect. To relieve poor health William spent winter months in Kyrenia, Cyprus, where he died on 25 Feb 1938.

18 Morgan, Tabitha, *Sweet and Bitter Island, A History of the British in Cyprus*, I B Tauris, London and New York, 2015, p 111

19 Memorandum to the Venerable H J Stuart, Chaplain-in-Chief, RAF, Ministry of Defence, London, 9 July 1982, D/C&G archive

20 Letter from Bishop Ashton to His Eminence Bishop Chrysanthos, Bishop of Limassol, 19 May 1976, D/C&G archive

21 "A Letter from the Bishop in Cyprus and the Gulf", *Bible Lands*, No 4, Vol XX, Autumn 1976, pp 74-75

22 "New arrangements for Larnaca Church", St Paul's Church Council, 5 Oct 1976, minute 76/99, (2) and (7a), St Paul's Cathedral archive, Nicosia

23 The bishop's house was bought on 24 July 1996 in the name of the JEMT (Cyprus), paid for by the diocese; the Paphos vicarage was bought on 17 March 2003 also in the name of JEMT (Cyprus), paid for mainly by the Paphos chaplaincy, with contributions from the diocese and other entities.

24 1st Annual Report of the Jerusalem and the East Mission Trust (Cyprus), p 1, D/C&G archive

25 A further Declaration of Trust was signed on 28 June 1976; a deed dated 4 Oct 1978 amended the provision of the Island Trust Deed, followed by Supplemental Deeds dated 9 July 1984 and 22 Sept 1992; on 15 Feb 1994 application was made by the JEMT (Cyprus) to register the charity as a trust in Cyprus, registered on 31 March 1995.

26 "A Letter from the Bishop in Cyprus and the Gulf, The Gulf", *Bible Lands*, No 4, Vol XX, Autumn 1976, p 76

27 Diocese of Cyprus and the Gulf, Diocesan Synod (Cyprus), Presidential Address, 1/76, p 1, D/C&G archive

28 "Occasional News Letter of the Episcopal Church in Jerusalem and the Middle East", from the office of the President Bishop H B Dehqani-Tafti, *The Presence*, No 5, Jan 1977, D/C&G archive

Chapter 9 - NEW BEGINNINGS, 1977-1979

1 *Bible Lands*, No 6, Vol XX, Summer 1977, p 120

2 Minutes D/C&G Synod (Gulf), 24 - 25 Feb 1977, 1/77 Presidential Address, pp 1-3

3 "The Parishes of Qatar and Abu Dhabi, 1977-1978", p 2, D/C&G archive

4 "Cyprus and The Gulf", *Bible Lands*, No 6, Vol XX, Summer 1977, p 118

5 "The Parishes of Qatar and Abu Dhabi, 1977-78", p 1, D/C&G archive

6 Letter from the Ven R A Lindley to Bishop Ashton, 28 June 1978, D/C&G archive

7 Bishop Ashton "Confidential Report, Larnaca Development", cc Mr Cecil Griggs and the Ven. Ralph Lindley, 15 Sept 1978, p 1, D/C&G archive

8 Ibid

9 2nd Annual Report of JEMT (Cyprus), 1 April 1974 to 31 March 1975, Nicosia, p 1, D/C&G archive

10 "Bishop's Occasional Letter, Larnaca Development", Sept 1978, p 1, D/C&G archive

11 Conversation between Mrs Susan Mantovani and the author

12 "scylla and charybdis", an idiom deriving from Greek mythology, meaning "threatened on either side by two different but equal evils"

13 Ibid

14 "St Helena's Larnaca Church Site Development", letter from the Ven A D H Northridge to Bishop L J Ashton CB, 22 Sept 1978, D/C&G archive

15 Ibid

16 Ibid

17 "Bishop's Occasional Letter, Larnaca Development", Sept 1978, p 1, D/C&G archive

18 Conversation between Mrs Susan Mantovani and the author

19 Bishop John Daly had retained a long association with All Hallows following his consecration in the church on 1 May 1935, throughout his episcopates in Africa, the Far East and England, and since his retirement in 1975.

20 The Revd Harvey Staal, the Revd Rodney Koopmans' predecessor, had moved to Salalah on the south coast of Oman to establish a mission bookshop.

21 Spring gathering at Launde Abbey Conference and Retreat Centre, Leicestershire; Summer gathering, AGM and Celebration Eucharist at All Hallows by the Tower, London; Autumn gathering at the Bar Convent, York

22 "News from Cyprus and the Gulf 1978", *Bible Lands*, No 9, Vol XX, Easter 1979, p 207

23 27 Sept 1962: formation of the Yemen Arab Republic (YAR), also known as North Yemen or Yemen (Sana'a)
    30 Nov 1967: formation of the People's Republic of South Yemen

24 Letter from Bishop Ashton to G Romeril, First Secretary (Consular), British High Commission, Nicosia, ref G9, G7/E, 18 Oct 1978, D/C&G archive

25 Letter from G A Romeril, First Secretary (Consular), British High Commission, Nicosia, to Bishop Ashton, ref. CON/226/1, 2 Nov 1978, D/C&G archive

26 Emails between Bishop Clive Handford and the author

27 "Saint Andrew's Church, Kyrenia", *Bible Lands*, No 10, Vol XX, Autumn 1979, p 242

28 Ibid

29 Ibid, p 243

30 Ibid

31 Letter from Winifred S Mogabgab, Hon Sec, St Antony's, Paphos, to Bishop Ashton, 17 Nov 1979, D/C&G archive

32 A Christmas letter from Douglas and Hazel Northridge, Nicosia, Cyprus, 1979, p 3, D/C&G archive

33 Tower Hill, *Bulletin of All Hallows by the Tower with St Dunstan in the East*, Gulf issue, July 1980, p 3, D/C&G archive

Chapter 10 - MILESTONES, 1980-1983

1 "Larnaca Inauguration", *Bible Lands,* No 11, Vol XX, Spring 1980, p 282

2 Ibid

3 D/C&G Synod (The Gulf), Report, 1/79 Presidential Address, p 3

4 "Archdeacon's Report - Cyprus", 1980, initialled ADHN, D/C&G archive

5 "The Protestant Church in Oman", Annual Synod Report - May 1980, typed signatories Alan Gates and Rod Koopmans, p 1, D/C&G archive

6 Ibid, p 2

7 D/C&G Synod 1980, Report, 1/80 Presidential Address, p 2, D/C&G archive

8 Jean Waddell served in the Middle East for just over twenty years, first as secretary to successive Archbishops in Jerusalem then in 1977 was invited by Bishop Hassan Dehqani-Tafti to be his secretary in Isfahan. She was shot by intruders on 1 May 1980. After her recovery, she was imprisoned. On 14 Feb 1981 she was released from Tehran's Evin prison with six other members of the diocese. Jean died in the UK on 26 April 2019, six days after her 97th birthday.

9 Resolution addressed to His Excellency President Bani-Sadr of the Islamic Republic of Iran, unanimously passed by the Synod of the Episcopal Diocese of Cyprus and the Gulf meeting in Cyprus from 7-10 May 1980, D/C&G archive

10 Ibid

11 "The Venerable Alan Douglas Hamilton Northridge", Bishop's Occasional Letter No 6, *Bible Lands*, No 12, Vol XX, Autumn, 1980, p 323

12 "Oman, The Church of the Magi, Salalah", *Bible Lands*, No 14, Vol XX, Autumn 1981, p 408

13 D/C&G Synod 1981, Report, 1/81 Presidential Address, p 5, D/C&G archive

14 Item 6 "Overall Impression", (ii), The Missions to Seamen, General Secretary's Report, Dubai, 30 Oct/1 Nov 1979, p 4, D/C&G archive

15 Ibid, "Overall Impression", (iii)

16 Letter signed by G C Handford, Archdeacon, and Alan J Horan, Chairman of the Fund Raising Committee, 10 Feb 1982, Attachment "St Andrew's Endowment Fund", p 1, D/C&G archive

17 Thompson, Andrew, *Christianity in the UAE: Culture and Heritage*, Motivate Publishing, 2011, p 106

18 "St Christopher's Cathedral, Manama and The Anglican Church, Awali, Report to Synod 1982", p1, D/C&G archive

19 Ibid

20 Sir Charles Belgrave KBE (9 Dec 1894 - 28 Feb 1969), Adviser to the Rulers of Bahrain, 1932-1957; his wife Lady (Marjorie) Belgrave, neé Lepel Barrett-Lennard (5 Aug 1894 - 19 Nov 1970); their son James Hamed Dacre Belgrave (22 April 1929 - 29 June 1979)

21 D/C&G Synod 1981, Report, 8/81 Diocesan Funds Appeal, (i) Capital Fund, p 14, D/C&G archive

22 Ashton, Leonard, Bishop in Cyprus and the Gulf, "Cyprus and the Gulf Report", p 2, D/C&G archive

23 D/C&G Synod 1981, Report, 8/81 Diocesan Funds Appeal, (ii) Project Fund, p 14, D/C&G archive

24 D/C&G Synod 1982, Report, 1/82 Presidential Address, pp 6-7, D/C&G archive

25 Ibid, p 8

26 Emails between Archdeacon Bill Schwartz and the author

27 D/C&G Synod 1982, Report, 1/82 Presidential Address, p 8, D/C&G archive

28 D/C&G Synod 1983, Report, 1/83 Presidential Address, p 3, D/C&G archive

29 Letter: Major Gerald Green to Bishop Ashton, 11 Jan 1983, author's archive

30 Letter: Bishop Ashton to Major Gerald Green, 26 Jan 1983, D/C&G archive

31 Letter: Major Gerald Green to Bishop Ashton, 23 Feb 1983, author's archive

32 D/C&G Synod 1983, Report, 1/83 Presidential Address, p 3, D/C&G archive

33 Ibid, p 4

34 Ibid, 5/83, d) Bishop's Report, p 14

35 Ibid

36 Ibid, Cyprus and the Gulf, p 7

37 Letter from Allan Brown, HQ British Contingent UN Force in Cyprus, to Bishop Ashton, 26 May 1983, D/C&G archive

38 D/C&G Synod 1983, Report, 7/83 "Appointment of a New Bishop", pp 21-22, D/C&G archive

39 Letter from C H Griggs, Chairman, The Jerusalem and the East Mission Trust (Cyprus), to the Rt Revd H B Dehqani-Tafti, 5 May 1983, D/C&G archive

40 Ibid

41 D/C&G Synod 1983, Report, 7/83 "Appointment of a New Bishop", p 23, D/C&G archive

42 Letter from G Meikle, Deputy Chairman, the Diocese of Cyprus and the Gulf, Standing Committee, to C H Griggs Esq OBE, 27 June 1983, D/C&G archive

43 *Hampshire Chronicle,* 7 Oct 1983, Hampshire Archives and Local Studies, Hampshire Record Office, UK

44 20 August 1988: Iran accepted an UN-brokered ceasefire

Chapter 11 - CONSOLIDATION, 1984-1987

1   Hertog, Steffen, "Gulf Economies: The Current Crisis and the Lessons of the 1980s", Carnegie Endowment for International Peace, carnegieendowment.org

2   Letter from Bishop Harry Moore to the Rt Revd P C Rodger, 3 Jan 1984, p 2, D/C&G archive

3   Ibid, p 3

4   Letter from Bishop Harry Moore to the Rt Revd P C Rodger, 20 Dec 1984, D/C&G archive

5   Letter from Bishop of Oxford to the Ven R A Lindley CBE, 1 Dec 1983, D/C&G archive

6   Conversation between Mrs Georgia Katsantonis and the author

7   D/C&G Synod 1984, Report, 1/84 Presidential Address, p 5, D/C&G archive

8   St George's Church, Baghdad, 1983-1984 Report to Synod, dated 10 Feb 1985, p 2, D/C&G Synod 1985, Report, D/C&G archive

9   St Paul's Church, Ahmadi, Kuwait, "1984 Annual Report, for Diocesan Synod 1985", p 1, D/C&G Synod 1985, Report, D/C&G archive

10 Parkinson, The Revd Canon John F, "Annual Report to the Diocesan Synod 1984: The Anglican and Episcopal Church in Bahrain", 3 April 1984, p 1, attached to D/C&G Synod 1984 Report, D/C&G archive

11 Ibid, p 2

12 Parkinson, The Revd Canon John F, "Bahrain Chaplaincy Report for the Diocesan Synod, May 1985", p 1, D/C&G Synod 1985 Report, D/C&G archive

13 Report from the Anglican and Allied Churches in Qatar, 1984, p 1, D/C&G archive

14 Ibid

15 Letter from Cecil H Griggs to Sir Donald Logan, 30 Aug 1984, p 2, D/C&G archive

16 D/C&G Synod 1986, Report, 1/86 Presidential Address, p 5, D/C&G archive

17 Quoted from Major Green's text when he presented the Episcopal Mandate to the Provost of St Christopher's Cathedral in Bahrain, during the Service of Thanksgiving, on Sunday 1 June 1986

18 Quoted from the Mandate and Declaration, signed and under "The Seal of Harry, Bishop in Cyprus and the Gulf"

19 At the Oct 1984 meeting of the Bahrain Anglican Church Council, it was unanimously agreed to ask Major Gerald Green to accept the position of churchwarden emeritus. On 30 Oct Major Green accepted the offer. Already, he had been part of St Christopher's activities for over twenty-eight years.

20 Quoted from Major Green's text when he presented the crosier to the Provost of St Christopher's Cathedral on 1 June 1986

21 Emails between Archdeacon Bill Schwartz and the author

22 "The Venerable John Edward Brown", comments by the Archbishop of Canterbury, July 1986, D/C&G archive

23 Brown, John, *Mainly Uphill*, p 54

24 Ibid, p 62

25 Ibid, p 63

26 Ibid, p 67

27 Ibid pp 69-70

28 Ibid, p 73

29 Ibid

30 Ibid, p 75

31 Ibid, p 77

464

32 "People of the Book" is an Islamic term referring to Jews, Christians and Sabians
33 Brown, John, *Mainly Uphill*, p 78
34 Ibid, p 84
35 Ibid
36 Emails between Archdeacon Bill Schwartz and the author
37 D/C&G Synod 1987, Report, 87/06 Report of JEMT (Cyprus) Trustees, p 12, D/C&G archive
38 Ibid, 87/01 Presidential Address, Abu Dhabi, p 4,
39 Ibid, 87/01 Presidential Address, Conclusion, p 6
40 When Derek Hearne's job contract was not renewed at the end of 1987, he returned to Wales where he was accepted as an ordinand by the Anglican Church in Wales, completed his training and in due course was ordained.
41 D/C&G Synod 1988, Report, 88/02 Presidential Address, p 2, D/C&G archive

Chapter 12 - THE DISRUPTIONS OF WAR, 1988-1992

1 D/C&G Synod 1988, Report, 88/02 Presidential Address, p 3, D/C&G archive
2 Brown, John, *Mainly Uphill*, p 116
3 D/C&G Synod 1988, Report, 88/02 Presidential Address, p 4, D/C&G archive
4 Ibid, pp 4-5
5 Ibid, p 5
6 Ibid, p 3
7 Email correspondence between Bill Schwartz and the author
8 In 2004, the Reverend Canon Peter Delaney became full-time Archdeacon of London. He retained his position as Commissary in the UK to the Bishop in Cyprus & the Gulf until April 2007 when the Rt Revd Clive Handford, 4th Bishop in C&G, retired.
9 Brown, John, *Mainly Uphill,* p 161
10 Ibid, p 163
11 Ibid, p 166
12 Ibid, p 167
13 D/C&G Synod 1989, Report, 89/06 The Bishop's Appeal, p 5, D/C&G archive
14 D/C&G Synod 1990, Report, 90/02 President's Address, p 2, D/C&G archive
15 Brown, John, *Mainly Uphill*, p 176
16 Ibid, p 189
17 Ibid
18 Ibid, p 193
19 Ibid, p 202
20 Ibid, p 203
21 Emails between Bill Schwartz and the author
22 Brown, John, *Mainly Uphill*, p 213
23 Ibid, p 249
24 Email correspondence between Canon Ian Young and the author
25 Brown, John, *Mainly Uphill,* p 261
26 Ibid, p 262
27 Ibid, p 268
28 Ibid, p 270

Chapter 13 - EVOLUTION, 1993-1999

1 The Reverend Bill Schwartz was funded by the Episcopal Church in the USA (ECUSA), a member church of the Anglican Communion
2 Email from Bill Schwartz to the author
3 Email from Professor Jonathan Warner to the author
4 The five members of the church council: Professor Warner; the Revd Philip Blair and Linda Bilton (lecturers in the English Department, EMU), Kathy Pagan from the USA (wife of a British professor at EMU), and Carol (whose surname cannot be recalled) from Trinidad (owner of the Moonwalker café)
5 Chaplain's Journal and Notes, 25 April 1993 to 22 April 1995, 27 June 1993, p 7, Christ Church Ayia Napa archive
6 Ibid, 25 March 1994, p 70
7 Blair, Patrick, Rural Deanery of Cyprus Report for 1994, p 3, inserted following p 177 of the Chaplain's Journal and Notes, 25 April 1993 to 22 April 1995, Christ Church Ayia Napa archive
8 The Jerusalem and the East Mission Trust Limited was registered on 27 Dec 1929. *See* the Glossary p 442.
9 Borner, Michael J W, Annual General Assembly 1995 of the Bahrain International Seafarers' Society, Chairman's Report, pp 1-2
10 Brown, John, *Mainly Uphill*, p 313
11 Ibid p 314
12 Ibid, p 325
13 D/C&G Synod 1995, Report, Appendix 1, President's Address, p 2, D/C&G archive
14 Brown, John, *Mainly Uphill*, p 331
15 St Paul's Cathedral Nicosia, 1996 Report to Diocesan Synod, p 3, St Paul's Cathedral archive
16 The Chaplaincy of Yemen, Chaplain's Report 1996, p 2, presented to Diocesan Synod 1997, D/C&G archive
17 Ibid
18 Report of the Chaplaincy in Qatar 1996, p 1, presented to Diocesan Synod 1997, D/C&G archive
19 Ecumenical Conference of Charity, Founding Documents, October 1996, p 13, St Christopher's Cathedral archive
20 Chaplaincy of Dubai & Sharjah with the Northern Emirates, Chaplain's Report for Diocesan Synod 27-31 Jan 1997, p 2-3, D/C&G archive
21 Ibid, p 2
22 Chaplaincy of Dubai and Sharjah with the Northern Emirates, Chaplain's Report for the Annual Diocesan Synod, 26-30 January 1998, p 1, D/C&G archive
23 D/C&G Synod 1999, Report, Appendix, Presidential Address, p 2, D/C&G archive

Chapter 14 - STEADFAST THROUGH STIRRING TIMES, 2000-2007

1 The Bishopric of the Church of England in Jerusalem, first formed in 1841 and reconstituted in 1887, had continued until July 1957 when an archbishopric based in Jerusalem was established. This ceased to exist on 5 January 1976, the day before the Episcopal Church in Jerusalem and the Middle East was inaugurated.

2   *Augeries of Innocence*, referred to by Bishop Handford as *Poems of Innocence*, were included in one of William Blake's notebooks now known as The Pickering Manuscript, believed to have been written in 1803.

3   D/C&G Synod 2000, Report, Appendix 1, Presidential Address, p 4, D/C&G archive

4   The Episcopal Church in Jerusalem and the Middle East, Proposals for the Structure of the Province, p 1, D/C&G archive

5   D/C&G Synod 2001, Report, Appendix 1, Presidential Address, pp 3-4, D/C&G archive

6   Before July 1974, the Ledra Palace Hotel was one of the largest and most glamorous hotels in Nicosia. Now it serves as the HQ for a contingent of the United Nations Peacekeeping Force in Cyprus (UNFICYP). In 2004, the Ledra Palace site became a crossing point in the Green Line.

7   D/C&G Synod 2001, Report, Appendix 1, Presidential Address, p 4, D/C&G archive

8   Bamforth, Marvin, "Planting a new church in Paphos", *The Olive Branch,* Spring 2001, No. 17, p 4

9   Ibid

10 Jebel is applied to different sized hills up to and including mountains. Jebel Ali is the height of a hill. One tradition is that Ali, the nephew of Muhammed, said his prayers there.

11 Bartholomew I, the Archbishop of Constantinople and Ecumenical Patriarch, has held office since 2 November 1991. He is regarded as the *primus inter pares* (first among equals) in the Eastern Orthodox Church, and as the spiritual leader of some 300 million Orthodox Christians worldwide.

12 The Reverend Canon Dr Herman Browne was born on 11 March 1965 in Liberia, deaconed in 1987; priested in June 1997 at Canterbury Cathedral, then served for five years as the Archbishop's Senior Adviser on Anglican Communion Affairs, during which time he was appointed a canon of Canterbury Cathedral.

13 *The Bahrain Anglican News,* Vol LXV, No 11, Dec 2001, p 3, St Christopher's Cathedral archive

14 Bait Al Qur'an in Bahrain was founded by Dr Abdul Latif Jassim Kanoo, a serious collector of Islamic manuscripts and art. This purpose-built arts complex opened in 1990, housing a mosque, school for Qur'anic studies, a library, a lecture hall, and the Al Hayat Museum where much of Dr Kanoo's collection is displayed.

15 On 11 September 2001 (known as 9/11 in America), Islamist extremists hijacked four commercial aircraft which had departed from airports in the northeast of the USA. Two were flown into the twin towers of the World Trade Center in New York; one was crashed into the Pentagon, the US military HQ in Washington DC; the fourth crashed into a field in Stonycreek township, Pennsylvania. 16   D / C & G Synod 2002, Report, Appendix 1, Presidential Address, p 2, D/C&G archive

17 The territory is composed of two Base Areas. One is the Western Sovereign Base Area (WSBA) which includes two main bases at RAF Akrotiri and Episkopi, plus Akrotiri village and parts of other village districts. The second area is Dhekelia Cantonment or the Eastern Sovereign Base Area (ESBA) which includes a base at Ayios Nikolaos and parts of twelve village districts.

467

18 Church of St Barnabas, Dhekelia Station, 50th Anniversary Service booklet, 11 March 2012, p 1

19 Province of Jerusalem and the Middle East, Provincial Commission, minutes of the meeting, 12 July 2001, Preamble, p 4, D/C&G archive

20 Minutes of the Meeting of the Standing Committee of the Central Synod of the Episcopal Church in Jerusalem and the Middle East (ECJME), 18 June 2002, p 2, SC 02/6, Matters Arising, b) Provincial Structures, D/C&G archive

21 Minutes of the Meeting of the Standing Committee of the Central Synod of the ECJME, 24 October 2002, p 2, SC 02/18, Matters Arising, b) Provincial Structures, D/C&G archive

22 During 2015, a circular labyrinth was laid out in the garden of St Paul's Cathedral, Nicosia, created by members of the diocesan Retreats Ministry.

23 Cheshire Homes were founded by Group Captain Leonard Cheshire who, after seeing the aftermath of the nuclear bombing of Nagasaki on 6 August 1945, devoted his life to setting up not-for-profit specialised residential care homes for adult persons with physical disabilities and victims of war.

24 On 5 Nov 2006 Saddam Hussein was convicted by an Iraqi court of crimes against humanity. He was sentenced to death by hanging, carried out on 30 Dec 2006.

25 The Coalition Provisional Authority was a transitional government of Iraq established following the invasion of the country on 19 March 2003 by the US-led Multinational Force and the fall of Ba'athist government.

26 In Jan 2002, after the events of 11 Sept 2001 had underlined the need for sustained efforts in developing better Christian-Muslim relations, the first "Building Bridges Seminar" for Muslim and Christian scholars was hosted at Lambeth Palace in London by the then Archbishop of Canterbury, Dr George Carey.

27 As reported by BBC correspondent Tabitha Morgan.

28 Youth for Christ is a worldwide Christian movement working with young people.

29 Interserve seeks to transform the lives and communities of the people of Asia and the Arab World through encounter with Jesus Christ.

30 Judy Cannan served with the Retreats Ministry until 2011 when she returned to her home in the Isle of Man.

31 Crooks, Peter, *Yemen, Heartbreak and Hope*, p 73

32 Email conversation between Bishop Clive Handford and the author

33 D/C&G Synod 2006, Report, Appendix 1, Brief Address, "Getting to Know One Another", p 1, D/C&G archive

34 AIDS, Acquired Immune Deficiency Syndrome

35 The signatories were Zayed M Al Kayrien representing The Public Authority for Planning and Construction Development, and Archdeacon Thomas Ian Young representing The Anglican Church.

36 Final Report, Finance Task Force, May 2006, p 5, D/C&G archive

37 John Banfield, for more than thirty years employed by Mobil Oil Corporation; Sarel du Plessis, a project management specialist; Kent McNeil, banking consultant; Colin Reeves, accounting consultant; Axel Schmidt, accounting consultant. Final Report, Finance Task Force, May 2006, p 14, D/C&G archive

38 D/C&G Synod 2007, Report, Appendix 1, Presidential Address, p 1, D/C&G archive

39 Murray, Angela, "Synod Highlights - 2007", *The Bahrain Anglican News*, Vol LXXI No 8, April-May 2007, p 5, St Christopher's Cathedral archive

40 Quoted by Bishop Handford earlier in the chapter

Chapter 15 - TOWARDS MATURITY, 2008-2015

1 D/C&G Synod 2008, Report, Appendix 1, Presidential Address, p 1, D/C&G archive

2 Ibid, p 2

3 Ibid

4 Ibid

5 Ian, Stephen and Bryan Tatman, "Memories of Baghdad", *The Olive Branch*, Summer 2013, p 4

6 "Fa'iz Becomes a Priest, St George's Baghdad, September 2011 by Bishop Michael", *The Olive Branch*, Winter 2011-2012, p 9

7 The Venerable Dr Bill Schwartz, Archdeacon in the Gulf; and the Venerable Dr John Holdsworth, Archdeacon in Cyprus, Executive Archdeacon in the diocese and Director of Ministry.

8 In 2004, following a request made by the Reverend Clive Windebank through HE Shaikh Nahyan bin Mubarak Al Nahyan, the Government of Abu Dhabi donated land in Mussafah for the construction of an Anglican church. Raising the finance to complete this project has proved to be more time-consuming than anticipated.

9 "St Luke Ras al Khaimah", *The Olive Branch*, Summer 2012, pp 14-15

10 The crematorium was built primarily to serve the Hindu community's needs

11 Lewis, Julia, "Angels of the Emirates" Part 2, *The Olive Branch*, Winter 2011-2012, p 14

12 Ibid

13 Lewis, Julia, "Angels of the Emirates" Part 3, *The Olive Branch*, Summer 2012, pp 12-13

14 Ibid

15 Tamil is an official language in Sri Lanka and Singapore, and in India, it is the official language in the state of Tamil Nadu and the Union Territory of Puducherry. It is also spoken in Kerala, Karnataka, Andhra Pradesh and Telegana.

16 Igbo or Ibo is the principal native language of the Igbo people, an ethnic group of south-eastern Nigeria, with about 27 million speakers made up of over 20 dialects.

17 Marathi is the official language and co-official language in the Maharashtra and Goa states of western India, and is one of the 22 scheduled languages of India.

18 Minutes of the Central Synod meeting, 9/10 Nov 2010, CS 10/14 Ministry of Women, D/C&G archive

19 Diocesan Synod 2011, Report, 2011/08 (b) Vocations, Training and Ordinands, p 10, D/C&G archive

20 The Eurogroup is the recognised collective term for informal meetings of the finance ministers of the eurozone, member states of the European Union, which have adopted the euro as their official currency.

21 At the AGM held on 21 April 2013 voting forms were distributed and members asked to place five names in order of preference. The top three choices were 1. Christ Church Ayia Napa, 2. Holy Trinity Ayia Napa, 3 All Saints Ayia Napa.

22 Email correspondence between Charlotte Lloyd-Evans and the author

23 Living water is a biblical term which appears in both the Old and New Testaments. "If you knew the gift of God and who it is that asks you for a drink, you would have asked him and he would have given you living water. (John 4:10)

24 Line 4, verse 3 of the hymn "The day thou gavest, Lord, is ended", written in 1870 by the Reverend John Ellerton (1826-93)

25 The Reverend Peter Crooks MBE and Mrs Nancy Crooks. "Christ Church and Ras Al Morbat Clinic Yemen", *The Olive Branch*, Summer 2013, pp 13-14

26 "Christ Church Aden", a paper written for the diocesan standing committee by the Reverend Stephen Miller and John Banfield, May 2008, D/C&G archive

27 D/C&G Synod 2014 Report, Appendix 1, Presidential Address, p 2, D/C&G archive

28 The Reverend Paul Burt, a CMS mission partner and assistant priest at St Christopher's Cathedral, Bahrain, 1988-1990; installed by Bishop Michael Lewis as an Honorary Canon of St Paul's Cathedral, Nicosia, 6 May 2018

29 D/C&G Synod 2014, Report, Appendix 1, Presidential Address, p 2, D/C&G archive

30 Ibid, p 3

31 Ibid

32 Ibid, p 4

Chapter 16 - LOOKING AROUND, LOOKING FORWARDS, 2016-2019

1 Islamic State (IS), also known by its Arabic-language acronym Da'esh, is a Salafi-jidhadist militant group, the adherents of which practice a religious-political ideology based on what they advocate should be a return to true Sunni Islam.

2 Synod 2016 Report, Appendix 1, Presidential Address, p 20, D/C&G archive

3 Ibid

4 Ibid

5 Ibid

6 "Harry Ching's Walk from Salamis to Paphos in the Footsteps of St Paul", *The Olive Branch*, Summer 2016, pp 15-16

7 The Home or House for Cooperation, a building in Nicosia within the Ledra Palace crossing in the UN Buffer Zone; essentially aims to act as a bridge-builder between separated communities, providing working spaces and opportunities for NGOs and individuals to design and implement innovative projects.

8 "Bishop Michael's Updated Report for the Cyprus and Gulf Foundation Meeting, May 2017", *The Olive Branch*, Summer 2017, p 7

9 In October 2018 the Reverend Jon Lavelle was appointed as Chair of the Selectors Panel to succeed the Very Reverend Christopher Butt who retired in April 2019

10 November 2019 to May 2022. *See also*: Primates, page 9

11 Email from Bishop Lewis to the author in October 2019

INDEX

476

478

479